T0315004

# GLOBAL DEVELOPMENT

# AMERICA IN THE WORLD

*Sven Beckert and Jeremi Suri, Series Editors*

For a full list of titles in the series, go to
*https://press.princeton.edu/catalogs/series/title/america-in-the-world.html*

# Global Development

## A COLD WAR HISTORY

### SARA LORENZINI

PRINCETON UNIVERSITY PRESS
PRINCETON & OXFORD

Published by Princeton University Press
41 William Street, Princeton, New Jersey 08540
6 Oxford Street, Woodstock, Oxfordshire OX20 1TR

press.princeton.edu

Library of Congress Control Number: 2019937862
ISBN 978-0-691-18015-1
ISBN (e-book) 978-0-691-18556-9

British Library Cataloging-in-Publication Data is available

Editorial: Brigitta van Rheinberg and Amanda Peery, Eric Crahan and Pamela Weidman
Production Editorial: Jenny Wolkowicki
Jacket design: Layla Mac Rory
Production: Merli Guerra
Publicity: Alyssa Sanford and Julia Hall
Copyeditor: Laurel Anderton

Jacket image: Prospecting for minerals. Zambezi River Basin, 1971.
Courtesy of Arquivo Histórico Ultramarino, Lisbon, Portugal

This book has been composed in Arno Pro

Printed on acid-free paper. ∞

Printed in the United States of America

10  9  8  7  6  5  4  3  2  1

*For Alberto*

CONTENTS

## ACKNOWLEDGMENTS

I HAVE BEEN FASCINATED by the theme of development for a long time. This book, therefore, is the result of years of research on this topic. Naturally, I want to acknowledge my debt to colleagues, librarians, friends, and students at the University of Trento who helped me to think about the questions in this book and supported my work throughout. Umberto Tulli has read many versions, and his thoughts have always been of great value. I have worked on the manuscript at several other places, too. Parts of this book have been written at LSE-Ideas; the Universität der Bundeswehr-München; the European University Institute (Florence); and the Weatherhead Initiative on Global History at Harvard University. I want to thank these institutions for hosting me and providing an ideal environment for moving on with my work.

I also need to thank the librarians and archivists who assisted me in my research: Archivio Centrale dello Stato (Rome), Archivio Storico Diplomatico del Ministero degli Affari Esteri (Rome), Archivio Storico del CNR (Rome), Politisches Archiv des Auswärtigen Amts (Berlin), Stiftung Archiv der Parteien und Massenorganisationen in der DDR (Berlin), Bundesarchiv Koblenz—Abteilungen DDR (Berlin), Politisches Archiv des Früheren Ministeriums für Auswärtige Angelegenheiten (Berlin), National Archives and Records Administration (College Park, MD), John F. Kennedy Presidential Library (Boston), Harvard Environmental Science and Public Policy Archives (Cambridge, MA), the National Archives (Kew, UK), LSE Library's Archive (London), Historical Archives of the European Union (Florence), Arquivo Histórico-Diplomático (Lisbon), Arquivo Histórico Ultramarino (Lisbon), the World Bank Group Archives (Washington, DC), the United Nations Archives (New York), the Columbia Center for Oral History—CCOH (New York); Biblioteca Nazionale Centrale (Florence), Staatsbibliothek zu Berlin, Bayerische Staatsbibliothek (Munich), Bibliothèque de Documentation Internationale Contemporaine (Paris), Library of Congress (Washington, DC).

Many are the colleagues and friends with whom I have discussed ideas that have entered this book at one stage or another and have influenced the final result. Special thanks to David Engerman, Marc Frey, Federico Romero, Antonio Varsori, and Arne Westad for their constant advice and encouragement.

Heartfelt thanks to Simone Bellezza, Elisabetta Bini, Francesco Cassata, Mario Del Pero, Giuliano Garavini, Malcolm Murfett, Leopoldo Nuti, and Silvio Pons, who have read the manuscript in whole or in part and suggested corrections, changes, and integrations.

Charles S. Maier, Sugata Bose, Tamis Parron, Casey Primel, Sybille Duhautois, and Liliana Obregon have discussed with me many chapters of this book while at the Weatherhead Initiative on Global History in 2016–17: I have learned a lot from them all. I have been inspired by exchanges and conversations with Michele Alacevich, Hubertus Büschel, Elena Calandri, Sebastian Conrad, Frederik Cooper, Nick Cullather, Victoria de Grazia, Andreas Eckert, David Ekbladh, Maria Cristina Ercolessi, Emanuele Felice, Jeremi Friedman, Mark Gilbert, Simon Godard, Andrea Graziosi, Stefan Hübner, Sandrine Kott, Piers Ludlow, Stephan Malinowski, Erez Manela, Michele Marchi, James Mark, Marc Mazower, Malgorzata Mazurek, Timothy Mitchell, Dirk Moses, Samuel Moyn, Molly Nolan, Timothy Nunan, Julia Obertreis, Jürgen Osterhammel, Jean-Marie Palayret, Niccolò Pianciola, Svetozar Rajak, Martin Rempe, Angela Romano, Luciano Tosi, Corinna Unger, and Berthold Unfried.

Special thanks for their constant support and friendship during research and writing to Monique Centrone, Maurizio Gentilini, Lorenzo Mechi, Guia Migani, and Dieter Schlenker.

This book was initially written in Italian as a history of development during the Cold War. Several people have made it what it is now, a much different book. I want to thank all those who helped me through this process, starting with the editors of the series "America in the World"—Sven Beckert and Jeremi Suri—and Brigitta van Rheinberg at Princeton University Press for believing in this work from the very start. I am grateful to the two anonymous reviewers who offered insightful comments and excellent suggestions for revision. My thanks to my editor Eric Crahan for pushing this project over the finish line, and to Amanda Peery, Pamela Weidman, and Jenny Wolkowicki for their assistance throughout. I am indebted to Aden Knaap, Laurel Anderton, and especially Martha Schulman, who helped me streamline my writing at different stages; while assisting me with the language, they also enhanced my clarity of thought.

My most significant debt, however, is to my family. My mother, Vittorina Moschen, never failed to support and teach me, and her balance and strength continually inspire me. My husband, Lapo Flavio Scarselli, has always encouraged me from near and far, and I am grateful for his love and patience. My son Alberto was just born when I began thinking about this project, and he has been a source of joy ever since, sharing with me the adventure of traveling around the world for research and writing. This book is for him.

# GLOBAL DEVELOPMENT

# Introduction

This foolish belief that the Cold War can be won by courting the weak.

—MANLIO BROSIO, 1960

ON 25 JUNE 1975, Samora Moises Machel, the first president of Mozambique, celebrated independence at Machava Stadium in the capital, Lourenço Marques, soon to be renamed Maputo. A jubilant crowd filled the arena. Hundreds of guests from the various countries and organizations that had supported FRELIMO, the Mozambique Liberation Front (Frente de Libertação de Moçambique), during the armed struggle for independence joined the celebrations. Machel had traveled from the Rovuma River in the north down to the Maputo River in the south: a triumphal march that lasted over a month. He hoped to convince his people to help construct the new state by spreading the news of independence and its significance. Machel promised the People's Republic of Mozambique that he would eradicate the remnants of colonialism and forever banish exploitation. He would build a new society, based on agriculture and propelled by industrial development, relying on its own forces with the support of its natural allies: the socialist countries and its African neighbors Tanzania and Zambia. Education, youth, and health were important parts of the plan; the emancipation of women was fundamental, along with social development within a community framework, the valuing of tradition, and the exchange of knowledge.[1]

Mozambique's bloody war of liberation from Portuguese colonialism lasted ten years (1964–74), during which FRELIMO received support from the Soviet Union and its Eastern European allies. They sent weapons, emergency supplies, advisers, and technicians and pledged to help construct the new state. Mozambique was ideally situated to become a new front of the Cold War, which in 1970s Africa often ran hot. Liberation, whether in Mozambique or elsewhere in Southern Africa, did not imply the end of conflicts,

1

and internal struggles continued, fueled by competing ideologies. President Samora Machel was the unchallenged leader of a paternalistic political elite anchored to an ethic of socialist development of the country. In 1977 during FRELIMO's Third Congress, the first after independence, the broad-based liberation movement became a vanguard Marxist party, built hierarchically and using central planning as its main development strategy. During the congress, the plans sketched at the moment of independence acquired a more precise shape, with Soviet-style modernization as its paradigm. One infrastructure project towered over the rest: the Cahora Bassa Dam, the huge work on the Zambezi River originally conceived in the 1930s by Portuguese authorities as a symbol of their power.

After complex and extended negotiations, in September 1969 a consortium of firms from Portugal, West Germany, the United Kingdom, and South Africa—ZAMCO—had signed a $515 million agreement to build the dam. Work was finally completed in 1974. Intended to supply energy to South Africa, the hydroelectric power plant symbolized the idealized union of white settler communities in Southern Africa. Owned and operated by a Portuguese corporation, Hidroeléctrica de Cahora Bassa (HCB), and inserted within the colonial development plan by Portuguese authorities, the megadam was associated with colonial oppression and had long been in the crossfire of both FRELIMO propaganda and warfare.[2] After independence, the dam became a challenge for the new ruling class: could the new government "tame the white elephant" and turn the colonial project into a tool for social revolution and the empowerment of the black population, by using the energy produced by Cahora Bassa's turbines in Mozambique? Machel's words and plans in this direction echoed those of earlier icons of national independence: Gamal Abdel Nasser in Egypt, Jawaharlal Nehru in India, Kwame Nkrumah in Ghana. Here, though, the rhetoric of liberation was clearly Marxist Leninist, promising a complete overhaul of the old socioeconomic order and a new model of a more equitable society. Ultimately, the dam did not serve the cause of socialist empowerment. Mozambique's postindependence political elite struggled to convert it into a symbol of emancipation within a plan for accelerated national modernization of economic and social structures where the state bore the burden of economic progress and social development. The imposition of collective forms of production and forced settlement into rural communities, often reminiscent of colonial methods, alienated big sectors of the population and nourished the raging civil war fomented by RENAMO (Resistência Nacional Moçambicana, supported by Rhodesia and apartheid South Africa) that transformed large areas into battlefields.[3] Cahora Bassa is a useful case study of development's entanglement with the colonial legacy and Cold War dynamics in Southern Africa. It is one of many examples of how economic decolonization mixed with Cold War interests, with local elites inviting superpowers in to help them achieve modernity and economic growth, often with mixed results.

This book is about the history of development as a Cold War global project from the late 1940s until the late 1980s, a period when the world's imagination was seduced by a concept that encompassed progress, modernity, economic growth, and welfare.[4] Development was crucial to colonial administrations, as the case of Cahora Bassa suggests. Used to appease both the European settlers and the local population, it strengthened empire. With decolonization, it ceased to be domestic policy for empires and became a form of international politics for their successors. How and on what terms would newly independent countries be integrated into the international system? Development became diplomacy's favored way to keep the emerging countries that Alfred Sauvy named the Third World, which could model themselves on either the West or the East, from following the wrong trajectory. In both the East and West, rich countries sought to help the decolonizing states catch up by offering both aid and an example of how a society could and should work. Development projects became a feature of international relations, part of the toolbox of both nation-states and international organizations. For the former colonial powers, development often meant resuming older commitments. It became development aid; once seen as investment at home, it was now a gift abroad, an act of generosity or enlightened interest. To the formerly colonized, however, foreign aid was a form of reparation, a duty for former colonizers who were expected to remedy the wrongs of imperial rule by helping correct global economic inequality. Using it effectively for the postcolonial state was a move of self-determination that national elites exploited to legitimize their rule. So crucial was aid in Asia, Africa, and Latin America that it is impossible to accurately discuss history in the late twentieth century without considering development projects, many of which were complex state-building operations that touched entire societies.

Narrating the political, intellectual, and economic history of the twentieth century through the lens of development means dealing with ideas as much as with material transformation, recounting the ways ideas and projects affected local realities, transnational interactions, and, eventually, notions of development. In describing this trajectory, *Global Development* makes three main points. First, it argues that the Cold War was fundamental in shaping the global aspirations and ideologies of development and modeling the institutional structures that still rule foreign aid today. Second, it contends that the role of the state was crucial, and that though development projects were articulated in global terms, as narratives to frame problems and provide solutions, they actually served national purposes. Third, it argues that development institutions tried to create a universal and homogeneous concept of development but ultimately failed.

German historian Reinhart Koselleck has remarked that a concept is both a product of its context and a factor shaping it.[5] Development was molded by the Cold War and, in turn, actively designed some of its structures. It predated the end of empires and the Second World War but acquired a special role with the globalization of American and Soviet ideological competition and the building of the institutions and ideology of an economic Cold War. At the very inception of the Cold War, with the Marshall Plan, development and foreign aid met, and development became a transnational project with potential global reach. It quickly became the preferred way to conquer the hearts and minds of poor people in Europe and—with Point Four in 1949—outside it. Postwar reconstruction valued cooperation highly, seeing it as the blueprint for dealing with backwardness. Even before the Cold War, it was the fear of communism that provided incentives for development. Economic aid was devised in the interwar years to counter the specter of revolutions fueled by social discontent and rising expectations. After the Second World War, anticommunism was clearly behind Truman's Point Four, but it was not until 1956 that aid became institutionalized as a tool for Cold War politics. It was then that Nikita Khrushchev took up the challenge by arguing that the socialist mode of production, with its system of cooperation on an equal base grounded in fraternal solidarity and stressing industrial development, possessed decisive advantages over the capitalist one. The combined effect of the collapse of European empires and the Cold War opened new space in international politics. To receive aid, newly independent countries were forced to choose a social and economic development model. This gave their leaders leverage, and as they showcased their needs and stressed the moral obligation of redressing colonial exploitation, they systematically threatened to align with the other side in order to receive aid for their favorite plans. In the late 1950s, development projects were competing against one another in terms of effectiveness and symbolic strength, which meant that Cold War politics determined the stakes, timing, and distribution of aid.

Development was also a tool of bloc consolidation and solidarity, with two rival groups, East and West, engaging in a worldwide tug-of-war for influence and clients. In the West, cooperation occurred through the Development Assistance Committee (DAC) in the Organization for Economic Cooperation and Development (OECD); in the East, through the Permanent Commission for Technical Assistance in the Council for Mutual Economic Assistance (CMEA or Comecon). These cooperative projects functioned both as a promotion of cultural values—Western democracy versus socialism—and as security ventures. In the West, the security dimension meant achieving social peace by granting extensive welfare. In the socialist countries, it meant strengthening international solidarity around the promise of an alternative system: an industrialized society with high levels of welfare and equality. But over time, donors on both sides were increasingly baffled by the security paradox: instead of enhancing security, aid nourished inefficient and autocratic governments that committed blatant violations of human rights and caused regional destabilization. The connection between foreign aid and security, a pillar of the system, did not hold. Disappointment with both the quantity and quality of aid was such that instead of bringing consensus, aid increased North-South tensions. In the 1970s, these tensions exploded within the United Nations, where the North-South divide inherited from decolonization and initially articulated through trade controversies became more prominent than the East-West divide. There were always new reasons for rupture on global issues such as resources, population, and the environment. And even when East-West détente lowered Cold War tensions, they continued at the local level, especially in Sub-Saharan Africa, where decolonization struggles persisted.

*Global Development* claims that notwithstanding their universal aspiration, development projects served mainly the national purposes of both donor and recipient countries. Donors wanted to promote their national self-interest, whether politically or economically, for instance by expanding markets for their products or securing strategic resources at favorable prices. Meanwhile, recipients were able to manipulate the interests of the donors to their own ends, sometimes national, sometimes for a specific group or even particular individuals. They systematically used the threat of moving to the other side of the Cold War, often exhibiting indifference to the source of aid in order to stress their independence and readiness to defect. In the hands of national elites in the "age of development" (1940–1973), economic growth became one with the national project, and planning and state investments were key—the conditions that created the developmental state.[6] All you need to fight poverty is a plan, Gunnar Myrdal bragged in 1956, but the plan was not just about economics—it was about constructing a new society. Joseph Schumpeter, upon meeting his former student Hans Singer, who was working on development for the UN Department of Economic and Social Affairs, remarked sarcastically, "I thought you were an economist."[7] Development, he claimed, was a matter for anthropologists, sociologists, or geographers. In the 1950s and 1960s, development concepts, however different their details, shared a faith in the state as an actor and in planning as a method, making it tempting to describe the history of development as a history of planning.

In the modernization era, the state was a powerful engine for development. The development field agreed that improving the living standards of the common people was a primary duty of governments. This belief, Myrdal enthusiastically noted in 1957, was brand-new in history.[8] In donor and recipient countries alike, policy makers extolled the virtues of development plans and technology's ability to promote growth. Big infrastructure projects such as dams and power plants were the ultimate symbols of modernity. And all of this was compatible across the spectrum of societal organization—it could be the product of capitalist ventures or be associated with hardcore planning the Socialist Bloc's way. Either way, it rested on an optimistic view of society and its future, on the feasibility of making the world a better place. The faith in the state, discourses of self-betterment, and the fundamental role of science and rational thought in replacing traditions ended in the late 1960s. And when the myth of invincible scientific-technological progress crumbled, development entered a long era in which there was a crisis of vision. Poor results also shook the optimistic view of economic growth automatically translating to generalized well-being. Poverty persisted despite economic growth: fresh tools thus had to be devised. New anxieties appeared, particularly resource scarcity, population, and concern for the environment. Trust in progress as linear development toward modernity collapsed. Historian Alexander Gerschenkron argued that linear development did not accurately describe European history, let alone global dynamics.[9] Linguist Noam Chomsky demolished the double myth of social sciences: political benevolence and scientific omniscience.[10] Together these destroyed the idea that the poor would eventually converge toward the rich. The main divide was not East-West anymore, but North-South, and trust in state planning was replaced by faith in the market. The costs of global modernization exploded, leaving national elites in recipient countries with huge debts that they were unable or unwilling to pay. They turned to more radical requests that challenged Cold War schemes and premises.

This global history of development shows how institutions promoted an unrealistic idea of development as a homogeneous system. The differences in interests and perspectives between North and South, East and West, and Europe and the rest were simply too great, and while there were temporary alignments, a stable consensus was elusive. The development galaxy was better described as a patchwork of regional plans with global ambitions than as a coherent system. Although cooperation—among allies and international organizations, between North and South, and among countries of what is now called the Global South—was fundamental to how aid was understood, this harmonious vision did not reflect reality. As this book reveals, coordination among allies was never simple, and it was not what made the system work. European countries had their own national interests and disparate visions on aid, regardless of whether they were allied with the Americans or the Soviets. These countries used the recipes proposed by the superpowers' experts or international organizations instrumentally, adapting them to their own needs. This happened in both the West and the East. Sometimes what seemed like just a slight difference in approach hid a substantial disagreement, as with Italy and its different ideas on the state's role in industrialization, or East Germany's preference for smaller projects in the processing industry rather than the big projects favored by the USSR. At other times, the opposition was more explicit, as with West Germany criticizing US program aid or Romania identifying with the Third World instead of with the Soviet Bloc. Development scholars often describe development as a global design with Western—usually American—ideas at its center. Indeed, many see it as a regime governed by Western concepts of morality and steered by the United States in cooperation with like-minded international experts.[11] Depending on the scholar's ideological view, the United States looms as either a generous patron or a malevolent, hegemony-seeking, neocolonial imperial power. However, although US-backed modernization theory and the policies it shaped were influential, they did not go unchallenged by national interests and alternative visions.[12] This book avoids the hegemony narrative by looking at the tensions and competing interests roiling beneath the even surface created when development is described as a single idea.

Typically, the economic Cold War has been explored in the classic bipolar framework by discussing the ways that Western and socialist views met and diverged.[13] However, Cold War development was much more than a competition between superpowers, and this book delves into national and regional archives, both public and private, to broaden this picture. This allows the appreciation of similarities and differences between and within the "First" and "Second" worlds during the Cold War. It brings in a wide range of actors, including state actors such as China, international organizations and their agencies, and Third World voices around the project for the New International Economic Order. One regional actor that rarely shows up in economic histories of the Cold War is the European Economic Community (EEC), which offered what it called a third way in development. The EEC discussions about how to structure a common aid program show the fundamental tension within development strategies over whether to take a regional or global approach. Regionalism, in this case, was a legacy of empire—the French especially cherished the geopolitical dream of Eurafrica—and this book tells the story of how it transformed itself into an alternative to the superpowers, something resembling Third World demands for a New International Economic Order.

The history of development shows that this concept underwent multiple transformations, yet there were also recurring ideas and models and long-term continuities in national strategies. Development was never linear. And while debates about aid have shifted from asking outdated questions such as "does aid work?" to strengthening aid mechanisms in specific situations, there are consistent through lines across decades. There is still a focus on food security and rural development, albeit with a stress on democracy in the case of US aid, on project aid with allegedly maximum control in the case of Germany, or the centrality of student exchanges in the socialist tradition, which remains part of Chinese aid.

On 9 March 2018, newspaper articles reported the "cold war" staged the day before at the Sheraton Hotel in Addis Ababa. Then US secretary of state Rex Tillerson and Russian foreign minister Sergey Lavrov crossed paths on Ethiopian soil, but though they stayed at the same hotel, they did not meet. Lavrov had visited Zimbabwe, Angola, Mozambique, and Namibia: traditional Soviet trade partners in Southern Africa. Tillerson, who then traveled on to Djibouti and Kenya, signed a $100 million loan agreement with the Ethiopian government and commented on China's presence on the continent. American aid to Africa focuses on training for military and police forces in peacekeeping operations and lessons in good governance and democratic traditions—the priority is security, just as during the Cold War. Russia focuses on weapons and mining industries, as it used to do in the 1970s, stressing the importance of noninterference in domestic affairs and supporting China against US accusations of predatory business methods. China, an important alternative socialist modernity described in this book, typically focuses on infrastructure. In Addis, for example, the Chinese have financed the new headquarters for the African Union and built the metro running from the airport to the city center, as well as the railway line connecting Addis Ababa with the port in Djibouti on the Gulf of Aden. Tillerson's and Lavrov's simultaneous trips to Africa—which continued geographical priorities established during the Cold War, and their interest in the classic intervention sectors—is just one example of how development mind-sets and aid dynamics still follow the paths laid out during the Cold War. In the history of development in the pages that follow, overriding trends and patterns are clearly recognizable, but regional and national specificities consistently complicate the picture, while the Cold War determines much—but not everything, and not always in the way that might be expected.

# 1

# Development as an Ideology for Empire

The great work of uplifting mankind.

—THEODORE ROOSEVELT, 1899

The real thing is that this time we are going to get science applied to social problems and backed by the whole force of the state.

—C. S. LEWIS, 1945

THESE DAYS DEVELOPMENT is a common word in everyday vocabulary and scientific phraseology. Its origin is recent, around the time of the industrial revolution.[1] In the nineteenth century, economic development was often referred to as modernization, westernization, or, most commonly, industrialization, and it had a prominent national or emancipatory character. Until the 1920s the word, filtered through German philosophy, was not widely used in the social sciences. To be sure, Joseph A. Schumpeter entitled his fundamental 1911 work *Theorie der wirtschaftlichen Entwicklung* (Theory of economic development), but he was very much the exception. As surprising as it may sound, development did not enter the technical language of economics until the 1930s and was little used prior to the Second World War. Economists largely used the language of progress instead. Only after 1945 did economic growth become crucial in developed countries and economic development a fundamental political goal.

Initially, development was a synonym for growth and was used for industrial economies only. Sun Yat-sen's book *The International Development of China*, written in English in 1918 and published in 1922, marks the first time the word was used in a non-European setting.[2] In the 1920s, economists at the London School of Economics, the place par excellence for colonial studies in the British Empire, started to systematically use the term "economic development" to refer to areas like India, China, and the less industrially advanced areas in the empire.[3] In the 1920s, colonial administrators started to use the active verb "develop" and to speak of developing peoples.

In the view of the internationalists and philanthropists of the early twentieth century, development was a civilizing mission. Conceiving imperialism as having a pedagogical side meant that advanced societies were required to take colonized peoples by the hand and teach them the rules of a modernity they had been excluded from.[4] This was a change: at the end of the nineteenth century, there were peoples who were thought to be unready for civilization, principally in Africa. The cofounder of the International Red Cross Gustave Moynier, for example, held that the 1864 Geneva Convention for the Amelioration of the Condition of the Wounded in Armies in the Field did not apply to Africans, who, he argued, lived outside civilization.[5] But colonial expansion meant taking responsibility. Jules Ferry, in the 1885 speech often considered a fresh start for French imperialism, described colonization as a political duty: the superior races had duties toward inferior ones, particularly in the promotion of science and progress.[6] Humanitarianism was a special element that started with abolishing slavery in all forms and limiting the excesses of colonialism. The struggle against slavery and slave practices was often used as a justification for intervention, as was the goal of undermining the influence of rival powers.[7]

This mind-set was also common on the other side of the Atlantic. The idea of uplifting colored people from their condition and bringing them civilization and Christianity was part of the political discourse. In 1899, President William McKinley used the civilizing mission as a pretext for annexing the Philippines.[8] Rudyard Kipling's poem "The White Man's Burden," now seen as a symbol of a brutal colonial mentality, was written to convince the public of the necessity of colonizing the Philippines. Kipling urged Americans to take up the burden of civilization, even though this meant being hated by subject peoples. In the United States, civilization was perceived as an element that bound Europe and the United States together in a global project. History was considered a movement from fragmentation to unity, and progress meant evolving toward a system of powerful nations that used a few rich and precise languages that everyone could understand.[9] Everywhere in the West the rhetoric of civilization flourished, albeit with different accents. The exception was Germany, where the concept of a civilizing mission was less familiar and the equivalent expression did not yet exist.[10]

## The Civilizing Mission in the Interwar Years

The enlightened paternalistic approaches to development common at the end of the nineteenth century shifted in the following decades. Imperial rivalries

at the turn of the twentieth century and the resulting First World War interrupted the cooperation and exchange of knowledge on colonial matters that
had reached an apex with the suppression of the Boxer Uprising in China
(1899–1902) by the Eight-Nation Alliance. At the First Universal Races Congress, held in London in July 1911, for example, each imperial model was
celebrated for its uniqueness. The coming of the First World War created a
different kind of solidarity: colonial powers fought each other, together with
their colonized territories. In this new era, dissimilarities rather than similarities were highlighted. After the war, this tendency intensified, as the two
major empires, France and Great Britain, amplified their differences and self-
identified as having divergent styles of colonial government.[11]

In the war's aftermath, the French and British Empires divided the
spoils of the vanquished. Rather than applying Wilsonian principles of self-
determination to the greater part of territories and peoples outside Europe,
the powers deemed them culturally and institutionally unprepared for self-
government and formalized rules and tools for colonial government in order
to reconstruct a world safe for empire.[12] One tool was the institutionalization
of the civilizing mission in international law: for the first time development
became a juridical principle governing international politics. The Covenant
of the League of Nations dealt with colonial issues in articles 22 and 23: article 23 was a charter establishing the duties of member states in issues such as
the just treatment of natives, while article 22 introduced the mandate, a mode
of governing whereby a power had a tutelary dominion over territories that
needed to be prepared for independence.[13] The mandate system translated
the civilizing mission into a written juridical norm, and the idea of stages of
development entered the language of law. Development had semantic dimensions that were far from obvious. It did not describe the economic dimension
but was rather a synthesis of noneconomic elements—social, demographic,
and cultural. Economic issues were dealt with separately, under the expression
"well-being."

The sacred trust the great powers placed in civilization reflected the belief
that colonial authority was vindicated by moral and material well-being and
social progress—in a word, civilization. Emancipation for colonial territories
was placed at some indefinite future point, pending political and administrative maturity. It was not conceived as imminent—not even for the former territories of the Ottoman Empire, which were classed as type A mandates and
thought to be the most ready for independence. Mark Mazower's study of Jan
Christiaan Smuts, the South African who invented the mandate system, clearly
shows that the road to self-government did not imply abandoning racist or even
segregationist policies. Smuts saw the British Empire as the model for world
government and considered the mandates a tool to accommodate nationalities

in Central and Eastern Europe. He did not think self-government was a viable prospect for "the barbarians in Africa," who needed to be under the rule "of the white race in South Africa."[14] Like many of his contemporaries, Smuts feared a global war between the races like the one vividly described in Lothrop Stoddard's 1922 best-selling book *The Rising Tide of Color against White World Supremacy*.[15] In the League of Nations, however, racial discomfort—whether the yellow peril or the prospect of losing control of African masses—did not take center stage. In its place was the optimistic prospect of the civilizing mission.[16] Humanitarian internationalism was oriented toward building the modern human: a standardized creature made on the Western model. The goal was to annul cultural differences. Since this mission was impossible to achieve, development was a potentially unending project.[17]

The mandate system and the legitimization of a civilizing mission it implied were typical of the climate of colonial revival in the 1920s. At that time, belief in the economic value of colonies was widespread, and there were new ideas about managing, modernizing, and rationalizing empire. A symbol of the new style was Sir Frederick Lugard's *Dual Mandate in Tropical Africa*, published in 1921, which brought together the spirit of mandate with colonialism. By "dual mandate" Lugard meant that an efficient use of the resources extracted by a colonial power must be coupled with an administration that promoted a civilizational drive. Lugard, then the most authoritative member of the Permanent Mandates Commission of the League of Nations, included article 22 of the Covenant as an appendix to his book, intending to show that according to modern principles of international law, the British Empire was an example of good administration.

Interestingly, several development projects dating back to the interwar years look modern today, since they focus on issues now perceived as innovative, such as education or the empowerment of women. French colonial minister Albert Sarraut outlined his plans for empire in his 1922 book *La mise en valeur des colonies françaises*. France, he claimed, did not hold old colonial mentalities based on racial inequality and the right of the fittest. Empire served the interests of the conquered, he argued. Culture was crucial, as were local institutions. Health, sanitation, education and training, microcredit, and the role of women were all part of his picture. The 1929 Colonial Development Act promulgated in the British Empire was similar in some respects.[18]

The interwar years in both the French and British Empires brought the organization of a new colonial bureaucracy charged with collecting revenues so that colonial territories could support themselves. Colonial bureaucrats were a "thin white line": a small group of whites administering an overwhelming majority of people of color.[19] Increasingly the administration absorbed locals who mediated between different political cultures, translating and modifying the principles of civilization. But civilization was thought to move from the metropole to the colony, so natives, even the highly educated ones called *évoluées*, could not aspire to higher ranks in their careers.[20] For white administrators, colonial experience, in the same or other areas of the empire, constituted an important feedback loop. Economic, political, and social modernity was forged through reciprocal influences.[21] Europeans in the field learned from natives how to deal with specific local problems and brought this knowledge back to the metropole. This, in turn, circulated back to other areas of the empire. In the 1920s, the model colonial officer was a man who "knew his natives," understood local customs and tradition, spoke the language, and could deal with locals and gain their loyalty. He had experience of the colonial world and was willing to test and adapt techniques used elsewhere.

In the interwar years, the rhetoric of modernity was used to justify all sorts of colonial policies. Modernization could imply violence, and the rhetoric of human rights began to accompany modernizing discourses, sometimes paradoxically. Forced resettlements, for example, were justified by the goals of achieving modernity and preventing civil war.[22] Imposing cultural practices, forced labor, and population transfers were all part of social engineering for economic and structural development. Development plans, presented as a technical fix, were in fact political tools for control and coercion.[23] Violence was a feature of administration in both colonies and mandates.

Since development was a tool for colonial government, for local elites it became the way to do politics, which can be seen in the modernization projects of postcolonial elites. Though they were presented as a break with colonial experiments and linked to local tradition, in many cases they reflected the methods of preexisting colonial administrations, ultimately replicating their failures. This is the case, for example, with rural development schemes in British West Africa, which resumed after national independence and proved as unsuccessful as their forerunners.

## Modernity and Authoritarian Rule

Making civilization a scientific enterprise became putative commonsense in the interwar years. In the period now called high modernism, science and rational thinking were the only sources of knowledge: traditions were linked to myth and the past and considered useless.[24] Taming nature and making it functional for human needs was typical of positivist thinking, and massive infrastructure works such as the Suez and Panama Canals were symbols of humans' ability to shape nature and make a huge, durable impact on society and the environment.

Colonial regimes were key sponsors of experiments in social engineering. The ideology of welfare colonialism, combined with the authoritarian power characteristic of empires, encouraged ambitious transformation schemes that often involved resettling local populations. Those in advanced nations were also affected, ending up as both protagonists and victims of experiments into the scientific management of production, or productivism. In the United States this translated into Taylorist modes of production. In Europe, this took the form of the organic state envisaged by Walther Rathenau and Wichard von Moellendorff of the Kaiser Wilhelm Institut für Arbeitspsychologie (1913), who hoped to construct an industrial planning pyramid, with representatives of workers, industrialists, and the government all working for the common good. The vision of a corporate state institutionalized in fascist Italy and propagated as a third way between Marxism and capitalism was reflected in the structure of the International Labour Organization (ILO), born in 1919 along with the Versailles Treaty. Workers needed to be appeased and involved in decision making in order to keep them away from Bolshevism.[25] The vision of a society in which technology and science were fundamental and growth and increased wealth would end conflict appealed to different and potentially competing philosophies; productivism, although basically a tool to promote the hegemony of capital, was for a time politically heterogeneous.[26] Even Lenin flirted with the Taylorist model, despite having initially described it as a scientific way to extract sweat. He lauded the principle of discipline, organization, and harmonious cooperation built on modern industry, mechanization, and the rigid system of responsibility and control.[27]

In the 1930s, the Soviet Union epitomized modernization, with planning seen as the means of cutting waste and capitalist inefficiencies. Soviet modernization also meant transforming society, sometimes drastically, as with Soviet internal colonization policies in Central Asia that planned settlements, fought backward traditions, and organized labor and social space in both rural and industrial districts.[28] Socialist modernization, with its propaganda campaign extolling the heroic construction not just of socialism, but of a new human to fit the new socialist society and the golden age of communism to come, caught the attention of intellectuals and public opinion the world over.

After the market crash, Stalin's Five-Year Plans captured widespread attention. The well-organized propagation of the Soviet myth transcended the borders of the communist movement.[29] Socialism's alternative path to modernity became credible, fascinating many intellectuals attracted by the Manichaean reading of the postwar years, which divided the world between a decaying bourgeois society and the prospect of a new communist civilization.[30] Intourist, the Soviet travel agency, designed visits to the so-called sites of communism to showcase the Soviet system: westerners visited exemplary sites to see Soviet solutions to social problems like rehabilitating criminals or providing for orphans and the homeless. Once socialism was fully realized, the propaganda promised, these model institutions would be the norm. Political pilgrims were not shown historical monuments, but rather model factories, representing a constructed reality of production in the Soviet Union. These sites, including collective farms, were carefully selected from a list of projects considered suitable for display. Visitors were taken to research and medical facilities, including reform houses for prostitutes (*profilaktoriia*) and sanatoriums. When opponents criticized visits to what they called Potemkin villages and unveiled continuities between tsarist and socialist styles in mounting colossal misrepresentations of reality, the Soviets tried to avoid less credible situations. Showcasing the successes of socialism remained a formula, but there were difficulties in persuading economic commissariats to open factories and industrial sites to visits. In 1936, the peak year for political tourism in the Soviet Union, the Commissariat of Heavy Industry attempted to curtail the number of visits per month per factory.[31]

Western sympathizers invited to the Soviet Union often praised the myth of the Soviet experiment, captivated by what George F. Kennan later called the romance of economic development.[32] This operation included showcasing a Soviet-style bourgeois culture, as part of an effort to create a Soviet consumption model, complete with luxury goods and warehouses.[33] Among those visitors were politicians like Eduard Herriot, who visited the Ukraine in 1933 right after the great famine, and intellectuals like Bernard Shaw, who met Stalin in 1931 and praised Soviet achievements. The model also fascinated later advocates of the New Deal like Stuart Chase and the intellectual elites in the colonial world.[34] In 1927, for example, Jawaharlal Nehru visited Moscow and was deeply impressed. Like Sidney and Beatrice Webb, he admired Soviet economic achievements, seeing glimpses of a new civilization in the Soviet model.[35]

With the success of the Soviet model, development became a weapon in the ideological clash. In his work on the "Three New Deals," Wolfgang Schivelbusch argues that a number of Western development projects were clearly born out of competition with Soviet achievements, with each project showcasing the goals, methods, and ideals of the political system that generated it.[36] Totalitarian regimes in Europe saw modernity as a technological, economic, and social enterprise. Nazi Germany pushed the Autobahn, an esthetic and technological revolution that embodied the promise of mass motorization. Fascist Italy carried out rural development projects, reclaiming land in the Agro Pontino, resettling peasants, and encouraging urban development. The plans developed in the Lazio countryside were then exported to the Italian colonies, where Le Corbusier's rational architecture and the theories of climatic axes found fertile ground. Italy extolled cultural and architectural unity in the Mediterranean as a means of promoting empire, and in the 1930s it rebuilt Asmara, the capital of the Italian colony of Eritrea, as a showcase for Italian modernity. The city's structure enforced racial separation, with one side used for administrative purposes and the other reserved for natives.[37] Other regimes used their colonies as places to try out ideas of economic and social development. For example, Japan experimented in Korea and Taiwan with implementing new models of urban planning, education, and health care. Inspired by Soviet planning, Japan built a Soviet-style industrial district in Manchukuo in the 1930s.[38]

The New Deal in the United States was entirely consonant with the prevailing zeitgeist, and some read it as a response to the success of European authoritarian regimes, both left and right. Like them, the New Deal had advanced technology and a fascination with planning, albeit in its Wilsonian variant.[39] The Tennessee Valley Authority (TVA), the regional development agency for modernization of the Tennessee River basin through hydroelectric power, was meant to prove that it was possible to promote economic development non-autocratically. David Lilienthal, its indefatigable director, never ceased extolling the importance of decentralizing decisions and involving civil society.[40] He embraced the ideas of his predecessor, Arthur E. Morgan, who fought to base the project on a system of small self-sufficient towns coupled with strong communitarianism.[41] The TVA became a cornerstone in American development thinking and practice, a regional development plan that was a model for global development, a scheme to repeat elsewhere. This vision was actualized in the 1950s, when President Harry Truman and Lilienthal discussed a TVA in the Yangtze or Danube basins, highlighting the power of development to transform society and promote peace and development.[42] A number of Great Dam Projects were explicitly inspired by the TVA: the Helmand Valley in Afghanistan, the Damodar Valley in India, and the quickly abandoned Danube TVA.[43]

Recognizing the transnational potential of the New Deal model, economist Eugene Staley set up a comprehensive plan for intervention for economic and social development in poor areas of the world, seeing such intervention as the basis for collective security against totalitarian aggression. Inspired by colonial policies introduced in the Philippines by Governor-General William Cameron Forbes, Staley was convinced that technical education could bring global change by creating a self-reliant generation. He envisaged laboratories where social experiments could be carried out under controlled conditions, first in China, then in other countries in Asia, Latin America, and Southern Europe.[44]

## The Second World War

The Second World War saw increased engagement with development at a time when planning as a method was spurred on by war logistics. European empires, although militarily and economically weakened by the war, continued to invest in their colonies to secure both political support and resources. The war economy was centrally directed, and the colonial offices acted on behalf of the dependent territories. Public funds were employed to promote colonial trade, and state intervention in the economy became the norm, with the state controlling wages and prices and allocating resources—both goods and labor. Revenue taxes were introduced to control inflation. In the 1920s, the idea had prevailed that colonies should support themselves and produce export goods to generate financial surpluses. It was now clear that colonies would not be able to find resources in financial markets and build infrastructure on their own. In 1940, fearing political and social instability, British colonial secretary Malcolm MacDonald set up a fund to finance development under the Colonial Development and Welfare Act. Facing general strikes, demonstrations, and riots, the colonial authority pursued security through development, allocating funds to create new jobs for natives and settlers and expand the construction of a welfare state in the colonies. The Colonial Development and Welfare Act used metropolitan resources to fund infrastructure and address housing, water management, education, and welfare for workers to secure higher standards of living in the colonies. The war sped up a process that had started in the 1930s but was now perceived as more urgent, given growing concern about securing the political and economic loyalty of subject territories. Things were not easy in Asia or Africa, with nationalism being fueled by economic complaints; general strikes spreading through the empire, starting in 1935; and conflicts erupting in rural areas over invasive colonial intervention.[45]

British colonial officers in the 1930s were aware of problems of production, population, and environment in the colonies. Facing backlash in both rural and urban areas, colonial officers looked for ways to stabilize populations and contain migration from the countryside. Anthropologists like Bronislaw Malinowski at the London School of Economics studied the consequences of the loss of a tribal dimension in African societies and the connections between health, diet, and food. Community development was devised to promote group well-being through better education and health without breaking with local traditions. Experts were employed to study changes on the ground, such as ecological or demographic imbalances in areas of India or in the Copperbelt in Africa. Colonial experts could see the links between high fertility rates, unemployment, and subversion, often related to population shifts from areas with a shortage of labor to areas with excess workforce. The 1920s myth of tropical riches had crumbled, and undernourishment was rampant in the colonies, but during the Great Depression, research focused on the betterment of export crops like sugarcane, cotton, rubber, coffee, palm oil, and tea and the introduction of high-performance or drought-tolerant varieties. Less attention was devoted to the production of food for local consumption.[46]

During the war, opportunities for colonial export increased, especially for white landowners. The war reduced supplies from Europe and boosted demand for colonial produce.[47] In the metropole, officials began thinking about how to apply productivism to the colonial economy. Experts in the British Colonial Office were confident that better standards of living in the colonies could be reached by enhancing production and yields through chemical fertilizers, rural mechanization, and new forms of cooperative organization. Modern development planning was introduced in the British Empire with the famous Caine Memorandum of August 1943. Sidney Caine, an economist on the rise in the Colonial Office, held that poverty and population problems could be addressed through a dramatic rise in productivity. Caine, who explicitly cited the Soviet Union and the TVA as models, had a new idea of the state's role in the British Empire. He saw the state as the engine of industrial planning, preferred urban to rural development, and was less interested in welfarist measures in education and health.[48] This vision collided with one more focused on labor approaches, a vision held by a young W. Arthur Lewis, who would go on to an influential career in development economics. Although in favor of industrialization, Lewis held that industrial centers had to be limited: better to concentrate resources than waste them on undifferentiated distribution to the colonies.[49]

At the end of the war, Great Britain and France took control of their former possessions and tried to create a more rational empire. Financing development never quite happened and was now no longer realistic. Struggling to hold on to their colonies, European countries had a new rhetoric of colonial partnership that tried to balance intensified economic relations with the promise of surrendering power. The effort was to selectively transform formal empire into informal empire, a system of satellites not in name but in fact. This was a second colonial occupation, with increased engagement in development projects that would be financed through local resources.[50] But conditions were poor. There was inflation, shortages of consumer goods, and a dangerously dense population in urban areas where poor services and miserable working conditions were the norm. Massive strikes were frequent, and when colonial powers used forced labor, the workers essentially deserted. Great Britain and France struggled to regenerate or reframe the imperial colonial ideal. William Keith Hancock in his *Argument of Empire* in 1943 gave a democratic-humanitarian raison d'être for empire, claiming that empire would preserve local society, especially in Africa, after which education via contact with the West could gradually take place. Since the colonized countries lacked a national community in the European sense, he claimed, a transfer of power would only create a tokenistic parliamentary democracy that benefited small oligarchies of educated people and left the masses at their mercy.[51]

State planning followed a sort of path dependency. In the postwar years, colonial administrations kept promoting lines of intervention that had been studied and debated in the years when colonial legitimacy was not in question. But development offered a new source of legitimacy. In Hitler's wake, racist theories and ideology had lost standing and there was a radical revision of the civilizing mission. Classic dichotomies of metropole-colony and civilized-primitive were reconceptualized. Development, which offered a new civilizational pair—developed-backward—to replace outmoded language, was the handmaiden of this turn.[52] With the urgency of countering colonial upheaval, the scale and intensity of development interventions rose dramatically. A new language entered the discourse not only of experts, but also of local nationalist elites, whose political speech now used the new terms coined by the colonial powers.

After the Second World War, an impoverished Great Britain could not regain the role of omnipresent investor and buyer it had designed for itself in the early 1930s at the beginning of the Commonwealth. The British Colonial Office drew up plans for Africa and Southeast Asia to be carried out by a newly minted Colonial Development Corporation. This corporation survived on revenues from the marketing boards born from trading colonial crops and raw materials, as well as the new income taxes raised in dependent territories. It was not able to build a consensus in the colonies where development projects were to be situated.[53] Planning continued, regardless of promises of self-government and self-determination. Initiatives ranged from pilot projects for water management and soil conservation to schemes for land reclamation and resettlement, mechanization of cotton or rice production, and improvements to infrastructure, health, education, and welfare. Rural cooperatives inspired by local traditions were tried in Jamaica and Kenya, with modest results. A bitter disappointment was in store for the East Africa Groundnut Scheme in Tanganyika, a scheme for the intensive cultivation of peanuts that planned to reclaim five million acres in five years and build a harbor and railway. Conceived poorly, then badly operated, the scheme caused costly deforestation of areas that proved impossible to farm, and revealed the dangers of misunderstanding ecological balance.[54] As Gunnar Myrdal prophetically stated, colonialism was on the brink of collapse now that the imperial system was proving too expensive.[55] But the Commonwealth was still considered a viable opportunity. The countries in the Sterling area kept their national currency and central bank. India retained association with the Commonwealth, as did postindependence African countries, turning empire into a series of postcolonial relations based on a common past.[56]

France followed a similar path, picturing itself as an exporter of the welfare state. Postwar France had an unprecedented consensus on imperial policies: colonies, all agreed, were fundamental for reestablishing national power. René Pleven at the imperial conference in Brazzaville in 1943 grandly announced that there were no peoples to free in the French empire and that the only freedom that mattered to colonial territories was the freedom of France. At first, reconstruction of empire was a shared priority, but colonial enthusiasm soon declined. The French public rapidly lost enthusiasm for colonial issues after the gruesome events in Algeria in May 1945, when local protests resulted in the killing of white settlers and subsequent indiscriminate and brutal repression. The railway strikes in West Africa and the Malagasy Uprising in 1947 lowered the popularity of colonialism even more. By 1946 nobody really supported the Union Française, a compromise effort to rebrand empire while providing a new progressive constitution for the French Fourth Republic. According to a poll of April 1947, half the respondents anticipated its quick collapse.[57]

The idea of a colonial fund for development had been abandoned in France as early as 1937 because of the lack of resources and expert enthusiasm in the face of the rather disappointing experiments of the 1920s and 1930s.[58] After the war, however, everyone still seemed to favor investment in dependent territories. A development fund, FIDES (Fonds d'Investissement pour le Développement Économique et Social), accompanied the birth of the Union Française. In 1947, 15 percent of the French GDP went to the development of overseas territories. Financial markets were restructured to meet credit necessities in the former colonies. Though economic advantages and investments were offered to overseas territories to keep them in the French orbit, too often FIDES looked like a continuation of colonial dependency. More than two-thirds of the goods exported by France's former colonies went to the French market, where they sold below market price. Between 1947 and 1958, France invested three times more in Francophone Africa than it had invested before the Second World War, an investment supported by the widespread belief that the African colonial market was indispensable. Meanwhile in Indochina, where independence was impending, French capital investments, partly from the state, partly from a few big companies, dropped by 30 percent in 1947, 1948, and 1951.[59] Leading intellectuals and political figures started claiming that colonies did not yield the expected returns, though nobody risked political suicide by raising the issue of the human tribute and financial costs imposed by colonial wars, especially in Indochina.[60]

Late colonial development projects were disappointing. They did not solve the dilemma of how to stabilize rural communities while promoting global imperatives of growth and accumulation. But what was their legacy for postwar development? Colonial ideas were transferred to the postcolonial elites in the newly independent countries and among international networks. The preference for state-centric ideologies and the state's involvement in development planning survived the colonial state. After independence, new national governments divorced themselves rhetorically and legally from colonial precedents but held on to their logic. Anticolonialism was a derivative discourse, which accepted the premises of modernity on which colonial domination was based.[61] Postcolonial regimes inherited the trappings of the late colonial state. Their redefinition of the state as constructed by the people according to the new needs was an extravagant promise.[62] They expanded bureaucratic power in the name of development and strengthened development machinery. And the development professionals now working within international networks of experts also inherited the practices and economic discourse typical of late colonialism.

# 2

# Truman's Dream

## WHEN THE COLD WAR AND DEVELOPMENT MET

Fourth, we must embark on a bold new program for making the benefits of
our scientific advances and industrial progress available for the improvement
and growth of underdeveloped areas.

—HARRY TRUMAN, 1949

ON 20 JANUARY 1949, when Harry Truman came onstage at the Capitol and
took his oath for the second term as the thirty-third president of the United
States of America, he probably did not anticipate that his words would be
included on the list of history's most influential speeches. As the fourth point
in his program, he launched a policy of making US scientific advances and
industrial progress available to underdeveloped areas in order to fight misery,
malnutrition, and illness.[1] Truman's Point Four, as it soon became known,
was presented as an absolute novelty. Enthusiastically acclaimed by his contemporaries, it is sometimes considered the start of a new era of world history.
But Truman's dream did not come from a void. It condensed the experience,
expectations, and projects of an entire generation of politicians, technocrats,
and intellectuals, not just Americans, who had worked in reconstruction and
relief after the war and were convinced of the need to build a Western political
community at the onset of the Cold War.

Experiments in modernization and development in the 1920s and 1930s,
colonial or not, had been primarily national. The move from national to transnational, from regional to global projection, happened after—and because
of—the Second World War. This is why historiography identifies 1945 as a
moment of political cleavage. Understanding the need to bring the international community together around a shared development assistance program, the United States made economic assistance a major foreign policy

tool. President Franklin Delano Roosevelt was crucial in shaping this cooperative view of foreign aid. He framed his postwar policy and plans in global terms—as his letter to the US ambassador in Tokyo in January 1941 put it, "The problems we face now are so vast and so interrelated that any attempts even to state them compels one to think in terms of five continents and seven seas."[2] In his famous State of the Union Address that year, Roosevelt announced a plan to restructure the world according to the four freedoms: freedom of speech, freedom of worship, freedom from fear, and freedom from want. The latter meant that the United States was ready to promote economic growth and well-being on a global scale.

Postwar development plans elaborated between 1942 and 1943 by the Advisory Committee on Postwar Foreign Policy, headed by Secretary of State Cordell Hull and his assistants Benjamin Sumner Welles and Leo Pasvolsky, were clear about the main features of the new international order.[3] Crucial to the project was the organization of the United Nations. Hull and his team envisaged a regional structure, with each superpower responsible for an area— the four policemen in Roosevelt's formula being the United States, the Soviet Union, Great Britain, and China. In the world the committee imagined, colonial empires would be replaced by a new regime of international trusteeship. Although this anticolonial radicalism was soon dropped in order not to prejudice relations with the British, the United States kept its promises, moving forward with independence for the Philippines once it was liberated from the Japanese occupation. A conservative anticolonialism, together with self-determination in the Wilsonian tradition and the fact that the United States had been a colony, was enough for other nations to credit it as an anticolonial power on the level of the Soviet Union, which had always claimed anti-imperialism as a foundational part of its identity.

The global character of Roosevelt's postwar vision translated into a series of interrelated projects. The word used back then was "reconstruction," which was synonymous with "economic, social, and political development or progress."[4] Politically, reconstruction was centered on the United Nations; economically, it was based on international economic organizations, particularly the International Monetary Fund (IMF) and the International Bank for Reconstruction and Development (IBRD), born in 1944 at the Bretton Woods Conference. Roosevelt, who did not intend to replicate Wilson's failures, prioritized US participation in world government to avoid the threat of postwar isolationism.[5]

Using the New Deal as a model for the linkage between modernity and American-style participatory democracy was crucial to Roosevelt and his associates, who saw New Deal methods as a means of managing demobilization, humanitarian relief, and reconstruction. International aid was also crucial, given the humanitarian crises in all the war theaters, particularly Europe and East Asia. Relief activity was placed in the hands of UNRRA, the United Nations Relief and Rehabilitation Administration, which was created specifically for this purpose in 1943 and heavily supported—with both personnel and resources—by the United States. UNRRA was directed by Herbert Lehman, a former Democratic governor of New York State, together with the extremely efficient Australian administrator Robert G. A. Jackson, former director of Allied Supplies in the Middle East. Between 1943 and 1947, UNRRA had twelve thousand employees in Europe and Asia and distributed hundreds of millions of dollars in aid. It created experts who went on to work for other American assistance plans or on the staffs of international organizations. This experts' community built the framework of important networks of knowledge across the globe. Criticized by the US Congress for giving aid to the Soviet territories of the Ukraine and Belarus, UNRRA was liquidated in 1947, when its original mandate expired.[6] The UN Economic Commission for Europe (ECE) was its natural successor, but the prospect of US funding going to the ECE was unacceptable to the US administration, which feared that US assistance to Central Europe would benefit the Soviet Union and its allies. As deputy secretary of state William Clayton commented, the United States "must run this show," by which he meant that US funds should strengthen the Western alliance.[7]

Soon after the war, the Grand Wartime Alliance (US, UK, USSR) was just a memory as the Cold War dominated international relations. During the 1946 Paris peace negotiations, the United States and the Soviet Union confronted each other vehemently, emphasizing their differences. Anticommunism became explicit in the reasoning of US policy makers. George Kennan, the father of containment, the strategy that prescribed continuous surveillance of the Soviets and the vigilant application of counterforce at a series of constantly shifting geographical and political points, was appointed assistant secretary of state under George Marshall. In May 1947, he suggested that US aid to Europe should be directed not to fighting communism as such, but to restoring the economic health and spiritual vigor of European society. This was the idea behind the Marshall Plan, the grand plan for economic aid to Europe announced shortly thereafter. "Our policy," claimed Marshall in his famous speech at Harvard on 5 June 1947, "is directed not against any country or doctrine but against hunger, poverty, desperation and chaos."[8]

The Marshall Plan, officially known as the European Recovery Program (ERP), has been described as the most ambitious aid plan in history. It lasted from 1948 until 1952 (ending a few months before its scheduled final date) and involved sixteen countries for a total expenditure of $13 billion ($146 billion at today's prices), about 1.5 percent of the US GDP at the time. A huge effort in terms of organization and vision, it had clear, albeit not always explicit, goals of containing the communist peril in Europe. Historians almost unanimously consider it a watershed and hold it responsible for both the onset of the Cold War and European integration.[9] In addition, the Marshall Plan introduced concepts and methods that were later used in other situations. It helped consolidate transnational networks of experts, bringing together the most brilliant economists and social scientists on both shores of the Atlantic with the most stubborn managers of relief networks, both public and private. This multifaceted reconstruction effort extolled the New Deal and its ability to bridge modernity and participative democracy; it united different strands of modernization thinking and made them tools for global influence.[10] Some conservatives worried about this New Deal revival. British foreign minister Anthony Eden, for example, feared that the United States, filled with missionary fervor, would impose a worldwide New Deal or see the TVA as an infallible model for shaping global society.[11]

While the Marshall Plan dealt with Europe, other areas, now left without UNRRA support, jostled for attention. Extending bilateral aid to East Asia and Latin America was often discussed, but it was not clear whether the Marshall Plan could be replicated elsewhere.[12] Although there was moderate optimism in the form of belief that the New Deal experience could be universalized as a blueprint for liberal transformation with economic growth, it was clear that Europe's situation was unique. The challenge there was to restore preexisting industry and return a labor force already trained in a modern cultural environment to work; the situation was quite different elsewhere. Some places seemed to have favorable prospects. In China, for instance, US business saw great opportunities, and a mission of the Economic Cooperation Administration (ECA)—the agency administering Marshall Plan funding—was opened in China in 1948 to reach out to active groups, including local communists, to promote the United States as a good trading partner. Aid for the industrial and rural reconstruction of China was included in title IV of the 1948 Foreign Assistance Act, but the mission was closed down in 1949, after the consolidation of communist power and the birth of the People's Republic of China.

Convinced that the right mix of planning, investment, and technology could produce economic growth everywhere, social scientists tended to minimize differences among backward countries. There was not yet a clear demarcation of development as a concept exclusively or mainly for underdeveloped areas outside Europe. The feeling was rather of a certain permeability. Developed and backward areas naturally cohabited, and development recipes were universally applicable and transferable from one setting to the other. Lord Hailey, a high official in the British Colonial Office, for example, argued in 1944 that the same treatment be used for backward areas in the British Isles and the colonies, and that achieving better standards of living in underdeveloped areas had to become a priority for reconstruction.[13] Reconstruction and development became intertwined, so that the World Bank, the international organization originally intended to restore the existing economy, inherited both tasks.

## Point Four

With Point Four, President Truman interpreted the spirit of the times and condensed ideas from many places, bringing together humanitarianism, the concept of development, and the Cold War. In slightly more than twenty minutes in his inaugural address, he emphasized the "four major courses of action" for US foreign policy: "continue to give unfaltering support to the United Nations and related agencies . . . continue our programs for world economic recovery . . . strengthen freedom-loving nations against the dangers of aggression," and, as a fourth point, "embark on a bold new program for making the benefits of our scientific advances and industrial progress available for the improvement and growth of underdeveloped areas." The speech started with a clear and resounding indictment of the "false philosophy of Communism," which, he claimed, was "based on the belief that man is so weak and inadequate that he is unable to govern himself" and which decreed "what information he shall receive, what art he shall produce, what leaders he shall follow, and what thoughts he shall think."[14] Truman explicitly linked the Marshall Plan, the plan for aid to Greece and Turkey (the March 1947 Truman Doctrine), and Point Four, which he introduced as a natural evolution of American thinking on foreign aid and reconstruction, claiming that Point Four had been in his mind "and in the minds of the government for the past two or three years, ever since the Marshall Plan was inaugurated."[15]

This picture, which envisions Point Four as a sort of obsession of his administration, is clearly exaggerated, given that—as historian Louis J. Halle recounts—it was added to the address on the eve of the speech.[16] Nevertheless, Point Four was not just a last-minute rhetorical gimmick. It was worked out beforehand by some of Truman's aides, who pledged to construct a positive picture of American global commitment, starting with the Marshall Plan. Among them was the plan's author, journalist Benjamin H. Hardy. In 1948, Hardy had written a report on the use of technology as a weapon against international communism. He believed that the United States had to invest in technological progress in order to capture world public opinion.[17] Notwithstanding the US State Department's skepticism, Hardy's ideas triumphed.

The launch of Point Four was a success. It transmitted the idea of discontinuity, allowing the United States to claim it was new. Newspaper headlines trumpeted Point Four, and the Truman administration immediately began turning the slogan into concrete measures. Planning and promoting Point Four, including plans to finance it, started straightaway and at an intense pace. How should it articulate the relationship between technical assistance and capital, between private and public, between American and international initiatives, and ensure the protection of investments?[18] Truman recalls in his memoirs: "I immediately instituted a series of conferences on the subject of how best to implement the Point Four program and ordered the Secretary of State to direct the planning necessary to translate the program into action."[19] He insisted that it be made clear that the interests of recipients would prevail over the interests of US business, and that recipients would make do with their own means, because American experts were there to instruct them on using resources efficiently.

In October 1949, at a business lunch to promote Point Four, Truman described his dream of launching TVA-like programs to transform vast areas in the Middle East, Africa's Zambezi basin, and the South of Brazil, all of which would require a massive injection of capital. Opinion within the administration was divided, with some convinced that private capital would flow in and others envisioning major state involvement. Among the latter was economic adviser Walter Salant, who was convinced that Point Four had to take more inspiration from the Marshall Plan and export capital along with know-how. Major investments, he maintained, were indispensable for creating the markets that would sustain European and US export ambitions in the long run. Institutionally, Point Four needed an ad hoc agency modeled on the ECA, the Economic Cooperation Administration of the Marshall Plan, he thought. The State Department argued instead for offering mostly training, with local costs of specific projects covered by recipients, as the Soviet Union had done in Central Asia.[20] In this view, aid was mainly education, offering models of community development.[21] The State Department won, and the idea of capital financing was put aside.

Point Four was presented to Congress in July 1949 with an appropriation request of $45 million. It took Congress almost a year to pass the Act for International Development, approving it on 5 June 1950. The $29.9 million appropriated for the first year included funding for nationalist China, Palestine, and UNICEF. The Technical Cooperation Administration (TCA) was in charge of Point Four technical assistance. It was constituted within the State Department and was headed by Henry Garland Bennett, who was assisted by a consultative committee, presided over by Nelson Rockefeller, that worked to involve civil society. NGOs participated with projects in education, training, and public health.

Several projects were started within Point Four: antimalaria campaigns in Chimbote (Peru) and Shan (Burma, now Myanmar), and rural development initiatives in Haiti, Mexico, Jordan, and India. Lauchlin Currie, a key New Deal figure, criticized Point Four, maintaining that the undertakings were limited and improvised—for one thing, experts were sent according to recipient request, not a general development plan.[22] From the very beginning, the Point Four administration suffered from excess bureaucracy and did not seem to be run effectively; in 1950, the new Mutual Security Agency (MSA) absorbed its activities. Point Four did, however, do well as a brand. In 1956, for example, the German Krupp company launched a new initiative called the Krupp Plan or "Point Four and One Half": it invited a consortium of private businesses to join it in offering technical assistance for profit-making projects.[23] The plan never took off.

Point Four has been described as the first case of implanting the Marshall Plan outside its original European framework. Both were masterpieces of political communication, born as empty shells to be filled with policies. They shared the same goals: peace, plenty, freedom, and the hope of keeping communism at bay by offering growth as the cure for social hardship. Technology was the key to increasing production and this, in turn, would grant peace and prosperity. Both programs were built on cooperation and the goal of strengthening regional alliances among countries identified with Western democratic values. The similarities between the two plans were also clear to the Soviets. *Pravda* commented that the two were complementary programs for economic expansion disguised by the rhetoric of anticommunism. The Soviet Union never failed to denounce Point Four as a variety of US imperialism intended to "seize the colonies and underdeveloped areas of the world in toto."[24]

The differences between the Marshall Plan and Point Four were, however, huge. Unlike emergency measures like UNRRA and the Marshall Plan, and despite its limited funding, Point Four was meant to carry on for longer. It was part of an economic development plan undergirded by "the expectation that better economic conditions would be more conducive to democratic institutions, and to a more peaceful world."[25] It was intended to prove that capitalism was better equipped than socialism to ameliorate the lives of the poor and underprivileged. ECA economic officer John D. Sumner maintained that development policy had to show that democracy was the best route to economic progress and political freedom.[26] Another key difference was that the backward countries were not offered the same conditions as Europe. Since resources were expected to come from private sources, the key point was to create the right environment for investments by taming nationalist and leftist tendencies among peasants and workers. Even though, as Truman pointed out, technical assistance was not "against Communism or anything else," it was made to serve as an antidote for communism. In Truman's words, "the Point Four program . . . was a positive plan of self-help for any country that wanted it. It recognized the historic fact that colonialism had run its course and could no longer be made to work for a few favored nations."[27]

With the escalation of the Cold War after the birth of the People's Republic of China and the outbreak of the Korean War, anticommunism became increasingly important. In 1950, the United States began intensely publicizing Point Four as a way to counter communist threats, with the aim of convincing politicians, public opinion, and academics of its usefulness. In March 1950, "Aiding Underdeveloped Areas Abroad," a special edition of the *Annals of the American Academy of Political and Social Science*, came out to explain the program and its goals. Willard L. Thorp, the economist in charge of Point Four, and his working group wrote most of the articles, which covered a series of topics, including relations with colonial powers in Europe and the Marshall Plan.[28] The July issue, "Formulating a Point Four Program," gave further details.[29]

## Studying Backward Areas: Social Scientists, the Marshall Plan, and the Limits of the Cold War

An emerging epistemic community came to exist around the issue of development. Centered in the United States, it interpreted development as a cooperative task of the international community.[30] The language of Point Four seemed to be purposely crafted to attract believers, activists, and internationalists of various kinds who were likely to be enticed into government service by the prospect of a universal mission. This community had been engaged in earlier projects, particularly UNRRA. Samuel Hayes recalls that Point Four was "heavily dominated by technical people—educators, agricultural extension people, public health people" who focused on their own specialty more than the broader picture.[31] For anthropologists, in contrast, who did not see development as a culturally neutral and universally desired norm, the project was a nightmare that would do violence to traditional cultures.[32] Point Four enthusiasts made no bones about this. Willard L. Thorp, assistant secretary of state for economic affairs, insisted on the cultural elements of development: it was necessary to change people's habits and convince them to use new techniques.[33] US experts had to plant their ideas in the minds of their partners, while convincing them that these ideas were their own original aspirations. Allen Griffin, former member of the ECA mission in China and then head of a special study mission in Indochina, maintained that the United States had to promote democratic (read: anticommunist) choices. It needed to provide a modern education that would supplant religious traditions that favored submissive attitudes, which hindered opposition to authoritarian rule.[34] NGOs identified education as the key to bringing local cultures into fruitful dialogue with the West.[35]

Within this community of social scientists, attention quickly moved from topics such as hygiene, health, education, employment, and urban quality of life to the economy. Academics had discovered poverty, and this discovery led to the gradual sacralization of economics.[36] In a talk held in Buenos Aires in the late 1950s, Italian top manager Aurelio Peccei, who would become famous as a founder of the Club of Rome (a think tank concerned with the predicaments of growth), observed that modernity had turned misery, once seen as normal, into something morally unacceptable.[37] Economists elaborated ad hoc tools that were thought to be able to read hunger, poverty, and development as comparable and measurable issues.[38] Their concepts of poverty built on the discovery of per capita income and the progress in comparative statistics. Constructing a universal index for measuring wealth had been a topic for cutting-edge research in the interwar years in Central and Eastern Europe, with the work of Polish economist Ludwik Landau standing out.[39] British economist Colin Clark was fundamental in further promoting a standard GDP.[40] Thanks to new aggregate tools of measurement, national or regional situations could be compared to common standards, bringing a revolution in poverty awareness. When in 1948 the World Bank set the threshold for poverty at $100 in annual GDP per capita, suddenly many were identified as poor and in need of assistance. Using economic-statistical language for a definition of well-being allowed underdevelopment to be read not as something ontologically different from development, but rather as one of its stages and thus a condition that could be acted on.

The Marshall Plan was the *trait d'union* between the tradition of foreign aid and development. Technocrats involved in the Marshall Plan had a special role in shaping the new discourse of development.[41] As Paul Hoffman, head of the ECA from 1948, one of the fathers of the UN Special Fund for Development in 1958, and later the first director of the United Nations Development Programme, explained in 1951: "We have learned in Europe what to do in Asia, for under the Marshall Plan we have developed the essential instruments of a successful policy in the arena of world politics."[42] Point Four used the new expert network that the Marshall Plan had put in place. It is intriguing to study the links between the Marshall Plan—that is, development and modernization through European reconstruction—and the new civilizing mission in underdeveloped areas.

The case of Italy shows the limits of the American approach to development. In the early years of the Cold War, Italy was a case study for the way regional development policies could be turned into global models for use in backward countries.[43] The Mezzogiorno was a laboratory of the kind envisaged by economist Eugene Staley in the 1930s, a place to export the "model TVA." David Lilienthal and his Development and Resource Corporation were active on the

Italian scene during postwar reconstruction.[44] Paul Narcyz Rosenstein-Rodan, a prominent economist in the Austrian School, well known for his works on marginal utility and the hierarchical structures of wants, saw Italy as the ideal laboratory for development. In the 1930s, he moved to Britain and then to the United States, where he worked as a consultant for the Marshall Plan.[45] In 1947, he followed the Italian case at the World Bank and became confident that Italy was indeed an ideal place to test comprehensive strategies aimed at turning a condition of backwardness into an asset, the perfect bridge between reconstruction in Europe and development in backward areas.[46] In his 1950 report on the development program of southern Italy, he was highly appreciative of the Italian development plan for the South, including the creation of the Cassa per il Mezzogiorno (Fund for the South), designed in May 1950 to promote economic growth in southern Italy, judging it the broadest and most attractive regional development plan in the world.[47] Italy thus received additional development funding.

In the 1950s Italy's southern provinces came into the spotlight because of the World Bank's commitment. For pioneers in development, the case was especially attractive.[48] Italy had a typical dual economy, of the kind described by W. Arthur Lewis during this period.[49] It was an ideal place to implement a plan that aimed at creating the preconditions for industrial development, starting with infrastructure. Albert O. Hirschmann, then working on the Federal Reserve Board, begged for an invitation to Italy in a letter to Italian economist and politician Manlio Rossi-Doria.[50] In his memoirs, Hollis B. Chenery recalls his period in Italy in the early 1950s as crucial. As a chief economist for both the State Department and ECA, he worked on input-output models to heighten the case for program lending.[51] The UN Economic Commission for Europe, presided over by Gunnar Myrdal, also devoted special attention to Italy in its study of depressed areas and how to promote development in them.[52]

The Association for the Development of Industry in Southern Italy (Associazione per lo Sviluppo dell'Industria nel Mezzogiorno; Svimez), a think tank created in December 1946 for the study of industrial development in backward Italian areas, was especially active. Rosenstein-Rodan was a member of its board (1954–1982) and worked with its Center for the Study of Economic Development (Centro per gli Studi sullo Sviluppo Economico), which trained experts and officials in developing countries.[53] The International Study Congress on Backward Areas (Congresso Internazionale di Studio sul Problema delle Aree Arretrate), held in Milan in October 1954, is the perfect place to see how Italians dealt with the development discourse of the early 1950s.[54] Organized around the discussion of the Italian case and its progress, the congress featured a special role for the state as an engine for development.

Point Four and its language were everywhere: the sense of mission, the stress on cooperation, the role of technology, the promotion of democracy, and the distance kept from colonial policies—these were all present in Milan. But the Milan conference also revealed the differences between Italian planners and the Americans who wanted to make their country a model for development. Italian social scientists preferred the public sector over the private sector and paid attention to anthropological elements and cultural specifics. They signaled discontent with US expertise and its one-size-fits-all approach and were resistant to standardized solutions imposed from above. They made it clear that they were not willing to serve as a laboratory for models designed abroad, especially not TVA-like policies. David Lilienthal soon abandoned the idea of working in Italy and used Italian technicians for his company's projects elsewhere. The ideas discussed at the conference clearly favored industrial development, following the lead of the arguably charismatic and symbolic figure of Italian developmentalism, Pasquale Saraceno. The Italian case, he contended, proved that developing agriculture and providing infrastructure were not enough to ignite the big push, the decisive move toward self-sustained growth theorized by Rosenstein-Rodan.[55] Foreign experts at the congress wanted to legitimize the Italian political economy just as much as they wanted to provoke scientific discussion. Italy's prospects as a worldwide model were severely limited by the lack of any real success story to tell, as Italy never fully completed the move from recipient to donor country.[56] Good only for a certain stage of development, the model was neither applicable to nor applied in former Italian colonies or in countries that were significantly poorer or less developed than Italy. The only case study on colonial areas offered in Milan was a report on Somalia from the Trusteeship Administration (Amministrazione Fiduciaria Italiana della Somalia, AFIS), which was disconnected from the *fil rouge* of the conference—that is, the state as a key agent for development through industrialization. As for the Cold War, the most notable sign of tension was the almost complete absence of participants from the Eastern Bloc. The only country representing socialist development was Yugoslavia. No contribution touched on development in backward areas in the Soviet Union; no significant mention was made of the socialist countries. The proceedings of the conference clearly show how, notwithstanding the pressure of the bipolar conflict, Cold War rhetoric and development discourse still had separate dimensions. In the 1950s, the reference to communism was not yet central to the development discourse. The case of Italian social scientists is paradigmatic of European resistance to fully identifying with US development strategies. The problems the United States encountered later, including the inability to fully make development a crucial weapon in the arsenal of the Cold War, echo the troubles of these early days.

# 3

# Socialist Modernity and the Birth of the Third World

These countries although they do not belong to the socialist world system can draw on its achievements in building an independent national economy and raising their people's living standards. Today they need not go begging to their former oppressors for modern equipment. They can get it in the socialist countries, free from any political or military obligations.

—NIKITA KHRUSHCHEV, 1956

We cannot tell our peoples that material benefits and growth and modern progress are not for them. If we do, they will throw us out and seek other leaders who promise more. And they will abandon us too if we do not in reasonable measure respond to their hopes. Therefore we have no choice. We have to modernize.

—KWAME NKRUMAH, 1958

"IF WE GET self-government we'll transform the Gold Coast into a paradise in ten years," Kwame Nkrumah, leader of the Convention People's Party, famously promised on the eve of the 1949 elections for the Legislative Council of Ghana, still under colonial rule.[1] Nkrumah, a leading figure of Pan-Africanism and a great protagonist of the history of independent Africa, was expressing a widespread sentiment in territories aspiring to independence: the belief that colonial rule was the origin of all evil, and that "once they became free to manage all affairs, all these problems would disappear."[2] If colonialism was the cause of backwardness, then independence would logically and automatically bring development. In Africa and Asia this attitude was shared by the educated middle class, the local elites of the colonies, formed by the generations that had been sent to study in Europe in the 1920s and 1930s and had come back fervent nationalists.[3] This view shaped what has been called the revolution of rising expectations and was part of an emancipatory discourse with global dimensions. Nationalism in newly independent countries was axiomatically anticapitalist because capitalism was associated with Western imperialism. How far did this also imply a natural inclination toward socialism? Several leaders in the developing world observed with great interest the Soviet model and its promise for redemption and progress—but it was far from obvious how and whether, during and after decolonization, socialism would take the form of a global project shared by postcolonial elites, and whether this would happen under Soviet leadership.

## Ideology Put to the Test on the Colonial Question

Marxism was originally ambiguous about the colonial project. Karl Marx, writing on British rule in India, claimed that the mission of the British bourgeoisie there was double: to bring down the old Asian order and prepare the ground for building Western society. This was commendable work. In a second stage, the fruits of the civilizing mission would be gathered when the working class overthrew the dominant classes or when Indians broke free of the British yoke. Economic development was the key to evolution, and the working class the engine to real civilization. This embrace of the civilizing mission inspired some debate in the Second International.[4] Some damned colonialism's violence; others justified it in the name of progress.[5] Karl Kautsky, for example, the leading promulgator of orthodox Marxism after the death of Friedrich Engels, was skeptical about the civilizing mission, maintaining that backward people could rule themselves. He praised cultural variety and self-government as values.[6] Reformist Eduard Bernstein, in contrast, saw socialism as building a future for colonies, a future with a higher, more modern, and more advanced culture.[7]

The Bolshevik Revolution altered things by disproving the assumption that capitalist economic development had to be achieved for revolution to succeed. In 1913, Lenin was optimistic about the prospects for revolution in Asia. His pamphlet *Imperialism, the Highest Stage of Capitalism* (1917) provided the basis for communist influence in the colonies and blamed economic oppression and colonial exploitation on financial capitalism.[8] With their successful revolution, the Bolsheviks became an all-around model—of an ideology of liberation, a successful revolution, and the construction of a modern state. In the Communist International, a new interest in the fate of peoples under colonial rule emerged. The Second Congress of the Communist International, or Comintern, held in Moscow in 1920, pondered the communist attitude toward liberation movements. Was nationalism to be considered a transitional stage toward socialism, or rejected as reactionary? The agreed-on line was unconditional support for the anticolonial struggle, which became a prerequisite for adhering to the Communist International. But this did not mean there was unanimity on this point. Mahabhendra Nath Roy, a central figure of "national cosmopolitanism," did not share Lenin's doubts on the revolutionary potential of the colonies. In his *Supplementary Theses on the National and Colonial Question*, Roy defended nationalists in the dependent territories, convinced that they could promote a successful revolution even without the complete formation of a working class.[9]

The national question was important for the populations inhabiting the former Tsarist Empire. The Muslim communist Mirsaid Sultan-Galiev, who preached communism and independence for the Tatar minority, was expelled from the party for promoting Islam's role in national liberation in Asia and advocating for a separate anticolonial international movement.[10] The First Congress of the Peoples of the East was held in Baku, Azerbaijan in September 1920. One topic was anticolonial strategy. The Soviet model was widely considered a great success, and many delegates formed a local communist party on their return from the congress. In the 1920s, communist parties were built in Indochina and Indonesia that promised to link nation building with distributive justice. As Nguyên-Aï-Quôc (later Ho Chi Minh) used to say, it was patriotism, not communism, that prompted him to believe in Lenin.[11] He officially joined the Communist Party in 1921. His 1925 book *Le procès de la colonisation* condemned French rule severely and promoted resistance and revolution as remedies to colonialism. Communists in the colonies were certainly inspired by social revolution along the lines of the Soviet model, but for them the conflict was not between workers and capitalists, but between colonized and colonizers.[12] The Bolsheviks quickly began working to export Soviet expertise—they saw little difference between propagating communism at home and abroad. Exporting a model meant exporting everything: forms of political organization as well as strategies for economic development. The Mongolian Revolution of 1921 offered a perfect opportunity for Bolshevik sympathizers, supported by the Soviet government, to experiment with setting up a people's republic in a backward area. Education, culture (including antireligious policies), collectivization, and rural development were all elements in this picture. The experiment was then exported to other parts of Central Asia.[13]

## The Age of Indifference

After this initial enthusiasm, a long period of apathy followed, coinciding with Stalin's rule. Between 1928 and 1943, national liberation movements ceased to be under the spell of the Comintern. The myth of Soviet modernity resisted, filtered through study trips and political pilgrimages organized under Stalinism, but the model was not easily transmitted. Latin American countries were not attentive and were geographically distant from the Soviet Union. Representatives from colonized territories in Asia and Africa had no opportunities to go to the Soviet Union; colonial powers did not invite dangerous political activists to the colonies. On the Soviet side, interest in promoting mutual knowledge and encounter was limited, and any hesitation in coordinating the anticolonial struggle with nationalists was justified by the Shanghai massacre of 1927. Secretary-general of the Communist Party of the Soviet Union (CPSU) Joseph Stalin had insisted on an alliance between the Chinese Communist Party and the nationalists of the Guomindang as a tribute to the Leninist line on cooperation in overthrowing imperialism. But in April 1927, the Guomindang purged members of the Communist Party and started an anticommunist campaign that culminated in the killing of thousands of people. The Soviet leadership then abandoned its promotion of modernity in Asia. In 1931, any discussion of China was prohibited, and in the great Soviet purges of 1937–1938, most of the people with Asian experience were removed.[14]

Political thinking also changed. In the 1920s, the key question was what relations could exist between socialist and capitalist countries of the West and the Orient (the word used to define all non-European areas, capitalist or not). The view spread that Asian countries had a special mode of production: a land property regime that made it possible to skip the stage of a bourgeois revolution. After the blow at Shanghai, special consideration for the Asian mode of production, on which the alliance with the Guomindang was based, was banished. Economic development was to be standardized along the path of the five historical stages prescribed by official ideology: primitive-communal and early slave-holding, slave-holding, early feudalism, capitalism, and finally communism. Economist Eugen Varga, an important and controversial figure in Soviet intellectual history, refused to relinquish the idea of an Asian mode of production. His thoughts remained marginal for quite a long time but were resurrected in the late 1960s, as a renewed interest in Asia and Africa grew.[15]

Although lack of reciprocal knowledge was a problem, in the interwar years the Soviet experiment became a model for nationalist elites aspiring to independence. After the Second World War, the Soviet miracle of modernization, economic growth, industrialization, and full employment was an important part of Soviet propaganda, even though Stalin was uninterested in decolonization and did not seem anxious to identify with the anticolonial struggle. He was convinced that after the war colonial peoples would rise against imperialists, but he did not get involved. The revolutionary nature of these movements was so self-evident that specific propaganda efforts seemed superfluous.[16] No communist party from the colonies was invited to the founding conference of the Cominform, in September 1947. The event was reserved for the mainstays of European communism. The convener, Soviet delegate Andrey Aleksandrovich Zhdanov, mentioned national liberation movements only in passing and never cited China. The "two camps" theory introduced there, which saw the camp of imperialism and the camp of socialism as being irreconcilably opposed, ruled out the possibility of the Soviet Union supporting nationalist movements in territories striving for independence. Stalin remained skeptical about the prospects for communism in China; he did not support the Chinese communists until 1948, when victory over the nationalist leader Chiang Kai-shek was virtually assured. In 1949, he recommended that the Chinese communists not overdo reforms like eliminating private property, collectivizing, and nationalizing industrial properties and land: he thought China's fate was democratic-revolutionary government, not communism. Even after meeting Mao Zedong and signing the Sino-Soviet Treaty of Friendship, Alliance and Mutual Assistance, in February 1950, he had doubts about the authenticity of Chinese communism.[17]

Some scholars assert that Stalin's caution was due to Europe's primacy in his strategic view: communism's success in China, Iran, or Southeast Asia might have threatened the consolidation of Soviet influence in Central and Eastern Europe.[18] But the war in Korea (1950–1953) became an opportunity to strengthen an alliance between the Soviet Union and China. Unlike Mao, though, Stalin did not see a direct link between decolonization and world revolution. He doubted the centrality of newly independent countries in international politics and tended to delegate Asian issues, saying that the Chinese Communist Party had to handle the situation in Indonesia, for example, where it could count on a large community of Chinese residents. The few suggestions delivered to Indonesian communists were delayed or lacked knowledge of the local situation and carried no great weight.[19]

Stalin did not like India, and he especially disliked its prime minister Jawaharlal Nehru, the leader of the Congress Party, whom he saw as too close to Great Britain and the United States. The aversion was mutual. Nehru preferred Fabian socialism to communism. In 1919 he noted poignantly that it was the discrediting of President Wilson that had raised the specter of communism in Asia.[20] The Indian Communist Party had failed to become a significant force in Indian politics and was split, with one group singing the praises of the Chinese model.[21] The Soviet opinion that the Congress Party was bourgeois and undeserving of protection did not help relations.[22] Nehru's sister, Vijaya Lakshmi Pandit, was appointed ambassador to the Soviet Union, but Stalin ignored her. Only in 1950 was the Indian Communist Party instructed to support Nehru. Two years later, when the Soviet Union sided with India on the Kashmir issue, bilateral relations began to improve. In 1953, the new Indian ambassador to Moscow, K. P. S. Menon, met Stalin just days before his death. He was struck by Stalin's vivid world vision, a sharp contrast to the dullness of Indian foreign policy. Nehru paid tribute to Stalin in the Indian Parliament; bilateral relations became smoother, even idyllic.[23]

With the launch of Point Four, a new kind of rivalry joined the silent competition between the development models of the interwar years. The Soviet Union attacked Point Four as "A Program for Expansion under a Screen of Anti-Communism" that was no different from older forms of imperialism.[24] In March 1949 at the United Nations, the Soviet Union accused the United States of a lack of clarity about the nature and conditions of the proposed aid to underdeveloped countries. It was plain to see that the Soviets were annoyed by the initiative. In 1948, when the UN Expanded Program of Technical Assistance, EPTA, was inaugurated, the Soviets had not contributed a single ruble. Now, while condemning American assistance, they applauded a fair aid policy that supported political independence and invested to promote national agriculture and industry. This signaled that they were open to joining a multilateral program and offering technical assistance and industrial machinery to underdeveloped countries, with a stress on equality and open criticism of imperialist dynamics.[25] But what would the Soviets contribute? Western analysts thought of expertise, while critics familiar with the Central Asian precedent worried about the repression of minorities. Only in 1954 did the Soviet Union respond with a plan for the Virgin Lands, the campaign to bring up-to-date farming and irrigation techniques to backward steppe regions in Kazakhstan. This became a paradigm for what socialist modernity could offer to less developed countries. In the coming years, the Soviet recipe would shift its focus to forced industrialization.

## The Afterthought

After Stalin's death, the Soviet leaders' view of newly independent countries willing to cut ties with their former colonial power changed—an attitude that has been called an afterthought.[26] But this revisionism actually started earlier, as the two camps formula came under increasing question. In May 1952, an international economic conference in Moscow discussed the possibility of an overproduction crisis hitting the Soviet Union and making it necessary to find markets for industrial output in exchange for raw materials. M. V. Nesterov, president of the Chamber of Commerce, claimed that the Soviet Union could send $3 million in machinery within two to three years, in exchange for cotton, jute, rubber, leather and nonferrous metals. In the spring of 1952, a new Soviet agency for foreign trade would sell machinery to developing countries. No action was taken until Stalin's death, however. An agreement was signed with

Afghanistan in 1953 and the Soviet Union started courting newly independent countries, especially in the United Nations.[27]

On 15 July 1953, at the sixteenth session of the Economic and Social Council of the United Nations (ECOSOC), the Soviet delegation abandoned nonparticipation and announced a contribution of four million rubles (then equivalent to $1 million) to the EPTA. It also granted bilateral aid, one loan at very convenient interest rates to Argentina and one to Afghanistan, and signed a long-term cooperation agreement with India. But these agreements were seen as strictly commercial, not as aid. Soon, however, the political economy of Soviet aid absorbed these initiatives, and subsequent ones, in a coherent propaganda offensive aimed at convincing underdeveloped countries to dissolve their traditional bonds with the West. This signaled an important shift in attitudes toward decolonization: a reevaluation of nationalists was occurring. A turning point was the 1955 trip of Nikita Khrushchev and Nikolai Bulganin, respectively the first secretary of the CPSU and the premier of the Soviet Union, to India, Afghanistan, and Burma: a friendly, but highly symbolic visit.[28] Confirming the new priority, two high officials in the Planning Commission, M. G. Pervikhin and M. Z. Saburov, were put in charge of the aid program.[29] At the end of 1955, the Soviets showcased their technology in fairs in Indonesia, Syria, Morocco, Argentina, and Uruguay. In India, the confrontation acquired new features, with the West held responsible for the country's underdevelopment. India was crucial for exporting the Soviet model to the Third World. It was here that the most fundamental element of nation building—national economic planning—became an international enterprise.[30]

India's Second Five-Year Plan took center stage. Drafted between 1954 and 1956, it was meant to cover the years 1956–1961. Its master was Prasanta Chandra Mahalanobis, longtime director of the Indian Statistical Institute (ISI), which served as a transmission line between international and Indian experts. Mahalanobis once told a student that while the first plan had been an anthology, a patchwork of different projects dating from the 1940s, the second would be a drama. It anticipated a growth in GDP of 5 percent per year, fighting unemployment with full-speed expansion. Like Nehru, Mahalanobis looked at the Soviet Union not as a political champion, but as a model for economic success. Although he had worked closely with Soviet experts and was an honorary member of the Soviet Academy of Sciences, he did not fully share their ideas. He did not have nationalization in mind, for example, even though he saw state enterprises prevailing over private ones in all strategic sectors. While working on the plan, Mahalanobis, who had been a member of the UN Economic Commission for Asia and the Far East, invited the most celebrated development economists to India. Michał Kalecki and Oskar Lange came from the Soviet Bloc; Ragnar Frisch, Jan Tinbergen, Simon Kuznets, Nicholas Kaldor, John Kenneth Galbraith, and Milton Friedman came from the West. In a 1969 interview, Gunnar Myrdal recalled that the commission had consulted all possible economic experts from Europe and the United States. Inviting foreign experts was probably a flag of prestige, given that their advice left little trace on the final plan.[31] Local experts did not accept criticism well: an Indian officer, confronted with Kalecki's criticism, commented indignantly that so many changes would in fact amount to rebuilding the whole country. Kalecki replied that in order to rebuild a country one should first make a revolution, not invite foreign experts.[32]

## The Age of Neutralism, or the Birth of the Third World

In the early 1950s, the world's less-developed countries began identifying as a homogeneous group. In the UN, and especially in the ECOSOC, the phrase used was "underdeveloped countries," but this was soon replaced by a much more evocative concept: the "Third World." The expression was coined in 1952 by French demographer Alfred Sauvy, who anticipated a collective awakening of the subject peoples previously ignored, exploited, and watched warily: a revolution like that of the Third Estate during the French Revolution.[33] The main reference was to the potentially subversive energy of the newly independent countries that were ready to take on a role commensurate with their demographic weight. In sum, it was one version of the Malthusian nightmare of excess population. Third World countries shared a Cold War political positioning: they claimed to be neutral. While initially this was not a key identifying element for the group, it became one during the Bandung Conference of 18–24 April 1955.

Convened by five Asian countries—Burma (now Myanmar), Ceylon (now Sri Lanka), India, Indonesia, and Pakistan—the Bandung Conference was the biggest and most influential meeting of Third World leaders ever. It was not the first time they had met, having been summoned in 1927 to the Conference of the League against Imperialism initiated by the Comintern to discuss the Chinese anti-imperialist struggle and the defense of the black race in Africa and America. For the first time, though, postcolonial leaders met at home. As President Sukarno claimed in the opening speech: "We do not need to go to other continents to confer. . . . We are again masters in our house."[34] The Bandung Conference called for worldwide decolonization. Twenty-nine countries and nineteen liberation movements were invited; prominent attendees included Hadj-Ahmed Messali from Algeria, Zhou Enlai from China, and Jawaharlal Nehru from India. Participants were all nonwhite and generally anti-imperialist. As Sukarno put it: "We are united by a common detestation of colonialism in whatever form it appears. We are united by a common detestation of racism. And we are united by a common determination to preserve and stabilize peace in the world."[35]

Bandung introduced a fundamentally anticolonial discourse.[36] Asian elites, commented African American writer Richard Wright, were "more Western than the West"—more modern, ready to innovate and burn bridges with the past.[37] In terms of political alignment, however, Bandung participants were less united. China and North Vietnam were aligned with the Soviet Union; Turkey, Pakistan, Thailand, and the Philippines were with the West; and India, Indonesia, and Burma were neutral. Being anticolonialist did not necessarily mean being procommunist: Sukarno opened the conference by citing the American Revolution. John Kotelawala, Ceylon's prime minister, asserted that countries in Central and Eastern Europe were also subject to colonial rule: by the Soviets. The pro-Western head of the Philippines' delegation, Carlos Romulo, paraded his blatant antipathy for hardcore neutrals, especially Jawaharlal Nehru, Gamal Abdel Nasser, and U Nu. He mocked India's condescension to China and was annoyed by the obvious sense of cultural superiority shown by Indian representatives.[38] Chinese Politburo member Deng Xiaoping confessed to Soviet ambassador Chervonenko that the struggle with bourgeois figures such as Nehru, Sukarno, and Nasser was "one of the most important problems facing the international communist movement."[39]

A large portion of the conference was spent discussing political issues, but economics was also crucial: Bandung rang the bell for economic decolonization. Ideas on postcolonial economic development traveled, becoming the collective knowledge of the postcolonial elites. Two ideas emerged above the rest: the obligation for countries in the developed North to give aid, and the reversion of sovereign rights over natural resources. There had been a Marshall Plan for Europe, but little more than chicken feed for Asia, protested Carlos Romulo. In the West, some feared the conference would translate into an accusation against the West and a collective move toward socialism. This did not happen—the call for help was directed at both sides. The final communiqué spoke of a deep concern about international tensions in an age of atomic weapons and urged "abstention from arrangements of collective defense to serve the particular interests of any of the big powers."[40] The formula was general because some countries, for instance China, were formally involved with the superpowers. Such ambiguities were dissipated in Belgrade in 1961, with the birth of the Non-Aligned Movement (NAM), in which only formally unaligned countries could participate. Non-Aligned Conferences—there were six in total—helped foster a sense of unity and a common platform for the newly independent countries.

# Khrushchev's Challenge

The apex of Soviet interest in the Third World coincided with the governance of the most Third Worldist Politburo member: Nikita Khrushchev. Under Khrushchev, the Soviet Union scaled down the two camps theory that had inhibited its actions and, after the Bandung Conference, adopted a new discourse. The zones of peace theory, although compatible with the two camps formula, considered the role of newly independent countries in world politics. Socialist countries and newly independent ones could cooperate in their many areas of common interest: peace, development, anticolonialism, anti-imperialism, and disarmament—Bandung's key points. In 1956, at the Twentieth Congress of the CPSU, Khrushchev stated that newly independent countries in Asia, Africa, and Latin America, although not part of the world socialist system, could profit from its success. They could receive modern machinery and advice from the socialist countries without political or military obligations and without having to beg from their former oppressors.[41]

Khrushchev's words were a wake-up call for the United States. The Soviet Union had accepted the challenge—an aid war was about to break out. Henry Kissinger described the feeling on the pages of the journal *Foreign Affairs*. "For several years," he wrote, "we have been groping for a concept to deal with the transformation of the Cold War from an effort to build defensive barriers into a contest for the allegiance of humanity."[42] Another prospective guru of US foreign policy, Zbigniew Brzezinski, wrote in slightly more alarmed tones that nondemocratic forces seemed to have an advantage over the forces of democracy in their ability to export their political structures to newly independent countries.[43] The Soviet interest in aid was interpreted as an offensive, and the reaction was immediate. In 1958, two works became available on the topic: the State Department published *The Sino-Soviet Economic Offensive in the Less Developed Countries*, and economics professor Joseph S. Berliner wrote *Soviet Economic Aid*.[44] The books lumped together Soviet policies with those of their allies. In the former, Soviet and Chinese assistance was made one and the same thing, while the latter described aid from the entire Socialist Bloc as Soviet aid.[45]

Although Khrushchev's words stressed technological advancement as the way to assist the newly independent countries to modernity, ideology and propaganda were still considered crucial means against the imperialist monopoly of the decolonizing world. The ideological resolve of Third World leaders needed strengthening whenever possible, with constant reference to the struggle against colonialism and imperialism to complement future economic investments. In this work East Germany—the German Democratic Republic (GDR)—had been a trusted ally for the Soviet Union since the early

1950s: it sent emergency aid to the national liberation movement in Algeria in 1954, immediately sided with Egypt in the 1956 Suez Crisis, and offered aid to Congo in 1960 and to Angola in 1961.[46] The division for international relations of the East German Communist Party, the Sozialistische Einheitspartei Deutschlands (SED), managed relations with national liberation movements, and the Soviet Union systematically consulted East Germans on the prospects of national liberation in Africa. East Germans were active in NGOs sponsored by the Soviet Union like the World Federation of Trade Unions, the World Federation of Democratic Youth, the International Union of Students, and the International Organization of Journalists.[47] The SED had a specific task: to make sure that national liberation movements followed Socialist orthodoxy.[48]

The Soviet Union was soon presented with several opportunities for direct competition with the United States. In July 1956, when Dulles withdrew the United States from the Aswan Dam project, Moscow made its offer, which was predicated on the Egyptians also rejecting Western aid for the project's next stages. In September 1956, the Soviets offered $100 million in aid to Indonesia, with the agreement ratified in 1958. In the same year, they signed an agreement with Guinea, which the West was boycotting as a punishment for rejecting colonial rule. In India, the USSR started a huge steel mill project in Bhilai. The Soviets concentrated on just a few recipients: in 1958, Egypt, Ghana, Iraq, Syria, Algeria, Indonesia, India, and Afghanistan received 80 percent of Soviet aid.[49]

## Features of Socialist Aid: Constructing the Ideological Framework

What were the main features of this aid? After 1956, there was an effort to clarify its characteristics, to elaborate a totally different rhetoric from the West and adapt ideology to the new framework. Decolonization was key: Eugen Varga asserted in 1957 that the disintegration of the colonial system was shaking imperialism at its foundations. The result of the general crisis of capitalism, it could not fail to make it worse.[50] As for the specific problems of development, the Soviet view was simplistic: underdevelopment was a consequence of colonial rule that persisted thanks to capitalist structures. The recipe for economic modernization was therefore equally simple: to cut relations with the West and introduce planning, nationalization, industrialization, and close relations with the Eastern Bloc. In 1958, the State Committee for Foreign Economic Relations (Gosudarstvennyi Komitet po Vneshnim Ekonomicheskim Svyazyam; GKES) defined "socialist development" using the Soviet experience in the Caucasus, the laboratory for socialist modernity, as the model. First came the establishment of modern, mechanized agriculture based on collective and state farms. Next came investments in infrastructure and industrial plants. Finally, the nascent industry had to be protected by limiting the presence of foreign capital and nationalizing existing enterprises so that the state was the only engine of growth.[51]

The new interest in noncommunist countries and the East meant that old Soviet institutions were reenergized and new ones created. In 1958, a special conference was organized at the Oriental Institute, the Soviet institution for the study of the history of non-European regions. Long forgotten, the institute was back on top after the Soviet Union's opening to the Third World meant that expertise was needed. Anastas Mikoyan did much to revitalize the institute after claiming during the 1956 Party Congress that it was still dozing, notwithstanding the awakening of the Orient. The study of the classic cultures of non-European countries took place in Leningrad (today's Saint Petersburg), while a new seat was opened in Moscow to focus on contemporary issues. In 1956, the Institute of World Economy and International Relations (IMEMO) was resuscitated as well. Shut down in 1947 after the final fracture with the West, it now had a new job. Instead of studying the possibility of compromise between the two systems, it collected data and analyzed social and economic trends. In 1959, a new Institute for Africa was opened, and in 1961, after the Cuban Revolution, an Institute for Latin America. The study of the cultures of recipients was crucial. Many underdeveloped countries had ancient and glorious traditions: well known is Sukarno's provocative question about why, when Europeans thought of undertaking a civilizing mission, they always ended up in places whose cultures were far more ancient than theirs.[52] The Soviets were well aware of the huge knowledge gap they needed to fill—they did not have the means to reverse Western influence, especially in Africa, even if they wanted to: they knew almost nothing about the continent.[53]

Soviet funding promoted economic liberation, but the Soviets had to find a way to justify supporting noncommunist economies. In the early 1960s, the theory of national democracy as applied to the Orient saw a coalition headed by noncommunists working to lead countries down the noncapitalist path of development, skipping the capitalist stage entirely. With the understanding that noncapitalist development was different from socialism, and that African, Asian, or Arab socialism was not necessarily scientific socialism, national democracies in developing countries were treated as the early stage of scientific socialism—and thus deserving of encouragement and support. In December 1960, at the Moscow Conference of Communist and Workers Parties, the Soviet Union proposed an alternative to the idea of the vanguard party revolting against the bourgeois structure born or strengthened with independence. The new model was a transition process whereby progressive forces—communists and progressive nationalists—would cooperate to guide a "national democratic state" wholly independent from "feudal and imperialist" bonds. Developing industry and a working class was a condition for more expedient passage to socialism, with assistance for modernization and industrialization granted accordingly. To get aid, national democratic states had to adopt land reform, seize foreign-owned properties, and orient economic relations toward socialist countries. The concept of national democracy was soon substituted for revolutionary democracy: when the working class was not yet ready to take the reins, noncommunist leaders could start the transition toward socialist revolution. This new line justified support for neutrals who opted for the one-party formula, even if they threw local communists out of national politics, as Ben Bella had done in Algeria, Nasser in Egypt, Ne Win in Burma, Sékou Touré in Guinea, and Kwame Nkrumah in Ghana. For the Chinese, nationalism was always backward, never revolutionary, and they criticized this policy, worsening their growing rift with the Soviets. In response, the Soviet Union branded the Chinese policy toward the developing countries as imperialistic.[54]

## The Political Economy of Socialist Cooperation

Socialist countries used a different language of assistance, one connected to the tradition of solidarity among anti-imperialist forces. Instead of the term "aid," they spoke of cooperation on an equal basis, or solidarity—a concept that became synonymous with socialist development aid.[55] Solidarity implied a variety of aid that helped both national liberation movements and independent countries cover essential needs in times of crisis. Credits for industrial or infrastructural projects were offered in nonconvertible rubles and were therefore de facto tied to purchases in the Soviet Union. Typically, the credits were offered in connection with the signing of long-term governmental agreements: complete plants in exchange for raw materials or manufactured products, with payment based on a clearing system that did not involve actual exchange of currency. The export of complete plants became significant in the USSR's trade with the Third World, especially after 1961. Although the USSR was preoccupied with aid to the industrial sector, most Soviet aid was actually concentrated in multipurpose projects involving transportation, electric power, irrigation, and communications. The Soviets insisted that their credits were loans to be paid back in local currency or exports. The extracting industry and the processing of raw materials were financed through credits. The preferred formula was a production-cooperation agreement, in which the Soviet Union acquired significant control of the production cycle of the enterprise, while the recipient country would retain sole ownership without being able to keep the profits until full repayment—in quotas of production.[56]

Khrushchev did not miss a chance to declare that, commercially speaking, economic and technical assistance to less developed countries was not in the Soviet Union's favor.[57] He also said that given the higher interest rates and the requirement of siding with the imperialists, Western aid was an economic and political burden. Soviet aid, in contrast, claimed to grant equality in entitlement (*ravnopravie*) and reciprocal advantage (*vzaimnaya vigoda*). The model, based on long-term trade agreements, was hugely successful at the UN with the many newly independent countries. In 1961, resolution 1707 of the UN General Assembly declared that international trade would be the main instrument of promoting economic development; in 1962, resolution 917 sanctified the principle of "trade, not aid."[58]

The Soviet recipe encouraged nationalization because only by controlling the means of production could the central government exert a guiding role in a country's economy. Establishing relations with the Soviet Bloc was seen as an infallible method of promoting development in the state-controlled sector of the national economy. It promised fast growth by emphasizing heavy industry and agricultural collectivization. The Soviet Union heralded a high socialist modernity that it hoped would allow it to realize the tsarists' failed project— equality with the West. The achievement of rapid growth in just one generation, the emphasis on heavy industrialization, and the prominence of state planning appealed to nationalist leaders yearning for development and hoping to cast off the burdens of the colonial legacy. The Soviets promoted their image with these countries, hoping to seduce their elites by stressing quasi equality, a position of primus inter pares. More than touting its role as a socialist vanguard, the Soviet Union promoted itself as a modern and pacific state, advanced in the sciences and arts.[59] The ultimate victory of communism over capitalism would be achieved through the demonstration that the socialist mode of production possessed decisive advantages over the capitalist mode.[60]

Modernization in Central Asia and the Caucasus was showcased for aspiring modernizers, politicians, and intellectuals in the Third World.[61] The idea of turning Central Asia into one of the most advanced areas of the Soviet Union was a legacy of the 1920s and 1930s, one that Khrushchev expanded. It was not just about rural development through infrastructure, but about turning Uzbekistan and Tajikistan from cotton producers into real industrial centers. The success of this operation was linked to an immense project, the Nurek Dam, which would produce electricity for building chemical plants, smelting aluminum, and producing electric components. These projects, which appeased local leaders who wanted to promote the region as a new industrial area and trigger urban development, went on until the 1970s and were the glue that held Khrushchev's political base in Central Asia together.[62] South African writer Alex La Guma, a leading representative of the African National

Congress who wrote for the elite, noted Soviet progress in Central Asia. He saw it as a model for the future South Africa, with railways, land reclamation, electricity, and the liberation of Muslim women all elements of Soviet modernity that could be transferred into African reality.[63]

As soon as Moscow adopted a more assertive line toward the Third World, it began aiding Afghanistan to counterbalance the alliance between the United States and Pakistan. Afghanistan had been the only example of the export of the socialist model in Stalin's years, and good relations between the two countries were deeply rooted: the Soviet Union had been the first to recognize Afghan independence, and it had immediately offered assistance. The first treaty, however, dated back to only 1953, and actual aid disbursement began two years later. An agreement was signed for the training of military personnel and the construction of factories and infrastructure, especially in the capital and the north. Sugar beets and even opium were considered cash crops. As for dam construction, the Soviets were competing with the United States, which had one in Helmand Valley, and with West Germany, which had a rural development project in Paktia. The Soviets had their own land reclamation and electrification project, the Darunta Dam, near Jalalabad. In addition, they set up infrastructure, building roads and tunnels to create connections to the north—Salang Tunnel in 1964 and the highway that connected Kushka, in Turkmenistan, with Kandahar via Herat in 1965. When natural gas was discovered in Sheberghan, in the northwest, it became an important source of revenue, triggering new investments, including the introduction of a social security system. In the 1960s and 1970s, Moscow did not plan to annex or Sovietize Afghanistan, but to secure its economic independence so that the United States could not establish a military base so close to Soviet borders.[64]

Several studies have documented the strengths and weaknesses of Soviet aid. Indonesia is a telling case. In 1954, as bilateral relations were initiated, the new Indonesian ambassador to Moscow, Subandrio, welcomed the Soviet Union as a development model for all Asia and claimed that economic growth was a precondition for ideological progress.[65] A large Communist Party supported the possibility of a political return for the Soviets, but President Sukarno did not take sides, submitting aid requests to other donors, too. Soon the Soviets, the Chinese, and the West were competing for influence. American modernizers, inspired by anthropologist Clifford Geertz, suggested mechanization of agriculture to overcome the legacy of Dutch colonial agricultural practices and the accompanying cultural backwardness.[66] Indonesian development planners, instead, believed in agricultural self-sufficiency and turned to the Soviet Union for better advice on industrial development. In 1956, Sukarno secured a significant credit agreement from the USSR. The aid protocol was signed in January 1959. According to Gosplan data, Indonesia received 789 million rubles in those years—21 percent of the amount given to all the nonsocialist countries combined. Much of it (701 million) was military aid. The Soviet-funded Senayan sports complex, near Jakarta, was quickly inaugurated and seen as a symbol of Indonesia's new international stature, which was boosted during the fourth Asian Games, held in late summer 1962. A hospital built with Soviet funding was also completed. But only a few projects were finished, and often not the most economically promising ones: in 1967, of the twenty-three projects funded, only three reached completion.[67] Much of the aid was used for military buildup, to support Sukarno and the central government during and after the 1958 civil war with Sumatra.

At the beginning of the 1960s, recipients were unhappy with the quality of communist aid, complaining about delays, low quality, and insufficient technical standards. Guinea featured prominently in the list of disappointed partners. After opting for immediate independence in September 1958—in what Western countries called a nationalist excess—France immediately terminated all assistance and withdrew all its personnel. New Guinean minister of economics Louis Lansana Beavogui invited the socialist countries to build the economic system of independent Guinea from scratch. The Eastern Bloc immediately mobilized huge resources, offering schools, hospitals and doctors, economists to change the economic and foreign trade system, agronomists to assist production of export crops, and aid for infrastructure (roads and railways) and communications. Trade and credit agreements were signed with the Soviet Union, Czechoslovakia, Poland, Hungary, and the GDR.[68] Guinea was the archetype of what would happen to newly independent countries once they cut off relations with the imperialist West, and the Bloc saw it as a place to showcase communism in Africa. East Germany was especially active, in the hope that Guinea would become the first African country to officially recognize the GDR government. The two countries signed a trade agreement in November 1958—the first international agreement concluded by independent Guinea. East German experts elaborated an ambitious aid plan. Mechanization of agriculture was to be introduced in the Kindia region and around Kankan, supported by GDR-sent agronomists, biologists, and other experts who would initiate irrigation and land reclamation schemes, provide diggers and tractors, and introduce electrification. Projects to be financed closer to Conakry, the capital, included wheat and palm oil mills, milk processing plants, slaughterhouses, and refrigeration plants. Paper mills and a government press completed the package.[69] This was all to be financed with governmental credits. Negotiations for the first East German five-year credit started in March 1959. Within the agreement, the GDR would build the promised government press and provide optical and photographic materials, chemical products, books, and consumer goods. It would be paid back in bananas imported by the GDR at a price substantially higher than the world market price.[70] Investments in extraction of mineral ores (bauxite) and in the communication system were also in view but required cooperation with the other socialist countries.[71]

Despite a socialist-looking national three-year plan (1960–1962), which promised political mobilization, socialization of the means of production, the creation of cooperatives, the mechanization of agriculture, and the nationalization of foreign trade, the Eastern Bloc was not Guinea's sole economic partner. From the very beginning, President Sékou Touré had declared that his country would take aid from all sides—and it did. Unhappy with the quantity and quality of socialist aid, Touré complained about military deliveries (Czechoslovak tanks were inadequate) and Soviet projects. A polytechnic, an open-air theater, a hotel, an airport, and a rice farm had been built, but more important works, for railroad development, the extraction of mineral ores and diamonds, and the introduction of a modern radio transmission system, were still under evaluation by Soviet authorities.[72] Trying to force a more effective engagement on the Soviet side, Touré expelled the Soviet ambassador in December 1961, and although he did not cut ties, he seemed ready to leap across the Iron Curtain. From then on, the Soviet Union took a more cautious approach toward investing heavily in dubious African allies, an attitude that came to be known as the "Guinean syndrome."[73]

Other privileged partners of the Soviet Union (Egypt, Mali, Indonesia) also complained about socialist aid. Self-criticism, however, was not a strength of the Soviets, and they attributed all problems to the recipients or to less than credible capitalist, bourgeois infiltrations. After 1965, they blamed less ideological factors like bureaucratic excesses, corruption, and overwhelming deficits. Influenced by the Western economic theories used in the United Nations, the new generation of Soviet economists started to question industrialization as a model. Georgi Mirsky, for example, one of the brilliant minds in IMEMO, the Institute of World Economy and International Relations, argued that heavy industry was good only for the bigger countries, not for all. He also said that nationalization could have drawbacks. Many social scientists held on to Soviet tradition, but some now began to claim that multiple roads could lead to industrialization.[74]

# 4

# Western Alternatives for Development in the Global Cold War

As military policy is too important a matter to be left to the generals, so is foreign aid too important a matter to be left to the economists.

—HANS J. MORGENTHAU, 1962

Economic aid should be the principal means by which the West maintains its political and economic dynamic in the underdeveloped world.

—EUGENE BLACK, 1960

WITH POINT FOUR, the United States had launched a development assistance policy imbued with Cold War tones. The response from the European allies, preoccupied mainly with reconstruction at home and the role of the state in regulating society and managing the economy, was mixed. European countries still saw themselves as empires, using first Marshall Plan and later Point Four funding to advance their dependent territories. Despite the imminent loss of empire, no major European country appeared to have abandoned a belief in its role as a global power. It was the effective decolonization of China after the Chinese Revolution in 1949 that "ultimately pulled the rug from under the colonial order in the Far East."[1] It also fueled the Cold War in Asia and drew the superpowers into the region. More concerned by the implications of rapid decolonization for Europe and Japan than by the anticolonial leaders' demands for independence, the United States backed the French effort at reconquest in Indochina, supported continued British control over Malaya, and acquiesced to Dutch efforts to reestablish control over Indonesia.[2] From Southeast Asia to Southern Africa, American alliances with current or former European colonial powers made winning the support of postcolonial elites more difficult. It required some intellectual acrobatics to criticize the legacy of European colonialism while financing development plans that continued colonial trade structures.

European empires were confronting decolonization their own way, still thinking within an imperial context. France, Great Britain, and the Netherlands all promoted the restoration of empire as a weapon against communism. They relaunched empire in a revised federal form such as the 1946 Union Française (later Communauté), the Commonwealth, or the 1949 Republic of the United States of Indonesia, imagining the continuation of informal empire in the framework of a united Europe.[3] The concept of Eurafrica, little known today, circulated widely in continental Europe in the years before decolonization. The political myth of a homogeneous bloc encompassing Europe and Africa that would restore Europe as a geopolitical third force had flourished in the 1920s and 1930s among intellectuals in France, Germany, and Italy and was at the center of Richard Coudenhove-Kalergi's 1923 manifesto for a United Europe, *Paneuropa*.[4] After the Second World War, Eurafrica was brought into postwar negotiations by British foreign minister Ernest Bevin, who hoped to link European forces in order to balance the resource gap with the United States.[5] In the discussion of the creation of a united Europe—referred to as European integration—an argument for including the colonies was that it would keep them out of the Soviet sphere. Newly independent countries were considered a European hunting reserve, even though at independence it became apparent that they could opt for other loyalties. In 1957, the former French overseas minister Pierre-Henri Teitgen, one of the politicians most cautious about Eurafrican relations, addressed the Council of Europe, the intergovernmental organization born in 1949 to promote political, economic, and cultural cooperation in postwar Europe. At independence, he said, African countries had several options: the American bloc, the Soviet world, the Bandung coalition, the Afro-Asian group, or Free Europe (Eurafrica).[6] The world he pictured was multipolar, not bipolar. Eurafrica was a project per se, manifestly different from neutralism or Pan-Africanism, but also distinct from the American idea of a Western-Atlantic bloc. The reference European leaders made to the Cold War was mostly instrumental to promoting the continuation of empire. European countries welcomed the fact that anticommunism took precedence over anticolonialism in US foreign policy and insisted on the role of empire in the expansion of containment, the US strategy to resist and prevent the global spread of communism.

Meanwhile, social scientists in the United States gave shape to their views of a process by which non-Western societies were transformed along Western lines. Known as modernization theories, these would soon become the basis for a much more interventionist foreign policy. This chapter explains how modernization worked its way into Cold War politics, how it influenced public discourse and foreign policy in the United States during the second half of the 1950s, and how, with the presidency of John Fitzgerald Kennedy (1961–1963), it became the representative Western ideology for waging the Cold War, even as other coexisting traditions of imperial origin offered rival methods of using development aid as a tool of foreign policy to face radicalization in the decolonizing world.

## The Inevitability of Foreign Aid as a Cold War Tool?

Foreign aid was already in the chromosomes of US foreign policy, but how this would be institutionalized was articulated more clearly during the 1950s, starting with Point Four. While Harry Truman saw development assistance as a way to increase security in the changing decolonizing world and as a tool in the Cold War, his successor, Dwight D. Eisenhower, did not share his enthusiasm. It was during Eisenhower's administration, though, between 1953 and 1961, that the Soviet challenge in the Third World became palpable and a discussion about foreign aid moved to center stage. Unable to reconcile anticolonialism with its overriding determination to contain communism, preserve ties with the European allies, and promote a liberal capitalist international economy, the Eisenhower administration endorsed conservative elites in the Third World, backed repressive regimes, and resorted to covert operations to prevent a communist seizure of power. As a result, it nourished the kind of revolutionary violence the Americans most feared. At the start, though, in an effort to curtail public spending and expand trade, the newly installed US government downgraded development assistance.[7] Aid was to be used in emergencies, not to cure the chronic malady of poverty and backwardness. For that, private investments worked more efficiently. The nexus between development and security was interpreted narrowly, and aid policies occasionally accompanied military aid—with the goal of stopping the spread of communism.[8] Aid in kind was also linked to military purposes. In the 1954 program Food for Peace, which dumped excess American food production into poor countries, proceeds were to be reinvested in either development projects or military sales in the recipient country.[9]

The Korean War (1951–1953) confirmed the impression of a larger strategy of communist expansion in Asia, and the 1954 Viet Minh victory against the French at Dien Bien Phu made erecting a barrier against upcoming communist movements an urgent priority. President Eisenhower often referred to the domino theory: once the first tile fell, the rest would follow. Seeing a communist revolution behind every corner, including in nationalist leaders, the United States accelerated aid plans that were already under way. It went to support the colonial powers, seen as the bulwark against communism. By 1954, the United States was paying most of France's war bill in Indochina; after the 1954 Geneva Accords ending French colonial rule, it stepped in.[10] A debate about foreign aid opened up immediately. In October 1954, at a meeting of the Colombo Plan (the cooperative venture for the economic and social advancement of the peoples of South and Southeast Asia within the Commonwealth, launched in July 1951), Harold Stassen, head of the short-lived (1953–1955) Foreign Operations Administration, pledged increased economic aid as an anticommunist measure and called for a Marshall Plan for Asia. Secretary of State John Foster Dulles, who held anticolonialism and neutralism to be immoral and myopic, also favored foreign aid, provided it was directed to the colonial empires to help them resist communist infiltration—he feared aid cuts would tip the Cold War balance.[11]

Powerful voices in governmental circles were at odds about offering foreign aid to newly independent countries. Some argued against economic assistance to nations not militarily allied with the United States, saying that since many of the so-called uncommitted nations were functionally socialist, or at least talked like socialists, there was no reason to promote their well-being.[12] Others saw Third World nationalists as worthy of cultivation. In November 1954, C. D. Jackson, a former Eisenhower aide, called for a "new world economic policy" and brought the president a report by MIT social scientists Max F. Millikan and Walt W. Rostow that recommended providing economic assistance to decolonizing nationalists. It was the only way, the authors said, to show that the Western way of life offered better chances than the communist. Modernization ideas were still in their formative stage. Another outspoken supporter of foreign aid was Henry Cabot Lodge, the US representative at the United Nations. He was often at odds with Dulles, who feared alienating NATO allies.[13] Lodge said that hallmark Cold War initiatives like Atoms for Peace in 1953, which promised states access to peaceful nuclear technologies in exchange for their relinquishing nuclear weapons, had earned the United States international acknowledgment. It was now time to impact people and countries more directly, with a "bold initiative in the field of economic development" that financed dams, roads, agricultural improvements, and water transport systems, outpacing the Soviets.[14]

By the spring of 1955, the Eisenhower administration had begun reconsidering a role for aid with trade. If aid was to become a constant feature of the international system, a permanent authority was needed. The International Cooperation Administration was created in 1955, and in 1957 it acquired a branch to deal with financial issues, the Development Loan Fund (DLF). Aid was given through grants and, preferably, loans. The EXIM Bank, offering export credits to developing countries, flanked the DLF. Eisenhower was never fully on board—between 1957 and 1960 there was only a modest increase in aid: a reflection of the idea that Third Word hostility resulted from

Soviet propaganda and that economic aid would not radically turn the tables.[15] The troubles in the Middle East, Africa, and Latin America, Dulles insisted, resulted from communist efforts to foment hatred against the United States, the United Kingdom, and France, not from nationalism, colonialism, or poverty. Confronted with mounting evidence of the Soviets' use of economic policy to extend their power and influence in underdeveloped areas like India, Indonesia, and Afghanistan, the United States resorted to propaganda to show that the alleged success of the Soviet precedent was being used as bait.[16] The Soviet Union promised development, it argued, but in fact offered "civil strife, political oppression and enslavement, material privations and exploitation, spiritual torture, and forced labor."[17] Having concluded that propaganda was important in determining the choices of Third World countries, the United States expanded psychological operations in Asia. After the Geneva Accords, the United States Information Agency (USIA) flooded South Vietnam with propaganda supporting the staunchly anticommunist Ngo Dinh Diem and trumpeting his government's social and economic development efforts. The "aggressive military, political, and psychological program" included spreading rumors about communist atrocities and exaggerating the rigors of life in North Vietnam.[18]

When facing a communist seizure of power from within—that is, when nationalist leaders opted to strengthen their ties to socialist countries—the first choice of the United States was covert operations. Emblematic were the interventions in Iran in 1953 against Mohammad Mosaddegh, the prime minister who worked for the nationalization of the Anglo-Iranian Oil Company, and in Guatemala in 1954 against President Jacobo Arbenz, who threatened the interests of the United Fruit Company. Convinced it would work again, American officials encouraged a similar operation in Indonesia. When it failed, they fell back on cementing ties through programs of military, technical, and economic assistance. Civilian and military leaders, though, wanted to accept aid without taking sides in the Cold War.[19] In the Middle East, where the overarching objective of the US national security strategy was keeping the region's oil resources from falling under communist control, the greatest threat was Gamal Abdel Nasser. All attempts at undermining Nasser's prestige in the Arab world failed. His defiance of the 1955 Baghdad Pact, the defensive organization promoted by the British in order to secure Western interests in the Middle East; the September 1955 Czech arms deal to purchase $200 million worth of advanced Soviet-made military equipment; and the 1956 Suez Crisis with the ensuing conflict all paved the way to Soviet influence in the region. The massive Aswan High Dam, originally intended to be financed by the World Bank with all the Western powers participating, became a symbol of Cold War politics—and Western defeat—when the Soviet Union stepped in to help build the most impressive high modernist development project in the Middle East.[20]

Between 1957 and 1958, several events prompted the US to shift toward a more active foreign aid policy: Khrushchev's renewed bid for competition between socialist and capitalist states in a speech before the Supreme Soviet in November 1957; the discontent voiced in Latin America during Vice President Richard Nixon's trip in May 1958; and the success of the Cuban Revolution in 1959. These events brought a consensus that a more vigorous approach to promoting economic growth and development as a way to contain communist influence was needed.[21] The question of improved coordination of development assistance among the Atlantic nations was also a factor. Most of Western Europe shared America's concern about Soviet penetration, and several members of the North Atlantic Treaty Organization (NATO) insisted on activating economic collaboration according to article 2 of the North Atlantic Treaty, using it to provide aid cooperatively.[22] Both France and Germany hoped that NATO would take care of security threats in Africa.[23] In 1958, the Federal Republic of Germany insisted on discussing the communist threat to the less developed countries. It argued that cultural exchanges, scholarships, and technical and financial assistance should be used to promote Western-style democracy in the Third World.[24] US undersecretary of state C. Douglas Dillon insisted that Europe had to provide more aid—and that the Organisation for European Economic Co-operation (OEEC) established with the Marshall Plan should coordinate that aid. He set up a group of eight leading capital-exporting countries within the OEEC to serve as a forum where major donor countries could consider particular problems and techniques of development aid while designing and monitoring procedures for assisting undeveloped countries. The Development Assistance Group (DAG), also called the Dillon Group, held its first meeting in Washington during 9–11 March 1960. Another option for coordination was the International Atomic Energy Agency (IAEA), born out of Eisenhower's Atoms for Peace proposal.[25] Since 1958, the IAEA had administered several nuclear assistance projects under its technical cooperation program, including training and facilities to promote civil use of nuclear materials in health and agriculture. Early ventures were small scale and time limited, but still they raised concerns in the Soviet Union, which, in the summer of 1961, on the eve of the Cuban crisis, presented the IAEA safeguard policies as designed to throttle the nuclear progress of developing countries.[26]

## Plans for Eurafrica

Busy with the collapse of empire, European countries were less preoccupied with Cold War dynamics. French and British intervention in the Suez Crisis in 1956 and the liberation war in Algeria (1954–1961) destroyed any remnants of political and moral authority for empire in North Africa.[27] Nevertheless, after the Treaties of Rome were signed in March 1957 to create the European Economic Community (EEC), all its members—France, Belgium, and the Netherlands, as well as Luxembourg, West Germany, and Italy—still believed in the resilience of the colonial system in Africa and thought of the EEC as an aid-sharing tool. European integration was a venture for joint imperial management. France intended to have Germany pay for empire in exchange for the possibility of joint exploitation of African riches. Dutch foreign minister Joseph Luns claimed that the EEC was the opportunity for "the continuation of [Europe's] grand and global civilizing mission."[28] Belgian Paul Henri Spaak, head of the committee that worked out the common market, believed that the project was the path toward "fulfilling the Eurafrica dream." For most European leaders, including West German chancellor Konrad Adenauer and his foreign minister Heinrich von Brentano, the inclusion of the colonies was a geopolitical imperative related to Cold War tensions, a particular concern for divided Germany.[29] The European idea, wrote German economist and naturalized British citizen Uwe Kitzinger, could bridge historical cleavages of all kinds: empire and the European community were one and the same, he claimed, and the EEC was "a Eurafrican as much as a European scheme."[30]

With the EEC, the "association" so typical of the French imperial tradition entered a second life. Eurafrica was to be constructed by granting complementarity between metropolitan areas and dependencies.[31] With the association of colonies included as part four of the EEC Treaty, European countries built a regional system they imagined would last, the looming end of colonial empires notwithstanding. The system had two elements: preferential trade between members and associated territories, and the European Development Fund (EDF), which was designated for the development of the associated regions. France had requested both elements in exchange for opening its overseas markets to other European countries. The Dutch and Germans were against the Development Fund, whereas the Italians complained because the colonial goods competed with the products of their own backward area, the Mezzogiorno. The decision, however, went as the French wished, with French prime minister Guy Mollet declaring in 1957 that "all of Europe will be called upon to help in the development of Africa."[32] According to Alexandre Kojève, a Hegelian philosopher and high-level official in the French Ministry of Economics, the way to transform European influence after the inevitable decolonization was a "colonialism of giving" (*gebender Kolonialismus*) focused on building infrastructure in the most promising area for development—the shores of the Mediterranean.[33] Grudgingly accepted by the other members, the EDF was not even submitted to African legislative assemblies. Although some leaders, including Félix Houphouët-Boigny, went to Brussels during the negotiations to support the project, no African representative participated in decisions on the EDF. The Senegalese politician and later president Léopold Senghor was utterly disappointed to discover that Eurafrica was not a tool to extend social democracy in Africa. He described the final European project as a "marriage of convenience." Africans, he said, might agree to be "the servants who carried the veil of the bride," but they certainly would not enter a bargain where they were the wedding present.[34] Pan-African leaders like Sékou Touré and Kwame Nkrumah and Third World–friendly intellectuals like Franz Fanon and Jean-Paul Sartre always spoke against a Eurafrican project.

In the Treaties of Rome, development aid had a significant role, and the introduction of the EDF was called "a new deal for the Dark Continent."[35] In the context of the patronizing rhetoric of the 1950s, the former colonists promised "real independence" for Africans. The EDF was modeled on the French development fund for the colonies, the Fonds d'Investissement pour le Développement Économique et Social (FIDES) and endowed with 581 million EUA (European Unit of Account) over five years. Of this, France and Germany were to pay the greatest part, 200 million each. When the EDF became operational in 1959, it did not follow rigid budget rules, like FIDES. Amounts were established on a five-year basis, and there was no strict financial control.[36] Recipients had to indicate their needs by submitting projects for funding; the European Commission controlled the apportionment of resources, following rules according to the geographical area and the project characteristics—that is, whether it was for economic or social development.

A large EEC bureaucracy was established, the Directorate-General of Overseas Development (DG Development). Its institutional architecture was shaped mainly by France: DG Development was a French enclave.[37] The first development commissioner, Robert Lemaignen, was a French businessman with long experience in African matters: former president of the Societé Commerciale des Ports Africains (1941–1958), vice president of the International Chamber of Commerce (1942–1958), and member of the board of directors of the East Africa Company (Compagnie de l'Afrique Orientale) and of the West African Bank (Banque d'Afrique Occidentale). He hired "the best elements available in France" for his team and asked them to separate themselves from a national vision and adopt the point of view of European Community institutions. The course of action he suggested, however, was imbued with a colonial mentality. Solving political or economic controversies in African countries, he condescendingly contended, depended more on the trust you inspired in your interlocutor than on the logic of your reasoning.[38] This suggested that patron-client relationships would weigh as heavily in EEC decision making as they had in the colonial era. In 1958, Lemaignen chose Jacques Ferrandi, a former colonial officer who had managed FIDES as director-general of economic affairs in Dakar, as his head of cabinet. Ferrandi was responsible for the EDF and established a system based on the indirect rule that former colonial officers had learned in colonial schools. A flexible governance based on personal relationships, trust, loyalty, and mutual obligation, the system was grounded on the principle that to deal effectively with the local population required adapting to their customs, even at the cost of violating the rules. This meant favoring specific groups and their interests—and presumably could lead to accepting bribery. Ferrandi, the éminence grise of EEC development aid, had the unconditional backing of Lemaignen and successors, Henri Rochereau (1962–67) and Jean-François Deniau (1967–73), operating with full autonomy for years.[39]

EEC development policies became a French fiefdom, but in the beginning their destiny was still open. There were two contending visions: the regionalist vision supported by France, reinforcing traditional trade and aid links with old colonies, and the world vision backed by Germany, EDF's other main donor. The global view was supported by Great Britain and the United States. The antagonism was reflected in the conflict within DG Development between Lemaignen and his director-general, former West German ambassador to Indonesia Helmut Allardt. Allardt made no bones about the gap between his views and the commissioner's.[40] He called for opening to a global perspective and general planning instead of diverting funds into "dozens of small pointless projects."[41] Within two years, he was forced to resign, allegedly because of his past as a Nazi Party member and Third Reich diplomat.[42] The more malleable Heinrich Hendus, formerly the German representative in Algeria, replaced him. The victory of the French approach meant that until the British entered the EEC, development policies were essentially French.

The empires hoped to keep decolonization from constituting a clear break with the past. The EEC was one of the options open to them to continue imperial structures and networks. Bilateral aid relations with former colonies were still pursued. In France, the architect of a decolonization process under the French umbrella was Jacques Foccart, known as "Mr. Africa." In 1960, Charles de Gaulle made Foccart the secretary of state in charge of African and Malagasy affairs with one mission: to anticipate and flank decolonization to avoid losing Sub-Saharan Africa the way France had lost Indochina and North Africa. Cameroon and Togo became anticommunist laboratories, while Congo-Brazzaville under Fulbert Youlou was considered the ideal outpost to keep the Cold War out of the Congo.[43] Technical assistance to accompany state building in Africa was crucial, and France signed agreements of aid and cooperation with each former colony.[44] The aid sector was entrusted to Foccart. Under his personal watch, it became the barometer of political relations with the former colonies in Africa, in a system that, according to the French, worked better with bilateral aid. The guiding principle was independence through interdependence: successful development initiatives were in the best interest of both partners, contended the French authorities. Continuity with late colonial traditions was assured by continuity in staff. "Envoye moi un colonial" (Send me a former colonial officer), replied the president of Gabon, Léon M'Ba, when consulted about the appointment of a new French ambassador in 1964.[45]

The United Kingdom also disliked multilateral aid, feeling that it weakened links with the Commonwealth. Throughout the 1950s and 1960s, at least 80 percent of British aid was channeled bilaterally to Commonwealth countries, with the UK seen as a banker to and a private investor in the Commonwealth countries. Financial aid was still provided through the Colonial Development and Welfare Act and, along with the 1951 Colombo Plan, had the goal of developing resources for the future independent countries. The legacy of empire was a double-edged sword. "Colonies and ex colonies regarded aid as a right," lamented British officials, while other (noncolonial) donors could claim that their aid was an act of generosity. The Commonwealth was both key to claiming a role as a world power, and burdensome because of the many responsibilities and limitations it implied. For example, entry into the EEC was unlikely because it was perceived as a betrayal of the Commonwealth. As in France, British aid programs had many continuities in people, projects, and institutions. Former colonial bureaucrats were systematically seconded to independent countries. However, British contributions risked being quickly eclipsed, lamented British officers, given that postcolonial states were eager to choose other donors and other models as soon as they achieved independence.[46]

Although decolonization was not perceived as imminent when the EEC treaties were signed, it was a pressing concern a mere three years later. The EEC structure for securing relations with African countries threatened to crumble, along with the idea of association. Independence meant that former colonies plummeted into a legal void, a no-man's-land. In June 1960, the German newspaper *Die Welt* revealed its fear that Europe would lose its influence on the African continent in its editorial "Läuft Afrika der EWG davon?" (Is Africa getting away from Europe?) and pressed for immediate action.[47] With independence, development aid, once considered domestic welfare policy, became foreign policy. The EEC still seemed to be an efficient way to externalize development and its costs, secure important structural continuities in people and projects, and give former empires a noncolonial identity. Links to the colonial past and ideology were underplayed accordingly in EEC discourse. The newly independent states in Africa, however, did not have a consensus about how to deal with the EEC. One group saw Pan-Africanism as a political project capable of countering colonial legacies and thus resisted cooperation with the EEC. Another, bigger group, fully aware of their dependence on former colonial structures, wanted to maintain existing links and preferential access to European markets. In July 1963, when eighteen independent countries in Africa decided to continue association by adhering to the Yaoundé Convention, which retained preferential trade with the Associated African and Malagasy States on a bilateral basis with reciprocal obligation, Eurafrica supporters cheered. The convention also guaranteed nondiscrimination and the continuation of the aid regime.[48]

## An Ideology for the Global Cold War: The Rise of Modernization Theory

With the collapse of European empires, the United States began to reassess the question of how to balance support for European allies against growing anticolonial demands. Needing new tools, the United States adopted an approach centered on concepts of development and resorted to modernization theory. This theory came from sociologists' and political scientists' efforts in the late 1950s to respond to an idea of development that had been viewed too exclusively in economic terms, and it generated great interest. "No economic subject more quickly captured the attention of so many as the rescue of the people of the poor countries from their poverty," recalled economist John Kenneth Galbraith.[49] Modernization theory was based on a set of cultural assumptions characteristic of the postcolonial transition: belief in industrial modernity and science as a common destiny, faith in capitalism supported by state regulation, and welfare provision to govern social conflicts.[50] There was a universally valid and historically defined trajectory of progress that required the spread of Western liberal capitalist democracy. It was the United States, of course, that would steer less developed countries along this path.

Modernization theory, inspired by the work of Talcott Parsons, Gabriel Almond, and Lucian Pye, was formulated by social scientists working at the Massachusetts Institute of Technology (MIT), and it found its bible in Walt Whitman Rostow's *The Stages of Economic Growth: A Non-Communist Manifesto*, published in 1960.[51] Originally a series of lectures Rostow gave in Cambridge in 1958, *The Stages of Economic Growth* argued that modernization always entailed five stages, from traditional society to high mass consumption. Once a country entered the fundamental takeoff stage, technological improvement would lead to industrial modernity, provided there were no distortions like communism. Rostow became a key reference for modernization theorists.[52] A former Rhodes Scholar at Oxford and a PhD student in economic history at Yale, he had worked on the UN Economic Commission for Europe in 1947, promoting European unity through economic cooperation in a global framework articulated at a regional level. He saw his intellectual mission as finding an alternative to a Marxian understanding of history. In the article "Marx Was a City Boy, or, Why Communism May Fail," he made a case for development anchored in the countryside.[53] His model called for improving agriculture and promised infrastructure at a later stage, along with urban development and the import of consumer goods within a global capitalist market. In 1950, he and Charles Kindleberger and Max Millikan founded CENIS, the Center for International Studies at MIT, a formidable think tank intended to convince the US government that aid was fundamental to winning the Cold War. *A Proposal: Key to an Effective Foreign Policy*, written with Max Millikan in 1957 and based on the concepts and ideas submitted earlier to the Eisenhower administration, became the most influential plan for turning modernization theory into political action. It claimed that aid to underdeveloped countries could promote growth and economic stability in the United States and argued that aid planning should be separate from military assistance. Unconcerned with distributive issues or social justice, it postulated that growth alone could create anticommunism, stability, and democracy. In the long run, aid was what would win the Cold War.[54]

Meanwhile, the East-West competition in foreign aid was being discussed in the public realm.[55] In 1958, the same year Rostow spoke at Cambridge University, an important piece of historical fiction was published. It jumped to the top of the sales charts, surpassing Vladimir Nabokov's *Lolita*, and spent seventy-seven weeks on the best-seller list, selling five million copies. *The Ugly American*, by Eugene Burdick and William Lederer, told of a US administration unable to interact with local communities abroad and unaware of the potential of its own nationals, underequipped compared to Soviet representatives, and incapable of dealing with the impending communist upheaval in Sarkhan, an imaginary Asian country.[56] According to the introduction, *The Ugly American* was "not just an angry dream, but rather the rendering of fact into fiction." It was both a mirror of the times and an anticipation of change.[57] The authors supported the use of development aid to wage a war on communism in Indochina, but they criticized the incompetency of the US administration. In the book, engineer Homer Atkins was the eponymous ugly American, a lay missionary who epitomized American values, solidarity with local populations, and genuine empathy. He and his wife assisted the peasants, solving problems with simple technologies like a cunning bicycle-powered water pump. The film adaptation was released in 1963 and focused on the book's military implications, but even with Marlon Brando as Atkins, it received a poor reception compared to the book. Aid momentum had already slowed. In 1965, Burdick and Lederer published a sequel, equally pessimistic but less successful, called *Sarkhan*. Written during the troop buildup for the Vietnam

War, the book described military operations and told how good Americans had gotten trapped by a conspiracy between American security forces and prospective dictators.

*The Ugly American* was a product of its time. A number of people, mostly within the Democratic Party, were working to make US involvement in the Third World more rewarding for both recipient and donor. In June 1957, while campaigning for the Democratic candidacy for president, Hubert Humphrey launched the idea of an American Peace Corps, "a genuine people to people program." He pitched it as the opposite of the grand development schemes and gigantic infrastructure projects beloved by donors (West and East) and recipients.[58] His inspiration came from community development, from visions of "development without modernization." Large-scale industrialization and state-centered processes of social transformation could cause disruptions, but alternative strategies could ease the way for modernization. Local populations could be mobilized through discussion groups, as with the TVA; these groups would also help assess community needs, in a decentralized form of participatory planning. Communitarian ideas were nourished by racial biases, an Orientalism sympathetic to the nonwhite peoples that associated them with tradition, community, and locality. "*Gemeinschaft* for them, *Gesellschaft* for us" (Community for them, society for us) was the patronizing principle underpinning community development.[59]

Around that same time, US representative Henry S. Reuss from Wisconsin was promoting similar ideas. He wanted the United States to stop allying itself with corrupt leaders and focus on the population instead by promoting primary education and teaching agricultural techniques and the crafting of simple objects.[60] In 1959, he submitted the idea of the "Point Four Youth Corps" to Congress. John Fitzgerald Kennedy picked it up in his presidential campaign, proposing a group that would counter the "hundreds of men and women, scientists, physicists, teachers, engineers, doctors, and nurses" from the Eastern Bloc prepared to spend their lives abroad in the service of world communism.[61] This picture, like the one in *The Ugly American* showing the Soviet ambassador having an enviable knowledge of the local language, geography, and customs, was a myth. A report to the Central Committee of the Communist Party of the Soviet Union (CPSU) written on 4 March 1959 described a very different situation, with only 48 Soviet specialists abroad, none with any knowledge of the local language. American experts numbered 924, British 1,143, and French 683.[62]

The Peace Corps went on to become a fundamental tool that the Kennedy administration used to reject the legacy of imperialism and defend the credibility of the United States amid challenges from communist rivals. The ideal supplement to the scarce skilled workforce in newly independent countries,

US volunteers could help underdeveloped nations overcome whatever kept their economies from further growth and delayed their arrival at the takeoff stage. President Kennedy put his brother-in-law, Sargent Shriver, in charge of the Peace Corps, which was kept separate from the State Department and the US establishment. Many countries, especially in Africa, received Peace Corps volunteers enthusiastically. Among them were Ghana and Guinea, which were close to the Soviet Bloc, leading President Kennedy to speculate that the Peace Corps could lead communist-oriented countries to turn to the West.[63] Popularized as the way to correct the shortcomings of US policy making in the Third World while helping new nations overcome colonial legacies, the Peace Corps is generally considered a great success.[64] That judgement is not unanimous, however: historian Julius Amin, for example, offers a more nuanced picture of the Peace Corps in Cameroon. He describes the training—480 hours in eight weeks, with much time spent on political education—as focused on the communist threat and representing American democracy abroad, with no time devoted to instruction in the local language. However, since most

FIGURE 1. President John F. Kennedy meets first Peace Corps volunteers, August 1961. Photo by Abbie Rowe, White House Photographs, John F. Kennedy Presidential Library and Museum, Boston. Record: AR6760-B.

recipients were accustomed to rougher colonial policies, the volunteers were well received, except for a few cases in which Peace Corps volunteers were sabotaged or expelled.[65] Their success is further confirmed by the fact that communist countries soon adopted similar formats—the most famous case being the friendship brigades, Freundschaftsbrigaden, that the German Democratic Republic (GDR) sent to Africa.[66]

## The Kennedy Administration: A Turning Point?

John F. Kennedy took the developing world seriously. While campaigning for president, he promised that the doctrine of massive retaliation that had characterized Eisenhower's last years would be replaced by a more engaged, committed approach that, he claimed, would make the world safer.[67] By supporting failing colonial states, he contended, America had ended up defending the status quo, leaving the Soviet Union to take the initiative for change.[68] This needed to be reversed. The most threatening security crises that Kennedy experienced in his tenure as president originated in the Third World: the Congo, Indonesia, Egypt, and Ghana were examples of countries at risk of falling under the influence of the Soviet Union.[69] Like his predecessors, Kennedy considered every setback a danger to US credibility and read international conflicts through the lens of the bipolar confrontation. However, he and his administration believed that military aid should go along with programs targeting politics and economics.

With Kennedy, modernization theorists, who had started to make their way into policy making during the Eisenhower administration, entered the control room. The revolution of rising expectations had to be steered toward Western- or American-inspired models. Many social scientists, especially economists, were associated with the Kennedy administration, including the putative father of modernization, Walt Rostow, who became special assistant of state, in charge of US policies in Southeast Asia. John Kenneth Galbraith was the US ambassador in India, Lincoln Gordon was the ambassador in Brazil, David E. Bell became administrator of the Agency for International Development (AID), Eugene Staley was a special adviser in South Vietnam, and Samuel Hayes worked in the Peace Corps. This was not just the ad hoc involvement of individual intellectuals—modernization theory succeeded in Cold War America because it crystallized widely shared ideas about the competition with the Soviet Union in the developing world: this was not a matter of Cold War skirmishes, but a fundamental clash of values and world visions. Kennedy believed that widespread poverty and chaos threatened US security, and that economic growth and democracy could and should develop hand in hand. In his aid message of 22 March 1961, he put forward his plan, which unified all food aid, technical assistance, and other scattered activities under a common umbrella; concentrated on national development plans with the aim of reaching self-sustaining growth; and used a multilateral approach to draw in other industrialized states on a larger scale. This reorganization was accompanied by a funding increase of one-third: $800 million more than the prior year's budget. The additional funding went to new programs for South Asia and Latin America and a somewhat enlarged effort for Africa. Addressing the international community at the General Assembly of the United Nations in September 1961, Kennedy underscored his commitment, calling for a "Decade of Development."[70]

This aid machinery was based on new theoretical underpinnings that pointed to the importance of significant investments in triggering self-sustained growth. With the exception of Food for Peace and the EXIM Bank, all US aid agencies were merged under USAID, the newly established Agency for International Development. The new resources invested in aid were a quantum leap compared to the efforts of previous years. Point Four had financed research, often partnering with private foundations like the Ford Foundation. In India, it had supported studies on urban planning, community development, land reform, and the peasants' response to economic incentives.[71] In Somalia, it had sponsored preinvestment studies and the drawing up of seven-year development plans.[72] Such technical assistance, however, was not enough to meet expectations for change or trigger the movement from backwardness to self-sustained economic growth. A big push like the one envisaged by Paul Rosenstein-Rodan required a focus on capital goods and infrastructure: roads, bridges, harbors, dams, and great reclamation and electrification schemes, which were also the projects developing countries wanted. Massive infrastructure became a symbol for modernization in the 1960s. Kennedy stressed the importance of rural development as the key to worldwide democracy, and dam building accompanied by huge land reclamation projects was for the United States what land reform was to the Socialist Bloc.[73] The United States was never alone in these megaprojects, sometimes partnering with private business, more often working in wide consortia supported by the World Bank.

USAID provided both project aid and more general program aid, but it preferred the latter, as program aid made it easier to impose conditions like fiscal reform, the opening of markets, and the promotion of private business and democratic and participatory institutions. American capital, both government and private, often went to energy projects, the extracting industry, transport, and agriculture. Technical assistance focused on human resources: education, training, and health. After an initial period in the 1960s when the United States offered generous loans, the debt problem led to a general increase in interest rates and a switch from local currency to dollars. Credit was increasingly linked to political alliances, and no aid went to countries that sold strategic supplies to Cuba. The recipients' best interests were not always paramount, and countries sometimes had to adopt principles of efficiency and rational funding usage linked to clauses favoring US interests.[74]

The use of aid as a security tool was tried in Latin America, where the priority was to avoid another Cuba. Communist inroads, Kennedy administration experts held, could be contained only with a program that would fundamentally alter the region's developmental course, one that combined political reform, economic prosperity, and the creation of new cultural values, within the framework of what was optimistically planned as a decade-long initiative. In December 1960, Kennedy summoned the influential academics Albert O. Hirschman, Paul N. Rosenstein-Rodan, Federico G. Gil, and Walt W. Rostow to get their opinion. The result came in 1961 in the Alliance for Progress: A Program of Inter-American Partnership, a ten-year, $20 billion foreign aid program for Latin America intended to promote economic growth and political reform in recipient countries. Kennedy described it as "a cooperative effort, unparalleled in magnitude and nobility of purpose."[75] In the months preceding the founding event, the Punta del Este meeting of Latin American leaders in August 1961, Kennedy received input from Latin American personalities like Felipe Herrera, the president of the new Inter-American Development Bank, and Raúl Prebisch, longtime principal intellectual at the United Nations Economic Commission for Latin America (ECLA).

The Alliance for Progress was based on the idea that poverty was a state of mind that could be addressed with the right guidance. As Rostow told a Mexican Chamber of Commerce meeting in 1963, with typical paternalistic tones, states stuck in the childhood that was premodernization could learn a great deal from more advanced countries—especially the United States.[76] With the new program, the United States would allocate capital and provide social scientists. American advisers would analyze the entire society as an integrated unit and identify the preconditions for rapid advancement. Although the Alliance for Progress was a regional scheme, funds were allocated on a country-by-country basis, with little connection between level of poverty and aid distribution. Regional AID project officers in the applicant country received projects and reviewed them in light of expected impact and relation to the nation's overall development plan.[77] Chile, Brazil, the Dominican Republic, and Colombia received almost 60 percent of all US funding. The alliance failed, and weaknesses in its administrative structure are usually blamed.[78] At the core, however, stood the flawed assumption (held for the whole developing world, not just Latin America) that foreign aid would convince leaders to change their policies and accept US ideas about development.

Foreign aid was also the ideal companion for a comprehensive counter-insurgency program for South Vietnam that integrated military action with social engineering. Peasant resettlement and village-level modernization programs were included early on as integral parts of the American counterinsurgency strategy under Eisenhower, when the United States replaced the French militarily, politically, and economically. The United States built facilities of all kinds in an effort resembling an American inflection of earlier colonial policies.[79] The Kennedy administration inherited these plans, with modernization theorists in the metropole tending toward a top-down approach, while in the periphery, experts in community development tended to prefer empowerment and local traditions to promote growth.[80] Lacking the area experts available in France and the United Kingdom, the United States relied on colonial expertise on the ground. One of the key consultants was Robert G. K. Thompson, head of the British Advisory Mission to Vietnam and a veteran of the successful attempt to fight Chinese insurgents in British Malaya. Thompson suggested measures to restore government authority and win the rural population, giving peasants "a stake in stability and hope for the future."[81] This view fit perfectly with modernization ideas, and it constituted the bulk of Operation *Sunrise*, launched in March 1962. Paradoxically, although Kennedy strategists thought of their altruistic, nation-building efforts as anything but colonial, they were influenced by colonial practices like the French *agrovilles* and British counterinsurgency plans, and they adopted colonial language: the idea of a moral mission based on generosity, benevolence, and protection.[82]

Modernization had become central to US policy making. The key was to get validation of the ideal and its specific projects from the recipients, but from the very beginning it was clear that many local leaders wanted aid but did not subscribe to the underlying logic of modernization—that is, the adoption of the American model. Another issue was how to get other Western countries to validate and share the model. That modernization could become the ideology of the West and the way it waged the Cold War was not a given. Integrating Europeans into the US plans for world development meant that they had to be convinced not just to share burdens, but also that this was the way to win the Cold War. This was difficult when the allies still believed in their old ideas of imperial management. These discussions happened in the Development Assistance Group, soon to be renamed the Development Assistance Committee (DAC) in the Organization for Economic Cooperation and Development (OECD), officially launched in December 1960.

# 5

# The Limits of Bipolarity in the Golden Age of Modernization

The trick here, at least for Africa, is to get the Europeans interested and, frankly, I don't know how to do it.

—DEANE R. HINTON, 1965

We fear that the experts would be too technocratic. The weak point of our current experts is neither their skills, nor their technologies, but their excess of skills and technologies, their inability to adapt these technologies to the country in which they are applied.

—JACQUES FERRANDI, 1964

IN THE 1950S, with the Soviet Union and its allies entering the development business, aid became a full-fledged weapon in the Cold War arsenal. Until then, talking about development meant singling out problems and suggesting solutions. Development plans extolled the virtues of modernity and modernity was conceived in the singular: there were several ways to solve the same problem, and experts had differentiated approaches, but they did not diverge drastically. With the entry of the Soviet Union as a potential donor rather than a distant model, development turned competitive. Models were now pitted against one another in a competition about effectiveness and symbolic strength. Technology was not neutral anymore, explained anthropologist Louis Dupree, referring to Afghanistan. Machinery and dams were products of a culture, and the choice of technology implied a choice of social organization, labor relations, and structures of production: it was a political choice.[1] Countries had to take sides in the Cold War, because the decision was a final and irreversible one between irreconcilable proposals.

Both the United States and the Soviet Union required loyalty from recipients. In exchange for being the sole partner, the superpowers offered the showcase projects and prestige buildings that leaders in newly independent countries, hungry to link their names to large symbols, cherished. Each side identified with an ideology that aimed to transform the world by creating progress that fit with its social and economic system—liberal democracy and socialism, respectively.[2] Meanwhile, recipients used the competition for their own ends. Development suited the ambitions of nationalist leaders who saw independence as a means to achieve rapid economic growth, welfare, health, and education. New elites needed to prove they were better than old colonial powers at improving their citizens' lives. Development got mixed up with national politics and its conflicts, and domestic ideological tensions meant that new elites often used development in an authoritarian way, ending up more intrusive and exploitative than the colonial authorities whose precedents they built on.[3] As for the Cold War competition, not only did recipients accept aid without taking sides, but under cover of neutrality, they played off their funders one against the other, threatening to rely on the other side in case of any rejection of their requests. This mechanism worked on both superpowers and their allies, especially in the 1960s. Divided Germany was often played this way.[4]

The history of development, or modernization as it was called in the United States between the mid-1950s and mid-1960s, makes a strong case for the existence of parallel histories during the Cold War. Coordination was essential on both sides of the Iron Curtain, and aid was one arena in which the superpowers had hoped to achieve unity. Instead, it was a source of tension. This chapter deals with differentiated priorities in the West and East as they emerged during the institutionalization of development structures and procedures. A special focus is the organs charged with coordinating aid: the Development Assistance Committee (DAC) of the OECD and the Permanent Commission for Technical Assistance of Comecon illustrate the differences in the paths toward modernity offered by the superpowers and their allies.

## The Cooperation Imperative in the West

The Marshall Plan was the official model for how Western countries could structure development assistance to backward countries. In 1955, Guido Colonna di Paliano, deputy secretary-general of the European Productivity Agency in the Organisation for European Economic Co-operation (OEEC), offered to use Marshall Plan experience to aid member countries in backward areas like Italy, Greece, and Turkey that would serve as laboratories, testing methods that could then be extended globally.[5] In the successor organization to the OEEC, the Organisation for Economic Co-operation and Development

(OECD), the United States asked for a Development Assistance Group that would cooperate on aid matters, starting with an exchange of information on aid.[6] Soon renamed the Development Assistance Committee or DAC, the working group, officially born on 31 January 1960, included Belgium, Canada, France, Germany, Italy, Portugal, the United Kingdom, and the United States, plus the European Economic Community (EEC). During the decade that followed, others were invited: Japan (1961), Norway (1962), Denmark (1963), Sweden and Austria (1965), Australia (1967), and Switzerland (1968).

The first chair of the DAC, Willard L. Thorp, had had a long career in economic diplomacy. He started working as an economic adviser in the State Department in 1944, helping to set up the Marshall Plan and Point Four. He represented the United States in the Economic and Social Council of the United Nations (ECOSOC). He had good contacts with European leaders and detailed knowledge of several European economic and bureaucratic systems, and because he had negotiated interim aid, Marshall Plan, and Point Four aid, he was familiar with American politics. No one could have been better suited for the job. Nevertheless, he encountered insurmountable problems in turning the DAC into a shaper of common rules and standards—the role the United States envisaged for the organization, according to Frank M. Coffin, deputy administrator of USAID and US representative to the DAC in 1964–1965. In his memories of the formative years of the DAC (he was chair from 1962 until 1967), Thorp calls his tenure a "learning process in the developed countries."[7]

Building a body of shared rules was not easy, even though the architects of what has been called the DAC's aid regime allegedly shared a culture. The DAC was a closed group, almost a club, and was meant to remain so.[8] No recipient country was admitted: the assumption was that no matter how different donor countries ideas about development aid were, they still had more in common with each other than with recipients. The question of how to promote a specifically Western political culture of democratic and liberal values through aid was discussed in NATO, too. A secret NATO working paper of August 1958 mentioned "propaganda for democracy": technical assistance that exposed communism's authoritarianism and promoted the Western model of "democratic humanitarianism."[9] However, a coordinated plan of this kind was never put in place in either NATO or the DAC.

In the 1960s, even within the mainstream believers in modernization theory there were differences. One early topic was the definition of aid, called Official Development Assistance, or ODA. The definition used today stems from a compromise reached in the DAC in 1969 (and slightly revised in 1972) after more than a decade of negotiations. Aid qualifies as ODA on the basis of three criteria: "it has to be undertaken by official agencies; it has to have the promotion of economic development and welfare as its main objectives; and it has to have a grant element of 25 percent or more."[10] An earlier definition, arrived at in 1962, included grants and long-term credit (over five years), but also export credits and reparations. From the very beginning, one bone of contention was tied aid, that is, money that had to be spent on goods and services from the donor country. Each donor had its own way of masking this habit. In the agreement finally signed in 1963, there was just a mere declaration of intent about limiting tied aid.[11] DAC members also cooperated via the two consortia set up in the OECD. The most well known is the consortium for Aid to Turkey, set up in mid-1962 to coordinate funding for Turkey's Five-Year Plan. It was governed by the West German diplomat Hans-Joachim Mangold—although why he accepted the position is a mystery, since he was not convinced of the plan's feasibility.[12] Although often described as successful because it attracted significant funding from all DAC countries, the consortium was hardly a bright example of efficiency: due to the complicated operation and supply mechanism, only 40 percent of the funds allocated on a specific project (project aid) could be spent. In contrast, almost all program aid—that is, funds allocated to the general development plan—was used. According to experts, the difference came at least partly from the lack of skill in project preparation.[13] Moreover, important projects that were fundamental to Turkey's development strategies were left out of the consortium. The Keban Dam project, for example, conceived in 1936 and carried out by the French-Italian group SCI-Impregilo between 1966 and 1974, was financed by an ad hoc international syndicate.[14]

## Disappointments: The United States and Bickering in the DAC

Despite "constant acrimonious debates about its foreign aid program," the United States managed to give a strong institutional structure to the DAC, quickly introducing an Annual Aid Review, a peer review process in which three members were picked in rotation to submit an annual report.[15] The aim was to improve the quality and quantity of aid. The Kennedy administration's idea was that the DAC would share the aid burden and redistribute its costs. According to the 1963 Clay Report, "There is evidence the American public feels strongly too that other prosperous industrial nations, having recovered their economic strength since the war with our assistance should assume much more of the foreign aid burden than they are now carrying."[16]

Instructions to US diplomats confirmed the perceived need to respond to these concerns. The first US representative to the DAC, George W. Ball, was specifically directed to press Germany and Japan. In 1961, on the eve of the first high-level DAC meeting, Ball toured Bonn, Paris, and London, hoping to "nail down" German foreign minister Heinrich von Brentano's commitment for a "continuing aid program at appropriate levels." Ball was aware that European allies were not yet ready, and he noted "too much too fast" on the margins of his instructions.[17] A 1962 draft paper argued that getting Europeans to share the burden of maintaining the Western system was "probably more successful in regard to expenditures for economic aid to LDCs (Less Developed Countries)" than military aid. It added that "the US should attempt to capitalise on desires for increased cooperation in order to persuade the European countries to make more resources available to the less developed countries than would otherwise be the case."[18] It was soon clear, however, that this would not be easy.

America preferred to reorganize the world with Germany than with the UK or France, which were still identified with colonialism. It saw Germany as an ideal partner to involve in a binary strategy because, as Ambassador McGhee claimed, it could use its Marshall Plan experience to help young nations in Asia and Africa.[19] It had no colonies, and, like the United States, its policy did not have a regional bias, and its anticommunism was not in question. From October 1961 on, the two countries regularly exchanged opinions on what they called "the economic offensive of the Eastern Bloc."[20] These perceived similarities, however, were a colossal misjudgment: the US-German strategic disagreement was like no other.

From the very beginning, relations were difficult. The Kennedy administration quickly launched the idea of cooperating in technical and financial assistance, but early study missions met with a distinct lack of enthusiasm from both sides.[21] The meetings that followed reached no agreement on important principles, including the very definition of aid. A memorandum of conversation at a meeting at the Foreign Ministry on 21 March 1961 during undersecretary Ball's visit to Europe, for example, shows that the West Germans did not like what they saw as the overstrict American definition of aid.[22] The German undersecretary of economics, Fritz Stedtfeld, who chaired the meeting, protested that he "failed to understand" why the US administration brought up burden sharing—something that had already been settled in NATO. Turning to the qualitative aspects of foreign aid, Stedtfeld wondered why the United States "proposed to leave out of consideration certain types of development assistance." Surely commercial credits and private investment had an important role to play in economic development and should be counted in any tabulation of the level of assistance. As Stedtfeld saw it, an important principle was at stake: the primacy of private investments. Placing too much emphasis on the public sector could contribute to the LDCs' "move towards collective economies." Germany would never agree not to count private investments and credits on commercial terms in the definition of aid.[23] The biggest disagreement, though, was about program aid versus project aid. The United States preferred program aid on a country basis because it allowed for an analysis of the recipient's overall prospects. The Germans resisted this approach—nonproject assistance, they argued, left the donor with inadequate control over funds. Germany thought it was better to select sound projects, implement them efficiently, and judge aid effectiveness by the time needed to complete the projects. Only 8.5 percent of German bilateral commitments in fiscal years 1962 and 1963 went to nonproject aid.[24] Germans were also opposed to soft lending.[25]

A few years later, in 1965, the prospects for bilateral cooperation with West Germany looked better. The United States and West Germany agreed on a set of principles, including self-help and noncooperation with Comecon.[26] But efforts to convince the West Germans to loosen the purse strings were in vain.[27] President Lyndon Johnson had no better luck in his talks with Chancellor Ludwig Erhard: he could not get any increase in the volume of German aid. The problem, US analysts said, was that the Federal Republic had "an economic philosophy which limits its generosity at home and abroad."[28] The disillusionment with aid as a political lever lessened their enthusiasm for foreign assistance, regardless of the public concern about economic relations between rich and poor countries.

## Rostow and the Idea of Binding Rules

Walt Rostow's aid plans were always ambitious. He saw aid as the key to world dynamics and wanted it established as a fixed feature of the system. Newly appointed as a special assistant of state in 1961, he launched a plan for increasing aid by 50–75 percent and securing an international agreement on the fixed share of GDP each country should devote to aid. This would prevent national parliaments from cutting commitments that their governments had pledged. The proposal included a commission to assist developing countries in submitting coherent development plans so that aid distribution would be more rational and repayments more likely.[29] His project was rejected by the other donors. Unable to impose automatic mechanisms, Rostow thought up the great powers club, an idea inspired by the DAC. In the DAC, the rule was unanimity, but any proposal backed by the United States, United Kingdom, France, and Germany was accepted. A separate consultative group of these powers, Rostow reasoned, would facilitate effective leadership and promote better agreements.[30] The Germans, however, fearing a tight bond like the one the 1963 Élysée Treaty enforced between them and France, declined the offer.[31]

Rostow insisted that President Johnson was considering "a quantum jump in scale and in conception" of aid to generate increased momentum in economic and social development in Asia, the Middle East, Africa, and Latin America, but he did not receive the hoped-for reaction, and discussions never began.[32] Deane R. Hinton, US ambassador to the Congo, candidly admitted: "The trick here, at least for Africa, is to get the Europeans interested and, frankly, I don't know how to do it."[33]

In January 1965, a disillusioned Rostow wrote to David Bell, the administrator of USAID: "Whatever the outcome of our own appropriation request this year, foreign aid is heading for slack times. The Germans lost no time in recommending a lower aid budget, the French are cutting down, the Italians plead poverty and instability and the Japanese say they can't keep up the little they do. A pall seems to be gradually descending over the enterprise. We all mean to become more 'hard headed'—as we grow richer."[34]

Rostow still thought that the United States, together with West Germany, could propose a "Wise Men's Group" of leading figures from the United States, United Kingdom, France, West Germany, and Japan, together with one or two World Bank representatives. This group would discuss long-term issues like the future of aid in North-South relations, forms of aid (multilateral or bilateral, regional or country based), and overall development strategy (rural vs. urban development, population policy, external vs. internal trade, trade and aid, incentives for private investments). In February 1965, AID administrator Ball left for Paris, Bonn, and London; during this visit, he advanced a proposal to create a new bilateral US-FRG aid relationship by inaugurating "policy level discussions on conceptual and longer-range questions of mutual interest." The rationale was explained in the background paper: to secure a larger German aid contribution and persuade the FRG to move from a project-by-project approach to a country program approach.[35] The US scheme addressed the organization of annual ministerial meetings in which general policy issues but also urgent country problems could be discussed. Ministerial meetings would alternate with periodic staff-level meetings of senior regional officials responsible for strategy review of performance in specific geographic areas. Other coordination activities included consultation between permanent representatives in the DAC and exchange of documents and information. The proposal also mentioned specific multidonor activities for the Kainji Dam in Nigeria and the Keban Dam in Turkey. Again, it was rejected.

Differences among the Western countries exploded in the United Nations, especially in the United Nations Conference on Trade and Development (UNCTAD), founded in 1964, and worsened with the stalemate in the Kennedy Round, the negotiations for curtailing tariffs in the General Agreement on Tariffs and Trade (GATT).[36] Although increasingly unrealistic, the idea of making the DAC work as an institution for policy coordination still featured in official US documents: "DAC should be used more intensively for policy coordination. The US, Germany and other major donors should consult closely on a bilateral basis and through permanent DAC representatives to provide more leadership for reaching full consensus in DAC on general aid issues and on particular LDC programs."[37]

Notwithstanding these hopes, after 1965 the DAC increasingly became a discussion forum for crucial choices and a tool for collecting and comparing data, not a coordinating body. One issue that required a common resolve was the debt issue. A report on the growth of the external liabilities of LDCs was submitted for consideration at the high-level DAC meeting scheduled for 22–23 July 1965.[38] Delegations were staffed with the highest-ranking representatives for the occasion—overseas development ministers, where available, such as in Germany or the UK. Thorp delivered a lengthy statement on enhancing aid effectiveness. He favored a move toward interest-free loans sponsored by international economic organizations.[39] His approach resonated with the ideas of World Bank president George D. Woods, who asked for an international agreement to provide more favorable concession terms.[40] Thorp was backed by the UK Labour government, with minister Barbara Castle assisted by development economist Dudley Seers as a member of the British delegation. West Germany, in contrast, opposed interest-free loans and expressed doubts about a multilateral agreement on untying aid. France's point of view, represented by Valéry Giscard d'Estaing, was the most categorical: softening the terms was just a palliative, while aid tying was perfectly reasonable because it made aid more acceptable to the public and thus was a prerequisite to aid increases. Aid was a national activity, he continued, and multilateralization was not even remotely in the plans of the French government.[41] The prospects for Western cooperation were discouraging: in a 1968 special issue of *International Organization* on development, economist Göran Ohlin claimed that the very notion of burden sharing had failed.[42]

In the mid-1960s, the Johnson administration was increasingly concerned with the growing competition in offering loans on better terms (the so-called credits race) introduced by East-West rivalry in the developing world. By 1966, several American politicians, including the president, were toying with the idea of involving Eastern Bloc countries in a joint strategy to develop the South. Recalling the 1965 Comecon hint about possible cooperation in aid matters (which had not originally been well received), the Americans offered to turn previous consultations on the red danger into a discussion about cooperating with socialist countries in aiding Africa.[43] Reluctantly, the new West German minister of economic cooperation Hans-Jürgen Wischnewski agreed that it would be unwise not to share the burden of aid—and the responsibility for failure—with the East. Under the new coalition government of Kurt Georg Kiesinger with Willy Brandt's Social Democrats as a driving force, West Germany consistently followed the path toward joint economic aid. In 1966, the West German government systematically pursued bilateral contacts with Eastern European countries to work on common projects in the developing world, especially Africa. If development aid was to be made more effective, Brandt claimed in 1969, cooperation between East and West in the Third World was necessary. In his *Ostpolitik*, such links could then evolve into a broader economic cooperation and eventually acquire enough strength to disentangle Eastern European countries from their economic links with the Soviet Union.[44]

## The European Economic Community Way

The European Economic Community, which counted France, Germany, Italy, Belgium, and the Netherlands—all DAC countries—as members, was also represented in the DAC. Its performance was submitted to evaluation just like that of the national donors. European Community circles, especially officials in the Directorate-General of Overseas Development (DG Development), mistrusted, even abhorred, the technocratic ideas that circulated in the DAC. They considered them as part of a distant Anglo-Saxon culture. They were no fans of modernization theory. Instead, they followed the teachings of Robert Delavignette, one of the most well-known French colonial officers in Africa (he served in Cameroon, Niger, and Upper Volta—now Burkina Faso), a long-time director of the École Nationale de la France d'Outremer, and director of political affairs in the French Overseas Ministry from 1947 to 1951. Delavignette praised traditional rural African societies and despised planners who "played with statistics," had no interest in local cultures, and were guided by what he saw as a blind faith in technology—a fanatic intolerance they considered progress.[45] The idea that local knowledge was crucial to designing effective aid plans became DG Development's guiding principle. Decision making on aid allocation was firmly in the hands of the head of the EDF, Jacques Ferrandi, and a small group that included his deputy Jean Chapperon and press officer Pierre Cros. This did not mean that ideas on aid performance were ignored: the EEC bureaucracy worked with feasibility studies and elaborated procedures granting publicity and transparency. It also claimed to have adopted objective criteria for its decisions.[46]

Development commissioner Henri Rochereau, who served between 1962 and 1970, made it clear that the Directorate-General was not a think tank, insisting that "we are no theoreticians of development, we are men of action and of good will." Associated countries, he contended, did not need to adopt a European way of life or European political conceptions. They would achieve progress "in their own way."[47] In his role as director of the EDF, Ferrandi was critical of ready-made recipes for development; he did not think that development was about "applying a solution developed in a lab onto a specific situation."[48] This hostility toward scientific modernization was sometimes expressed as a rebuttal of perfectionism, of the "perfectly tailored technical solution" that might fit Europe but did not match African requirements. Ferrandi also rejected development doctrines that predicted a project's success without considering its economic and social context. The thinking of DG Development was not so removed from what was called the Latin thought on development typical of people like Giorgio Ceriani Sebregondi or some of the ideas of 1950s-era Social Catholicism.[49] As it disdained industrial planning, this interpretation was a sharp departure from the doctrines then prevailing in the international system.

The peculiarities of the EEC aid system emerged very clearly in the detailed annual aid review of 1964, when the regime of the first convention with not-yet-independent associated territories was replaced by the Yaoundé Convention, signed in 1963 by the now-independent countries. The director-general of DG Development, Heinrich Hendus, stressed the novelties, conveying the message that the EEC was conforming to mainstream ideas on development prevailing in the DAC and intended to increase aid volume and diversify financing methods. Aid programming criteria were also changing: investments in infrastructure that had largely prevailed under the first scheme would be replaced by "directly productive operations in agriculture and industry," in cooperation with the private sector. Similarly, while the first convention provided only grants, Yaoundé provided loans, too. Hendus had to admit that EEC aid still lagged because of the shortage of qualified personnel in recipient countries after the departure of Europeans at independence. Local bureaucracies were not able to prepare plans and submit them for funding, so the EDF had to make allocation decisions centrally.[50]

What kinds of projects were funded with EEC aid? Jean Durieux, adjunct director-general of DG Development in 1964, claimed that Africa was not yet ready for industrial development, and much aid went to create the necessary preconditions.[51] Many Ferrandi-era EDF projects went toward improving rural production and the living conditions of rural populations. The review presented to the DAC in 1964 focused on investments in the rural sector in Upper Volta (Burkina Faso), where EEC aid amounted to $26 million for drilling wells and small dams, plus another $3 million available for a school. Another case mentioned in the review was Somalia. Here, natural conditions made it difficult to think of diversification purely in terms of rural development. Emphasis was laid instead on processing agricultural produce for local consumption and export, with a view to modifying the economic structure. This industrial development was to include canning plants, flour mills, sugar refineries, and textile plants for the processing of cotton. An interesting view of aid to Somalia "from the outside" that allows a comparison of EEC aid with that from bilateral donors is offered by a remarkable 1969 report by the British Embassy in Mogadishu. The report ruthlessly points out Somali lack of commitment to development that enraged all donors, from the West Germans, disillusioned by the lack of progress in their projects, especially the Gelib-Kisimayu road, to the Russians, firmly in control of the armed forces but reluctant to embark on new initiatives. The EEC was as a "medium league" donor to Somalia ($20 million to $30 million)—the "big league" included former colonial power Italy, the United States, and the USSR. The EEC built and staffed the hospital in Mogadishu and funded various roads that required continuing foreign aid for their maintenance. According to estimates of the United Nations Development Programme (UNDP), total EEC grants amounted to nearly $27.5 million.[52] Rural diversification projects are well documented in the EEC archives, and the Alaotra project in Madagascar, intended to improve rice cultivation for export, stands out.[53] The reports describe wells, dikes, small dams, bridges, canals, and small irrigation projects, accompanied by the provision of simple technology and the introduction of pesticides.[54] Facing indifference from the local population, development experts involved in Madagascar were skeptical about sustainability. What strategy should the EEC adopt? Should it force progress on the recipient countries against their will, or should it let them get on with their own ideas? In order to apply efficient farming methods, even simple ones, European assistance, they could see, would be needed for a very long time.[55]

Along with rural diversification funding, the EEC provided aid for the preparation of five-year plans. In 1964, Cameroon, Chad, Dahomey, the Central African Republic, and Mali managed to file their programs, thanks to the assistance of the local EEC missions. Planning was expected to ensure that aid allocation was based on the quality of the projects, but distribution would still be biased, given that it was easier to find sound projects in the wealthier seaboard countries than in the interior. Geographical criteria, introduced with Yaoundé, were thus merely indicative, and action was required for some countries to bridge the gap. This margin of discretion made the activities of the EDF opaque. Existing networks of clients and patronage could continue: Ferrandi was especially criticized for his reliance on political connections—he responded that politics was made of relationships, and that he did not have a policy, he had partners. There were requests for more objective criteria in EEC aid distribution—bigger and more advanced countries such as Senegal and Ivory Coast, for example, objected to the amount of aid provided to small countries like Gabon.[56]

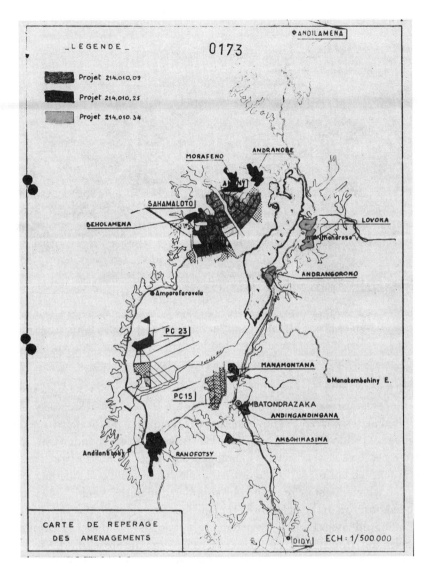

FIGURE 2. Project Alaotra, hydroagricultural development map, 1970. Historical Archives European Union (HAEU), CEE/CEEA Commissions—Fonds BAC, 25/1980 783.

A summary of the discussions following the 1964 EEC aid review is essential to understand how much the EEC intended to represent a different way to deal with aid. In Cold War terms, the remarks about the political side of aid were revealing. The US representative asked whether the commission could "use the weight of its financial contribution to guide the policy of the states

FIGURE 3. Project Alaotra, hydroagricultural development, canalization works. Historical Archives European Union (HAEU), CEE/CEEA Commissions—Fonds BAC, 25/1980 783.

which were aided" and whether "an analysis of the policies of the associated states" was "used as a frame of reference for the grant of aid." Essentially, the United States wanted to know whether the recipients' political orientation influenced allocation decisions. The EEC representative responded that "the Commission is less subject to psychological and political pressure than a bilateral donor; it had therefore laid down the rule that it would not undertake any action which might be motivated by consideration of this kind."[57] The principled position of the delegation, though, failed to mention that criteria for granting aid under Ferrandi were remarkably variable and that they included preventing African leaders from seeking funds from the Soviet Bloc.[58] To the US request about whether EEC aid could finance a general development program, for example by granting loans for the import of raw materials or semi-finished products, the EEC representative answered in the negative: under its statute, the EEC commission could not.[59]

How to assess the efficiency of aid remained an open question. Studies on effectiveness were introduced in the 1960s in Rwanda and Burundi, Congo (in the Equator province), Mali, Ivory Coast, Somaliland, and the Central African Republic.[60] The EEC Commission had technical controllers in all associated countries who were charged with reporting on the progress of funded projects—however, the system needed reform to ensure that controllers did not act solely as paymasters but could suggest how to adapt projects to emerging necessities. In 1970, the controllers acquired increased responsibilities. Director-General Hans-Broder Krohn introduced a system whereby external technical personnel, balanced by national origin, were made project supervisors. Called *contrôleurs délégués*, these supervisors gradually became a network of diplomatic representatives of the Community. Recruiting procedures and a system of rotating assignments were introduced. The supervisors became prefects who took care of a particular territory and promoted Community action.[61]

One of the main issues of EEC aid as a whole was the pipeline problem; that is, resources were allocated but were not spent. This phenomenon was a generic flaw of project aid, where resources got stuck because of the lack of good projects that met financing criteria. All systems where project aid was important (the German system, for example) had huge pipeline problems. In the case of EEC aid, the issue was acute. In 1966, during the high-level DAC meeting devoted to food and agricultural questions, Jean Durieux explained the solution devised to "shorten the pipeline": the introduction of an intermediate step, an "operational program" to detail how individual projects would work within the bigger plan.[62] Programming became the new buzzword for the EEC as well as for other international organizations. Notwithstanding the many uncertainties in a system that was constantly under construction during the 1960s, European aid practices are believed to have positively influenced development. Historian Martin Rempe, for example, makes a convincing case for the positive impact of EEC projects on diversification in Senegal.[63]

## Coordination among Socialist Countries: The Permanent Commission for Technical Assistance in Comecon

In the 1950s, the Eastern Bloc thought of the international economic system as two world markets. Socialists assigned newly independent countries to one of the two sides—usually the capitalist, albeit of a special kind. The Eastern Bloc was a clear alternative to the West, and its aid was intended to be qualitatively different from that of the West. Socialist countries did not use the term "aid": they did not have to give aid, because they were not imperialists repenting for colonial legacies. They also rejected the distinction between donors and recipients, using the word "solidarity." Policies toward the newly independent countries were discussed both at a bilateral level and in multilateral settings: in the Advisory Committee on Foreign Policy in the Warsaw Pact, in meetings of the International Departments in the Communist Parties, and especially in Comecon, the organization established in 1949 to encourage economic cooperation and integration among the socialist countries of Bulgaria, Czechoslovakia, Hungary, Poland, Romania, the Soviet Union, Albania (since 1949), and East Germany (since 1950).[64] Soon it included others as observers and potential members: Yugoslavia, Mongolia, the People's Republic of China, North Korea, and North Vietnam. Mongolia got membership in 1962, and Yugoslavia became an associate in 1964. This inclusiveness was stressed in the 1960s, and the formula "integration through equality" was presented as a possibility for newly independent countries. In a world divided into two economic and social systems, choosing scientific socialism would open Comecon doors for developing countries—Cuba joined in 1972, Vietnam in 1978.[65]

In 1957, a year after Khrushchev offered to aid newly independent countries, a working group was formed in the Permanent Commission of Foreign Trade in Comecon to deal with them by forging new trade channels and offering economic assistance. It was not a coincidence that the group was established just a few weeks after the European Economic Community was born, with its program of technical assistance for former colonies, now connected through the association system. The working group changed its name several times before being formalized as the Permanent Commission for Technical Assistance in June 1961. And given the Cold War's parallel history, it was no coincidence that the DAC was institutionalized in the OECD just one month later.

The commission's original plan was to harmonize long-term agreements for importing food and raw materials and exporting complete plants, with the hope of eventually signing multilateral trade agreements.[66] For socialist countries, it was impossible to offer credits to support the national development of a country or projects where the donor's participation was not part of the deal. Ideally, participation meant following a project throughout its lifespan, as in the offer of complete plants with technical assistance and experts to help start production.[67] In the 1960s, the socialist countries increasingly offered turnkey plants, covering all construction costs, assembly, and starting operations. Included in the deal, and typical of cooperation among Comecon countries themselves, was technology transfer and patent exchange. This could include the transmission of technical documents, training of experts, and specific operating advice, but also—as in the scientific and technical cooperation agreements (WTZ: Wissenschaftlich-Technische Zusammenarbeit) granted by the GDR—organization of vocational training and education or commitment to joint research projects.[68]

Socialist countries never managed to structure full multilateral cooperation centered on Comecon.[69] At the first meeting, in June 1961, each delegation was supposed to present ideas, but most members left the floor to the Soviet Union, assuming that the Soviets already had a plan. Guidelines for the GDR's delegates put it quite bluntly: "In the interest of good relations with the Soviet

Union, it is not expedient to express any critical observation on this point," referring to the plans for the commission.[70] This deferential attitude, how-ever, should not be misread. East Germany, like other Eastern Bloc members, was not always malleable in Comecon: cooperation was limited to members' common interests and based on mutual agreement.[71] Made up of experts in economics and international trade, the commission met once in the spring and once in the fall. In 1963, high-level meetings of deputy ministers were introduced.[72] Comecon's commitment was fostering relations with newly independent countries by promoting trade and securing supplies of strategic raw materials to Comecon countries. The developing countries' needs hardly figured in the equation.

The documents of the commission are puzzling to those familiar with the discourse of anti-imperialist solidarity and the Eastern Bloc's public discourse. The word "solidarity" is absent, revealing the marginalization of a dimension that was otherwise heavily publicized. The topics discussed were technical issues connected to trade or, occasionally, the supply of machinery or great infrastructural works. The Socialist Bloc did not share the definition of needy countries based on per capita income, as its members identified with progress and modernity and did not accept the label of underdeveloped. Nevertheless, some members, especially Romania and Bulgaria, tended to identify with the developing world. They rejected the Soviet Union's idea of an international division of labor that meant they would continue producing low-added-value supplies and thus remain relatively backward.[73] Friction emerged when the Soviet Union discussed such a division of tasks as a way to avoid duplications.

Comecon members, especially the Soviet Union, devised coordination schemes to avoid being played by developing countries, which tended to submit wish lists to several potential donors and accept aid from different sources for the same project.[74] In 1962, Khrushchev advanced a proposal based on comparative advantages called the "Basic Principles of the Social International Division of Labor." The focus, however, was not on promoting Comecon as a means of fostering multilateral cooperation but on confirm-ing the strength of bilateral links tying each Eastern European country to the Soviet Union. In the commission, a division of labor emerged quite neatly: Czechoslovakia offered projects for the energy sector, the steel industry, and light industries (leather, shoes, textiles, sugar); Hungary specialized in light machinery, hydroelectric power, and pharmaceuticals; East Germany in tele-communication and electronics; Poland in mining, naval construction, and wood processing; Romania in oil processing technology and petrochemical production. The specialization made it harder for recipients to play one coun-try off another. In 1965, Eastern European credits financed mainly the follow-ing sectors: steel mills (26 percent), electric power (26 percent), metallurgy

(11 percent), and chemistry (5 percent). India, Afghanistan, and Egypt, the countries where several Comecon members worked jointly on infrastructure projects, received 70 percent of bloc aid.[75] The Comprehensive Program for Socialist Economic Integration of August 1971, also known as the Bucharest Plan, retraced the "Basic Principles," with explicit reference to the desirability of equal development levels and thus to favoring less developed member countries in accessing advanced technologies and credits.

The debt problem burdened relations with developing countries from the very beginning. The commission had long discussions about how to avoid the risk of insolvency. The 1950s rule of sticking to the principle of balanced trade had proved ineffective, as poor countries rarely managed to export goods of sufficient quality and quantity to keep trade balanced. In October 1963, at the fifth meeting of the commission, the Soviet mandate was unambiguous: developing countries had to make clear how they intended to pay their debts to be granted new credits. Several Eastern European partners argued that a strategy focused on the promotion of small business could facilitate loan repayment. General rules for credits were set forth. Governmental credits were connected to the sale of complete plants—the term used for any bigger industrial structure, whether for producing energy, extracting or processing raw materials, or manufacturing. Governmental credits lasted ten to twelve years and carried an interest rate of 2.5 percent, while commercial credits generally lasted five years, with an interest rate between 2.5 and 6 percent. In special cases, they could be extended to eight or ten years. Favorable conditions were reserved for countries with friendly relations with the Eastern Bloc.[76] Keen to coordinate actions for building bigger plants, the Soviet Union required members to agree to full disclosure of information on agreements for exporting plants. Eastern European allies were often skeptical about big projects, favoring smaller ones with simpler technology that responded to local requests.[77] East Germany argued for cooperation on smaller productions where it could compete in terms of quality—for example, optical products. Eastern Bloc technology, contended Walter Ulbricht, secretary-general of the Sozialistische Einheitspartei Deutschlands (SED), was at once too backward to compete with Western technology and too advanced to meet the needs of backward societies—Comecon countries should offer simpler material to African countries.[78]

Unlike the West, socialist countries did not often formalize consortia before the 1970s. In 1966, a mere 3.7 percent of the complete plants exported to developing countries by Comecon countries were the product of cooperation between two or more Bloc members.[79] In the construction of the Aswan High Dam, for example, described by historian Elizabeth Bishop as a failed attempt to transfer the Soviet planning culture to Egypt, no other Eastern

European countries were officially involved.[80] Elite Soviet technicians were carefully selected for this showcase project run by Ivan Komzin, the Soviet hero who had built the Kremenchuk Dam on the Dnieper, in Ukraine. In 1962, however, Egyptians complained about the construction, demanding Western European technicians and machinery. In 1963, Soviet personnel were ousted, reappearing only when Khrushchev visited in 1964. The credit line stayed open, but Soviet technology was replaced with Swedish drills and British motors, while the West Germans of Hochtief Aktiengesellschaft and Rheinstahl Union Beckenbau sent turbines and hydraulic structures made of steel.[81]

## Responding to External Challenges

Comecon was also the place where socialist countries decided how to react to the challenges posed by changes in the international economic system. The confrontation with Western models, especially the European Economic Community, was raised in all coordination arenas of Socialist Bloc countries, including bilateral talks. East Germany was especially sensitive on the topic, given that EEC aid was conditioned on an acceptance of the West German view of the German question—that is, nonrecognition of East Germany as a legitimate member of the international community. Its attitude vis-à-vis the EEC was contradictory. On the one hand, East Germany constantly attacked the EEC as a form of collective colonialism, using the terms circulated at the Pan-African conference in Cairo (March 1961).[82] On the other hand, East Germans argued that the EEC was worth imitating, because developing countries wanted the socialist countries to provide a unitary policy like that of the EEC. The undersecretary of foreign affairs, Otto Winzer, coming back from a 1963 tour of Ghana, Mali, Guinea, Morocco, and Algeria, insisted that Comecon should adopt a trade and aid policy similar to that of the EEC.[83] Another reason the East Germans admired the EEC was because it focused on agricultural cooperation. Agriculture had to turn socialist too, with state farms and rural cooperatives that used modern technology, fertilizers, and pesticides to increase productivity. East Germans were not comfortable with offering rural development: until 1975, they financed just thirty-seven rural development projects, model farms, or irrigation schemes, generally paying instead for projects in the processing industry.[84] In September 1967, East German trade representative Hartmann pressed for urgent consultation within Comecon to provide joint support to rural development plans in Tanzania.[85] The urgency, shared by the GDR and Yugoslavia, came from the feeling that Tanzania had been neglected and pushed into the arms of China and the imperialists. Comecon should intervene and grant at least the teachers requested by Tanzanian president Julius Nyerere. The GDR sent seventeen out of fifty—other countries should now deliver the rest.[86]

In the 1960s, cultural policies and education were not at home in the Commission for Technical Assistance, despite East German and Czechoslovak efforts to bring them up. Discussion of common educational policies took place in Moscow in 1963, with Romania objecting to expanding the commission's portfolio. Nonetheless, educational aid such as sending teachers, hosting students, instructing journalists, educating trade union or party personnel, sending books and films, and organizing exhibitions eventually took off, because it was considered a reasonably inexpensive way to influence developing countries. Higher education of a technical-scientific character and for medical doctors, in addition to experts in planning and foreign trade, was preferred over primary schooling.[87] Only in 1966 was a specific coordination plan launched—one with the somewhat overstated goal of burying Western cultural influence.[88] Once a neglected area, in the 1970s education became a preferred means to counter imperialist influence, extolled in the propaganda materials that introduced Comecon. Nongovernmental (so-called social) organizations were also involved in education in the Third World.

In the GDR, the SED with its international relations department superintended political cooperation with like-minded (progressive) parties in developing countries, including regular consultations, study delegations and exchanges, and education for cadres in the Party schools of the GDR. Other organizations were active, including the Journalists' Union, Verband der Journalisten der DDR (VDJ), with its well-known "Solidarity school" for journalists from Asia and Africa. In 1963, the Council of Ministers of the GDR approved the plan for a socialist version of the Peace Corps, the Freundschaftsbrigaden, made up of young East Germans, most highly skilled technicians. They were sent to newly independent countries with the aim of "developing friendly relations and instructing personnel for future bilateral relations."[89] Depending on the agreement with the host country, the Freundschaftsbrigaden took part in pilot projects and vocational training camps, helped with harvesting, or offered maintenance support for GDR machinery. They were seen as ambassadors for East Germany and were expected to propagate socialism. The first brigades were sent to Ghana, Guinea, Mali, and Algeria in 1964; by the 1970s they also went to the Central African Republic, Guinea-Bissau, Angola, and Mozambique.[90] Medical aid was equally crucial, although often the language, which was cast in terms of civilizational differences, limited its appeal.[91]

In 1964, governmental credits were stepped up throughout the Soviet Bloc, a response to UNCTAD and the increase in aid by the United States. UNCTAD posed a real challenge to socialist countries. How to react to the requests of the G77 (the seventy-seven countries constituted in 1963 to act as a pressure group within the United Nations for the developing world) was discussed in several arenas, especially Comecon.[92] The G77 requested that developed countries in both the West and East import processed or semiprocessed goods. East Germany advanced the point in the Commission for Technical Assistance—a common line was needed, it argued, to face the threat of overpriced or poor-quality products flooding the market as a consequence of the opening. The issue became thorny in 1966, when other problems, related to export licenses and the quality of products, were discussed.[93] Despite Romania's resistance, the commission decided to meet the G77 demands. The main interest was ensuring the Eastern Bloc's import of essential raw materials, starting with copper, nickel, cotton, and rubber. Mixed companies, involving one socialist country and one developing country, could produce and trade goods that were needed by the socialist countries.[94]

In the mid-1960s, the Comecon opinion of coordination was essentially positive. It remained active in the following years with a new axiom: mutual advantage. Great projects were preferred.[95] With limited strong currencies, Eastern European countries cooperated to import raw materials that the Soviet Union no longer provided at subsidized rates. In return, they offered weapons, complete plants, technicians, and experts.[96] Increasingly, however, it was clear that the socialist countries could not offer enough economic assistance to cover the huge requests coming from the less developed countries, which perceived trade with Comecon as a mere enlargement of their market, able to grant a welcome stability on the demand side.[97] Recipients were often dissatisfied with the Eastern Bloc's aid performance; not surprising, considering how little attention the socialist countries paid to recipients. In the Commission for Technical Assistance, for example, discussions revolved around donor concerns, and the commission rarely discussed specific aid features. It was left to the mixed economic committees established at the bilateral level in the 1970s to collect complaints—the most common were about the lack of spare parts, slow provision of supplies, and low technological standards.[98] These issues eventually undermined East-South relations. In the global Cold War of the 1960s, neither side was really able to achieve serious, permanent success using aid as a political tool. Both East and West worried about mounting debts, and between 1964 and 1968 this occasionally led to fleeting ideas of limited East-West cooperation in aid giving. Neither East nor West had many political gains to point to. Recipients did not show gratitude: they expected aid as a form of restitution for colonial plundering and requested more and more from the rich North, hardly differentiating between the different social and economic systems. LDCs choosing the Eastern path of development was a remote possibility, and the overthrow of "socialist" Kwame Nkrumah in Ghana in 1966 proved that socialist development paths were reversible. For that matter, Guinea and Tanzania, which professed a socialist orientation, still partnered with the West.

Modernization theory did not seem to work, nor was it unanimously shared, as suggested by the frequent disagreements in the DAC and, even more clearly, by EEC development policy, which was based on different assumptions, distant from the ideological pillars of modernization. Criticism was directed against both the policies and the theory, including the implicit idea that progress implied convergence. French sociologist Raymond Aron first criticized this point in his lecture series at the Sorbonne, published in 1962 under the title *Dix-huit leçons sur la société industrielle*. He criticized the idea of the universally valid stages of growth and its corollary, that similar industrial societies could be spread all over the world. In 1964, Zbigniew Brzezinski and Samuel Huntington addressed the lack of historical awareness in the discourses of convergence.[99] The debate received new impetus with the 1968 publication of John K. Galbraith's *The New Industrial State*, which opened by stating, "Capitalistic or communistic, all states tend to converge in character under the imperatives of technology." Galbraith applauded modernization, seeing a brilliant outlook for planning in the industrial state in the West and the East alike.[100] This idea of convergence was anathema to socialist orthodoxy, which rejected convergence as an intolerable misunderstanding of the socialist system. Economists like Gunnar Myrdal, Jan Tinbergen, and François Perroux, all of whom somewhat endorsed convergence, were called propagators of ideological mistakes by the Eastern Bloc and accused of advocating imperialism disguised as humanitarianism.[101] In contrast, nationalist leaders in the South, such as Léopold Senghor, saw convergence as a useful analytical tool because it brought the rich countries of the North under the same umbrella and allowed a different understanding of world politics, less as an East-West, Cold War confrontation and more as a global struggle between the "have" nations (including the Soviet Union) and the "have-not" proletarian nations.[102]

# 6

# International Organizations and Development as a Global Mission

It's more like sending missionaries than sending goods, somehow.

—WILLARD L. THORP, 1971

For many years I have looked for the brain which guides the policies and operations of the UN development system. . . . The search has been in vain.

—ROBERT G. A. JACKSON, 1969

"WELCOME TO THE new United Nations, with a large developing country majority," American ambassador Richard Gardner commented ironically, recalling the moment when Nigeria first took its seat at the United Nations in 1960. The American delegation was shocked by the nasty words of Ambassador Jaja Wachuku, Nigeria's permanent representative in the General Assembly. Reacting to the welcome speech of US representative Adlai Stevenson, who reiterated the US commitment to helping African countries, the ambassador responded with what Gardner called a terrible statement: "Well, the West will have to pay for its decades of colonialism, and we are not here with our hand out asking for your charity, Ambassador Stevenson. We want a whole new world economic order based on justice. We want higher prices for our exports, and different terms of trade. We want control over multinational corporations." The clash between the superpowers and newly independent countries exposes some fundamental characteristics of General Assembly discussions in this period. Sometimes they harmonized with external events and sometimes they ran counter to them, but they always reflected Cold War dynamics. Gardner later recalled that "by this time the Russians were working not only behind the scenes, but very overtly, to form an alliance with the most radical part of the Afro-Asian group against the United States."[1]

Nigeria's speech came as a shock because the new administration supported the creation of an international aid system. US president John Fitzgerald Kennedy, addressing the UN General Assembly on 25 September 1961, called for a strong international commitment: "Self-determination is but a slogan if the future holds no hope. That is why my nation, which has freely shared its capital and its technology to help others help themselves, now proposes officially designating this decade of the 1960s as the United Nations Decade of Development."[2] Economist Hans Singer recalled that Kennedy's determination surprised the audience.[3] The Decade of Development became the setting for expanding and coordinating UN development programs. The hope was that research, technical assistance, and pilot projects would transform development into a cooperative venture involving the whole international community.

The UN was the ideal place for East and West to meet. In General Assembly sessions, political confrontation was the rule, but in the more technical institutions, dialogue often prevailed. The growing awareness of the global dimensions of development had made international organizations, especially the United Nations, crucial to development thinking and practice. The word "underdeveloped"—or more precisely, the word as applied to a country—was first used in an international organization, the International Labour Organization (ILO), before the Second World War. Wilfred Benson, a former British colonial officer linked to Fabian socialism, employed the term in his report *Social Policy in Dependent Territories*, where he called for the adoption of supranational welfare policies.[4] International organizations' involvement in development proceeded in stages, converging toward "one size fits all," universal technocratic knowledge, and solutions unconnected to cultural specificities, even if distinctive in their ideological orientation. In the 1990s, the naturalized French diplomat Stéphane Hessel wrote that development was a concept that informed the whole structure of the United Nations and gave it meaning.[5] He claimed it took forty years to move from the black-and-white reasoning of the 1950s toward a more nuanced view. The story of this transformation is told here. International organizations that had acted as agencies of civilization in late colonial times became arenas in which different ideas of modernity were articulated. Some, like the World Bank, were clearly the expression of a Western capitalist mind-set, whereas others, like the United Nations, provided a home for both technocratic thinking and anti-imperialist ideas that differed from the prevailing modernization theory.[6]

## Precedents: The League of Nations

In 1945, Belgian law scholar Maurice Bourquin, longtime diplomat and professor of international law at the Institut Universitaire des Hautes Études

Internationales and Geneva University, witnessed the first General Assembly of the United Nations as a member of the Belgian delegation. Thinking back to the League of Nations, he wrote that the League's greatest success was as an incubator for international technical organizations that created a new way of doing international politics: as technocratic work.[7] The technical role of the League of Nations was often praised. Stanley Bruce, together with the Special Committee on the Development of International Cooperation in Economic and Social Affairs, of which Bourquin was a member, wrote the famous Bruce Report, published 22 August 1939. In it, he argued for a clear separation of political and technical activities in the organization. His ideas were later used to form ECOSOC, the UN Economic and Social Council.[8]

In the interwar years, it was widely thought that economic crisis was a primary cause of instability and that growth and humanitarian measures were the tools to mitigate its impact. Intervention in the economic and social realm was thus seen as a preventive measure. Rooted in nineteenth-century philanthropic internationalism, this view survived the crises of the 1930s and 1940s, motivating the League of Nations to engage with economic and social security and making it the ideal place to deal with emerging development policies. Jamie Martin has recently studied how in the 1930s, the League's economic and financial department and its head, Arthur Salter, thought of implanting corporatist models of economic management in India and China by introducing National Economic Councils where colonial experts and international officers could work together on development policies. These were early examples of international cooperation of a new kind, sometimes called a civilizing mission without empire.[9] Asia was the first site of these global networks, and several Americans prophesied that it would soon turn into the world's factory.[10]

The first project sponsored by the League of Nations, a technical assistance program centered on rural cooperatives, was requested by the nationalist government of China. Sun Yat-sen's *The Economic Development of China* had appeared in English in 1922; in it he suggested that technocratic management of development could counter imperialism. He advocated that "the vast resources of China" could "be developed internationally under a Socialist scheme" in a sort of "great trust owned by the Chinese people."[11] After years of foreign domination under unequal treaties, Sun Yat-sen considered bilateral aid unacceptable. The League of Nations, however, did not intend to offer multifaceted and expensive reconstruction plans. Salter and Chiang Kai-shek created an economic planning committee that elaborated a three-year development plan modeled on the Soviet five-year plan and used experts familiar with Soviet planning. Under the technical assistance agreement that Chinese finance minister Song Ziwen signed with the League of Nations in 1931, China would receive technology and financial support for nation building. Because of natural catastrophes, work did not start until 1933, when the League sent twenty-six experts, including doctors, engineers, and agronomists, who dealt with public health, education, water management, transportation, and agriculture. The general principles guiding the League of Nations were promoting free trade and increasing industrial production; however, it did not have a unitary idea of modernity. The agricultural development experts sent to China in 1933, Briton William Kenneth Hunter Campbell, Italian Mario Dragoni, and German Max Brauer, were influenced by different intervention approaches— "liberal" colonialism, fascist corporatism, and a moderate strand of European socialism—and held different ideas about developing rural cooperatives.[12] Local elites and experts ended up choosing what suited their political agenda.

In the 1930s, particularly between 1936 and 1939, Chiang Kai-shek did not rely exclusively on the League of Nations. He also had a personal consultant, H. D. Fong, an economist and Yale graduate who wanted to develop heavy industry under state control, as in Germany or the Soviet Union.[13] His ideas contrasted sharply with those of the League of Nations' expert, John Bell Condliffe. Previously at the Rockefeller Foundation, by 1932 Condliffe was working on a World Economic Survey for the League of Nations. He contended that promoting the natural evolution of the economy was key to development, while economic nationalism blocked growth. In his view, individual rights should prevail over the nation-state. Technological innovation should be encouraged only if it took root autonomously. Condliffe doubted that China could industrialize in a short time. A few years later, the Rockefeller Foundation, still working on its fantasy of constructing a Free China, hired Fong as its leading expert. In 1944, Fong returned to China to submit his plan to Chiang Kai-shek, and the Economic Commission for Asia and the Far East, founded in 1946 by ECOSOC, took up his plans for reconstruction and development.

## Development as Profession after the Second World War

China illuminates the continuities between the interwar and postwar years. It also reveals the strong connections between governmental and nongovernmental international organizations, whose staff and ideas frequently moved back and forth. While in the colonial tradition experts had specialized in a place and its culture, in the League of Nations the model officer was a theorist of the laws of economic development, an ambassador of progress, a specialist in regions considered underdeveloped by Western modernity. This professional could eradicate malaria, organize a school system, teach new farming techniques, or deal with workplace litigation.[14]

Whether in the imperial system or international organizations, the classic technocratic move still occurred: a political and moral issue was transformed into a technical one.[15] As described by anthropologist James Ferguson, this reflected the idea of development as an "anti-politics machine" based on the objectivity of scientific-technological thinking.[16] Development became a special area. Economist and US ambassador to India John Kenneth Galbraith was an eyewitness to this transition. He explains how in 1949 development economics hardly existed, but within fifteen years, with contributions from private foundations such as Ford, Rockefeller, and Carnegie, attention to poverty and its conundrums had increased exponentially.[17] The language of development traveled through conferences, study programs, and specific experience. Often people who had participated in US-funded postwar reconstruction ended up working in development. Development officials were the product of a homogeneous cultural and intellectual climate dominated by trust in a modernizing revolution that would create a future in which all societies had high levels of industrialization, urbanization, mechanization of agriculture, rising living standards, and common (Western) values.

International networks of experts became powerful conduits for the dissemination of a potentially global project.[18] Meanwhile, international organizations became the place where Truman's dream—as described in chapter 2—could be achieved. Poverty, like peace, work, and health, was now a global issue to be resolved by international organizations applying international principles. At the director level, experts with strong colonial backgrounds were involved in the new internationalist project. John Boyd Orr, for example, the biologist who became the first director-general of the Food and Agriculture Organization (FAO), worked with colonial administrations in South Africa, Kenya, and Palestine in the 1920s.[19] Julian Huxley, who headed the United Nations Educational, Scientific and Cultural Organization (UNESCO) after the Second World War, had been a consultant in the British colonial administration in West Africa. Scientists and technicians specializing in colonial issues ended up working for international organizations or, sometimes, newly independent countries.[20]

An international class of supposedly apolitical specialists emerged, with a strong sense of mission and a reliance on applied science for problem solving. Trust in the social sciences was widespread, though those afraid of a dehumanized international society created in the name of technical knowledge had reservations. Alva Myrdal, the director of the social sciences department at UNESCO between 1951 and 1955, worried about what she called the philosophy of technical assistance. She was disturbed by the nightmare of automatic perfection, represented in literature by George Orwell and Aldous Huxley, and warned about the dream of a mechanized society. She saw in industrialization the looming threat of the enslavement of entire peoples: economic and cultural development, as well as the promotion of human rights, needed to be carefully synchronized.[21] Before planting the seed of economic development, one must prepare the cultural terrain, Myrdal claimed. Convinced that education was crucial for successful development, she feared that progress could be suffocated or, worse, retarded, by uprooting cultural traditions: not all problems could be solved uniformly by one international standard.[22] The role of the United Nations was to digest knowledge produced by experts, international philanthropists (she expressly mentioned the Rockefeller Foundation), and missionaries, and to turn it into expertise accessible to the scientists of the future.[23] One of Myrdal's main worries was population control, which she wanted to promote, and which was both a factor and a product of this cultural work. A better education for women was one of the key elements for change.[24] Her ideas were ignored.

By the end of the 1940s, international organizations were creating projects in the hundreds. Some organizations were specifically devoted to development, like the World Health Organization (WHO), the International Labour Organization (ILO), the FAO, and the World Bank.[25] Typically, these organizations started first in Latin America and then moved into Asia and Africa. Assuming that modernity required the uprooting of tradition to raise standards of living and solve the perceived problems of backwardness, they ignored the warnings of anthropologists.[26] Development projects often implied a great deal of social engineering, and official documents did not hide the fact that adjustments could be painful. A 1951 UN Department of Social and Economic Affairs report, *Measures for the Economic Development of Underdeveloped Countries*, for example, claimed that "ancient philosophies have to be scrapped; old social institutions have to disintegrate; bonds of caste, creed and race have to burst; and large numbers of persons who cannot keep up with progress have to have their expectations of a comfortable life frustrated."[27] It felt that very few communities would be ready to pay the full price of economic progress, but they would have to, as this was the road to modernity.

## The World Bank

The institution that statutorily interprets development as a global project is the World Bank. Born as the International Bank for Reconstruction and Development (IBRD), its twofold mission was reconstruction and development. The World Bank, however, was and is a bank, not a development agency. From its beginning, many were suspicious of it. Investors saw it as a place for dreamers, not one that would prioritize revenue-generating investments.[28] To encourage private capital investments, Eugene Mayer, president of the bank in 1946, insisted on profitability as the first criterion for loans. His successor, John McCloy, tried to win Wall Street's trust by stressing the outstanding professionalism of the bank's personnel, highly trained cadres who saw past their national identity. They aligned with McCloy when he insisted that criteria for loans be economic, not political. The president's view, however, contrasted with that of executive directors in the bank, who were required to prioritize politics. The East-West conflict was mixed up in decisions right from the start. At the end of the 1940s, Poland requested a loan to reconstruct its mining industry. That industry should have sold its produce to Western Europe in exchange for dollars or gold that would have let it repay the loan. The project was viable, but by Cold War logic it was not permissible to offer Western resources to a communist country. As a consequence, Poland was judged unable to pay it back and the loan was not granted at all.

When the Marshall Plan started operating in Western Europe, the World Bank could focus more clearly on the other element in its name: development. John McCloy made this explicit in a meeting with the executive directors in 1947: "I think we are going to be driven into a very different field sooner than I thought, into the development field."[29] At least initially, reconstruction and development did not seem so separate. Italy, a recipient of World Bank aid for the Mezzogiorno, for instance, received Marshall Plan aid both for reconstruction and for development of its backward regions.[30] The move from reconstruction in Europe to development in backward areas outside it occurred when Eugene Black was bank president (1949–1963). Black was eager to think in Cold War terms, and he often urged Western countries to join forces against the Soviet Bloc. The Aid-India Consortium, for example, an international scheme to support the economic development of India and Pakistan, was introduced to German chancellor Konrad Adenauer in July 1959 as a tool to act against the Soviets.[31]

The first study mission in a developing country was in Colombia between 11 July and 5 November 1949.[32] Called the General Survey Mission, it had the goal of formulating "a development plan designed to raise the standard of living of the Colombian people," and it was intended to serve as a model of good practice and a pattern for future missions. It was motivated by the belief, typical at that time, that growth, once ignited, would become self-sustainable. The commission, made up of eleven international experts, started work under the direction of Lauchlin Currie, a Keynesian economist close to Franklin Delano Roosevelt and D. H. White, the creator of the Bretton Woods system. The commission's report revealed its faith in self-sustained growth: "Only through a generalized attack throughout the whole economy on education, health, housing, food, and productivity can the vicious cycle of poverty, ignorance, ill health and low productivity be decisively broken. But once the break is made, the process of economic development can become self-generating," it claimed.[33] The plan was never fully put into practice.

The hope of promoting economic growth through low-cost operations quickly faded. Teaching techniques, sharing models, and spreading entrepreneurial and technological strategies were not enough to spark self-sustaining growth. What was needed was capital, which was to be secured by introducing a guarantee scheme. To this end, in 1956 the International Finance Corporation was born. Although its director was autonomous, it shared staff, structure, and experts with the bank. In the same year, an Economic Development Institute was built to educate recipients on the methods, ideas, and language of the World Bank and to increase its planning capacity. Educating recipient government staffs from the Third World helped replicate the bank's ideology and promote the capitalist system in opposition to the Soviet challenge. The Economic Development Institute, which availed itself of the assistance of the Ford and Rockefeller Foundations, emphasized US planning, especially the TVA, in its educational programs. In the minds of World Bank experts, the system of dams, hydroelectric plants, and irrigation schemes was an ideal model thanks to the great injection of capital under government control.[34]

The World Bank promoted an idea of efficiency based on the theory of comparative advantage. It encouraged solutions in which poor countries exported raw materials while advanced countries produced and exported technology, and it did not approve development plans that contravened this logic. For example, it rejected financing for Juan Domingo Perón's Argentina. Not because of outrage at his dictatorship, but because the policies envisaged in his plans—nationalization, import substitution, regional integration—were considered ineffective and bad for the health of the economy. Political issues, including evaluations of the democratic character of the recipients or their respect for human rights, were not considered in the loan-making process; the environment or the rights of local communities still less. This approach was occasionally criticized; Sir Robert G. A. Jackson, former deputy director of the United Nations Relief and Rehabilitation Administration (UNRRA), was particularly harsh. He bluntly denounced the decision to withdraw support for the Aswan Dam in Egypt and the rejection of Tazara (a railway project to connect Tanzania and Zambia) as political blindness. Both projects, he contended, were rejected because fierce neutralist governments promoted them, while loans were accorded to the colonels' regime in Greece. For years the World Bank had forgotten the goal of promoting democracy, wrote Jackson in 1971 in a letter to Margaret Joan Anstee, his partner in both life and development.[35]

## The United Nations and Development: The Place for an Alternative?

Development, like anticolonialism, was not the original mission of the United Nations. That role was given to economic organizations. However, the

Economic and Social Council of the UN (ECOSOC) soon became a place to discuss development ideas via the studies of the regional economic commissions ECOSOC instituted. Unlike international economic organizations, UN commissions included socialist countries. In 1946, a Sub-Commission for Economic Development was constituted, with the United States, the Soviet Union, China, India, Brazil, Mexico, and Czechoslovakia as members. The sub-commission discussed strategies for capital financing, land reform, income redistribution at the national level, and technical assistance. Its goals were better living standards, full employment, social progress, and development, as well as full use of natural resources, energy, and capital. This would be achieved by Western-style industrialization: diversifying the economy, introducing key industries and advanced technology, and pursuing rural development.

After 1945, humanitarian intervention through the United Nations was about structuring large-scale assistance networks, a project that culminated in the creation of UNRRA, which handled emergency relief. UNRRA's mandate ended in 1947: Cold War warriors disapproved of the relief it provided to the socialist countries of Central and Eastern Europe. Isolationist senator Robert Taft said that for the United States to finance United Nations programs was insane, since these programs supported socialism.[36] Although UNRRA ended, some of its operations were carried on by specialized agencies. FAO resumed the projects against rinderpest in China, WHO continued the antimalaria program, and UNESCO worked on universal primary education. And later international development organizations were often staffed by UNRRA alumni, often Americans who had been active in the New Deal and served in Europe during the war.

UNRRA had another important legacy: the idea that technical assistance was crucial to postwar reconstruction.[37] The vision of expanding and coordinating actions for development through the United Nations had been around since the League of Nations, and it fitted within the tradition of Western philanthropic thought that considered aid the key to a better future. The first step was a program of technical assistance in line with the spirit of Point Four. In 1950, as part of a Twenty-Year Peace Program based on the idea that technical assistance promoted peace, UN secretary-general Trygve Lie launched the Expanded Program of Technical Assistance (EPTA) for the economic development of underdeveloped countries. Freedom from want promised increased social peace and security.[38] In the wake of Point Four, the UN began making plans: full employment, capital investments in underdeveloped areas, and regulation of international markets and prices. The idea was a managed system that could redistribute wealth on a world scale, a vision distant from economic liberalism and the views promoted by the US administration.[39]

From its foundation, ideas on development played an important role in the United Nations. Its economists and social scientists believed that development had to be financed by loans at subsidized rates and that international trade was the key to growth. Polish economist Ignacy Sachs later recalled that the first generation in the UN, coming from a career in military administration or the League of Nations or UNRRA, was committed, politically involved, and animated by trust in full employment, planning, the priority of social questions, and anticolonialism.[40] Three reports commissioned by ECOSOC and published between 1949 and 1951 reveal how these views shaped the UN: these were *National and International Measures for Full Employment* (1949), *Measures for the Economic Development of Under-Developed Countries* (1951), and *Measures for International Economic Stability* (1951). The key expert involved was the West Indian economist W. Arthur Lewis. His work *The Principles of Economic Planning* (1949) came with an appendix, "On Planning in Backward Countries," that became compulsory reading for UN officials. In it, Lewis stressed the necessity of devising planning instruments for poor countries and keeping development plans commensurate with administrative capacity: overambitious schemes would engulf poor countries' weak administrative structures. He also claimed that both the rural economy and the processing industry had to be promoted in order to produce for export.[41] His *Economic Development with Unlimited Supplies of Labor* (1954), about the concept of the dual economy, became a milestone of development economics and earned him the Nobel Prize for economics.[42] Lewis was a professor in Manchester but also worked in the early 1950s as a consultant for the UN on technical assistance. He was brought in by David Owen, a British diplomat who had a crucial role in setting up the UN structure for technical assistance.[43]

At the core of UN actions was the principle of balanced development. This meant encouraging growth by transferring labor from low-productivity to high-productivity areas, from rural to urbanized zones. In 1953, an ECOSOC report on the choice between agriculture and industry, written with the participation of Arthur Lewis, Jan Tinbergen, Simon Kuznets, and Barbara Ward, concluded that it did not matter whether agriculture or industry was prioritized. What was important was promoting a balanced growth of all sectors, and raising living standards by constantly improving the effective use of all factors of production.[44]

The UN's other focus was the role of trade in development. Here the studies of Hans W. Singer, an economist in the UN's statistical office, were key. In his 1949 *UN Report on Relative Prices of Exports and Imports of Underdeveloped Countries*, Singer identified the problems of trade in underdeveloped countries: the price volatility of the goods they produced and the worsening of the terms of trade. When his study on the terms of trade was published in 1950 in the *American Economic Review*, it had a major impact.[45] The data he used—collected by the League of Nations and covering the period 1876–1948—did not confirm the predictions of classical theory.[46] What should have happened, the theory said, was that prices of raw materials, primary products, and metals would increase relative to other manufactured goods. Singer's data showed different dynamics: the terms of trade for goods exported by poor countries tended to worsen, while the terms of trade for manufactured goods tended to improve. These conclusions, which showed that underdeveloped areas contributed to growth without receiving the same advantages as developed countries, shocked economists. In the UN Economic Commission for Latin America (ECLA), Argentine economist Raúl Prebisch's *The Economic Development of Latin America and Its Principal Problems* pointed out the political consequences of Singer's work.[47] The ECLA report was presented in 1951 in Havana, together with *The Economic Survey of Latin America*, a survey of production trends that drew on a huge set of newly available data, including regional data on population, transportation, foreign trade, inflation, and the balance of payments.[48] In his presentation of the report and survey, Prebisch provided the context and offered ideas for a UN action plan. The Prebisch-Singer doctrine, as it became known, was born. The doctrine argued that technical progress in manufacturing increased profits, whereas progress in the production of food and raw materials led to lower prices. Industrialized countries thus got the best of both worlds—high prices for the goods they sold and low prices for those they bought—while underdeveloped countries lost on both counts. The theory immediately influenced economic policies in Latin America and India, since the idea of worsening terms of trade could be used by those in developing countries looking to diversify their exports.[49] Although it was produced within the UN, the ECLA report was never fully owned by it. Secretary-general Trygve Lie wrote the introduction to the document, but he failed to endorse it.[50]

Underdeveloped countries were (and are) chronically short of capital, a key factor for economic development. Where to find the needed capital? This crucial question was discussed at the outset of the ECOSOC. For industrialized countries, the rationale for contributing capital was that improving standards of living in poor countries would awaken a new demand for the import of manufactured goods, thus helping rich countries solve their unemployment problems. The EPTA, the UN's technical assistance program, had provided mostly training and tutorials, but Hans Singer and Paul G. Hoffman, the former administrator of Marshall Plan aid and indefatigable supporter of development initiatives, worked to expand its investments. "If we do our job well, we will be out of business in 25 years," Hoffman liked to say.[51] But the drive to create a fund for economic development encountered huge problems. In 1952, ECOSOC retrieved an early 1949 plan and transformed it, hoping to overcome the hostility of many developed countries.[52] The proposal for the UN Fund for Economic Development (UNFED)—the name was soon changed to Special UN Fund for Economic Development (SUNFED), to avoid the unpleasant acronym—landed in the General Assembly in 1953. It proposed a base of $250 million, plus additional voluntary payments, to be used for financing the development plans of participant countries. As soon as the Soviet Union endorsed it, SUNFED became a symbol of East-West competition and the object of a Cold War propaganda campaign. The Eisenhower administration was not interested in multilateral cooperation on development, nor could it countenance investing in a program co-managed by the USSR. Even less palatable for the United States was the prospect that SUNFED might legitimize the Soviet rhetoric of moving resources out of the arms race and into development.

Discussions over SUNFED intertwined with the McCarthyite anticommunist obsession and political tensions around the war in Korea.[53] McCarthy's committee had an office in the UN building, checking for communist influences there, and from 1950 to 1953, during Trygve Lie's weak secretariat, he scared off or fired many excellent specialists. Hans Singer was accused of plotting with the communists because of his support of planning and SUNFED.[54] After the first version of SUNFED was abandoned because of the West's communist phobia, discussions turned to smaller projects: for example, the funding of surveys or feasibility studies to alert less developed countries to available natural resources, or the construction of research centers to apply modern technologies to development and instruct the local workforce. In 1955, new energy was injected into UN development when Hoffman turned down the post of US ambassador to India to take charge of the US mission to the United Nations. SUNFED returned to the agenda, and while Hoffman reiterated US objections, he also pushed the United States to announce a "bold new development program" of participation in multilateral initiatives other than SUNFED.[55] In mid-1956, another brutal press campaign hit SUNFED and its supporters. The plan was described as a UN socialist plot to bankrupt the United States.[56] Nonetheless, a draft was passed by ECOSOC in 1957, which the United States, the United Kingdom, and Canada voted against. The rift was mended via a compromise that involved a new agency of the World Bank group, the International Development Association (IDA), that would offer long-term credits at subsidized rates payable in local currencies to be used to build infrastructure. The idea of a far-reaching development fund financed within and run by the UN was dropped.

Singer argued that the UN should offer credits on favorable terms (soft lending) in partnership with the World Bank, but the bank claimed that donors would not entrust their money to the UN, which they saw as radical, utopian, and politically naive. Only by operating on its own could the

World Bank ensure its credibility. In 1956, the bank promoted the International Finance Corporation to attract private capital into development projects.[57] As for the UN, in 1958 it created a more modestly endowed Special Fund, directed by Paul Hoffman, with W. Arthur Lewis as his deputy. To differentiate itself from the World Bank, the fund, at Singer's suggestion, was described as an organ to finance preinvestment studies and research.[58] Hoffman was a committed supporter of aid as enlightened interest, believing that without aid, the so-called revolution of rising expectations would end in violence, war, and chaos.[59] Anticommunism and anti-authoritarianism were part of his rhetoric, and he got more funds through his program than any other UN agency dealing with social and economic issues.

Histories of development at the United Nations tend to downplay the role of planning and industrialization in its programs, but a close analysis proves the opposite. W. Arthur Lewis, for example, a leader of UN development thought, was especially keen on industrialization as the engine for growth. Voicing the impatience of the leaders of newly independent countries, Lewis proposed that labor-intensive industries be financed through foreign capital attracted by favorable fiscal conditions: a sort of industrialization by invitation.[60] UN-sponsored initiatives often included education policies, city planning, or projects modeled on the TVA, like the development of the Mekong River basin promoted by Hoffman. The plan had been studied by the United Nations Economic Commission for Asia and the Far East (ECAFE) in 1957, and ECAFE's report *Development of Water Resources in the Lower Mekong Basin* recommended a huge system of five dams that would irrigate 90,000 square kilometers and produce 13.7 gigawatts of electricity. It was conceived as the first in a series of similar Asian projects. The UN controlled works through one of its field officers.[61] It then naturally fell prey to Indochina's Cold War dynamics, so that historiography typically describes the Mekong River Project as the schoolbook example of American-style modernization, ideal for illustrating US policies in the 1960s, including the Peace Corps, and devising new counter-insurgency strategies. However, the project originally resulted from a network of international organizations, both governmental and nongovernmental, and national development agencies, which shared ideas and people. To be sure, the United States jumped on board with enthusiasm; it sent so many TVA experts to UN headquarters and to the field that the Johnson administration eventually appropriated the project entirely.[62]

## UNCTAD

The best-known aspect of the UN action for development, and the most innovative, was the creation of the United Nations Conference on Trade and

Development (UNCTAD), which became the site for coordinating Third World political action and offered a neutralist alternative to the system centered on the World Bank. UNCTAD resulted from the less developed countries' disappointment with the failure to endow UN programs with significant capital. UNCTAD came in the wake of the Bandung Conference, when a group of newly independent countries reunited around the cause of economic decolonization. Formalized in 1963 with the *Joint Declaration of the Seventy-Seven Developing Countries*, the G77 group requested changes in the structure of international trade, especially the prices of raw materials.[63] Just as the OECD coordinated the actions of the Western developed countries, the G77 was meant to coordinate those of the underdeveloped countries. However, it lacked research and organizational capacities. "Trade, not aid" was the principle put forward by the G77 and agreed to by ECOSOC in 1962 with resolution 917 (XXXIV) for convening a Conference on Trade and Development before mid-1964: UNCTAD.[64]

UNCTAD's success in becoming the place for devising political strategies for the Third World is directly linked to its first general secretary, Raúl Prebisch. After the first ECLA report, Prebisch established headquarters in Chile's capital, Santiago de Chile. ECLA became the think tank of a new approach to development. Prebisch was a celebrity who enchanted masses as he toured Latin America with his ideas. His 1964 document "Towards a New Trade Policy for Development," in which he described his vision of North-South relations and proposed ways to improve them, was widely circulated.[65] Facing a widening of the trade gap between less developed and developed countries, Prebisch offered strategies, and, before UNCTAD, a place to discuss them. Trade was positive, but it needed adjustment through compensatory finance that stabilized the price of raw materials and promoted export of manufactured products, with a preference system to avoid custom duties. As Singer recalls, this idea revived Keynes's old design for world currencies based on primary commodities. Jan Tinbergen, Nicholas Kaldor, and Albert G. Hart produced a memorandum for Prebisch based on this idea of a commodity-based currency, but after a long debate stabilization was left to future agreements on individual commodities.[66]

Placed at the bottom of the UN's priorities, the opening of UNCTAD in Geneva was expected to be a flop. Instead, held between 23 March and 16 June 1964, with two thousand delegates from 121 countries, it captured public opinion and became a major event. Three groups coordinated their policies: Western countries in the OECD, the Socialist Bloc, and the G77. Socialist countries hoped to use UNCTAD as a propaganda opportunity. As early as 1956, the Soviet Union had requested the institution of an economic conference within the United Nations, but the Economic and Financial Commission blocked the proposal in the General Assembly. The socialist countries agreed with the demands of newly independent countries; they lamented discrimination in East-West trade, protested quantitative restrictions and the embargo on strategic materials, and attacked reciprocal tariff reductions in European free-trade areas. The G77 was not in principle against including East-West trade on the agenda. However, facing the strong opposition of the West, Prebisch tried to keep the Cold War out of proceedings.[67] UNCTAD thus remained relatively impervious to Cold War ideological battles and served mainly as an arena for North-South confrontation in which compromise resolutions could be reached.[68]

It was not clear what UNCTAD would be. Was it to be a permanent organ, or just a periodic meeting, as its original architect, Polish economist Wladek R. Malinowski, had envisaged? Malinowski, a representative of regional commissions and then secretary of ECOSOC, was convinced that the key to North-South relations was political, not economic.[69] It was Prebisch who pictured a permanent UNCTAD secretariat, able to encourage South-focused activities while maintaining its intellectual independence. But what did this mean in this context: independence from the United Nations or from the Anglo-American academic establishment? Originally, UNCTAD was devised as a research organ of the G77. But the G77 was large, and it was almost impossible to come to full agreement when members had such different needs. Self-sufficiency was good for India or Brazil, but not for smaller countries.[70] In the end, a permanent South Center was created, headed by Manmohan Singh, later prime minister of India. However, the center had very limited resources—limited financing came from the Scandinavians and the Dutch—and ended up being a podium for charismatic politicians from the Global South, such as Julius Nyerere.

In the first UNCTAD (1964–1968), negotiations on commodity agreements stalled immediately, and many G77 members became impatient and pressed for an agreement on a generalized system of preferences. In 1968, everyone agreed that UNCTAD's achievements had fallen far short of original expectations, which were too great. Although successful as a forum, it was not effective in terms of accomplishments. The final declaration disappointed Prebisch, who had hoped for more.[71] He resigned, officially for health reasons. His departure was perceived as the end of a way of understanding North-South relations. On 13 December 1968, the *Economist* ran an article titled "The End of an Era?"

## Assessing Aid at the End of the First Development Decade

At the end of the 1960s, two reports were published in quick succession: the Pearson Report of the World Bank and the *Capacity Study* on UN technical assistance.[72] They were intended to raise public awareness of development and encourage financing from national parliaments.

The development community within the United Nations had grown during the First Development Decade, as had the resources devoted to development. In 1965, technical assistance (EPTA) and capital assistance (the Special Fund) joined forces and created the United Nations Development Programme (UNDP). In 1967, synergies between the United Nations and the World Bank looked promising. World Bank president George Woods, together with famous journalist and indefatigable promoter of development initiatives Barbara Ward, called for a grand assize to evaluate the results of development policies and overcome the allegations of financial mismanagement that surrounded this whole field. A Commission on International Development was charged with writing a report for the World Bank. Canadian Lester B. Pearson, Nobel Peace Prize winner and a founder of FAO, headed it.[73] He had no direct experience of North-South issues, but other members did. Douglas C. Dillon, the early architect of the DAC, was the US representative in Kennedy Round negotiations at the GATT; Robert E. Marjolin had served as the commissioner for economics in the European Community; Saburo Okita had long headed the Commission for Economic Planning in Japan; Wilfried Guth had spent a career at the World Bank and was now working for the Kreditanstalt für Wiederaufbau, a West German development agency; and former British minister of education Sir Edward Boyle was well known for his antiapartheid stance. Two members, W. Arthur Lewis and Brazilian economist Roberto Campos, could be considered representatives of the Southern view. The Pearson Report, *Partners in Development*, was both a diagnosis and an agenda. Since its goal was to increase support for development, its intended audience was the general public, not governments. As a result, it received widespread publicity.[74] It is probably the document that best describes social democratic humanitarianism as a global project, a moral imperative to fight poverty. It set astronomical growth rates for poor countries, 6 percent a year—a real boom. It also introduced the well-known minimum figure of 0.7 percent of GDP as the required amount of aid for each donor: a target destined to stay constant in the following decades.[75]

In February 1970, the *UNESCO Courier* devoted an entire issue to the Pearson Report.[76] In the same month, Barbara Ward organized a conference at Columbia University to promote it.[77] W. Arthur Lewis opened the conference by elaborating the report's methodology and goals, insisting on the merits of development. Pearson gave the closing remarks. Some of the speakers, especially in the section on "The Aid Relationship," were famous: Albert Hirschmann, Mahbub ul Haq, Richard Jolly, I. G. Patel, and Samir Amin. Many were critical, arguing that the partnership between developed and underdeveloped countries was an illusion, and that the document did not deal with real problems like poverty, inequality, and unemployment, not to mention the environmental consequences of development projects, the evils of uncontrolled urbanization, and the conundrums of poor public health systems. The report did succeed in shifting the focus from the Cold War bickering that had held public discourse on development captive. Even President Richard Nixon began reasoning on the basis of needs instead of East-West conflict, claiming that aid was about morality and that a great nation like the United States could not "close [its] eyes to the want in this world."[78] Pearson fervently defended development from its critics, describing aid as the missing link in the evolution of a society from poverty to well-being, and proclaiming that developed and developing countries had no choice "but to face together with honesty and energy the difficult, frustrating, but vitally important problems that are caused by the grossly uneven pattern of world growth."[79]

A Study of the Capacity of the United Nations Development System was commissioned by Paul Hoffman to Robert G. A. Jackson. Jackson was a controversial personality in the history of development. Former architect of the Middle East Supply Center during the Second World War and an illustrious UNRRA administrator, he represented the grand view of development, the faith that megaprojects could improve thousands of lives. Contrary to Arthur Lewis, who criticized Nkrumah's Volta River Dam plan for being too grand, too expensive, and unresponsive to the needs of the African population, Jackson supported both the plan and Nkrumah.[80] Entrusted with the management of Ghana's Development Commission, with his wife, Barbara Ward, he encouraged Nkrumah's view that the dam was an act of liberation, proof that Africans could handle big TVA-style projects on their own.[81] Jackson also promoted an International Development Authority to coordinate development efforts at a global level. In a talk at Syracuse University in 1959, he held that developing newly independent countries was a necessity for the developed world, too. A change in mentality was needed in order to understand that the Earth's well-being required better living conditions for all.[82] Hoffman shared Jackson's view on the priority of improving the living conditions of people worldwide, and to that effect he put Jackson in charge of rationalizing the UNDP. Jackson had a talent for firing the inefficient—which made him one of the most detested people in the UN and kept him from maintaining a career there.[83] In charge of surveying the jungle of UNDP projects and suggesting ways to trim them, he set up a huge structure of consultants, high-level officers in international organizations (UN, UNDP, World Bank, WHO, ILO, FAO, UNESCO, UNIDO), and representatives of both developed and less developed countries, from both sides of the Iron Curtain. European Economic Community officers like the powerful Jacques Ferrandi and high-profile UN hands such as Prebisch and Tinbergen were also consulted.[84]

The result of his analysis was a tome of more than five hundred pages, plus tables; the report itself was only the first chapter. Sometimes called the Jackson Report or Capacity Study, it appeared in 1968 and has been described as the most disruptive document in UN history, possibly because it mocked the system as a gigantic brainless machine, as big and stupid as the dinosaurs— and destined for the same end. "The UN development system," it claimed, "has tried to wage a war on want for many years with very little organized 'brain' to guide it."[85] Given Jackson's background as a supporter of development, his indictment of the system was even more damning. Jackson was very critical of organizational flaws that made the UN system a nightmare. The main problem he identified was balancing the interest in grand development strategy with smaller local development projects. He proposed a stronger center that would direct diverse regional articulations with a view of simplifying a huge, complicated, expensive, and slow system. The study emphasized fieldwork as the way to resurrect the development mission and suggested a special school to train personnel in development management, plus the use of a corps of volunteers. Offended by the report, Hoffman locked it in a drawer. The 1970s would soon spur further a different line of discussion.

# 7

# Multiple Modernities and Socialist Alternatives in the 1970s

We are all planners today, although very different in character.

—MICHAŁ KALECKI, 1976

"WE ARE NOT Marxist-Leninists, and most of us have never read a single line of *Das Kapital*. So what interest do you have in our participating in your doctrinal quarrels? I have had enough, when I am eating a sandwich, of being accosted by someone who asks me what I think of the Soviet position, and, when I am drinking coffee, by someone who questions me about the Chinese arguments."[1] This remark from a Kenyan delegate to the 1964 Afro-Asian People's Solidarity Organization meeting in Algiers summed up the feelings of many Africans. In the 1960s, Africans did not hesitate to defy the large communist powers and were often involved in intermural disputes. In the West, Soviet and Chinese actions were often depicted as part of a single plan, but the reality was rather different.[2] During the Cold War era, multiple, often incompatible modernities were on offer.[3] In the 1970s, development assistance models offered an array of radical alternatives to the capitalist system. Three different models stand out: the Second World around the Soviet Union, the Chinese model of self-reliance, and Third Worldism with its project of a New International Economic Order.

## The Soviet Union Reinterprets the Two Worlds Theory

By the end of the 1960s, the Soviet Union and its allies were disappointed with the prospects for socialism in newly independent countries. The discontent was mutual, since the developing world did not appreciate either the Soviets' aid provisions or their political stance, which was perceived as too conservative.

Facing increasing aid requests, Leonid Brezhnev, Khrushchev's successor, sought to rationalize Soviet economic assistance plans. His use of cost-sharing provoked bitter frustration in recipients who received less money and more advice on topics such as nationalization, planning, redistribution, mobilization of domestic resources, and balanced development.[4] Scholars have often stressed the shift in the 1970s when the Soviet Bloc moved away from ideology and toward realism, pragmatism, and caution.[5] During the Khrushchev years, aid to the Third World had been costly and yielded little: revision was required. Political instability meant more constrained investment options. Political reversals like that of Ghana, where Kwame Nkrumah, the Pan-African leader who had famously opted for African socialism, was overthrown in 1966, suggested that the support of individual personalities did not always pay. The new guidelines implied institutional development and societal transformation.[6]

According to official ideology, Comecon and its formula of "integration through equality" was the future of North-South relations: the admission of developing countries to Comecon—Mongolia in 1962, Cuba in 1972—was offered as proof that the world would eventually be divided into two social systems. Comecon's Permanent Commission for Technical Assistance was the setting for discussions on aid. Developing countries were treated as a special form of capitalist countries that did not necessarily deserve the anti-imperialist solidarity given to socialist allies.[7] In the international division of labor, poor countries were still mainly suppliers of raw materials—in the 1950s and 1960s exchanges revolved around cash crops like cocoa from Ghana and bananas from Guinea, while in the 1970s there was a turn to minerals and fuel. After 1967, the Soviet Union made it clear that the Eastern Bloc was expected to obtain raw materials from the Third World rather than to rely solely on the USSR. Details on how to get better conditions for the import of fuel and other raw materials were discussed in meetings of the Commission for Technical Assistance and of the deputy ministers for foreign trade, held annually under the Comecon umbrella. The USSR was willing to sign agreements with the producers and then provide subcontracts to other socialist countries. Weapons and turnkey plants with technicians able to teach locals how to operate them proved to be the ideal bargaining chips. In April 1971, at the Moscow meeting of the deputy ministers for foreign trade, the expectation was even clearer: the Soviet Union declared itself unable to satisfy its partners' demands for oil, offering to mediate oil purchases from other sources instead.[8] From then on, capital investments had to be profitable and grant the supply of fuel, raw materials, and metals from outside the Eastern Bloc. The industrial modernization of the developing world was now secondary.[9]

As for the exploration of new sources of strategic raw materials, the predicament of Eastern European countries is well documented in Comecon sources:

unable to finance huge projects on an individual basis, they had no alternative but to join bigger projects financed by the Soviet Union.[10] In turn, the Soviet Union was keen to embark on cooperative and multilateral initiatives. Its experts contended that "great opportunities reside in multilateral cooperation," which meant building joint-export enterprises, mutually providing technical assistance, and pooling resources in training personnel. Indeed, commission meetings from 1971 to 1974 focused exclusively on the joint import of raw materials. Africa and the Arab countries were seen as especially promising new sources of oil and phosphates needed for the production of fertilizers. Discussion focused on specific projects, for example, oil in the deserts of Libya, phosphates in Egypt's Western Desert (Abu-Tartur), and the Kindia project to extract bauxite in Guinea.[11] Other interests in Sub-Saharan Africa included oil from Nigeria, chrome from Sudan, and copper from Zambia.[12] As for financial relations with Third World countries, the economic integration plan of August 1971 foresaw the gradual adoption of the convertible ruble to settle accounts among Comecon countries and with developing countries. A socialist countries' development bank, funded with one billion transferable rubles, was implemented in January 1974 to promote economic and technical assistance to developing countries. This, the Socialist Bloc maintained, was a great opportunity for developing countries to finance projects in the extractive industries. Once again, the hunger for raw materials drove aid offers.[13]

Fearing that the data could be used to discredit the socialist system by showing low growth rates, socialist countries opposed having their development level evaluated by Western statistical tools.[14] They insisted that irreconcilable differences separated them from Western notions of modernity: rather than copy the stages of growth in the capitalist system, they would, as their motto said, surpass without imitating.[15] Besides, development was an imperial legacy: colonial exploitation had caused both underdevelopment and the political pressure on colonists to clear their conscience by providing aid. Only Romania abstained from this view.[16] In the early 1970s, First Secretary of the Romanian Communist Party Nicolae Ceaușescu called his country a Socialist Developing Country. Relations with countries "at the same level of development," he contended, were preferable to Comecon's international division of labor.[17]

Developing countries were important trade partners for Comecon, and official publications stressed this, focusing on the increase in trade with the Third World—in 1975, for instance, the volume of trade was seventeen times higher than the 1950 figure. Highlighting the rise in manufactured products, they pointed out that they were meeting UNCTAD's requests on structural changes in economic relations. They hailed the expansion of multilateral cooperation, the introduction of scholarships, and the opening of credit lines in

Comecon's international bank.[18] At the end of the 1970s, Comecon discussed the admission of non-European members, especially Vietnam (1978). Some countries that had adopted scientific socialism were accepted as observers: Afghanistan, Angola, Ethiopia, the Democratic Republic of Yemen, Laos, Mozambique, and Nicaragua. Could they all be admitted irrespective of their stage of development? Many European members doubted it.[19]

## Convergence and Interdependence

"If you cannot beat them, join them," said Aroon K. Basak, deputy director of the World Bank responsible for the United Nations Industrial Development Organization (UNIDO) cooperative program, about the 1970s Socialist Bloc strategy, especially the move toward Tripartite Industrial Cooperation (TIC).[20] By the end of the decade, interstate agreements for cooperative activities and joint East-West companies in Third World markets experienced a steady growth. Typically, tripartite projects started from tenders from the developing country. Western firms provided management and the most advanced technology and equipment; the Eastern Bloc provided the intermediate level of machinery and know-how; developing countries supplied labor and raw materials. Oil-producing countries, hoping to expand their influence, paid the bill.

One of the developing countries most active in negotiating trilateral cooperation was Libya. Interested in promoting its influence in Africa and the Middle East, Muammar Gaddafi chose the German Democratic Republic (GDR) as a partner. He was fascinated by the new activism of Werner Lamberz, the architect of the East German Africa Policy, or *Afrikapolitik*, in the early 1970s. A prominent member of the Politbüro of the Sozialistische Einheitspartei Deutschlands (SED) and a longtime leading figure of its Commission for Agitation and Propaganda, Lamberz was a key personality in Erich Honecker's government. He was convinced that trade with developing countries needed to be integrated into the GDR economy as a way to overcome the economic crisis of the early 1970s. At the turn of the decade, the GDR became a crucial economic partner for African countries—ranked second after the Soviet Union among Eastern European donors.[21] In June 1977, Lamberz visited Yemen, Ethiopia, Angola, Zambia, Nigeria, and the Congo, hoping to sign agreements on raw materials in exchange for rural or industrial development projects or state building. On 20 December 1977, the SED Politbüro endorsed Lamberz's view and decided to form a special commission for developing countries, headed by party secretary for economic affairs Günter Mittag and named the Mittag-Kommission. The commission began studying the prospects for mixed enterprises, starting with Libya.[22] An agreement for oil in exchange for development projects in Syria, Ethiopia, Angola, and Mozambique was discussed but never signed, as Libya did not like the GDR's conditions, which were less attractive than those the Italians were offering. Lamberz's death in a plane crash over Libya in March 1978 blocked further developments, but the model was applied by the GDR elsewhere.

More often it was the Soviet Union that cooperated in developing projects for industrial plants in exchange for raw materials. Trilateral projects were common in the energy and oil sector, increasing dramatically after 1975, but the reality was that trilateral cooperation was more "cooperation in" rather than "cooperation with" developing countries.[23] This encouraged those who talked of convergence and claimed that the West and the socialist countries were no different from each other. While in the 1960s the Eastern Bloc abhorred the idea of convergence, in the 1970s in the new climate of détente, it essentially rehabilitated it via the related concept of interdependence, which was the precursor of globalization. Soviet intellectuals and party officials who networked with the West admitted that capitalism reacted well to the crisis and was successful in attracting developing countries. Karen Brutents, an important member of the Department of International Relations in the Central Committee of the CPSU and a top expert on Africa and Asia, wrote in *Pravda* in 1978 that capitalism adapted to decolonization by enacting new and more sophisticated forms of exploitation.[24] Comecon also changed its mind about exclusive relations with newly independent countries. By then, not many believed in complementarity between socialist and developing countries, as the economic systems of both were based more on the supply side than on the demand side. Both were hungry for investments, and they often competed with one another. In the mid-1970s, one top economist in Central and Eastern Europe, Michał Kalecki, suggested that the West was the better match for both.[25] Margarita Maximova, head of the Soviet Scientific Council of Philosophy and Global Problems, remarked that "despite all the differences and contradictions," the two world markets found themselves "in a definite mutual interaction," with common tendencies that operated in the world economy as a whole.[26]

This change in approach did not fail to influence East-South relations. Among Eastern European and Soviet economists, the issue was promoting in developing countries a mixed economy with a role for both domestic and foreign private capital.[27] The growth in international cooperation suggested that there might be mutually agreeable solutions for problems connected with the backwardness of developing countries.[28] Leon Zalmanovich Zevin, director of the Division for Relations with Developing Countries at the Institute for the Socialist World Economic System of the Academy of Science, insisted that developing countries needed to cooperate with developed countries, "including those with different social systems," to succeed.[29] He suggested that tripartite cooperation including both socialist and Western countries could help developing nations rid themselves of their one-sided attachment to the world capitalist economy. Radically, integrating LDCs in Comecon was no longer the favored strategy. The most striking manifestation of this change came in 1981, when Mozambique was refused entry, an event signaling the collapse of rhetoric of a special East-South solidarity: not all Third World countries were equal or had the right level of development to integrate with the socialist system. Radical leaders in the Third World perceived this new line as a betrayal.

## Third World Visions

Relations between socialism and Third Worldism were always ambiguous.[30] Socialist countries considered the Third World unity a myth. In 1979, Karen Brutents wrote authoritatively in *The Newly Free Countries in the Seventies* (an English edition came out in 1983) that groupings of newly independent countries were huge conglomerates of countries that had important differences. Therefore, he concluded, Marxism-Leninism rejected any concept of the Third World as a single unit and saw attempts to group newly independent countries into a special theory or development mode as scientifically flawed.[31] Soviet scholars argued that national liberation movements did not share a common platform and that nonalignment did not, strictly speaking, exist: newly independent countries maintained strong links with former colonial powers and were therefore tout court on the side of the West. After the meeting of the Non-Aligned Movement in Lusaka in 1970, when the Third World upheld its differences from the socialist countries, the Soviet Union pointed out the ambiguity in the different social and economic orientations within nonalignment.[32]

The Soviets thought they could profit from the discomfort poor countries felt in the capitalist system.[33] They did so with Cuban support. During the 1960s, Cuba had often confronted the Soviet Union, but relations improved in the early 1970s, when CPSU general secretary Brezhnev repeatedly stated that Cuba's approach to international relations had matured.[34] The two countries carved out separate spheres of influence and adopted different strategies but consulted on the prospects of nonalignment in multilateral settings. Cuban aid programs had a stronger emphasis on solidarity and did not really involve transportation or strategic resources, focusing instead on the exchange of medical school students, schoolteachers, doctors, and others.[35] In Angola, the country in which Cuba was most involved, Cubans replaced Portuguese personnel, and in 1977, 3,350 Cubans were sent there.[36] Through the good offices of Salvador Allende's Chile, Cuba joined the G77 in 1971 and sided with the

Soviet Union, holding that capitalist and socialist countries clearly expressed radically different visions of international relations.[37] It made the same point in gatherings of the Non-Aligned Movement, UNCTAD, UNESCO, and the UN General Assembly. In exchange, Cuba received weapons and aid from the Soviet Union and achieved greater visibility and a position as mediator between Southern African liberation movements, especially in Angola and Mozambique, and the Soviets.[38]

In the 1970s, Soviet social scientists claimed that only those countries close to scientific socialism should be considered nonaligned. If nonalignment was equal to anti-imperialism, countries calling themselves nonaligned should not accept capital from international economic organizations or host Western military bases. They needed to have an active antiapartheid stance and a consistently favorable attitude toward détente.[39] A collective work published in 1985 studied specifically whether nonaligned countries met those conditions.[40] Socialist orthodoxy maintained that antagonist classes could not be neutral. Therefore, nonalignment did not mean forming a third bloc.

The Soviets also rejected the North-South divide and the idea of a racialized color line to classify countries, as they felt that accepting the color line would imply that the Soviet Union was like the capitalist countries. Any idea of a Third World outside the two economic-social systems was dubbed a "false Maoist notion."[41] In September 1975 Jacob Malik, the USSR's representative at the UN General Assembly, officially rejected any definition of a North-South conflict that put the Soviet Union on the same side as the capitalist North. The Soviets took a harsh view of dependency theorists, particularly Samir Amin, seeing him as a personification of the theoretical radicalism of the Third World establishment that grouped socialist countries with the capitalist North.[42] Although Soviet members of government and academics began recognizing that establishing an alternative, worldwide economic order patterned on integration agreements set up in Comecon was unrealistic, the view that "the practice of international division of labour and cooperation within the Comecon" offered a "just solution" to many of the problems of the developing world coexisted along with views that saw potential for cooperation with the West.[43] International organizations did not buy Comecon's view. UNCTAD, for example, did not accept the principle that political orientation trumped economic development, and it included Cuba, Vietnam, and Mongolia in the group of developing countries in Africa, Asia, and Latin America.[44]

## China's Development Alternative

Both an aid recipient and a donor, China had a special role in development. A huge laboratory for the development strategies of US and international organizations in the interwar years, it became the main recipient of Soviet aid after the Sino-Soviet Treaty of Friendship, Alliance and Mutual Assistance of February 1950.[45] After Bandung, it also became a donor, aiding the African continent and contending with the Soviet Union for Third World influence. Development aid was crucial to promoting the picture of China as a power capable of entering the donors' club and deserving the prestige that went with it.[46] The link to Africa was essentially political, rather than cultural or economic, and grounded in the Bandung legacy of shared involvement in the Afro-Asian group. In his 1963–64 trip to Asia and Africa, Zhou Enlai and his deputy Chen Yi visited thirteen countries.[47] During the trip, Zhou recalled a past of Chinese contacts across the Indian Ocean dating back to ancient Chinese travelers. Recalling Bandung, he mentioned the principles of cooperation that China's policies were founded on. Along with equality and mutual benefit came others: China never attached conditions or asked for privileges; it tried to lighten the burden of recipient countries as much as possible; it helped recipient countries gradually achieve self-reliance; it strove to develop aid projects that required less investment and yielded faster results; it provided the best-quality equipment and materials of its own manufacture; it saw to it that the personnel of the recipient country fully mastered necessary techniques; and it did not allow its experts to make special demands or enjoy special amenities. China promoted its experience as a model, described in 1965 by Yong Longgun in an article titled "Afro-Asian People's Path to Achieving Complete Economic Independence." The goal was to inculcate self-reliance so that developing countries achieved economic autonomy and stopped relying on foreign aid. The steps to be followed included eliminating all foreign privileges; promoting social democratic reforms to increase productivity; granting the bare necessities such as food and clothing; increasing productivity to earn foreign exchange; training national cadres; and developing domestic science and industry so as not to rely on foreign powers.[48]

China inaugurated a policy of aid on concessional terms, lending at a zero interest rate. It was a move that the Soviet Union criticized immediately as a tool for discrediting Comecon aid. The Sino-Soviet rift was devastating to the Afro-Asian People's Solidarity Organization, AAPSO. Begun in Cairo in December 1957, AAPSO was sponsored by the World Peace Council, and its original members included the European countries of the Socialist Bloc. By the 1960s, only the Soviet Union retained its membership, but at the third AAPSO meeting, in 1963 in Moshi, Tanzania, China and a pro-Chinese group requested the Soviet Union's expulsion on the grounds that it was too white a country to be considered Afro-Asian. As Marxist George Padmore once said, whatever their ideology, the Russians could not fulfill the African desire to be mentally free from Europeans.[49] The Soviets reacted by stressing their Asian dimension. They cited the Soviet victory over economic and cultural backwardness, recalling the Virgin Lands Campaign in Central Asia and Soviet industrial development in Baku, Alma Ata, Frunze, and Tashkent. They also offered military support for national liberation movements to dispel doubts instilled by Chinese propaganda, which labeled peaceful coexistence as a counterrevolutionary strategy contrary to the interests of national independence movements.[50]

China became very active in Africa beginning in 1963–1964 with propaganda materials of various kinds, including more than seven hundred hours of radio broadcasting in twenty-five languages reaching as far as Latin America—an effort surpassing that of the BBC.[51] It planned to set an example for African countries. Initially, the political dimension prevailed. The success of the revolution in 1949 led several Asian and African leaders to promote China as a model. Mao's guerrilla techniques from the late 1940s were especially popular, though they did not work optimally because of differences in the field and because the discipline required by Chinese guerrilla warfare was more demanding than what most Africans were willing to embrace. However, leaders of African liberation movements such as Julius Nyerere and Samora Machel praised their effectiveness. The Chinese planned to gain influence in the Congo area. To this effect, they offered their military and economic assistance to Congo-Brazzaville, Burundi, and the Central African Republic. In 1966, Fulbert Youlou, the overthrown first president of Congo-Brazzaville, wrote J'accuse la Chine, which blamed the Chinese for planning to turn Africa into a gigantic rice paddy.[52]

With the Cultural Revolution (1966–69), China set aside both old structures and the traditional values linked to them. Experts in planning and foreign policy were ousted, leaving little in terms of contacts or knowledge of international relations.[53] The Cultural Revolution interrupted China's efforts in Africa, but in the early 1970s, China was back, albeit with policy changes. Political motives were still crucial, particularly the quest for support for its bid to take over Taiwan's seat at the United Nations. Competition with the Soviet Union, which had gained new momentum in Africa, was also important in orienting China's political choices.[54] Mao launched the Three Worlds theory. Each world was defined in terms of economic development, wealth, and possession of atomic weapons. The United States and the Soviet Union were in the First World; Japan, Europe, Australia, and Canada belonged to the Second; and all other countries occupied the Third World. The language Mao used was that of class conflict, because he identified the First World with exploitation and oppression.[55] He shared his theory with Zambian president Kenneth Kaunda in February 1974 and shortly thereafter with the president of the Non-Aligned Movement, Algerian Houari Boumedienne. On 10 April

1974, Deng Xiaoping, the Chinese vice premier, illustrated the theory of the Three Worlds and the Four Modernizations in the General Assembly of the United Nations. Development took center stage.

In the 1970s, China reoriented its priorities. Geographically, it focused on Southeast Africa. Tanzania and Zambia received aid, while requests from West Africa, like the railway between Guinea and Mali or the potentially profitable Manantali Dam in the Senegal River basin, were systematically rejected, even if they came from politically friendly governments. Countries that severed relations with the Soviet Union also received Chinese aid: in 1977, for example, China took over the Soviet role in Somalia and financed the Fanoole Dam, completing an unfinished Soviet work in four years. The dam was meant to produce electricity and irrigate rice fields, but civil war soon made it unusable.

No longer did China offer unconditional aid to national liberation movements.[56] Sponsorship of Maoist groups was replaced by a less ideological approach that targeted governments in power, including military regimes.[57] This strategy, justified by the application of noninterference, tarnished the Chinese among left-oriented African governments.[58] The backing of revolutionary regimes was supplanted by a totally different discourse based on productivity. Economic rationales had more weight, and China often asked recipient countries for financial contributions to support experts' living costs or pay for spare parts.[59] In the 1970s, China suggested that African governments privatize their economic structures or look west to gain further assistance. Economic growth, more than revolution, was the key to success, stressed Deng Xiaoping in 1974. In 1979, he bluntly claimed that a strategy of economic openness, which included accepting aid from the United States, was more likely to achieve economic growth.[60] In 1988, he advised Joaquim Chissano (Mozambique) and Mengistu Haile Mariam (Ethiopia) against adopting scientific socialism.[61] Development aid became the focus of China's external relations and the key to instituting a new global political and economic order, not necessarily based on the ideological adoption of socialism.[62]

## Self-Reliance? Tanzania between the
## Tazara Railway and *Ujamaa*

For at least a decade, Julius Nyerere's Tanzania was the ideal African laboratory to test the Chinese model. Nyerere was an intellectual leading a country with several ministers who had experienced colonial government, and China's Tanzania projects began with the coming of independence: Urafiki, the Friendship Textile Mill in Dar es Salaam, started in 1964.[63] After 1965, China offered military aid in the form of advisers and weapons. Tanzania became the place to test the idea of self-reliance, and the place where the Chinese promoted modernization without imposing burdensome political or economic conditions.

On 5 February 1967, Nyerere and his party, the Tanganyika African National Union (TANU), promoted their new strategy for African development in the Arusha Declaration. *Ujamaa*, a revolution in politics and culture, was intended to recover tradition and create self-reliance. Its goal was autonomous development, independent from the international economic system and built on an artificial idea of premodern autarchy. Nyerere's African socialism was based on collective property, not on centralized economic control, planning, or industrial development. China helped turn the Arusha Declaration into a concrete plan, offering aid in a different kind of South-South solidarity.[64]

Nyerere visited China thirteen times, and he claimed he modeled *Ujamaa* on China's experience.[65] The point was to assemble the population in rural areas and initiate cash-crop production: for it to work, peasants had to be convinced to cooperate, which meant they would be involved in the process of modernization and state building.[66] Nyerere hoped that rural cooperatives that operated on a voluntary basis could prevent the so-called kulakization of Tanzanian agriculture—that is, the birth of a class of rich peasants who hired other peasants as laborers.[67] Organization of *Ujamaa* happened in stages, the first suggesting minimal time working in common plots, with more significant communitarian organization concentrated in *Ujamaa* villages that farmed in common at least three days a week, with profits shared among the community.[68] According to a 1961 World Bank report on planning in Tanganyika, agricultural strategies based on mechanization, like the ones Nyerere devised, had been failures.[69] Nonetheless, *Ujamaa* villages adopted colonial ideas of modernization, including scientific agriculture, mechanization, bureaucratic centralism, and modern education. The villages were built next to communication routes, but in places that were not traditionally inhabited and were therefore unlikely to turn a profit. From a structural point of view, the model for the *Ujamaa* village was the Ruvuma Development Association, an organization that united fifteen villages in the Songea District in the southwest part of the country. It was a blow for the whole project when in 1968 this community, the incarnation of the *Ujamaa* ideal, with local control and nonauthoritarian organization, refused to adapt to the centralized scheme.[70]

Facing popular resistance, Nyerere turned to coercion. In December 1973, organization within villages became compulsory, and the expression "*Ujamaa* villages" was replaced by "operation planned villages." *Ujamaa* moved from a democratic policy inspired by tradition into a more classic mode of planning, one that figured prominently as a case study in conferences of the 1970s that discussed the viability of planning.[71] Expectations for the Tanzania experiment varied. Nyerere's original plans were widely endorsed: the Catholic Church, for instance, praised the role of education, particularly the fact that Nyerere did not intend to dismantle the country's missionary-based educational structures.[72] But skepticism came quickly: "violence, forcing, injustice, and failure" were the words the Episcopal Conference used to describe the early experience of those in *Ujamaa* villages.[73] The concentration of power in local authorities who abused that power by favoring client networks was a problem, as was the authorities' violent response to local resistance.[74] The villagization campaign produced economically unproductive communities that refused to cooperate with the state. The strict surveillance was too similar to the repressive policies of colonial times, and forced population movements recalled the campaigns against sleeping sickness, which had moved large masses. Belief in the mechanization of agriculture and, more generally, in farming with modern techniques was also associated with colonialism.[75] *Ujamaa* villages did not meet Nyerere's expectations. In 1979, he said that although 60 percent of the people were now living in socialist villages, they did not live as socialists.[76] Overall, the plan was economically counterproductive and disrupted the ecological balance of the traditional rural economy.

The project that served as the symbol of China's ability to offer an alternative to the superpowers and traditional European donors was the 1,060-mile-long Tazara Railway, also known as Africa's Freedom Railway. Built between 1968 and 1975, it cost $400 million: China offered a long-term loan at zero percent after the Soviet Union and Western donors rejected the project as economically unviable. The railway would allow Zambia to export its copper without depending on the railways and ports still under white minority rule in Rhodesia, Angola, and South Africa, and despite being an old colonial enterprise, it was now reinterpreted as a project for national identity.[77] The refusal of support by other donors made it the ideal showcase for Chinese aid, courage, and skill. The cooperation between Zambia and Tanzania—two former colonies uniting against white imperial rule—added ideological meaning. The railway was completed before the original deadline, which was considered a testimonial to Chinese and African labor efficiency. Acceleration of the schedule was a typical Chinese approach, and because of the project's great international visibility, only the most qualified workers had been chosen.[78] Since the workers came from Zambia and Tanzania and represented several ethnic groups, the project was also a way to build solidarity. The workers learned technical skills through example on-site, a necessity that was soon translated into pedagogical and ideological principle. Although socialization between the Chinese and Africans was complicated, the local population loved the Chinese medicine

Figure 4. Building the Tazara Railway, 1967. From *Beijing Review,*
*http://www.bjreview.com.cn/special/2014-04/24/content_615209.htm.*

that came along with the railway work. They thought it was more advanced than Western medicine, just as socialism was more progressive than capitalism.[79] While there was and is much propaganda extolling the project's virtues, China was not wholly satisfied, and the hugely expensive project diminished Chinese enthusiasm for aid.

Tazara Railway stations were incorporated into *Ujamaa* villages, thus uniting the two big projects and symbols of Chinese aid. The first resettlements started in 1973 and were to be completed by 1977. Later, communities were expected to provide security to the new infrastructure. Workers who had built the railway were to serve as settlers, an avant-garde of modernizers who would catalyze settlement.[80] This did not happen. Locals saw the population transfers as utter violence.

## Third Worldism and the New International Economic Order

"For a long time prior to their independence, the developing countries had been seduced by the idea of the class struggle; but today they realized that the essential problem for them was the elimination not so much of the proletariat classes as of the proletarian nations."[81] This was how Doudou Thiam, the foreign minister of Senegal, summed up the Third World's view in 1967. Aid was not about begging for charity, nor was it solely a moral issue. It was a juridical obligation, he argued, and as such needed to be codified into a legal right. Talking to the United Nations General Assembly one year earlier, he had insisted on the right to development and imagined an "Economic Bandung" that would draft a new charter for the world economy.

The demand for a profound change in the international economic order grew stronger in the 1970s. The crisis and obsolescence of the Bretton Woods system after 1971 helped Third World claims, which also enjoyed the support of the rebellious youth movements in the West.[82] Third Worldism had a huge influence on large sectors of the political left, which were captivated by champions such as Frantz Fanon, the psychologist and leading anticolonial thinker who called for the use of violence in the decolonization process—an author who was rather alien to orthodox Marxism.[83] In its list of assets, the Third World could count on the crucial strategic alliance with the oil producers united in the Organization of the Petroleum Exporting Countries (OPEC), who were reclaiming sovereignty over natural resources. In the 1960s, oil-producing countries had successfully demanded their share in oil concessions, which—argued Fouad Rouhani, the first secretary-general of OPEC—was not only anachronistic, but immoral in a postcolonial world. In 1965, Saudi oil minister Abdullah al-Tariki, cofounder of OPEC along with Venezuelan minister Juan Pablo Pérez Alfonso, had denounced petroleum colonization. His appeal to nationalization found enthusiastic followers in the revolutionary regimes that came to power in the Mediterranean at the turn of the decade. Libya, under Colonel Muammar Gaddafi, was the front-runner: it nationalized all the holdings of British Petroleum in November 1971. Algeria and Iraq soon followed. The ability to acquire control over means, technology, and levels of production was crucial to economic development and industrialization, the insurrectionist oil elites argued.[84] They were supported by the Soviet Bloc, which was eager to offer technology and acquire Arab raw materials through long-term agreements. In the 1973 Arab-Israeli War, the Arabs used oil as a weapon, with oil producers cutting production and imposing an embargo in concert with non-Arab OPEC members, causing a dramatic rise in prices. OPEC backing gave the Global South a new contractual power, putting it in an ideal position to promote an ambitious scheme for economic decolonization: the New International Economic Order (NIEO).[85]

The NIEO monopolized public discourse between 1973 and 1974. It was exactly what Thiam had called for in 1966: the completion of the work started at Bandung. Rich countries conceded political self-determination to the South only after securing the continuation of economic dependence, Houari

Boumedienne claimed: it was time now to complete the work of independence. The Third World elaborated a political economy agenda based on rapid growth and global redistribution of wealth.[86] The focus of Cold War neutrality became economic; it was about alternative models of development, with the Global South supporting its own project to redress global economic inequality.[87] In the 1970 Lusaka Declaration on Non-Alignment and Economic Progress, the crucial point was how to use international mechanisms to rapidly transform the economic world system. The nonaligned summit in Algiers in September 1973 adopted the economic platform of the G77 and called for reducing military expenditures and investing the savings in development. Led by Houari Boumedienne, the platform, known as the Charter of Algiers, was radical, demanding a new foundation of international economic relations, a new and more equitable division of labor, and a new international monetary system. Nonalignment, announced Boumedienne, would no longer be defined in the negative, as a mere denial of Cold War logic: it would become an active politics reclaiming the rights of the emerging world.[88]

When it arrived at the United Nations within the Special Session of the General Assembly, the NIEO project was articulated in the following instruments, all approved in 1974: the declaration of the New International Economic Order, a Program of Action, and the Charter of the Economic Rights and Duties of States. It was on the agenda at the Sixth and Seventh Special Sessions of the General Assembly in New York in 1974 and 1975, the fourth session of UNCTAD in Nairobi 1976, and the Paris Conference on International Economic Co-operation (CIEC), more widely known as the North-South Dialogue. The discussion then called Global Negotiations on Raw Materials lasted until 1980. Requests included a long list of rights: sovereignty over natural resources, controls on foreign investments, better trade terms, easier access to the markets of developed countries, reduction in technology costs, more aid, a moratorium on debt and its eventual reduction, and the redistribution of power within the World Bank and the IMF. The tools devised to meet these goals included the promotion of producer cartels on the OPEC model, the abolition of trade and nontrade barriers, the creation of buffer stocks to limit the market volatility of raw materials, and the promotion of stable currency exchange rates through compensatory finance.[89] Alas, this long list did not appeal to the Western industrialized countries, which saw the NIEO as an attack on the establishment. They saw any revolution in international economic relations as a problem of public order within a worrisome systemic upheaval.[90] The Soviet Union was no more supportive—no surprise, since the NIEO's spokesperson attacked the Soviet Union regularly. In the United Nations, however, socialist countries were broadly supportive but complained that they lacked opportunities to consult with the G77.[91] The

Chinese, in contrast, fully supported the Third World countries, agreeing to sponsor whatever language they wanted, and approving "their sacred desire to safeguard national sovereignty [and] their struggles against control and plunder by imperialism and the superpowers."[92]

In front of the General Assembly, Soviet representative Andrei Gromyko repeated the Soviet ideological refrain of anti-imperialistic solidarity between socialist and newly independent countries. "These states," he said, "ever more comprehend their responsibilities in the struggle against foreign monopolies in rebuilding international economic relations on the basis of equality and justice." He pointed out that peace was inseparable from social and economic progress and that peace and security were a prerequisite for development. Only by strengthening their ties with the Eastern Bloc could poor countries oppose foreign monopolies and make their economies independent.[93] Free from historical responsibility for colonial exploitation and not part of the Western economic and monetary system, the Soviet Union did not feel it ought to be attacked by the poor countries. According to Gromyko, the developing countries were not thinking creatively. The NIEO aimed to correct capitalism, not wipe it out; a mistake, as only momentous changes in social structure would develop productive forces in Afro-Asian countries.[94] The "amorphous ideology of development" was not universal, given the fundamental division between socialism and imperialism—only Comecon could provide a real alternative to capitalist servitude.[95] The Soviet Union rejected the world seen through the lens of the North-South divide, not surprisingly, since an automatic redistribution of income in favor of poor countries and the foregrounding of North-South trade over East-West trade was especially inopportune for the Soviets.[96] In the early 1980s, Soviet hostility waned, and Comecon offered support to the nonaligned countries' program.

The Soviets criticized Third World intellectuals because of the conceptual weaknesses in their ideas, particularly the paradox of rejecting Western models while hoping for Western support and the way that Third Worldist ideas remained fundamentally connected to Western thought, a tendency that Gilbert Rist has called a generalized ethnocentrism.[97] The NIEO was not so new: it was clearly connected with the progress narratives of positivist thinking, the idea of history repeating itself, of poor countries catching up with the rich ones. Its language was universalist and shaped by internationalism—it was not Marxist, and its most representative intellectuals were not Marxists.[98] The NIEO made some of UNCTAD's requests its own and shared with the Singer and Prebisch theses the fundamental tenet that trade was the main engine of development. It saw a correlation between the growth of the world economy and that of poor countries: the expansion of world trade within a capitalist market was considered progress. It viewed technology as crucial to development and demanded better and easier transfer procedures to access it—but only one technology, the West's. In sum, the NIEO's goal was integration within the capitalist system, for which it was attacked not only by the Soviets, but by radical critics including Andre Gunder Frank and Immanuel Wallerstein.[99]

# 8

# Resources, Environment, and Development

## THE DIFFICULT NEXUS

I do not wish to seem overdramatic, but I can only conclude from the
information that is available to me as Secretary General, that the members of
the United Nations have perhaps ten years left in which to subordinate their
ancient quarrels and launch a global partnership to curb the arms race, to
improve the human environment, to defuse the population explosion, and to
supply the required momentum to development efforts.

—U THANT, 1969

"I have no apologies to make to anyone that we do things in a big way. Why
shouldn't we be proud that America . . . accounts for more than half the consumption of energy on this planet?"[1] Unremarkable as these words were when
David Lilienthal said them in 1949, as a new environmental awareness emerged
some thirty years later, they sounded out of place. The linkage between state
power and large-scale projects that ruled during the modernization years
entered a crisis in the 1970s, when modernity ceased to be an end in itself and
new sensibilities replaced what in 1958 Nehru—otherwise known for calling dams the temples of modern India—called the "disease of giganticism."[2]
While development struggled to keep its promise to quickly grant underdeveloped countries wealth and well-being, problems related to industrialization appeared in the form of ecological imbalances. At the turn of the decade,
development was considered a failure as a Cold War weapon, and there was
widespread doubt about planning.[3] Though ideology was still unyielding in
the periphery, where international crises and civil wars stemming from decolonization and the failure of new states continued to fuel Cold War dynamics,

in international organizations the East-West conflict rarely challenged the fundamental underlying agreement on global issues. Instead, a major cleavage ran along the old color line, between a rich, white, developed North and a colored, poor, underdeveloped South.

## The End of Technological Optimism?

In the modernization years, technological optimism prevailed. Technology solved problems. In France, for example, in the early 1960s, René Dumont, formerly a colonial agronomist and later the French Green Party presidential candidate, defended the Green Revolution and the intensive methods imported from the United States. In 1961, Louis Armand, longtime head of Euratom, wrote *Plaidoyer pour l'avenir*, an elegy for technical progress, big machinery, and humanity's conquest of nature.[4] Armand saw technology as key to well-being. Only a few people questioned the usefulness of science and technology or worried about the consequences of technological innovation and scientific experiments. One prominent skeptic was US president Dwight Eisenhower, who in 1961 alerted the world to the threat of a scientific-technological elite.[5]

Pollution and overpopulation were not yet part of this scenario. The obsession with population growth, common among social scientists in the first half of the twentieth century, was not yet dominant. The UN Population Division, for instance, was more worried about European demographic decline than population growth elsewhere. In 1954, Eugene Black commissioned a World Bank study on the consequences of population growth in less developed countries. Ansley Coale, a demographer at Princeton, and Edgar M. Hoover, an economist at Berkeley, envisioned three scenarios, all negative, and called for birth control in the South.[6] No action was taken, however. Throughout the 1950s, modernity was seen as the key to changes in values and reproductive patterns that would result in population control. Population imbalances were considered a temporary feature of demographic transition, although the move to lower fertility was slowed both by progress in medicine and by traditional cultural values that promoted high fertility and rejected family planning.[7] A galaxy of opposed interests grew around the population issue: committees and pressure groups, private foundations large and small, international organizations, and governments, mainly oriented against population control.[8]

In the late 1950s, British zoologist Charles Elton wrote an influential work on ecological explosions showing how the enormous increase in some organisms threatened the ecological balance. He argued that overreliance on chemicals had not made food supplies more secure; in fact, because of the indiscriminate use of pesticides—an "astonishing rain of death upon so much of the world's surface"—supplies were actually more vulnerable.[9] His ideas influenced others, most notably biologist Rachel Carson, whose 1962 *Silent Spring*, now seen as the spark that ignited the 1970s ecological movement, condemned the overuse of DDT in farming.[10] Increased pollution also contributed to the environmental revolution, as did a series of toxic incidents. There was the 1952 Great Smog in London and the nuclear fallout after thermonuclear tests at Bikini Atoll in 1954, which inspired both *Godzilla* (1954) and the documentary *Daigo Fukuryū Maru* (1959). In the 1960s, there were acid rains in northern Europe, and severe mercury poisoning in Niigata, Japan. Other disasters, including the Torrey Canyon oil spill in 1967, which contaminated miles of Cornish and French shores, and the devastation caused by chemical weapons in Vietnam, were featured regularly on television. In the 1960s, a vast literature on technology's unwanted consequences flourished. Scientists tried to predict the effects of a total war, nuclear or otherwise. They studied biological warfare, then called bacteriological warfare, by conducting experiments on pests, chemical weapons, and epidemic disease. They considered the social responsibility of science and warned against the unchecked rise in population, wild industrialization, and vulnerability to infectious disease. The issues, data, and people involved in this new awareness became the protagonists of environmentalism.[11]

By the 1970s, the utopia of technological modernization had given way to pessimism focused on the limits of growth and development, an attitude seen earlier in futurology journals of the late 1950s that focused on resource scarcity.[12] Although ecology had a long history, it gradually became less descriptive, focusing instead on elaborating predictive models and raising concerns about the environment, resources, and population growth.[13] As it migrated from biology departments into public opinion, it combined with the protest movements of the late 1960s in an almost explosive mix.[14] On 10 November 1967, *Science*, the journal of the American Association for the Advancement of Science (AAAS), published an influential article: "Population Policy: Will Current Programs Succeed?" by Kingsley Davis. Davis criticized population policy, arguing that overcoming resistance to family planning required governments and agencies "to develop attractive substitutes for family interests, so as to avoid having to turn to hardship as a corrective."[15] He was clear that cutting population growth required either cultural change or, failing that, coercive state intervention.

His ideas sparked multiple responses, including Garrett Hardin's "The Tragedy of the Commons" in *Science*, and Paul Ehrlich's *The Population Bomb*, both published in 1968, the two best-known examples of catastrophic environmentalism in the tradition of Malthus.[16] Both saw population growth as an urgent problem that had to be addressed immediately to save humanity. Zero-growth options that allowed only the births necessary to replace deaths was the part of the argument that many found morally shocking. Hardin, however, reversed concepts of morality, arguing that "freedom in a commons brings ruin to all" and that the freedom to breed was itself immoral. His reasoning turned parenthood from a right into a privilege. Ehrlich was equally dramatic, defining population increase as a cancer requiring immediate action. Connecting demography and ecology, Ehrlich saw zero population growth as the best path toward environmental protection. He founded the organization Zero Population Growth in December 1968, hoping to influence governments. The demographic challenge of the 1970s, he claimed, was how to reduce fertility worldwide.[17] In December 1970, in Chicago at the annual meeting of the AAAS, the link between excess population and the environmental threat became a fixed principle, with two symposia out of four focused on the issue—"Reducing the Environmental Impact of a Growing Population" and "Is Population Growth Responsible for the Environmental Crisis in the United States." Key Neo-Malthusians appeared on the second panel: George Wald, Ansley Coale, Barry Commoner, Paul Ehrlich, and Garrett Hardin.[18] Ecologists were divided mainly into two groups: those like Commoner who blamed technology for environmental distress, and those like Ehrlich who leaned toward demography. For the journal *The Ecologist*, founded to immediate popularity in 1970 by Edward Goldsmith, the problem was the combination of the two.

In 1970, British biologist John Maddox published *The Doomsday Syndrome*, an explicit attack on Ehrlich. Ecologists, he argued, were both exaggerating the problem and underestimating the transformative power of technology. His argument was contradictory, however. On one hand, he considered the impact of human activity negligible in comparison with natural cycles; on the other, he thought technology was powerful enough to produce nourishment and energy for all and to fight pollution.[19] Another optimist was microbiologist René Dubos. In his *Reason Awake*, he acknowledged that pollution and the invention of weapons of mass destruction were threats. Nonetheless, he insisted that science and technology were tools that could solve ecological problems. What was missing, he argued, was a positive utopia, a vision for the future.[20]

The most influential Neo-Malthusian document was *The Limits to Growth*, a report published in February 1972. It originated in the initiative of the Italian industrialist Aurelio Peccei.[21] Peccei's biography reflects the shift from the optimism of modernization to the demographic pessimism of 1970s environmental thinking. After years at Italconsult, a state group that exported technology to the Third World, in 1969 he penned *The Chasm Ahead*, in which he criticized what he called a technological hurricane that forced developing countries to move ahead recklessly. Aid in the form of technology, he argued, just assuaged advanced countries' guilt and let them cover a history of abuse and dispossession.[22] Though he still believed in Western supremacy and a civilizing mission, Peccei thought global problems had to be solved via an all-embracing outlook, in cooperation with the Eastern Bloc. In September 1967, in Akademgorodok—the Siberian "City of Science"—speaking to scientists from various disciplines, he underscored the necessity of "universal programs" to deal with global challenges such as the population explosion, megalopolises, intergenerational conflict caused by longer life expectancies, the plundering of natural resources, the waste and abuse of the planet's riches, and air and water pollution.[23]

In 1968, together with the Scottish scientist Alexander King, head of the Scientific Affairs Directorate in the OECD, Peccei founded the Club of Rome, an independent think tank to deal with the "World Problematique," as it came to be known: the question of how to secure humankind's survival in the face of population growth, resource depletion, increasing pollution, and the growing technological chasm between advanced industrialized countries and Third World countries. This "Predicament of Mankind" had to be dealt with through a global planning approach, Peccei and other club members, including Turkish systems thinker and cyberneticist Hasan Özbekhan, maintained.[24] The club commissioned a study of the implications of world growth that was carried out at MIT under the direction of Dennis Meadows, who used a computer-aided analysis developed by pioneering systems scientist Jay Forrester to study complex systems with multiple factors—in this case, population, agricultural production, natural resources, industrial production, and pollution. The ensuing report was meant to showcase development trends rather than to offer scientifically accurate data. It was titled *The Limits to Growth* and published as a book that concluded that the world should abandon the idea of steady economic growth.

In "The Computer That Printed Out W*O*L*F*," a long review for *Foreign Affairs*, Carl Kaysen objected to both the methodology and the content, mocking the work and its alarmist tone.[25] The *New York Times Book Review* called the report empty and misleading, worse than pseudoscience.[26] Robert Solow in *Newsweek* called it a piece of irresponsible nonsense.[27] The German weekly *Die Zeit*, in contrast, was more worried about the psychological consequences and called it "a bomb in a paperback format."[28] Academics questioned the project's scientific validity. Others were less critical. World Bank president Robert McNamara, for example, established a task force drawn from the bank's Central Economic Staff and chaired by economist Mahbub ul Haq to perform a comprehensive review of the document.[29] Ul Haq, a believer in regional models rather than global schemes, judged that it was necessary to think of the North and the South as two distinct systems.[30] Others at the World Bank were more supportive. Senior adviser on development policy Ernest Stern, for example, admired the report because it raised "precisely the kind of questions about the relationships between the rich and the poor that we have struggled with within the development community."[31] McNamara was aware of ecological issues and of the need to factor the environment in the bank's strategy for development. In January 1970, referring to the Murchison Falls project in Uganda, he claimed that the bank should undertake systematic reviews of projects in which ecological problems were likely to arise.[32]

## Recasting the Problems of Modern Society

At the turn of the decade, uncertainty over the future of the world economy led to a multifaceted malaise.[33] Notwithstanding high growth rates and low unemployment and inflation, there was a feeling that poor economic performance had caused political radicalization in both the Third World and developed countries. Global containment of communism as envisioned in the years of Kennedy and Johnson was not considered viable or desirable anymore. Modernization theories based on the acceleration of history and rapid transition to modernity lost their following. A pervasive sense of Western cultural and economic decline infected development thinking, throwing it into disorder.[34] Development, claimed British economist Dudley Seers in November 1969, had been identified with its economic dimension only, with growth. But it was simplistic to think that economic growth would solve social problems; in fact, growth could introduce new problems. If the GDP went up but poverty, unemployment, and inequality went up as well, growth was not real.[35] Even the United States conceded that development was not just economic growth and that widespread participation in the labor market and equitable income distribution were as important as increases in total productive capacity.[36] In early 1971, OECD secretary-general Emiel van Lennep declared that well-being and growth did not necessarily coincide: all told, the concept of growth was facing a crisis of doubt. The OECD studied the problems of modern society and concluded that qualitative factors mattered—but it took until 1977 for the DAC to point out the advantages of fewer social imbalances.[37]

US president Richard Nixon (1969–1974) and his assistant for national security Henry Kissinger shifted foreign policy priorities and opted for a new "realism" based on easing Cold War tensions. The first step was a recognition of the status quo in Central and Eastern Europe, together with an opening to Communist China in hopes of disengaging from the war in Vietnam, which had become politically and economically burdensome. As détente made economic Cold War less urgent, aid as a political tool lost momentum. "At present our foreign assistance program is dead," the Nixon administration claimed as it set up a task force to study reforms to an aid system it considered unsuited to the times.[38] In March 1970, a task force of prominent private citizens chaired by Rudolph Peterson, former head of the Bank of America, published *U.S. Foreign Assistance in the 1970s: A New Approach; Report to the President from the Task Force on International Development.* The Peterson Report laid the foundations for future planning. It stressed the "profound national interest of the United States in cooperation with developing countries" and the need to make development "a truly cooperative venture." The report continued:

> This country should not look for gratitude or votes, or any specific short-term foreign policy gains from our participation in international development. Nor should it expect to influence others to adopt U.S. cultural values or institutions. Neither can it assume that development will necessarily bring political stability. Development implies change—political and social, as well as economic—and such change, for a time may be disruptive. What the United States should expect from participation in international development is steady progress toward its long-term goals: the building of self-reliant and healthy societies in developing countries, an expanding world economy from which all benefit, an improved prospect for world peace.[39]

These words reveal the disappointment with the results of earlier development policies.

In the same year, Edward M. Korry, the US ambassador to Chile, criticized the Marshall Plan legacy. That early success in Europe, he argued, was the original sin of development assistance, as it led to the belief that foreign aid produced political stability. By the 1960s, he continued, this mistake had become the rule, and progressively "the principle of assisting others in their economic development was elevated to the level of an end in itself." The reality was that providing development assistance did not ensure political support in return, he contended, and even though the 1970s saw "a growing congruence of international political interest between the US and the USSR," other issues were emerging like the explosive increase in world population, with the connected problems of food sufficiency and qualitative and quantitative environmental changes.[40]

In earlier years, large private foundations like Rockefeller and Ford had studied farming, seeing food as a technological issue.[41] Research on new seeds and fertilizers, pesticides, and weed killers paved the way for what would be known as the Green Revolution—a term coined by USAID director William Gaud in March 1968 when he saw that year's extraordinary harvest. Seemingly the solution to all problems, progress in agriculture appeared likely to solve the problem of hunger. Just behind the corner, however, lurked an unsettling reality: good harvests did not translate to food security, the elimination of poverty, or social peace. Instead they revealed failures in distribution.[42] "There are problems of race, of the dispossessed, and of the disadvantaged," Korry said, "that are global, endemic, and amenable to resolution only by persistent effort over a long period of time."[43] The answer he envisaged was to move toward making US aid more multilateral to maximize depoliticization—but was this a viable solution?

President Richard Nixon revised US priorities by recasting the problems that needed to be addressed. Instead of focusing on world development, the mission of the United States should be to care for the environment and world resources. The United States could become the locomotive of global environmentalism, starting off with projects on air quality and ocean pollution.[44] He was so convincing that the French minister of the environment, Robert Poujade, called America "the Mecca of environmentalism."[45] The United States brought the issue to NATO, making the case that environmental matters had a clear security dimension. Inspired by the OECD's Committee on Science and Technology Policy, NATO requested a Committee on the Challenges of Modern Society (CCMS). The former was begun in 1967 and placed within the Scientific Affairs Directorate headed by Alexander King in the working group on "Economic Growth and the Allocation of National Resources."[46] Nixon thought that replicating this structure in NATO would force members to promote research, share information, and use the knowledge as a basis for political action. The committee was constituted in July 1969 and headed by Italian ambassador Manlio Brosio; Daniel Patrick Moynihan, an expert on urban affairs, represented the United States.[47] Historians have tried to explain Nixon's romance with the environment. At the time, some commentators saw it as an effort to distract public opinion from the Vietnam War. If this was the goal, it was a double-edged sword, since Vietnam, the prototype of war as environmental catastrophe, was itself a classic reference in environmental criticism. Others saw it as a way to extoll the role of the United States in the Western Alliance and of the West in international organizations, promoting the image of a cohesive group that cared about the world's well-being. Some believed the United States thought it would be easier to prevail against the Socialist Bloc or the Third World in the environmental sphere.[48] Others thought it was a way to keep allies busy while the superpowers discussed more important security issues.[49]

In his 1960 electoral campaign, Willy Brandt warned that the environment was bound to become an obsession, much as unemployment had been in the 1930s.[50] By 1970, his prophecy was realized, with doomsday scenarios feeding a feeling that has been defined as collective hysteria. Some unlikely personalities shared a sense of ecological urgency, including George Kennan, the father of containment and a key US Cold War strategist, who published an article titled "To Prevent World Wasteland" in *Foreign Affairs*.[51] Under media pressure, Western European countries followed the lead of the United States. In 1970, environmental protection became central in the press on both sides of the Atlantic, with German and Italian investigative journalists doing exceptional work.[52] In Italy, Antonio Cederna reported on the landscape and the excesses of rampant urbanization.[53] In Germany, the environment made the front page in 1969, when millions of fish killed by pesticides turned up in the poisoned waters of the Rhine.[54] First Great Britain, then Germany and France instituted a Ministry for the Environment.[55] On 22 April 1970, the first Earth Day was celebrated worldwide and the Council of Europe, which in 1968 had promulgated a European Water Charter, made 1970 the European Conservation Year.[56]

The European Economic Community joined the environmental surge in 1971. Altiero Spinelli, the European commissioner for industry, led a working group on the environment. On 18 April 1972, the European Parliament discussed environmental protection. Sicco Mansholt, European commissioner for agriculture, was under the spell of the 1972 Club of Rome Report. He was against pesticides and for taxing pollutants, and he warned against automation, pollution, and environmental degradation. On 9 February 1972, he wrote to Malfatti, president of the European Commission, to call Europe to action. Mansholt claimed that inflation and unemployment were minor problems compared to population growth or the consumption of energy and raw materials in developed countries.[57] He immediately became the target of left-wing critics who accused him of representing technocracy and serving forces of social regression because he was not prioritizing labor issues. Attacks on a perceived collusion between ecology and big business became a common leftist critique. Giovanni Berlinguer wrote "Ecology and Politics" for the Italian Communist Party journal *Rinascita* (Rebirth). He mocked what he called the new ecological business and described the Club of Rome as a camouflaged polluters' society.[58] It was true that big polluters took care to exhibit environmental concern. One of the most blatant episodes involved ENI—the Italian state-owned Hydrocarbon Corporation—and its subsidiary Tecneco, which specialized in water cleanup. In the early 1970s, ENI financed two important reports: an ENI-ISVET study on the economic costs of pollution in June 1970 (translated into English as *Economic Costs and Benefits of an Antipollution Project in Italy: Summary Report of a Preliminary Evaluation*), which tried to convince developing countries that their cleanup technologies were effective,[59] and a Tecneco study on public intervention against pollution in 1973.[60] Believing that technology could clean what it had fouled, and keen to safeguard the interests of the ministry of industry and public works, the Italian government tended to devolve responsibility onto semiprivate consultancies working at a local level.[61]

# The Emergence of Global
# Environmentalism: Stockholm, 1972

Held in Stockholm on 6–15 June 1972, the UN Conference on the Human Environment had such a huge impact that it is identified with the birth of global environmentalism. It called for incorporating environmental issues into development thinking, thus setting the stage for the concept of sustainable development. Institutionally, its most remarkable result was the birth of the United Nations Environment Programme, or UNEP. The conference came out of an earlier one, the UNESCO-sponsored Biosphere Conference held in Paris in September 1968. That conference's conclusions were summed up in twenty points: number 19 explicitly referred to the ecological consequences of big development projects. The Biosphere Conference dealt with science: political issues were left for the UN arena. In 1969, the General Assembly adopted resolution 2581 (XXIV), convening the Human Environment conference, presented as a way to help developing countries prevent environmental problems.[62] But tensions between development and environmental protection still lurked in the political and scientific communities.

The secretary-general for the Stockholm Conference was Maurice Strong. He had a puzzling record—a rapid rise in the oil business combined with a calling for international service.[63] Formerly president of the Canadian International Development Agency, Strong was an ideal choice: keen on compromise and open to requests from developing countries, he stressed compatibility between business, development, and environmental protection. He saw environmentalism as an issue for both East-South and North-South relations, of interest to all, and helped pressure the United Nations to adopt the environmental cause. The conference's goal was to produce a report on environmental conditions, a declaration on the human environment, and an action plan.[64] Three commissions worked on this. The second dealt specifically with resources and the environment-development nexus.[65] A crucial meeting to prepare for the conference took place in Founex, Switzerland, on 4–12 June 1971. Also headed by Strong, it involved experts on issues related to the environmental consequences of big development projects, especially dams.[66] By now it was obvious that big projects—Aswan was a much-cited case—had tremendous adverse effects on the ecology of developing countries and that these effects had been underestimated and had aggravated social unrest. Megadams and large irrigation schemes had been evaluated according to political, economic, and engineering parameters, not by the environmental disruption they caused or their social and medical consequences.[67]

The fundamental idea in Founex was that the environment was crucial to securing the success of a development plan. Every country needed to establish minimum environmental standards that would take into account its stage of development and social and cultural goals. The Founex report suggested ways to avoid mistakes and distortions typical of old ways of doing development and stressed the problems of poverty and underdevelopment rather than industrialization. These problems included traditional agriculture, given population increases and the decay of cultivated land; the problems of modern farming, including the chemical war against weeds and pests, soil salinization, soil erosion, flooding induced by irrigation, river basin development and the resulting resettlement and endangered wildlife; and pollution caused by industrialization.[68] The report was discussed at a regional level in summer 1971 by the UN Economic Commissions: for Asia (Bangkok, 17–23 August), Africa (Addis Ababa, 23–28 August), and Latin America (Mexico City, 6–11 September); and by the Social and Economic Office in Beirut (27 September–2 October). Scientists were also involved: the working group constituted by the Scientific Committee on Problems of the Environment (SCOPE) discussed the report in Canberra (24 August–3 September 1971).[69]

The Stockholm conference was accompanied by efforts to target public opinion, particularly youth, via exhibitions, radio, and TV. The primary educational document was *Only One Earth: The Care and Maintenance of a Small Planet*, written by Barbara Ward and René Dubos, experts on environment and development.[70] Commissioned by Maurice Strong for the Stockholm delegates, the book contained the collected views of intellectuals and scientists with a range of opinions about the ecosystem's adaptability; humanity's role in the natural environment; and technology, including nuclear energy, which some considered a useful option and others "absolutely out of place" in the biosphere.[71] The book conveyed both urgency and optimism.

One hundred and twelve national delegations came to Stockholm, along with UN specialized agencies, forty-four international NGOs, and more than fifteen hundred accredited press representatives. The Environmental Forum, a counter-conference organized by environmentalists, hosted the liveliest debates. A key speaker was Barry Commoner, whose "Motherhood in Stockholm" appeared in *Harper's Magazine* on the eve of the conference and became a critical manifesto for it. Commoner argued that proceedings in Stockholm were threatened by long-standing political conflicts: atomic war was the worst-case scenario for human survival, but it could not be discussed in Stockholm because it was reserved for superpowers' summit diplomacy. At the conference, the potentially disruptive clash was the conflict between rich and poor, between whites and nonwhites. For the poor, remarked Commoner, "the world's most dangerous issue" was a matter of social justice, of distribution among nations and races.[72]

Intended to deal with global issues in a climate of détente, the conference ended up amplifying both East-West and North-South tensions. Eastern

Bloc countries, with the exception of Romania and Yugoslavia, boycotted the meeting in protest against the exclusion of East Germany—the still unsettled German question was interfering once more with international politics. One novel aspect of the conference was the participation of the People's Republic of China—soon to be admitted to the United Nations—which used the conference to regain a significant role as a representative, along with India and Brazil, for the developing countries. Deep political divisions threatened to render the whole project meaningless, and international crises, especially the Vietnam War, cast a pall over the proceedings. In opening the conference, Secretary-General Kurt Waldheim and Swedish prime minister Olof Palme explicitly condemned war, Waldheim referring to it as the most detestable form of pollution, and Palme specifically referring to Vietnam as an ecological war, given the destructive herbicidal warfare program of the US military.

Eager to get to the main issues, Maurice Strong began where he had left off at Founex. He argued that the no-growth paradigm aimed at limiting growth and influencing population policies was unacceptable, and stressed the importance of harmonizing environmental and developmental needs. Development was a priority for poor countries, and thus a prerequisite for dealing with environmental problems. Three results were expected from the conference: a move from unalloyed development toward more cautious resource use, some restraint on population growth, and a way to facilitate the gradual catching up of developing countries. Only economic growth got attention, however, as the environment-development nexus was always the center of discussions.[73] The secretary's indirect approach, intended to defuse tensions, was reflected in the forum as well, with both economist Barbara Ward and anthropologist Margaret Mead highlighting the rapacity of consumerism and overpopulation without identifying a culprit.[74] After Stockholm, key forum speeches were collected in the volume *Who Speaks for Earth?*[75] In it, Barbara Ward, René Dubos, Thor Heyerdahl, Gunnar Myrdal, Carmen Miró, Solly Zuckerman, and Aurelio Peccei discussed the ecological predicament of humankind. Although the authors offered a warning, like the conference itself they adopted a mild tone, clearly hoping to have both development and environmental protection.

Developing countries, however, were not willing to reconcile the two. They saw environmentalism as a pretext for escaping obligations on the aid front—a distraction from the problem of poverty. In their minds, the environment was an issue solely for the rich. Developed countries had caused environmental decay, and they should pay the price. In a speech delivered on 14 June 1972, Indira Gandhi put it this way: "The inherent conflict is not between conservation and development, but between environment and reckless exploitation of man and earth in the name of efficiency." Pollution, she argued, was not a technical problem: it was a political one. Science and technology were not at fault; rather, it was shortsightedness and a willingness to ignore the rights of others.[76] Pollution and other environmental issues were the inevitable result of developed countries' reckless use of the world's resources.

One of the most controversial questions was population control. According to critics of unchecked demographic growth, strategies for development and environment would fail without population control. But the population question was pushed to the margins and the final conference document did not refer to it. The Third World opposed any reference to population growth as a factor in maintaining ecological balance, as did the Vatican delegation. Ever since Pope Paul VI's March 1967 encyclical *Populorum progressio* on "the development of peoples," the Catholic Church had acquired an important role in these discussions. The principles of Catholic social teaching listed in the encyclical—such as the right to a just wage, employment security, fair and reasonable working conditions, and, especially, the universal accessibility of resources and goods—resonated with the requests of developing countries. In his message at Stockholm, the pope warned against the excesses of progress and called for a radical change in mentality. He urged the international community to pursue "not only ecological equilibrium but also a just balance of prosperity between the centers of the industrialized world and their immense periphery."[77] Excluded from the official conference, demography entered the forum, where the Club of Rome report, with its recipe for saving resources and protecting the environment by limiting population growth, was harshly contested. Demography and pollution were labeled problems of rich Northern countries, whereas the problems of the South were war, the arms trade, and colonialism.[78]

Given these tensions and the fact that some delegations were distracted by issues they considered more urgent than the environment, some observers doubted that the conference would produce meaningful results. In the final days, Chinese delegate Tung Ke insisted on a complete overhaul of the Declaration on the Human Environment, also known as the Stockholm Declaration, the product of eight months of work by an ad hoc committee. Notwithstanding opposition from some members, including the United States, the declaration was discussed again and amended. The most radical change was in the ranking of priorities: development was now first, although a healthy environment was also a goal. The key, though, was dynamic economic and social development.[79] The burden of creating ecologically viable solutions was not to fall on developing countries. This was reflected in the principles of additionality and compensation included in the final draft of the declaration, a novelty of Stockholm. Additionality meant that additional aid was to cover the costs of environmental protection, and compensatory aid was to be paid for environmental damage caused beyond the polluter country's jurisdiction.[80]

The Stockholm conference had broadened the environmentalists' agenda beyond conservation and pollution to include development plans and strategies as well as issues of North-South trade.

## Environment and Development as Seen from the East

Given the absence of most socialist countries, the Conference on the Human Environment did not function as a site for détente. Anticipating the possibility of a boycott, the Soviet Union had tried, unsuccessfully, to depoliticize the conference by turning it into an experts' meeting. The Soviets considered disarmament a prerequisite for investing in both development and the environment; without them, disarmament was little discussed in Stockholm.[81] The connection between development and security was addressed by the United Nations, however. In 1955, France requested that resources saved from a gradual reduction in armaments be collected into an international fund, 25 percent of which would go to development. Other, similar proposals followed—a Soviet initiative in 1956, a Brazilian project in 1964—but in the Cold War climate they were not credible. The General Assembly discussed the issue in 1973. That year's Nobel Prize for Economics went to Wassily Leontief, who in 1961 had published an influential essay for *Scientific American* on the relations between disarmament and development.[82] Using input-output analysis to examine disarmament, "The Economic Effects of Disarmament" claimed that reallocating resources from military expenditures would benefit both consumption and employment. Leontief was chosen to elaborate the UN response to the Club of Rome's *Limits to Growth*. His report *The Future of the World Economy* was published by the UN in 1976. It used a comprehensive input-output framework to study the relationships between development, resource use, and pollution. It concluded that in most scenarios there would be a substantial shift in the terms of trade leading to a redistribution of income favoring the less developed countries.[83] Another expert group on disarmament was constituted by the UN General Assembly in 1978, and its head, Inga Thorsson, picked up Leontief's point. The *Relationship between Disarmament and Development* was completed in 1981.[84] The notion of using military industry to civil ends was technically termed "conversion."[85] Many recommended disarmament as an environmental priority, including Nicholas Georgescu-Roegen, whose *Entropy Law and the Economic Process*—a fascinating study of thermodynamic principles applied to the economy—advocated a stationary state, a stable condition in which economic processes merely reproduced themselves and both consumption and population growth were limited. The prerequisite of such a state would be the prohibition of war and all instruments of war, which depleted energy and matter.[86]

Environmental security landed at the Conference for Security and Cooperation in Europe (CSCE), held between July 1973 and August 1975, with a spot in the so-called second basket, devoted to cooperation in the fields of economics, of science and technology, and of the environment. The ideal place to discuss cooperation on environmental issues was, however, the International Institute for Applied Systems Analysis (IIASA), founded in Vienna in 1972. The institute came from an agreement signed in 1967 by President Lyndon Johnson's special envoy, McGeorge Bundy, and Dzhermen Gvishiani, vice chair of the State Committee for Science and Technology of the Council of Ministers of the USSR.[87] Gvishiani was a philosopher and sociologist, as well as the son-in-law of Soviet premier Kosygin, and the head of the Laboratory for Research into Complex Problems of Management of the Institute for Concrete Social Research in the Soviet Union. He worked on the analysis of complex systems, which he thought was the future of planning.[88] He was in touch with Peccei and the Club of Rome, and though he did not share the pessimistic conclusions of the *Limits to Growth*, in November 1972 he prodded the Soviet Academy of Science to organize a conference to discuss the club's report.[89]

Twelve countries participated in the IIASA: England, France, Italy, West Germany, East Germany, Poland, Bulgaria, Canada, Czechoslovakia, and Japan joined the United States and the Soviet Union. Scientists from participating countries worked on three-year multidisciplinary projects. IIASA also engaged in data collection—its research groups covered biomedicine, ecology and the environment, energy systems, industrial systems, urban and regional systems, and hydropower.[90] At this moment, the height of the energy crisis, IIASA's primary focus was the global aspects of energy systems over a fifteen- to fifty-year time frame. The first energy study was the Energy Systems Program. It started in May 1973 and included a working group sponsored by UNEP, the World Meteorological Organization, and SCOPE. It dealt with "energy and climate," or how nuclear, solar, and fossil energy affected the environment. There was minimal faith in solar energy, but atomic energy was seen as highly promising: no surprise, given that the adjunct director of the institute was a West German nuclear physicist, Wolf Häfele.

The first general IIASA conference was held in 1976 to report on its first three years of research. Opened by Austria's chancellor Bruno Kreisky, it was managed by Gvishiani in a spirit of technological optimism: wisely employed, science and technology would greatly benefit humanity.[91] Gvishiani trusted system analysis, informatics technology, and modern management and their ability to predict, evaluate, and manage the social repercussions of scientific and technological advancement. One case study discussed at the conference was the social and economic reorganization required after constructing big dams, based on a comparison of the TVA and the Bratsk-Ilimsk Complex in the Soviet Union, both described as successful.[92] The last IIASA conference on global models was held in 1981: later in the decade, both the belief in system analysis and the willingness to share information that it required were dragged down by new East-West tensions.

## The Legacy of Stockholm and the Invention of Sustainable Development

With the energy crisis in the fall of 1973, caused by the OPEC oil embargo, a new security discourse that included resources, the environment, and population emerged. In late 1973 the German weekly *Der Spiegel*, which had previously given huge space to environmental issues such as water and ocean pollution, devoted every front page of its November issues to what was called "the oil shock." In a special edition published on 19 November 1973, the editors asked whether the oil crisis meant the end of consumer society. In his column, director Rudolf Augstein did not fail to cite the nightmare of overpopulation, arguing that the crisis was an opportunity to rethink the future of humankind.[93] The general discourse moved from the environment to the energy shortage to reflections on pollution as a way to reconsider consumerism. Malaise had turned into crisis. With currencies floating free after the 1971 collapse of the Bretton Woods system and the specter of increasing raw material prices, rich countries in the North felt vulnerable. They were hit hard by the phenomenon of stagflation, a combination of low growth and high inflation, and its social consequences, especially unemployment. This could not fail to alter long-term goals. The question now was not about how to make growth better, but how to get growth at all. In December 1973, prominent European social democratic leaders Willy Brandt, Olof Palme, and Bruno Kreisky met in Schlangenbad and Vienna to envision a postcrisis future. What were the prospects for social democratization on a global scale in a time of crisis?[94] According to them, rethinking consumer society and envisaging a more effective role for the state in the economy looked like an important agenda for a Third World split in two, with one side rich in oil and the other, the so-called Fourth World, prone to deaths from hunger. Social issues had now acquired global dimensions on a scale that could hardly have been imagined earlier, or so Palme and the others said.

In the year of the energy crisis, a discourse connecting austerity with environmental necessity emerged, used in many European countries as an argument for the reduction of oil consumption. However, this was not a surefire argument, as President Jimmy Carter (1977–1981) discovered when he admitted being skeptical about the future and doubting prospects for growth.

His infamous 1979 "Malaise" speech was so ill conceived that many think it cost him reelection.[95] Environmental concerns seemed unable to survive or outweigh economic hardship: environmentalism was indeed the product of wealth.[96]

The tension between environmental protection and development persisted up to the early 1980s.[97] The Club of Rome embraced the view of the developing countries on the primacy of development over environmental issues, also picking up some of the refrains of the NIEO and the criticism of the Western model of consumer society. In February 1974 Peccei organized a meeting in Salzburg, hoping to involve Third World elites in his plans. Luis Echeverría Álvarez from Mexico and Léopold Senghor from Senegal joined Bruno Kreisky and Olof Palme as speakers. In March 1974, Peccei commissioned Jan Tinbergen to write a new report. The team of experts was meant to include the Eastern Bloc, but the Soviets, represented by Gvishiani, were skeptical. The final document, *Reshaping the International Order* (the RIO Report), was presented in Algiers in October 1976. Its title echoed that of the New International Economic Order; this, along with the decision to present the report in a capital with great symbolic value for the Third World, heralded a new age for the Club of Rome.[98] Gvishiani and the Soviets still supported the club, convinced that détente would help solve significant world problems like ecology, energy, and food. Their attitude on environmental issues was inconclusive, however, since their enthusiasm for global models went hand in hand with inadequate environmental protections in their own territory.[99] The real key to saving the planet, the Soviets claimed, was complete and generalized disarmament.[100]

At the end of the 1970s, the Club of Rome was a shadow of its former self, producing reports with ever more vague technocratic accents. Disappointed by the low level of discussion, Strong excoriated the first meeting he took part in, in Stockholm in September 1977. He asked rhetorically whether the Club of Rome had exhausted its mission and now had just a vague global agenda and outdated concepts.[101] Still the soul of the club, Peccei wrote alarmist introductions to the reports, filled with words like disorder, disaster, ignorance, and indifference. Proposals were much less radical and increasingly resorted to a language of participation, respect for religion and values, and global solidarity. Pollution, so crucial in the first report, virtually disappeared. The concern with population growth remained, but the focus shifted to resources and restructuring international relations politically and institutionally. One key point was that development could be funded by the money saved by ending the arms race. Eventually, the club's 1988 report *Beyond the Limits to Growth*, written by Eduard Pestel, broke with the past. It reversed the club's views on a zero-growth-oriented policy, which it now considered a disaster. Technology should meet the needs of the South and be ecologically acceptable, though it was not clear what this meant beyond the gradual abandonment of fossil fuels.[102]

The idea of sustainable development, meaning development that respected the ecosystem, was launched in an UN-sponsored seminar. The term was first used in a 1980 study titled *World Conservation Strategy: Living Resources Conservation for Sustainable Development*, promoted by the International Union for Conservation of Nature and Natural Resources (IUCN). It became a development mantra in the 1990s and remains one today. Used by the Brandt Commission in *North-South: A Programme for Survival* and *Common Crisis North-South*, and by the Palme Commission in *Common Security: A Blueprint for Survival*, after the 1987 Brundtland Commission Report, *Our Common Future*, the term became the most famous oxymoron in the history of international relations.[103]

# 9

# Responding to the Challenges from the Global South

## NORTH-SOUTH DIALOGUES

Human beings have basic needs: food, shelter, clothing, health and education . . . any process of growth that does not lead to their fulfilment—or even worse, disrupts them—is a travesty of the idea of development.

—BARBARA WARD, 1974

"HERE WE STAND after two decades of development trying to pick up the pieces, and we simply do not know whether problems associated with dire poverty have increased or decreased or what real impact the growth of GDP has made on them," World Bank economist Mahbub ul Haq commented bitterly at the World Conference of the Society for International Development in Ottawa on 17 May 1971. In 1968, the Pearson Report had unveiled the limits of past achievements and pronounced aid a moral duty, pressing for more commitments. But did growth, when achieved, result in reduction of the worst forms of poverty? Evaluation of past experience suggested that it rarely did. Did this mean that the challenge of the age—scaling up the welfare state to the world stage—could not be achieved?

The financial cataclysm of the early 1970s was a symptom of a global reshaping, and the West was concerned about the international economic system's durability. The Global South responded to the crisis with a proposal for global economic justice, the New International Economic Order (NIEO). Their challenge was supported by a strategic alliance with the oil-producing countries united in the Organization of the Petroleum Exporting Countries (OPEC). In the rich North, the financial crisis implied a general retreat from state financing of development: major donors became unwilling to sustain earlier levels of state-to-state aid, let alone to make greater structural concessions. How would they respond to the challenges from the developing world? New concepts and strategies had to be devised to face the new North-South divide that seemed to be replacing the classic Cold War conflict. By the 1970s, the United States and the Soviet Union were conservative status quo powers that had more in common with each other than with the Global South. The Cold War was embedded in the international system and worked at much lower levels of tension than in earlier years.[1] Would an East-West cooperation to deal with the Global South be viable? The Soviet Bloc did not appear to be keen on discussing a joint path out of the global economic turmoil, which it interpreted as the long-awaited crisis of capitalism. It was the European Economic Community (EEC), instead, that stood up as a distinctive actor, claiming to be distant from its members' imperial past and to offer a third way for the Third World, with goals that were not those of the Cold War superpowers.

## The Birth of Basic Needs in the Second Development Decade

"It is amazing how two such innocent, five-letters words could mean so many different things to so many different people," commented ul Haq in 1971 about the phrase "basic needs."[2] Development should consist of a "selective attack on the worst forms of poverty," he claimed—malnutrition, disease, illiteracy, squalor, unemployment, and inequalities. In Cocoyoc, Mexico, the great popularizer of development Barbara Ward was categorical: "Human beings have basic needs: food, shelter, clothing, health and education," she said, and "any process of growth that does not lead to their fulfilment—or even worse, disrupts them—is a travesty of the idea of development."[3] Almost overnight, this new approach became the focus of development thinking.[4] International organizations took up the challenge of meeting basic needs. The aims of the Second Development Decade were set out in a series of proposals prepared by a committee of the United Nations Economic and Social Council (ECOSOC) under the leadership of Jan Tinbergen.[5] The Tinbergen report called on the developed countries, including the central planned economies, to help stabilize commodity prices, remove trade protection on manufactures, and intensify technical assistance efforts, with a goal of 1 percent of GDP in resource flows. Along with an average annual rate of growth of 6–7 percent for the less developed countries, it made specific reference to housing, health, education, and employment and included better distribution of income and wealth as a specific development objective. The basic needs revolution—as this new development trend came to be called—was discussed in the International Labour

Organization (ILO), too, which had received the Nobel Peace Prize for its work on social justice in 1969. In September 1970, ILO director David Morse announced that satisfying the minimum needs of a country's citizens was the new standard by which to measure the country's success.[6] Despite criticism from both the right, which saw basic needs as dangerously close to Chinese or Cuban communism, and the left, which saw the concept as a capitalist conspiracy to deny industrialization and modernization, basic needs became the focus of the 1976 World Employment Conference. The conference's final report set out a minimum standard of living that addressed food, housing, clothing, and essential services, including access to drinking water, transportation, health care, and education.[7]

The basic needs strategy conquered American foreign aid, too. In 1970, the Peterson Report had recommended a shift of US development aid to multilateral channels, recommending that capital development aid should be provided through the World Bank group and the regional development banks (Asian Development Bank, Inter-American Development Bank, and African Development Bank). It also recommended that the US bilateral program be primarily technical assistance, redesigned to experiment with new forms of development cooperation such as the financing of rural development banks. Military assistance should be totally separate from aid.[8] The report's recommendations were never adopted because of objections to the move toward multilateralism—but that rejection was just a preview of the much more aggressive attack by US conservatives on foreign aid, which torpedoed the foreign aid bill in 1971–73. Only in 1973 was the deadlock broken, with the move toward basic needs. Founded on a reorganization of AID from an agency defined by geographical categories to one based on three functions—food and nutrition, population planning and health, and education and human resources—the strategy was intended to "increase substantially the participation of the poor in the [recipient] country's development."[9]

In the mid-1970s, the World Bank—influenced by ul Haq—took ownership of the basic needs paradigm, which became the buzzword during Robert McNamara's long presidency (1968–1981).[10] Under his tenure, the bank seemed to change course, with a new interest in promoting development worldwide and the conviction that poverty threatened security. McNamara brought the modernization spirit that had characterized the US foreign aid program in the 1960s to the World Bank. In the 1970s, when the US administration gave up on aid and moved away from North-South aid relations, the World Bank adapted some of the methods of the previous decade for the new one. Rejecting arguments that foreign aid was money down the drain, McNamara stressed that development was morally, economically, and strategically important. A Marshall Plan for the world was necessary because political instability meant "less markets for our products," as he explained on TV in 1971.[11] Influenced as well by Barbara Ward, McNamara elevated poverty to the top of his agenda, in the form of an effort to identify and eliminate whatever stopped economic growth from reaching the poor. Growth focused on industrialization without redistribution could cause poverty instead of eliminating it. Poverty alleviation was introduced not simply as a second-best solution but as the key to tackling the real problems of developing countries: aid was to provide the minimum resources for long-term physical well-being.

Not only did the World Bank become the fulcrum of a reorientation of aid toward antipoverty programs, it also increased the function of study and analysis begun in the late 1960s with the Pearson Report. In a meeting hosted by West German development minister Erhard Eppler in Heidelberg on 19 June 1970, major personalities in politics and development discussed the opportunity for a world economic report. Among them were secretary-general of UNCTAD Manuel Pérez-Guerrero; his predecessor Raúl Prebisch; Emiel van Lennep of the OECD; the secretary of the forthcoming UN Conference on the Human Environment, Maurice Strong; the head of UNDP, Paul Hoffman; the author of the UN proposals for the Second Development Decade, Jan Tinbergen; and the director-general for economic cooperation in the Ministry of Foreign Affairs of Japan, Masao Sawaki.[12] The World Development Report had its origins in this initiative: begun in 1978, it would become the flagship publication of the bank.

## The Lomé Revolution

While the United States was dismantling its aid program, the EEC took a different path. Europe, contended the early activist of European integration François Duchêne, was "a civilian power," a dispenser of civic and democratic standards worldwide, promoting social justice and fighting poverty in the Global South.[13] The 1972 Paris Summit, remembered as the starting point of a European foreign policy, listed cooperation with the Third World as its top priority.[14] With Great Britain finally admitted as a new member in 1973 and the association of Commonwealth countries with the EEC system, did a Eurafrican dimension still make sense, or was a radically different framework needed? Claude Cheysson was the man charged with turning the old structure into something new that would accommodate these changes. A diplomat in the French foreign service after the war, he was removed in the mid-1950s because he supported Algerian independence. He then became secretary-general of the Commission for Technical Co-operation in Africa South of the Sahara (CCTA), revolutionizing its composition and function. Under his lead, the discussion chamber for white colonizers became a political body governed by black Africans. In 1962, Cheysson chaired the Organisme Saharien, the Franco-Algerian cooperation body for management of subsoil resources, where he strove to involve Algerians in decision making. He was French ambassador to Indonesia (1966–1970), then president of Entreprise Minière et Chimique (EMC) and the Compagnie des Potasses du Congo (1970–1973).[15] Appointed development commissioner in 1973, he ruled European aid until 1989, with a parenthesis as François Mitterand's foreign minister (1981–1984).[16] With an expertise that brought him tremendous credibility among African countries, Cheysson reshaped Euro-African relations. "Tomorrow's Europe has its extension in the Third World," he contended, trying to win African support for a new agreement to replace Yaoundé.[17] But Third World voices still considered the EEC policy to be disguised imperialism, fully continuous with Eurafrican ideas of the interwar years.[18] That initial African skepticism, however, was overcome during negotiations, largely because the draft agreement embraced several requests advanced in UNCTAD by the G77.

The resulting Lomé Convention of 28 February 1975 extended association with the EEC to forty-six countries.[19] The bulk of these countries were part of Eurafrica, but the terminology changed significantly: association was replaced by partnership, and associated countries became ACP countries (Africa, Caribbean, and Pacific). As in the Yaoundé agreement, there were two kinds of policies: trade and technical assistance. The main novelty was the abolition of reverse preferences, or systematic mutual reductions of customs duties. The United States had long asked for the termination of this legacy of colonial trade, especially in the GATT. Agricultural and mining products would now enter Europe free of duties, without any reciprocity clause. Commodities that competed with European products were governed by quota systems negotiated separately. The most lauded innovation was Stabex (short for Système de Stabilisation des Recettes d'Exportation), a mechanism for price stabilization of raw materials. Requested by Third World countries, Stabex protected against price volatility by stabilizing revenues from trade in primary commodities. In the event of imbalances, it would provide emergency funds. As for the aid provisions, Lomé introduced a new industrial cooperation and funding for technical assistance amounting to three billion ECUs or European Currency Units, the new unit of account. The British asked for a change in the European Development Fund (EDF), the organization responsible for planning and managing the EEC's technical assistance projects, starting with a switch from project to program aid, so that consistent development plans rather than single projects could be evaluated and financed. The French position, whereby France contributed 30 percent to the budget but its former colonies received 80 percent of the funding, was adjusted.[20] The new agreement was welcomed on all sides, including by its former detractors. Félix Houphouët-Boigny, initially critical, described Lomé as a starting point for a new era, "one of the greatest adventures in the Century."[21]

The next big shakeup came with the departure of Jacques Ferrandi, the technocrat who had long ruled the EDF and embodied the French idea of Eurafrica. Ferrandi resigned just after Lomé: "Le patron du FED s'en va" (The EDF boss is leaving), blared the headline of the Dakar, Senegal, newspaper *Le Soleil* on 10 December 1975.[22] With his departure, EEC development assistance policy became more European. With the contribution of British officer Maurice Foley, a harsh critic of the previous mode of operating, DG Development began rationalizing procedures and embracing international standards on development aid. "Ferrandi style" rules gave way to new criteria for resource allocation, more in line with international practice. A key factor was the move to measuring poverty by per capita parameters that favored overpopulated Asian countries over Africa.[23] Country programming and evaluation, as requested by the British, entered the EEC system.[24] However, procedures did not change that much: the commission still relied on ad hoc political choices, insisting that funding decisions were political matters that could not be wholly based on automatic, computational methods.[25] Only in the 1980s did new development commissioner Edgar Pisani consistently stress programming over the project approach. The key intervention areas in the 1970s were rural development and transportation. Projects were not radically different, with an idealized vision of African reality that saw traditional agriculture as the sector in need of investments still in effect. This commitment was endorsed in *The Courier*, the in-house organ of DG Development that published several special issues on rural development and infrastructure.[26] Rural cooperatives were considered the structural basis for community projects, and while participation was voluntary, surveillance was prevalent enough to recall coercive colonial methods. These features persisted into the 1980s, when innovations like the introduction of microcredit appeared. Although commissioner Pisani extolled the novelties, the projects of the 1980s, like those of the Ferrandi era, were based on soil conservation, rotation of traditional crops, and distrust of modern technology: responding to the need for development did not necessarily mean transferring the most advanced technologies, but rather finding an adequate solution to local problems.[27]

Development commissioner Cheysson saw Lomé as a model of political economic cooperation that could be replicated at a global level.[28] Since he did not believe in universalism, he planned to promote multiple regional agreements resembling Lomé.[29] The ACP policy of general preferences, agreements on commodity prices, and more and better aid including industrial cooperation would be tried elsewhere.[30] Traditionally, regional and world approaches had clashed, but the EEC managed some remarkably inventive thinking in the early 1970s, claiming that it was wrong to see regionalism and globalism as conflicting; they could, in fact, reinforce each other. Cheysson fashioned European policies as an affirmative answer to the demands of the NIEO and presented the European strategy as complementary with nonalignment, which explicitly competed with socialist discourse.[31] The Europe of tomorrow, he claimed, would describe its relations to the Third World in terms of interdependence and offer a policy different from the nation-states'—bolder and less connected to the past.[32] Europe and the Third World needed each other: prosperity and growth would come from building deeper and more integrated ties. Cheysson saw the developing countries as waging an international class struggle against the rich North. The Third World was the world's proletarian class and as such it was entitled to the benefits claimed by the European working class in the nineteenth century: rights, security, and a fair share of wealth.[33] "It is not excessive to state that we will be saved by the poor," he maintained.[34] He also directly attacked the Soviet Union, claiming in a 1978 interview, for example, that the USSR was not a good development partner, and that its history proved the inadequacy of Soviet technical capacity. The Soviets were excellent support in a war of liberation, but with peace their aid went back to risible levels.[35]

Socialist countries fought back. UNCTAD offered a perfect stage for denunciation: in Santiago de Chile in 1972, for example, Hungary and Bulgaria joined with Brazil and Algeria to attack EEC agricultural protectionism.[36] They frequently described the EEC as collective colonialism, typically referring to the Scramble for Africa and the 1885 Berlin Conference.[37] The Lomé Convention was a neocolonial policy, a compromise between packs of imperialist wolves, with all parties trying to impose their will at the expense of others, said commentators from the Soviet Bloc.[38] Lomé offered a broader regional community, but it did not change the division of labor. Association agreements, maintained Hungarian economist Tibor Palàmkai, brought only short-term advantages and paved the way for multinationals through industrial cooperation. EDF and Stabex were too underendowed to have any real impact.[39] In sum, European regionalism was just a way to divide Third World countries so that those with preferential agreements with Europe would not join the bigger cause of Third Worldism or attack EEC protectionism in the United Nations.

## A Regional Plan: The Euro-Arab Dialogue

In the 1970s, with peace on its way in Vietnam and détente lowering East-West tensions, the Mediterranean seemed to be the most explosive area in world politics. Muammar Gaddafi's radical coup in Libya in 1969 and the conflict between Greece and Turkey over Cyprus (1971) added to the wounds of the 1967 Arab-Israeli War, the tragic situation of the Palestinian refugees expelled from Jordan in September 1970, and the PLO attack at the 1972 Munich Olympics. Little surprise, then, that Western Europe, dependent on oil supplies from the Arab countries, focused much of its political efforts there. Houari Boumedienne from Algeria, in a 1973 interview for the Belgian daily newspaper *Le Soir*, argued that now that Europe was assuming a global role, it could choose whether to ally with American imperialists or work with the developing world for their mutual advantage. In the *Manchester Guardian* in January 1974, Saudi prince Abdul Aziz spelled out the terms of this mutual advantage: "We need European expertise in the field of land reclamation, industrialization, and armaments. The Europeans need our oil, our other raw materials, and our markets."[40] Europeans responded both at the EEC level and with single country initiatives, especially from France. The rhetoric of "the new European exceptionalism" promising a third way between East and West, based on partnership and social justice as in the "Lomé model," was tested in the Mediterranean.[41] A Global Mediterranean Policy (GMP) articulated in bilateral agreements had been launched first in 1972. Agreements were structured in three main chapters, including commercial cooperation with preferential tariffs; financial and economic cooperation with capital aid in different forms; and social cooperation, where the EEC pledged to improve the standard of living of immigrant workers in its countries. The first GMP agreement was signed with Israel in 1975; Morocco, Algeria, and Tunisia followed in 1976; and Egypt, Jordan, Lebanon, and Syria in 1977.

With the 1973 oil crisis and the growing concern about securing energy sources, the nascent GMP was flanked by another, more political, initiative: the Euro-Arab Dialogue. Launched in Copenhagen shortly after the October War and the oil embargo, the Euro-Arab Dialogue was a scheme to promote cooperation and networking expertise in the Mediterranean. It created a contractual relationship with Syria and the countries on the southern shore of the Mediterranean (Algeria, Morocco, Tunisia, Egypt), patterned on the Lomé precedent, promising "consistent actions in finance, technology, energy, employment, environment."[42] The problems of the Arab countries, Cheysson argued, had to be dealt with by Europe as domestic issues, and the growth of the Arab world had to be turned into a trump card for Europe.[43] Europe was working for global leadership by setting the Mediterranean at its center, he said.[44] The working paper prepared by the commission in 1975 spoke of harmonizing economic development, addressing industrial cooperation in the petrochemical sector, differentiating industrial activities, and extending training and technology for rural development.[45] The aid component made limited headway: plans for rural development in the Juba Valley in Somalia, prefeasibility studies on potato development in Iraq, and meat production and marketing in Sudan were the projects that occurred first.[46] The Euro-Arab Dialogue was defined as a contract of civilization (*un contrat de civilization*),[47] but while the Europeans prioritized economic issues, Arab countries were keen to discuss politics, especially the Arab-Israeli conflict. In 1975, in an effort to promote cultural affinity, the commission sponsored the journal *Eurabia*, published by the Comité Européen de Coordination des Associations d'Amitié avec le Monde Arabe and headquartered in Paris, whose contributors included intellectuals supporting Euro-Arab unity.[48]

Henry Kissinger dismissed the Euro-Arab Dialogue as an element of tension and confusion, just as he did with any European initiative that did not fit his plans.[49] The Trilateral Commission, the powerful think tank created by David Rockefeller in 1973 to bring together leaders from government and the private sector from North America, Europe, and Japan to discuss issues of global concern, gave the dialogue quite a different reception. Here, EEC action was praised as a regional contribution toward a global understanding.[50] The EEC was acting for the whole West, insisted Cheysson when he spoke at the Trilateral meeting in 1975, highlighting the European role in the Mediterranean and North-South economic relations and pointing his finger at "the relative absence of the Soviet Union and Eastern European states from North-South dialogue and action."[51] Cheysson's Mediterranean dream was now cheered by African leaders like Léopold Senghor who had initially been skeptical. Senghor, facing hardships at home with the move toward a multiparty system and the progressive democratization of Senegalese politics, hailed the economic community of Europe and the Arab countries as a laboratory for civilization centered on the Mediterranean. In his talk at a Club of Rome meeting in Stockholm in September 1977, he described it as a step toward Eurafrica, a solution to African balkanization that would be able to include all its components, black and Arab, even, eventually, Israel and Iran, an unlikely geopolitical imaginary.[52] Expanding the Lomé method to the southern Mediterranean did not yield the desired results, however, as countries there resisted horizontal economic partnerships with each other and had no interest in creating a real community.

## North-South Dialogue: The Global Dimension

While the EEC was cultivating joint Mediterranean plans, its members promoted other strategies. French president Valéry Giscard d'Estaing, for instance, started direct talks with President Gerald Ford (1974–1977) on how to respond to the world economic crisis. The result of this initiative was a summit in Rambouillet (France) on 15–17 November 1975. The meeting included the big five

Western countries: the United States, Japan, France, Germany, and the UK, plus, at the last minute, Italy. The starting point was the recognition that in matters such as defense, energy, trade, and development aid, individual efforts could "only have lasting success if supported by the contributions of all." Much of the discussion revolved around the topic of "Energy, Raw Materials, and Development," particularly oil shortages and their impact on Western societies, especially on employment.[53] Notwithstanding the blow the oil shock had given to Western confidence, everyone at the table believed that prices were about to go down and that the answer was reducing dependency on OPEC oil imports by diversifying energy sources. British prime minister Harold Wilson was alarmed by the OPEC syndrome—that is, the rapid growth of associations of producers of raw materials: phosphates, bauxite, bananas, tin, sugar, cocoa, coffee, wheat, copper, and tea were all under consideration. German chancellor Helmut Schmidt was the most supportive of EEC ideas, planning to initiate "something analogous to the Lomé agreement" (i.e., Stabex): a global system of price stabilization. Concerned with preventing a bloc of developing countries from ganging up against the West under OPEC leadership, the United States wanted to promote consumer/producer dialogue.[54] Insisting on its leadership in mediating between North and South—nothing in this area can work without our support, read the memorandum prepared for the meeting—the United States did not bother to hide its annoyance at the EEC's autonomous initiatives. The Third World, noted Henry Kissinger, was no monolith: poor LDCs (the Fourth World) and OPEC could be split off from each other; Japanese prime minister Miki agreed.

The Rambouillet Summit was considered a success, and summits became the new system of governance in trans-Atlantic relations. President Ford hastily organized another high-profile conference to emphasize Western cohesion and leadership, in Puerto Rico, 27–28 June 1976. Canada was also invited, and from then on, the yearly summit where international economic issues could be discussed informally was called the G7. In Puerto Rico, they debated North-South political issues, especially how to reach a common approach to conditions for Third World aid and to terms of credit for the Soviet Bloc countries. The US administration planned to use aid as a bargaining tool in Asian, Middle Eastern, and African negotiations, while dramatically cutting back on the multilateral front.[55] Kissinger was blunt about this: "Virtually all North-South aid comes from the developed democracies or their close association—so we need not be defensive at international conferences—or act competitively with each other." He asked for more discussion on the commitment of the industrialized democracies to aid LDCs: development came from the major countries, and the LDCs had to be clear that they had no other place to go. In terms of aid, however, ideas were distant and the meeting inconclusive.[56]

Notwithstanding, Kissinger ended on a positive note, denying the picture of a Soviet Bloc on the offensive and Western democracies on the decline in response to those who believed that, in the final act of decolonization, the world was going the Soviets' way.[57] This argument was based on the resurgence of Eastern Bloc international initiatives. The collapse of the Portuguese empire had opened up new avenues for Soviet influence in Africa, where the Soviets had had friendly contacts with national liberation movements since the early 1960s—with FRELIMO and its People's Republic in Mozambique and with the People's Movement for the Liberation of Angola (Movimento Popular de Libertação de Angola, MPLA), where, along with Cuba, they had intervened in the civil war.

After a whole year of discussions in vain, in 1975 the tone around the 1973–74 NIEO proposal started changing.[58] The United States and West Germany resumed dialogue, distinguishing between the poorest countries (the least developed and those that were landlocked) and more advanced ones. The latter would receive agreements facilitating access to the markets of developed countries rather than aid. North-South relations were discussed along these lines in a special arena: the Conference for International Economic Cooperation (CIEC), also called North-South Dialogue, which began as an international conference on energy among OPEC members, the industrial countries, and non-oil-rich developing nations. The CIEC met in Paris between December 1975 and June 1977 to deal with oil, trade, development, and the financial crisis. Its work was organized in four thematic commissions (energy, raw materials, development, and finance) that discussed position papers. Developing countries thought of the CIEC as an UNCTAD-like agency where they could advance requests for industrial cooperation and technology transfer. Developed countries, instead, wanted a permanent forum on energy, which they hoped to use as a counterweight to OPEC. US policy in the North-South Dialogue involved blaming OPEC for poor countries' rising energy bills and debt, while showing openness to discussing some of the developing countries' requests. Helmut Schmidt saluted the CIEC as the ideal place to break up the unholy alliance between the LDCs and OPEC by exposing the connection between debt problems and skyrocketing oil prices. "We can make the point that the newly rich countries have to take part in new development aid in accordance with their new riches," he contended, and convince LDCs of the West's genuine interest in their well-being by having an open attitude toward price stabilization for raw materials.[59] The CIEC should thus set in motion cooperative programs by producers and the industrialized nations that would ease the financial burdens of LDCs coping with high oil prices. The EEC had already set a precedent with the Cheysson Fund, an emergency package for developing countries hit by the oil shock, which was endowed with 500 million ECUs.[60]

The North-South Dialogue was often discussed at the G7, where key participants were in no position (many faced elections) to promote decisive actions and insisted that only existing international economic institutions could provide solutions to the problems of the Global South as an alternative to the NIEO.[61] The eighteen months of the CIEC brought minuscule results. In June 1977, agreement was reached on just a few points, including a Special Action Program to help meet the urgent needs of individual low-income countries ($1 billion, of which the US share was to be $375 million, and the EEC's contribution $385 million), a Common Fund to finance buffer stocks for raw materials exported by the less developed countries (to be discussed in the UNCTAD), and a pledge to increase bilateral aid. Comprehensive reports about the CIEC were all negative. The detailed account in *Foreign Affairs* by Iranian economist and ambassador at large Jahangir Amuzegar was called "A Requiem for the North-South Conference."[62] The memorandum prepared by the US undersecretary of state for economic affairs, Richard Cooper, was called "Post Mortem on CIEC." Developing countries, Amuzegar said, were disappointed because the agreement fell short of promising a path toward a New International Economic Order: no long-term solutions for their problems of development aid, raw materials export, and debt had emerged from the CIEC. The industrial countries, which had offered certain concessions in the expectation of pledges from LDCs in energy prices and supply but had received nothing in return, were also baffled. The lesson learned, concluded Amuzegar's opinionated article, was twofold. The electorate in the affluent parts of the world had to learn that an international economic system still based on colonial relationships and unequal partnership between the haves and the have-nots had to change—for everyone's good, developed and developing countries alike. The Third World public, in turn, needed to realize that age-old global injustices and inequities could not be redressed in a short time and that dialogue with the industrial countries was still the best way to achieve results. The US delegation's take-home message was more one sided: "We have allowed the developing countries to seize the moral ground," Cooper said in his report. Yes, some elements were encouraging, especially the lack of acrimony and hostility that had accompanied the North-South Dialogue at the height of the oil crisis. However, developing countries were still after the New International Economic Order, and they planned to threaten to use oil prices to attain it, or so it seemed from the words of Manuel Pérez-Guerrero, now Venezuelan minister of foreign economic affairs and cochair of the CIEC.[63]

What was missing from the North-South Dialogue was the Soviet Bloc. US president Jimmy Carter raised the issue during negotiations at the CIEC in 1977; at Rambouillet, Italian prime minister Aldo Moro had insisted on a Socialist Bloc contribution to multilateral aid institutions as a condition for better East-West economic relations. In Puerto Rico, Helmut Schmidt had raised the point of countering Soviet weapons sales to the Southern Hemisphere.[64] In January 1977, Carter wrote to Brezhnev relaunching détente; there was much that the two countries could cooperate on: "development, better nutrition, and a more meaningful life for the less fortunate portions of mankind."[65] The idea of opening up East-West cooperation on North-South issues was thoroughly discussed in the Trilateral Commission, which included President Carter and several key personalities of his administration.[66] In 1976, Carter's prospective national security adviser Zbigniew Brzezinski, also a Trilateral Commission member, had prepared a document on reforming the international system, "Towards a Renovated International System," which was discussed at the Trilateral meeting in Tokyo, 9–11 January 1977. But under his scheme, the World Bank would control aid, and what was the likelihood of the Soviets following the guidelines of a Western-controlled institution that excluded them?[67] The report of the Trilateral task force on "Constructive Communist Global Involvement" considered cooperation desirable in all nine areas of global concern—food, energy, oceans, space, weather, earthquake warning, development aid, trade and monetary policy, and nuclear nonproliferation. But while East-West trade and nuclear nonproliferation were promising, other areas, including development aid, were less so.[68] The analysis prepared by the Policy Planning Staff for Secretary of State Cyrus Vance in June 1977 on "Prospects for Expanded Soviet Bloc Role in North-South Problems" was equally pessimistic. The Soviets did not intend to dilute the political impact of their assistance by incorporating it within the broader efforts of the industrialized (Western) nations. Their focus on arms and military equipment gave them a huge short-run political impact—in Southern Africa and the Horn, for example, where in 1977 Ethiopia's Mengistu Haile Mariam had opted for scientific socialism and obtained Soviet military aid. They would never renounce that strategy and were happy to leave the Western countries with the more burdensome and controversial longer-term economic aid. In authentic Cold War spirit, the report to Vance concluded that "a genuinely cooperative effort" with the aim of dampening East-West political competition had hardly any chance of success, whereas revealing Soviet inadequacies and exposing the Soviets to criticism on the part of the developing countries could still be useful.[69]

## Development and Human Rights

In the mid-1970s, an animated debate took place on whether the New International Economic Order was compatible with international law. Third World legal scholars articulated their requests in sophisticated legal language; international law was a creature of the West, but if adapted to the changed environment, it could be used to the advantage of the decolonizing world.[70] Latin American jurists, like International Court of Justice judge Alejandro Álvarez, had long advocated a regional approach to law and requested limits on exploitation of natural resources.[71] Throughout the 1960s, reclaiming sovereignty over natural resources achieved outstanding results from the Third World's point of view, and the oil elites had been successful in reversing the colonial legacy of the concessionary regime. Mohammed Bedjaoui, an influential legal scholar close to Boumedienne's Algeria, questioned the rulings on successor states that bound newly independent countries to agreements signed during colonial rule. He contended that international law should be changed to accommodate the Third World's requests.[72] Advocates of the NIEO made the case for a new discipline, international development law, that would regulate relations between developed and developing countries. The classic Western principles of equality, reciprocity, and nondiscrimination needed adjustment in order to compensate for structural inequality.[73]

In the mid-1970s, human rights gained new prominence in international politics, largely because of campaigns initiated by advocacy groups, most notably the human rights NGO par excellence, Amnesty International.[74] After a long delay, in 1976 both the International Covenant on Civil and Political Rights and the International Covenant on Economic, Social and Cultural Rights, adopted by the United Nations General Assembly in 1966, finally entered into force. Third World legal scholars rephrased the NIEO program in human rights terms. In the 1973 report *The Widening Gap*, Iranian diplomat Manouchehr Ganji made the case for granting social and economic rights to the Third World.[75] Western public opinion, contended Amuzegar, Iran's ambassador at large in Washington, had to understand that human rights embraced not only the right to free speech, assembly, and political association, but also the right to a decent life free from desperation, despair, disease, ignorance, and idleness.[76] He was clearly critical of approaches where the commitment to a classic concept of human rights prevailed over development. President Carter, in fact, in the first postelection articulation of his foreign policy, the famous Notre Dame commencement address on 22 May 1977, spoke in favor of equal trade, which would help countries help themselves. This formulation nodded to both traditional concepts of US foreign aid (self-help) and developing countries' requests for equality. His position was sufficiently ambiguous, sympathetic to the Third World but still distant from the idea of structural changes claiming social justice through compensation in favor of less developed countries.

Carter had campaigned on adopting a more accommodating policy toward the developing countries, but his administration was clearly betting that Third World unity would not last. Indeed, it disrupted what was left of it by seeking cooperation with the most advanced countries and providing charitable aid to the poorest. In December 1975, prospective national security adviser Brzezinski outlined his ideas on foreign affairs: along with trilateral cooperation among the advanced democracies, détente with the Soviets, and the courting of China, relations with the Global South figured prominently.[77] The plan was twofold: closer relations with the emerging Third World countries went along with compassionate multilateral aid for the Fourth World. These lines were then developed in "A Memorandum to the President Elect," which spoke of the United States' recent history as the most hard-nosed of the industrial countries in resisting the demands of the developing countries for the NIEO.[78] It recommended that the new administration soften the anti-NIEO rhetoric and correct the "growing and embarrassing shortfall on the multilateral front" by paying its promised contribution to the World Bank and its soft loan affiliate, the International Development Agency (IDA).[79] An injection of staff from the Overseas Development Council (ODC), notably Senior Fellows Roger Hansen and Guy Erb, who joined the National Security Council, led to a major rethinking of foreign aid.[80] Hansen suggested that the United States embrace both human rights and basic economic rights. A basic human needs approach, he argued, could provide a comprehensive framework that would help break the North-South Dialogue's deadlock.[81] In order to "reinforce positive human rights and democratic tendencies in the Third World," the focus should be on the "promotion of economic and social rights," with the goal of a more equitable and humane social and economic order.[82] In an idealized conception of global community, every nation cared for both economic justice and economic growth.[83]

The Carter administration tried to refashion North-South dialogue along these lines by moving it away from trying to restructure the NIEO to finding pragmatic ways to improve it. This task had to be embraced with determination. Undersecretary Cooper lamented: "I feel that we are in a defensive position on too many fronts. . . . Our policies can be described by one word, containment." Luckily for the United States, for the time being the Soviet Bloc was not involved in the North-South Dialogue, and Chinese influence was limited.[84] What road to take, then? In August 1978, Cooper sketched a strategy based on two lines of action: regaining the initiative in moral and humane values and promoting US technology on the model of Truman's Point Four.[85] Neither of these objectives aligned with the NIEO, and Third World leaders like Venezuelan president Carlos Andrés Pérez were clearly disappointed by the US attitude.[86]

The tension between a macro and a micro approach to development—that is, the tension between the global redistribution of power centered on the state (NIEO) and the antipoverty strategy centered on the individual (basic needs)—dominated the second half of the 1970s. Debates about the compatibility of the two ideas raged in the social sciences and international law. The NIEO was a codification of international social justice, aiming at a better distribution of wealth among countries, whereas basic needs were a codification of intranational social justice, working on domestic redistribution within individual poor countries. The first requested a radical reform of the system and the recognition of the right to development as a human right. NIEO helped countries accumulate economic surpluses, but there were no guarantees that these surpluses would be used to meet basic needs and fight poverty, or so said basic needs supporters. On the other hand, NIEO advocates considered basic needs a distraction from the core principle of achieving international economic justice by addressing structural inequality. Since the basic needs approach applied predominantly to the Global South, leaders of the Non-Aligned Movement, meeting in Belgrade on 25–30 July 1978, saw it as a ploy for obscuring "the urgent need for fundamental change in the world economic order," if not a blatant attempt to slow down the growth of the Third World by reducing capital assistance.[87] In the UN Human Rights Commission, Indian delegate Vijaya Lakshmi Pandit pointed out that the basic needs strategy implied that the only problem of developing countries was providing a minimum standard, whereas the real problem was much bigger: a problem of international economic and social justice.[88]

Economist Paul Streeten, senior adviser at the World Bank, countered that basic needs by no means interfered with the NIEO. But were minimum levels of nutrition, health, and education fundamental human rights? Or were human rights themselves basic needs?[89] Making development itself a right would bring the Global South's demand for equality within the emergent human rights revolution. But was it possible or even fair to identify the cause of development with the cause of human rights? The NIEO requests were human rights neutral and thus could be consistent with human rights violations.[90] In 1977, the General Assembly discussed the idea of a Human Right to Development, which the members of the Third World claimed would support the quest for a more just global order. On the other hand, the NIEO was based on a recognition of legal inequality that would clash with the structure of the United Nations, which was (and is) based on the principle of sovereign equality. The UN Commission for Human Rights requested that the secretary-general undertake a study of "the international dimensions of the right to development as a human right," considering the right to peace, the requirements of the NIEO, and fundamental human needs. Submitted in 1979, the report was pretty anodyne: it stressed that the human person is the subject of development and that development requires satisfaction of both material and nonmaterial basic needs, including political and civil rights, but also employment and education.

Parliaments in the West were increasingly concerned with respect for individual human rights, intended in the narrow sense of basic rights of the person, a definition that was appropriate to deal with the problems in the countries under military dictatorship in Latin America—Brazil starting in 1964, Chile under Pinochet, Argentina with the *desaparecidos*—and Greece under the Colonels. The Global South was a place where gross violations of human rights could no longer be silenced, but human rights were also an issue in the delicate balance of détente, with dissidents in Central and Eastern Europe calling on the Soviet Union to respect the human rights clauses of the 1975 Helsinki Final Act. In the first three months of his term, President Carter cut economic aid to several countries in Latin America, Asia, and Africa because of their human rights violations.[91] The US Congress was concerned that development funds were being used to prop up abusive regimes in the developing world.[92] Between 1973 and 1979, the European Parliament passed 530 resolutions on human rights, claiming to be "the conscience and the critical voice of Europe."[93] The issue entered the negotiations of the second Lomé Convention. In case of flagrant violations of human rights, "public opinion, workers, and young people in our countries would . . . withdraw their support for a real joint development policy with the Third World," Cheysson declared.[94]

Should the EEC officially make development assistance in Asia, Africa, and Latin America dependent on respect for human rights? Since the 1950s, Third World countries had urged the international community to take up the question of human rights, articulating it in terms of self-determination and taking a stand against gross violations such as apartheid and torture in South Africa: Why would they now not be willing to make respect for human rights a general principle?[95] The issue was complicated. Cheysson doubted that stopping aid was an "effective means of helping downtrodden populations that are denied the most basic human rights."[96] The public, though, pressed for making foreign aid conditional on a minimum standard of respect for human rights. The exemplary case was Idi Amin's Uganda, where the regime's crimes were condemned by NGOs such as Amnesty International and there was public backlash against aid. Given that sanctions in cases of violation of human rights were not in the Lomé agreement, the EEC intervened in 1977 with the so-called Uganda guidelines, which suspended aid disbursements. Equatorial Guinea in 1978, the Central African Republic in 1979, and Liberia in 1980 were likewise sanctioned because of gross human rights violations. A specific clause on political conditionality went into the new Lomé Convention, Lomé II (1981–1985).[97] However, the clause was watered down and did not mention cases of gross violations of human rights. Instead, aid would be suspended if norms of fair working conditions established by the ILO were unmet.[98] Conditionality remained unresolved through the turn of the century.

The introduction of human rights into the development equation was a massive shift. From the Global South's point of view, human rights looked like a pretext, given the decades the West had spent supporting anticommunist dictators. Rights talk was just another example of cultural arrogance from a Global North that now used interdependence and basic needs to offer patronizing palliative solutions: clearly, these were no consolation prize for the denial of distributional justice.[99]

"For international purposes we should act together," warned Julius Nyerere in 1977. "We may criticize tyrannical, brutal, or unjust governments and regimes in the Third World, but we must not do this in the context of the North-South debate."[100] This warning was not enough to make the Third World a cohesive and organized force. In 1979 at the nonaligned summit in Havana, the rift between the moderates (India, Egypt, Indonesia, Sri Lanka, and Yugoslavia) and radicals (Cuba, Iraq, Libya, and Vietnam) widened.[101] In the 1980s, with the worsening of the financial condition of Third World countries plunged in the debt crisis, the NIEO was not on the agenda anymore, not even in UNCTAD. In Belgrade, at UNCTAD's sixth session in June 1983, the NIEO was officially declared dead.[102] A new topic emerged: mismanagement of aid by the recipient countries. In the NIEO, revolution and conservation had shared the stage. Revolution was reserved for the international system and the global distribution of power: bringing down existing hierarchies and structures would create the ideal conditions for Third World development. But domestically, the opposite held sway, and they were totally opposed to changes in resource management and income redistribution. The new developmental wisdom prescribed that what needed reform and modernization was the state, not the international system: it was no longer about restructuring international trade, but about reforming domestic policies.[103] The failure of the NIEO exposed the weakness of the South vis-à-vis the North.

# 10

# The Dynamics of the Lost Decade

The one common characteristic of the Third World is not poverty, stagnation, exploitation or skin colour. It is the receipt of foreign aid.

—PETER T. BAUER, 1984

"IN THE HALLS of this building, there is much talk about the right to development. But it is becoming ever more evident that development is not a right in itself. . . . Those who advocate public solutions to the problem of development should take into account that free market is the alternative to development and this is the only right way. Unlike many other ways, this one leads to the goal. It works." These were the words of US president Ronald Reagan in 1987, at the forty-second session of the United Nations General Assembly.[1] They signaled the divorce of American hegemonic projects from development. An abyss separated Reagan's words from the project of the New International Economic Order that had dominated debate just a few years earlier. In Ronald Reagan's plans, there was no room for development. At home and abroad, Reaganomics—as his economic policy was called—advocated deregulation and reduction in government spending. As for security, rearmament and militarization trumped soft power.

The 1980s are often described as the lost decade in the history of development, when the allegedly universal crusade against poverty failed to deliver the expected results.[2] In 1968, one book anticipated an incipient systemic aid crisis.[3] It featured two opposing views on development: one from Barbara Ward, then a Carnegie Fellow at Harvard University, the other from Peter T. Bauer, a development economist at the London School of Economics. Ward's essay "A Study in Frustration?" was optimistic about the prospect of moving the funds saved by disarmament into increased aid. Bauer, in contrast, was pessimistic. Titled "Foreign Aid: An Instrument for Progress?," his essay answered its question with a definite "no." Bauer argued that aid compromised efficient allocation and was damaging for everyone, and in the 1970s and especially the 1980s, he became the spokesperson for this revisionist view of aid. He upended the discourse on morality characteristic of the aid culture of international organizations and central to publications such as the Pearson Report. Aid, he contended, was immoral, especially if paid for by public money. It was a waste, a nonessential element of world development.[4] Calling aid by its real name of "government to government subsidies" would dispel its beneficent aura and allow for a more objective evaluation of spending. There was no significant correlation, Bauer argued, between aid and development. The latter happened mostly without external assistance, in Europe and elsewhere. The narrative of aid as an enlightened policy was told to promote security or the political interests of donors and was modeled on post–World War II successes that were long past.[5]

"Without aid," Bauer claimed, "there is no such collectivity as the Third World or South. Foreign aid is, therefore, the source of North-South conflict, not its solution."[6] Aid had unleashed the forces behind persistent civil wars, induced politicization of the economy, and distorted the rules of the game. Altruistic or reparative motives were just a smoke screen for political or financial interests. In his study of India, Bauer claimed that technologically grand programs would not do the job of promoting development. His solution for fixing development focused on liberalizing domestic trade in recipient countries.[7] What was needed for growth was ability, motivation, traditions, institutions, and working in concert: indeed, "a society which cannot develop without external gifts is altogether unlikely to do so with them."[8] In the end, what accounted for success was the existence of a civil society fabric that could support development.[9] Maladministration was responsible for failure, channeling investments in unproductive sectors, while political divisions within the country blocked potentially efficient minorities.[10] Bauer's teaching had a major legacy in both Western policy making and in the theory, most notably through the works of Dambisa Moyo and William Easterly.[11]

Criticism à la Bauer became the norm in the 1980s, which development enthusiasts describe as an era of "crisis in hegemonic vision."[12] At the same time, new emergencies surfaced, including famine. Given the optimism about the Green Revolution, in 1975 the versatile philosopher, sociologist, and pedagogue Ivan Illich said in *Medical Nemesis* that it was incredible that malnutrition was still "by far the most important threat to modern man."[13] In the 1980s, food scarcity, along with climate change, illness, refugee flows, and distributional bottlenecks in Asia and Africa, began to be seen as a security threat.[14] When the Brandt Report, commissioned by World Bank president Robert McNamara in 1977, came out in 1980, it revived awareness of food issues. Initially, the former West German chancellor's Independent Commission for

International Development set out to see where development stood ten years after the Pearson Report. Although inspired by the prospect of democratic social reform on a global scale, possibly through a redistribution of the profits from taxing the world arms trade, the report was much less groundbreaking than planned. It dealt with basic needs, especially food, outlining four lines of action: a massive transfer of resources, the inauguration of an international energy strategy, the institution of a world food program, and reforms in the global economic and financial system. Equitable economic relations were considered crucial to the promotion of peace and security.[15] UN secretary-general Kurt Waldheim greeted the report as "a welcome basis" for a new effort to create a breakthrough in the North-South Dialogue.[16]

Meanwhile, discussions on North-South issues followed the dual path designed during the 1970s. On one side there was the UN, with the G77-led discussion on the New International Economic Order, and on the other, the North-South Dialogue, steered by the developed countries in the West. In 1979, the UN General Assembly had called for global negotiations on raw materials, trade, energy, development, and finance. It resumed discussion on the NIEO under a new name: Global Negotiations on International Economic Cooperation. The G77, Japan, Canada, and the "EC10" (the nine member states plus the EEC Commission) confirmed their attendance. Unwilling to discuss NIEO again, neither the United States nor the Soviet Union took part in the preparatory phase, thus confirming the South's view that the two superpowers were more similar than they admitted. US secretary of state Alexander Haig had promised "a fresh American approach" and the guarantee of being radically different from the Eastern Bloc: "We support economic development; the East does not. We assist the refugees, the East refuses relief. We offer the peaceful mediation of dispute; the East offers only arms of conflict."[17] The trumpeted differences were destined to remain unnoticed, given that talks on global negotiations that were to have begun in December 1980 never made it onto the agenda.[18]

Yet discussions on North-South issues resumed on another stage: the North-South Summit convened in Cancun, Mexico, in October 1981. Called for by Austrian chancellor Bruno Kreisky and Mexican foreign minister Jorge Castaneda, the Cancun Summit was meant to give an impetus to the global-round negotiations that had started in the UN framework "by means of achieving a real meeting of minds."[19] Given the inclinations of the participants, though, the summit was highly unlikely to bring change. New leaders Margaret Thatcher and Ronald Reagan intended to talk about opening markets and encouraging private investments, which was not what developing countries had in mind.[20] Instead of discussing the international economic order, industrialized countries insisted on debating the inflationary impact of petro dollars on the international economy, which, they said, threatened all the nonoil countries, rich and poor alike.[21] In a meeting with Secretary-General Waldheim, German chancellor Helmut Schmidt claimed that a new international economic order could not solve the problems of the Global South, nor could an increase in development aid. It was the price of oil that was destroying the developing countries, he contended. In the climate of the Second Cold War following the Soviet invasion of Afghanistan in December 1979, Schmidt held that development did not enhance security. East-West tensions "originated in the developing countries because of interference by the industrialized countries in the Third World."[22] The changed political context was fatal to global negotiations; the developing world's attempt to bring the US-dominated Bretton Woods institutions, the World Bank and the International Monetary Fund, directly under United Nations control failed miserably. It was, as the US State Department commented without regret, "the last gasp of a decade-long effort at multilateral diplomacy."[23]

In his review of the historiography of development, Joseph Hodge highlights the convergence of criticism from the left and right in the 1980s.[24] It made for strange bedfellows: critics included those like the Ayatollah Khomeini in Iran, for example, who denounced Western civilization as evil and corrupt and saw progress as disruptive of higher values, and neoliberal followers of Peter Bauer, like economists Deepak Lal, Bela Balassa, or Ian Little, who equated developmental failure with state failure. On the left, some postmodern thinkers rejected modernity, preferring a romantic idea of the rural Third World, while systems thinkers such as Immanuel Wallerstein attacked capitalism as the most exploitative system ever devised, at least for the vast majority on the periphery.[25] Criticism also came from those who had participated in the global aid system and now renounced it. One was Brigitte Erler, who had served in the West German Ministry of Cooperation, but who in the mid-1980s wrote a book that unmercifully described the mistakes of West German development aid in Bangladesh and pointed out the racism inherent in the patronizing idea of foreign assistance.[26]

In the early 1980s, neoliberal criticism of development continued apace. Critics railed against the social engineering underlying development and extolled the virtues of the market. The World Bank made no exception, as it moved away from Robert McNamara's basic needs–based policies, now considered harmful (because they fueled debt) rather than useful. During the 1970s, while major donors retreated from bilateral lending (Official Development Aid from OECD countries decreased from 0.65 percent of GDP in 1965 to 0.23 percent in 1979), the World Bank had increased its commitments from $1 billion in 1968 to $13 billion in 1981.[27] Cynical developing countries thought that it was "the rich countries' substitute for the NIEO."[28] But results were poor, and key elements of the system came under attack: the overextension of the public sector with duties beyond normal governmental functions, excessive emphasis on physical capital and the resulting underestimation of human capital, and the proliferation of economy-distorting controls. The African case was seen as exemplifying the distortions caused by antipoverty World Bank policies. It was studied by a World Bank report entrusted to economist Elliot Berg in 1979 and published two years later as *Accelerated Development in Sub-Saharan Africa: An Agenda for Action.* Poor performance in African economies, the Berg report argued, was not attributable to the legacy of colonialism or declining commodity prices, but to population pressure, modest agricultural outcomes, and perverse and wasteful government policies compounded by external indebtedness. Domestic policy inadequacies such as overvalued exchange rates, protectionist trade policies, and overextended public sectors were reinforced by a consistent bias against agriculture. Accommodating the great variety of economic structures in Sub-Saharan Africa, the report offered a solution: a clear focus on the rural economy, a more efficient public sector, and a greater reliance on the private sector were the ways to address African underdevelopment.[29]

When the long-latent debt crisis surfaced with the default of Mexico in August 1982, the effort to consider the ethics of globalization received its final blow, and the neoliberal political economy became the real new international economic order. In 1985, the World Bank made its move away from basic needs and its watered-down compromise for global justice explicit with the document *New Research Priorities: The World Has Changed—So Has the Bank.*[30] Mirroring the West, especially the United States, the World Bank had reoriented its priorities. With the electoral success of conservatives in the United States, Great Britain, and West Germany, supply-side economics was in its glory. Neoliberal policies could free the market from excess state rules, reduce taxation, privatize state companies, liberalize the labor market, and minimize the welfare state, or so conservatives claimed.[31] A structural adjustment policy—that is, a standard package of reforms that cut public expenditure and the role of the state—was prescribed to the countries asking the World Bank and the International Monetary Fund for assistance: a strategy that came to be called the Washington Consensus. Structural adjustment promoted situations of economic security that granted investors as much as possible. The focus on country programming, absorptive capacity, and project feasibility that had largely oriented the bank's policies since the 1950s was now reemphasized. McNamara's revolution was quickly forgotten. Poverty reduction ceased to be a goal, and growth was again a top priority.[32]

The new antistate doctrine was anathema to developing countries. Unwilling to succumb to the North's ideological agenda, they saw structural adjustment as a violation of their national sovereignty and tried to avoid the harsher measures of the neoliberal counterrevolution.[33] At the end of the 1980s, several studies analyzed the adverse impact of structural adjustment on poverty, the environment, and gender issues.[34] "When this talk of liberalization and deregulation came in," recalls Gamani Corea, UNCTAD secretary-general from 1974 to 1984, "it was not enough to clear the stage" and remove what the neoliberals called the obstacles in the way.[35] The prior emphasis on state power, he claimed, had come not from a socialist orientation, but from the practical reality that the state was usually the only strong actor in these countries, many of whom were "too weak to rely on the private sector to do the things that developed countries encouraged them to do." Neoliberals, in contrast, saw the state as the origin of inefficiency and development failures. The key to growth was cutting expenditures and promoting openness. The success stories they used to support their view were the so-called Asian Tigers—Hong Kong, Singapore, South Korea, and Taiwan—small countries with export-oriented economies. Curiously enough, neoliberal advocates did not mention that strong state structures had been crucial to making the Asian Tigers' economies work.[36]

As for the Soviet Bloc, by the end of the 1970s it increasingly saw development as a global problem to be handled with comprehensive tools. In 1979, at UNCTAD III, the Soviet Union adopted a new attitude, its previously harsh tones giving way to an openness toward East-West economic relations.[37] Discussions about international trade rules should not cover only North-South relations: they should be generalized. Nonetheless, the attack on multinational companies typical of the 1970s was still a part of Soviet discourse. While the West moved toward neoliberalism, the East moved toward de-ideologization, in business in and with the Third World. Trilateral projects, where West and East worked together in a developing country, functioned satisfactorily, and the Soviet Union continued to partner with multinationals. One example was the Cuanza River basin in Angola, a 1982 cooperative project with a Brazilian engineering firm, Oderbrecht, financed by Portuguese capital, to construct a hydroelectric power plant and prepare a land reclamation scheme.[38] As a global strategy, though, trilateral agreements were less widespread, because the West considered them a tool that socialist countries used to reap political advantages at a reasonable price.[39]

For the USSR, the notion of the Third World was still critical, even though Soviet orthodoxy went out of its way—and closer to the Western point of view—to point out the differences and cleavages within a group that claimed to be cohesive. At the Twenty-Sixth Congress of the CPSU, Leonid Brezhnev reiterated the words of Soviet social scientists: the vast majority of developing countries were still fixated on the idea of catching up via capitalist-type growth—that is, at all costs and without regard for social consequences.[40] Another approach was to argue that the very concept of the Third World was a conceptual error, as historian Nodari Simonia did in 1985; it was just as wrong as the idea of a third way, which did not exist. Nonalignment and "compound and multi-structural systems" did not qualify as a distinct world system. Before independence, the "countries of the East" (the collective term Simonia used to mean what we now call the Global South) had been part of the world imperialist system, "specifically its politically oppressed and economically exploited component." This legacy still influenced their international economic relations.[41] While the Soviet Union did not talk of the "Third World," other socialist countries did. For example, the mixed East German and Hungarian historians' commission constituted in 1987 used the expression "Third World" in criticizing the notion of a dichotomy between a wealthy North and a poor South.[42] Reflecting the greater dependence of their countries on world trade, Eastern European studies of the Third World were less ideological and much more dispassionate than Soviet ones in addressing the developing countries' needs, prospects, and problems.[43]

The Soviet analyses in the 1980s were as hostile to Third World leaders as the West was, often accusing them of abusing their bureaucratic powers. A collective volume published in 1982, with writings by Karen Brutents, Rostislav Ulianovsky, Andrey A. Gromyko, and Yevgeny M. Primakov, among others, spelled out the many ways that Third World states with socialist orientations fell short of genuine socialism. It focused on the numerous problems posed by the economic, social, and political underdevelopment of countries like Afghanistan or the People's Republic of the Congo, rather than acknowledging the progress in economic and political governance achieved by, for instance, Algeria. It further argued that widespread illiteracy and the lack of sharp class differentiation made it difficult to introduce progressive economic reforms and organize a vanguard party with close links to the masses.[44] The lack of a bourgeois class in most places made it impossible to start a Marxist-Leninist revolution. According to this analysis, backwardness was not just the legacy of imperialism but had local causes as well. There was a revival of studies of Eastern societies—that is, of Asia, North Africa, and the Middle East—with Simonia writing several important pieces. In *Destiny of Capitalism in the Orient*, he argued against the notion that capitalism was universal and would fit all, claiming that Eastern cultures struggled in vain to adopt principles of Western capitalism. Western modernization theories were simplistic and doomed to fail, as would all formulas that did not take local traditions into account. Technology could not solve the problems of underdevelopment; industrialization on its own would not bring success; expelling peasants from traditional sectors of the economy was not the answer. Soviet cooperation with developing countries was about scientific and economic development, not just growth, and this was the only path to economic independence.[45] Traditional structures were reactionary and could not promote change. In developing countries, state capitalism prevailed in its various forms: Bonapartist in Iran, feudal in Saudi Arabia, republican-bureaucratic in India and Indonesia, authoritarian but parliamentary in Malaysia. In these places, social revolution was not viable.[46]

When Mikhail Gorbachev came to power in 1985, disengagement with the South was anticipated, with the substantial subsidies and military aid of the 1970s expected to cease because of the "Afghanistan syndrome," an aversion to commitment in developing countries as a consequence of the unexpected and costly Afghan defeat. This expectation was only partially confirmed: Gorbachev's approach to strategy and security considered ideas of interdependence and ecological concerns that had been part of 1970s Soviet thinking. Engagement in the Third World was a cost, certainly not a source of profits.[47] Soviet aid in the 1980s did not compare to Western aid. In 1987, DAC countries offered $65.7 billion in foreign aid, whereas—according to OECD sources—Soviet aid in 1988 amounted to $4.2 billion, two-thirds of which went to three countries: Cuba, Mongolia, and Vietnam. The CIA counted $7.77 billion in Soviet aid, not including military aid. Soviet data from the Institute of World Economy and International Relations (IMEMO) gave a higher figure of 63 billion rubles for 1981–1986, with an annual average of 11 billion rubles—around $17.4 billion at the official exchange rate.[48] Figures were hard to compare, given that rubles were not convertible and the exchange rate was overestimated.[49] Still, the gap with the West was enormous. Under Gorbachev, participation in multilateral programs increased and was partially revised. Nodari Simonia, now deputy director of IMEMO, offered openness as the new recipe for Third World countries. A closed system, he claimed, was doomed to fail. Traditional structures and colonial legacies needed to be abolished, and even the role of the state could be reduced in order to avoid industrialization without growth, bureaucratization, and corruption.[50]

New Soviet thinking supported disarmament as a way to finance development assistance, but this linkage between peace and development was not universally accepted by the critics of imperialism, with some radicals attacking what they called a false capitalistic peace.[51] In November 1986, however, Gorbachev met with Rajiv Gandhi in New Delhi. The Delhi Declaration called for a nuclear weapon–free and nonviolent world and added that "only disarmament can release the enormous additional resources needed for combating economic backwardness and poverty."[52] During the years of nuclear brinkmanship, the environmental consequences of an atomic war had fueled nightmarish nuclear winter scenarios.[53] In the United Nations, the discussion was also fed by the 1987 Brundtland report on sustainable development that came after several monumental environmental crises: the Bhopal gas tragedy in India (1984), the Sahel drought in Africa (1982–84), and the Chernobyl nuclear power disaster (1986). Development aid was initially a tool for security, but by the end of the 1980s, it was clear that for it to serve this purpose, a new, comprehensive approach that factored in environmental crises and their consequences was needed.[54]

# Conclusions

We believe that the failure of a great many development projects to achieve
even the most fundamental objectives is due to a reluctance on the part of
development practitioners to appreciate the significance of history.

—WILLIAM RAY ARNEY, 1991

WITH THE END of the Cold War, development was to be given a new lease on
life, as resources freed from the arms race were reinvested in the South. Would
this open a new stage in North-South relations? US president George H. W.
Bush (1989–1993) thought so, speaking along very different lines from his predecessor, Ronald Reagan, who had openly opposed aid. Bush saw an opportunity to "shape a new world": "If we succeed, the next decade and the century
beyond will be an era of unparalleled growth—an era which sees the flourish-
ing of freedom, peace and prosperity around the world."[1] However, his vision
of liberal democracy's uncontested worldwide success—this triumphalist idea
of "the end of history"—did not last long.[2] Nor did the hope that the end of
the Cold War would free up new capital for development. During the Cold
War, countries in the Global South had played the superpowers off each other,
achieving almost unchecked aid during decolonization—but this approach
no longer worked. Economists and social scientists attacked the Cold War,
claiming that the aid distributed then, while abundant, had been distorted by
politics, with negative consequences for national economies. Cold War aid,
they said, fostered inefficient distribution, thwarted institutional development
in newly independent countries, propped up failed states, and nourished civil
wars with weapons and ideology. The Cold War was a perfect scapegoat.

During the Cold War, aid was used for a variety of purposes: building permanent links, reorienting trade, redesigning the political economy in recipient
countries, and consolidating leaderships that would otherwise have fallen.
This book shows that development was—and is—bound to national projects

of both donors and recipients. It reveals development's many expectations other than humanitarian motives: political loyalty, broader markets, personal or group legitimacy. It describes the tensions between different actors and the competing interests below the seemingly even surface of development. Historian Jürgen Osterhammel, interviewed by *The Guardian* in relation to his monumental work *The Transformation of the World*, reads modern history as a set of multiple globalizations, a series of contradictory developments.[3] This book also recounts a plural history, seeing the global history of development as made up of projects with worldwide aspirations but clearly framed for national purposes and within regional dimensions. The image of development as a single design, the concretization of a hegemonic view, a global faith, a center around which global polity is organized, is, this book contends, a simplified representation.[4]

The Cold War contributed to framing global approaches. Both superpowers promoted universal ideas: for the West, development was associated with international aid; in the East, it was seen as a way to build solidarity. Both approaches, not coincidentally, were useful for transmitting ideas and values to recipients. During the 1950s, development was absorbed into East-West competition, becoming a battle to conquer hearts and minds, potentially on a global scale. It became a cultural project that required donors and recipients to see eye to eye on concepts of modernity and the paths to reach it. Projects like land reclamation and river basin development were ideologies in material form, embodying culturally specific values and ideas of social progress. Not that development planners admitted this. They saw development as synonymous with efficient control over both the environment and society and thus the ideal tool to defeat poverty. The spirit of the times was "one problem, one solution." But below this seeming uniformity, each donor and recipient country had its own individual plan.

International organizations also defined development in homogeneous and universal terms. Foreign aid is a central component of world development, claimed Hollis Chenery, vice president of the World Bank in charge of economic research, in 1981.[5] Since their birth, international organizations had sought a legitimizing ideology that proved that big bureaucratic supranational structures were needed. Development was the ideal fit: global entities could offer impartial solutions to local development problems. The epistemic community clustered around the applied scientific methods of international organizations, working out universal techniques and experimenting with case studies whose results could be transferred elsewhere, regardless of the specificities of the local context. Inevitably, this practice promoted a one-size-fits-all mentality.

This book details both the efforts to construct a global myth of development and, more crucially, the obstacles those efforts encountered. In the vast fresco of development, everyone, whether recipient or donor, had space and retained wide liberties. Difference and disagreement occasionally came to the surface but were mostly covered up by the imperative of coordination and cooperation, two development buzzwords. There was to be cooperation among allies, cooperation within and among international organizations, North-South or South-South cooperation—but this harmony was wishful thinking, and even among allies, coordination was mostly mythical. Held up as a goal—sometimes genuine, sometimes for propaganda purposes—it was neither easy nor complete. The donors, wanting their choices to seem legitimate, argued that they were shared, that aid was a universal value. In reality, several visions, each with global ambitions, confronted one another. During the Cold War, both superpowers, even if they reasoned in what were potentially universal terms, operated via regional frameworks. The DAC coordinating Western aid was one such regional framework. So was Comecon in the communist world. Even more regional was the European Economic Community, which in the 1970s formulated a theory of turning regionalism into a global tool. Regionalism could become the answer to the one-size-fits-all approach.

Politically and intellectually, aid was one of the greatest disappointments of the twentieth century, because it could never accomplish the many diverse goals all the different actors hoped for. Imagined as a means to secure alliances, aid could not orient governments to the degree that donors hoped. Born as a device for improving security and based on the conviction that widespread well-being limited social discontent and might bring peace at home and abroad, aid never created political stability. In the minds of former colonialist donors, aid was meant to offer redemption from the colonial past; in antisystem ideologies like communism and Third Worldism, it promised liberation from exploitation. However, aid policies could not erase dissatisfaction, poverty, and inequality—among individuals, social groups, or countries.

In the 1970s, widespread discontent with the prospects of growth created new tensions between North and South, tensions born of trade issues that exploded during discussions about the environment. The linkage between development and security, a pillar of the system, no longer held: by the 1980s, economist Peter Bauer could contend that aid was the reason for North-South conflict, not its solution.[6] The North-South divide replaced the old grudges developed along Cold War fault lines. After the collapse of the bipolar system, social scientists spoke of a new global era, and in the 1990s, globalization became the new catchphrase. Debates about globalization brought discussions about governmentality and security, with development still identified as useful for ensuring both, even as most attention went to issues considered crucial to the well-being of global capitalism—the networked economy, multinationals, money markets, and complex financial instruments.[7]

Foreign aid has long been a key foreign policy tool. In the Cold War years, there was hardly a government too brutal or corrupt to receive assistance, provided it was on the right side of the East-West battle. Recipients could be inefficient and autocratic; they could violate human rights, abet violence, and destabilize their regions, and still they received aid. Of course, this gave aid a bad name. The Cold War, in its global form, constructed the institutions, concepts, and discourse around foreign aid that survive today.[8] By the end of the Cold War, development aid had become a massive system, multiplying institutions and minimizing evaluation and responsibility. It was a business built out of local, national, and international agencies and organizations—both governmental and private. A galaxy of actors who talked and lived development promoted a system of knowledge and a certain way of thinking, while competing with each other for predominance. It was a community that constantly interrogated itself about its effectiveness. "Does aid work?" asked economist Robert Cassen in 1986 in his book of the same title, which presented the results of a task force on development commissioned by the World Bank and the International Monetary Fund.[9] His answer was yes, albeit not in the way or measure hoped for.

Development assistance did not wipe poverty from the Earth, but there are remarkable success stories. World Bank data confirm that poverty indicators are improving worldwide. Recent data establish successes in the reduction of extreme poverty. At the aggregate (world) level, the number of people living below the extreme poverty line declined from 34.8 percent in 1990 to 10.7 percent in 2013.[10] Intransigent interpreters will, however, point out that the situation is much worse when the data are disaggregated. They point out that numbers do not properly reflect the disproportionate impact of global warming on developing countries. They remind us that much of the global change is due to China's exceptional economic growth, and they point to the Gini coefficient that measures inequality, which tells a story of poor results in promoting efficient distribution—an issue that became crucial to development thinking after the end of the Cold War.[11] In East Asia, the so-called Asian Tigers (Hong Kong, Taiwan, South Korea, and Singapore) have extolled the virtues of governed market policies and corporatist arrangements and created the developmental state—that is, a state focused on economic development that takes the necessary policy measures, including state-led economic planning, to accomplish that aim. It is a model that remains valid for development theory today.[12] Africa, which offers a more discouraging picture, is now on the front line of development efforts.

Aid's effectiveness remains a vexing question. In donor countries, conservatives criticize aid agencies for wasting money. Aid activists, instead, fear that aid might corrupt governments more than it helps them.[13] After the Cold War, aid flowed through structures that formed a sort of parallel state, sometimes rivaling the actual one: donors fed money into their programs and then assessed those programs themselves, making the whole development business a closed circle with limited accountability. An OECD study of the late 1990s concerning aid effectiveness in Mali, for example, shows that donors relied on project implementation units independent from the local government rather than on national bureaucracy.[14] This case study gives helpful evidence of a parallel structure of foreign aid experts disconnected from local bureaucracies, and therefore not able to transmit good practices in the view of sparking self-sustained growth. Observers concerned with evaluation commented that "despite the billions of dollars spent on development assistance each year, there is still little known about the actual impact of projects on the poor."[15] Others complained about tied aid—goods that have to be bought from donors' companies, which can mean that if aid does turn out to help the inhabitants, it is merely an incidental benefit—a complaint heard since the 1960s, as we have seen.

Traditionally, the Cold War was blamed for weakening the states born with decolonization. However, almost thirty years after the fall of the Berlin Wall the allegation that aid undermines recipients more than it helps them is still heard. Disappointment with aid to Africa is often connected to a governance issue. The World Bank has argued that the underlying causes of Africa's development problems are the poor-quality institutions, a weak rule of law, limited or no accountability, tight control over information, and the high levels of corruption that still characterize many African states. A 2004 study by Deborah Bräutigam and Stephen Knack argued that high levels of aid go hand in hand with weak governance and low tax revenues in African countries.[16] Development economics thus prescribes selective funding in order to avoid a vicious cycle of poor governance and economic decline. This paradigm has recently been applied to Liberia, where aid, despite having built roads and schools, is accused of having quietly weakened the state. According to this argument, because aid meant that all activities were run from the outside, it actually distorted the government's plans and undermined its authority.[17] In the last few years, countries like Liberia, Chile, and Indonesia have jump-started growth the capitalist (Western) way through American-educated economists, but they remain fragile states. In these states, donors decide what to invest in and governments often agree without questioning. Infrastructure is still preferred: a new road is more visible than, say, expanding education. In the last two decades, development economists have argued that the ideal recipients of foreign assistance are poor, well-governed countries, but the need is greater in fragile states whose governments barely function. These states are often regional security threats, and rebuilding infrastructure is often a waste of money because of the recurring outbreaks of war, both external and civil.[18]

In poor and desperate situations in Africa, where poverty and security threats are especially destabilizing, state building was long thought to be a Sisyphean task. However, even there, success stories exist. One is Rwanda under President Paul Kagame, in charge since 1994. Rwanda is now called "the best-run country in Africa," a result few would have predicted when the country was in ruins after the genocide, when most of the middle class was dead or in exile and hardly anyone had enough to eat. The country was transformed in two decades, with aid playing a part in what is sometimes called the "Rwandan miracle." In 2006, aid was a quarter of Rwanda's GDP and half the government's budget—those figures are now down to 5 percent and 17 percent, respectively. Per capita yearly income has risen from $150 to $700, and Rwanda is growing at a rate of 8 percent a year, making it one of the world's fastest-growing economies. Between 2011 and 2014, poverty fell by 6 percent, down to 39 percent, and the Gini coefficient that measures inequality improved slightly, from 0.49 to 0.45 percent.[19]

The myth of US hegemony and Western predominance, long a feature of simplistic readings of Cold War era development, is now even less accurate. US hegemony seems in decline, and China is on the rise. Hardly a day passes without a report on China's advances, while the West is shown retreating.[20] Thus despite the end of the Cold War, the trope of communist threat can still be used regarding China, especially since its rise as a global investor in the early 2000s.[21] Western media tend to stress aggressive actions (China buying up Africa) and aggressive use of political conditionality (aid flows to countries that vote for China in the UN).[22] They also stress financial support for corrupt dictators and point to the fact that China does not fuss over democracy and seldom objects to loans being spent on grand projects. China's soft power, they claim, is promoting a so-called Chinese model of authoritarian, state-driven development and undermining Western efforts to spread liberal democratic capitalism. Analysts, however, have worked to deconstruct this Cold War–like picture of aggressive Chinese expansion. Bräutigam, for example, argued that by 2012 a misleading image of Chinese agricultural engagement in Africa appeared to have solidified in the public mind. Stories of Chinese land grabbing in Southern Africa, Zambia, Mozambique, and Zimbabwe captivate the media, but in truth, she claims, Chinese agricultural activities are marginal, often exploratory ventures from private businesspeople. In other cases, like Mozambique, traditional assistance in reviving the historical irrigated rice production under the Portuguese is a continuation of aid given right after independence, when Chinese agronomists assisted Mozambique in developing the seven thousand hectares of the Moamba State Farm.[23] From the beginning,

Chinese-sponsored friendship farms were meant to boost rice production, with self-sufficiency (a mythic goal) in mind.

As in the 1960s and 1970s, China offers its history as a model for climbing out of poverty. It roots its effort in historical solidarity and presents its assistance as mutually beneficial cooperation. Building on both the tradition of socialist aid and its experience as a recipient of Japanese aid in the 1970s, since the mid-1980s China has adopted investment-for-resource swaps and signed compensatory trade agreements that provide equipment and machinery but defer payment until the recipient can pay in kind.[24] Like the Soviet Bloc used to, China supplements aid with political training programs that involve members of ruling parties and trade unions. This model has a long history as the low-cost strategy of communist countries. During the Cold War, such measures were not coupled with advanced technologies or sufficient capital and thus disappointed recipient expectations. Has China learned this lesson? Is it now providing adequate resources and advanced technology? Afrobarometer, a Pan-African research network that surveys democracy, governance, economic conditions, and related issues in Africa, suggests that the answer is yes. According to its survey, 63 percent of people interviewed in sixty-three countries consider China a positive influence, although China's development model ranks second after America's.[25] Chinese loans and contractors have reshaped much of Africa's infrastructure, paying for and building new ports, roads, and railways. In many cases, this was accompanied by investments in mines and manufacturing plants. No other country, a recent McKinsey report found, "matches China's depth and breadth of engagement."[26] Still, some traditional criticism persists—China provides no-strings financing and is therefore especially desirable to the African countries as a development partner, but recipients complain about the poor quality of materials and technology.

Academic analyses such as David Dollar's *China's Engagement with Africa*, written for the Brookings Institution, show that just half of the announced Chinese investments actually materialized. Western media often portray China's involvement as enormous, potentially overwhelming Africa, and the secretary-general of the Communist Party and president of the People's Republic of China, Xi Jinping, contributes to this exaggerated picture, having recently spoken of spending $1.6 trillion on infrastructure and development in Asia, Africa, and the Middle East over the next decade. In December 2015, he pledged $60 billion in support for African development. The amounts eventually disbursed will still be significant, but much lower than that $60 billion. Chinese direct investment in Africa was $32 billion at the end of 2014, less than 5 percent of total foreign investment there.[27] And, of course, not all investments prove equally useful. Consider Tazara, which helped China's reputation but cost a fortune. This could happen with other big infrastructure investments—two prominent examples are the railway between Mombasa and Nairobi in Kenya, and the one connecting the resource-rich southeastern Katanga province and Matadi, the Democratic Republic of the Congo's Atlantic port, built in exchange for concessions of copper and cobalt. China, commentators say, may find itself in the position once held by the West, which, after repeated disappointments, wrote off many of its loans to African governments.

In 2016, Official Development Assistance, which includes grants, loans, technical advice, and debt forgiveness, reached a new peak of $142.6 billion, an increase of 8.9 percent from 2015 after adjusting for exchange rates and inflation.[28] Most funding comes from the usual advanced centers—Berlin, London, Paris, Tokyo, and Washington, though the Nordic countries are generous relative to their size. More than two-fifths of the money flows through multilateral institutions such as the World Bank, the UN, and the Global Fund. In 2016, 9 percent was spent on refugees in donor countries, reflecting the surge of migrants to Europe.[29] The tendency to use aid as a tool of foreign policy lives well beyond the Cold War era: either against today's political enemy—not communism, but radical Islam—or, in the case of the European Union (EU), as a reward to African and Middle Eastern countries who cooperate in migration management, nowadays one of the thorniest aid-related issues. Poverty, often linked to war or environmental crisis and climate change, ultimately results in mass migration. In this new version of the population scare, the idea is to use development to help prospective migrants stay home—an updated version of the official goal of the late 1940s to "help them to help themselves." Despite studies proving the opposite, economic growth and aid are considered ideal tools to help reduce migration flows,[30] and this view is widely used to justify EU aid expenditures. EU development aid—especially for countries in the Mediterranean basin—is now conditional on help controlling people's movements from these countries. This instrumental use of development aid has been criticized by development practitioners but is widely supported by the citizens of donor countries. The popularization of aid as a tool to curtail migration keeps approval of development aid at high levels. The 2011 Eurobarometer, an extensive survey conducted in all EU member states, shows that nine Europeans out of ten think that development aid is an important expenditure.[31] In Italy, where aid includes a disproportionately high level of in-donor-country refugee costs, the connection between development assistance and migration policies is essential. A 2013 discussion in the Italian Parliament over reforming development assistance made this link explicit; it is why both right and left continue to support development aid.

The security nexus so characteristic of the history of development is still fundamental today. On the eve of the 2017 G20—the outreach forum created by the developed countries to help developing economies raise financial and monetary management to the standard of the developed world—the German government hosted an Africa conference in Berlin. The aim was to establish new relations between Europe and Africa based on peace and development and to reduce migration—a phenomenon the European public increasingly perceives as a colossal security threat for European welfare and identity.[32] "If we don't give young people any prospects, if we don't invest in education and qualifications, if we don't strengthen the role of girls and young women, the development agenda won't succeed," Angela Merkel said in her speech, addressing a distinguished audience of the heads of state of Ivory Coast, Egypt, Ghana, Guinea, Mali, Niger, Rwanda, Senegal, and Tunisia. The plan put forward by the German Ministry of Cooperation (Bundesministerium für Zusammenarbeit, or BMZ) and immediately called the "Merkel Plan" by Alassane Ouattara, the president of Ivory Coast, was described in the original proposal as "A Marshall Plan for Africa." Like its explicit model, it hopes to attract private capital to Africa, which it describes as a resource-rich continent where "poverty, hunger, malnutrition, and want could be overcome in just a decade."[33] Africa needs African solutions, the plan says, echoing both the spirit of the Marshall Plan and the rhetoric of the 1975 Lomé Convention. The legacy of Cold War era discourse and ideas is still with us.

"We believe that the failure of a great many development projects to achieve even the most fundamental objectives is due to a reluctance on the part of development practitioners to appreciate the significance of history," say development professionals hoping to find solutions for the future in the past.[34] Thinking historically has always been a tool for reshaping the future, for thinking critically about what is to come.[35] History can indeed provide examples of both failure and success in efforts to manage huge questions like famine, poverty, drought, tyranny, and bad governance, but development policies are often victims of amnesia: policy makers and practitioners forget about past strategies and how they worked or did not work, and why. As we have seen, development strategy has cycled between essential project approaches and gigantic, state-led planning and has still not solved the challenge of reconciling development and the environment. Today, the key concept in aid discourse is sustainability. Originally, sustainable development meant factoring the environment into development projects, understanding that development and environmental protection were intertwined. Increasingly, though, with the Global South claiming its right to develop, sustainability means customizing aid according to the desired mix of growth, domestic social justice, and environmental damage. In terms of preserving the environment, the developing countries argue that cutting consumption is the responsibility of the industrialized countries, the original big polluters. The right of countries to pursue their national economic development as they please continues to be an obstacle to any global agreement on environmental issues. International cooperation on climate change—the most urgent global issue today—remains elusive, as national elites prioritize national economic goals over environmental imperatives, and some important leaders, including American president Trump, even go so far as to deny climate change. Thirty years after the end of the Cold War, development, far from being a global project, is still closely bound to nationalist economic and political priorities.

## Introduction

1. Department of Information—FRELIMO, Lourenço Marques, *Mozambique Revolution*, Independence Issue, no. 61, [1975], 13–23, accessed December 2016, *http://freedomarchives.org /Documents/Finder/DOC50_scans/50.mozambique.independence1975.pdf.pdf.*

2. On the Portuguese development plan around Cahora Bassa, see Arquivo Histórico-Diplomático, Ministerio dos Negocios Estrangeiros, EAA 36 Cabora Bassa; and Arquivo Histórico Ultramarino, Cabora Bassa; MU M/Cx57,2.

3. Corrado Tornimbeni, *Cento anni su una frontiera africana: Dal sogno dell'oro al parco naturale tra Mozambico e Zimbabwe* (Milan: FrancoAngeli, 2017), 117–123; Allen F. Isaacman and Barbara S. Isaacman, *Dams, Displacement and the Delusion of Development: Cahora Bassa and Its Legacies in Mozambique, 1965–2007* (Athens: Ohio University Press, 2013), 151–166.

4. Frederick Cooper, *Africa since 1940: The Past of the Present* (Cambridge: Cambridge University Press, 2002), 85; also Basil Davidson, *The Black Man's Burden: Africa and the Curse of the Nation-State* (Oxford, UK: James Currey, 1992).

5. Reinhart Koselleck, *Vergangene Zukunft: Zur Semantik geschichtlicher Zeiten* (Frankfurt, Germany: Suhrkamp, 1992), 120.

6. Frederick Cooper, "Writing the History of Development," in "Modernizing Missions: Approaches to 'Developing' the Non-western World after 1945," ed. Stephan Malinowski and Corinna R. Unger, special issue, *Journal of Modern European History* 8, 1 (2010): 11.

7. Thomas G. Weiss, Tatiana Carayannis, Louis Emmerij, and Richard Jolly, eds., *UN Voices: The Struggle for Development and Social Justice* (Bloomington: Indiana University Press, 2005), 187.

8. Gunnar Myrdal, *Economic Theory and Underdeveloped Regions* (London: Gerald Duckworth, 1957), 80.

9. Alexander Gerschenkron, *Economic Backwardness in Historical Perspective* (Cambridge, MA: Harvard University Press, 1966).

10. Noam Chomsky, *American Power and the New Mandarins* (New York: Pantheon Books, 1969), 23–32.

11. Gilbert Rist, *The History of Development: From Western Origins to Global Faith* (London: Zed Books, 1997); Annalisa Furia, *The Foreign Aid Regime: Gift-Giving, States and Global Dis/order* (Basingstoke, UK: Palgrave Macmillan, 2015); Immanuel Wallerstein, *The Politics of the World Economy* (Cambridge: Cambridge University Press, 1984), 173–175; Arturo Escobar, *Encountering Development: The Making and Unmaking of the Third World* (Princeton, NJ: Princeton University Press, 2012).

12. David Ekbladh, *The Great American Mission: Modernization and the Construction of an American World Order* (Princeton, NJ: Princeton University Press, 2011); Nick Cullather, *The Hungry World: America's Cold War Battle against Poverty in Asia* (Cambridge, MA: Harvard University Press, 2010); Michael E. Latham, *Modernization as Ideology: American Social Science and "Nation Building" in the Kennedy Era* (Chapel Hill: University of North Carolina Press, 2000); Nils Gilman, *Mandarins of the Future: Modernization Theory in Cold War America* (Baltimore: Johns Hopkins University Press, 2003).

13. Odd Arne Westad, *The Global Cold War: Third World Interventions and the Making of Our Times* (Cambridge: Cambridge University Press, 2007).

## Chapter One

1. Reinhart Kößler, *Entwicklung* (Munich: Westfälisches Dampfboot, 1998); Heinz W. Arndt, *Economic Development: The History of an Idea* (Chicago: University of Chicago Press, 1987).

2. Sun Yat-sen, *The International Development of China* (New York: Putnam, 1922).

3. Heinz W. Arndt, "Economic Development: A Semantic History," *Economic Development and Cultural Change* 29, no. 3 (1981): 458.

4. James Hevia, *English Lessons: The Pedagogy of Imperialism in Nineteenth-Century China* (Durham, NC: Duke University Press, 2003).

5. Albert Wirz, "Die humanitäre Schweiz im Spannungsfeld zwischen Philantropie und Kolonialismus: Moynier, Afrika und das IRKK," *Traverse* 5 (1998): 95–111. On the controversial relationship between humanitarianism and colonialism, see Martti Koskenniemi, *The Gentle Civilizer of Nations: The Rise and Fall of International Law, 1870–1960* (Cambridge: Cambridge University Press, 2001), 98–166.

6. Rist, *History of Development*, 51–52. Raymond Betts, *The False Dawn: European Imperialism in the Nineteenth Century* (Minneapolis: University of Minnesota Press, 1975).

7. On the Congo Reform Association, see Jürgen Osterhammel, " 'The Great Work of Uplifting Mankind': Zivilisierungsmission und Moderne," in *Zivilisierungsmissionen: Imperiale Weltverbesserung seit dem 18. Jahrhundert*, ed. Boris Barth and Jürgen Osterhammel (Konstanz, Germany: UVK Verlagsgesellschaft, 2005), 403–408.

8. Osterhammel, "Great Work of Uplifting Mankind," 364.

9. John Fiske, "The Theory of a Common Origin for All Languages," *Atlantic Monthly*, 1881, quoted in Frank Ninkovich, "Die Zivilisierungsmission der USA im 19. Jahrhundert," in Barth and Osterhammel, *Zivilisierungsmissionen*, 297.

10. Barth and Osterhammel, introduction to *Zivilisierungsmissionen*, 7–12.

11. Ulrike Lindner, *Koloniale Begegnungen: Deutschland und Großbritannien als Imperialmächte in Afrika, 1880–1914* (Frankfurt, Germany: Campus Verlag, 2011), 95–100; Véronique Dimier, *Le gouvernement des colonies, regards croisés franco-britanniques* (Brussels: Editions de l'Université de Bruxelles, 2004).

12. Erez Manela, *The Wilsonian Moment: Self-Determination and the International Origins of Anticolonial Nationalism* (New York: Oxford University Press, 2007), 197. On the continuation of empire, see Susan Pedersen, *The Guardians: The League of Nations and the Crisis of Empire* (New York: Oxford University Press, 2015).

13. Frances P. Walters, *A History of the League of Nations* (New York: Oxford University Press, 1952).

14. Jan C. Smuts, *The League of Nations: A Practical Suggestion* (London: Hodder and Stoughton, 1918), accessed May 2014, *https://ia600202.us.archive.org/17/items/leagueofnationsp00 smutuoft/leagueofnationsp00smutuoft.pdf*; Mark Mazower, *No Enchanted Palace: The End of Empire and the Ideological Origins of the United Nations* (Princeton, NJ: Princeton University Press, 2009), 28–65.

15. Lothrop Stoddard, *The Rising Tide of Color against White World-Supremacy* (New York: Scribner, 1922).

16. Marilyn Lake and Henry Reynolds, *Drawing the Global Colour Line: White Men's Countries and the International Challenge of Racial Equality* (Cambridge: Cambridge University Press, 2008).

17. League of Nations, Secretariat, *The Aims, Methods, and Activity of the League of Nations* (Geneva: Secretariat of the League of Nations, 1935), 164–180.

18. Albert Sarraut, *La mise en valeur des colonies françaises* (Paris: Payot, 1923), 19; Clive Whitehead, *Colonial Educators* (London: I. B. Tauris, 2003).

19. Anthony Kirk-Greene, "The Thin White Line: The Size of the British Colonial Service in Africa," *African Affairs* 79 (1980): 25–44.

20. Andreas Eckert, "Die Verheißung der Bürokratie: Verwaltung als Zivilisierungsagentur im kolonialen Westafrika," in Barth and Osterhammel, *Zivilisierungsmissionen*, 278–279.

21. Tony Ballantyne and Antoinette Burton, "Empires and the Reach of the Global," in *A World Connecting, 1870–1945*, ed. Emily S. Rosenberg (Cambridge, MA: Belknap Press of Harvard University Press, 2012), 297.

22. Dirk Moses, "Partitions and the Sisyphean Making of Peoples," *Refugee Watch* 46 (50), (December 2015): 36–50; Stephan Malinowski and Moritz Feichtinger, " 'Eine Million Algerier lernen im 20. Jahrhundert zu leben': Umsiedlungslager und Zwangsmodernisierung im Algerienkrieg 1954–1962," in Malinowski and Unger, "Modernizing Missions," 107–133.

23. Frederick Cooper and Randall Packard, eds., *International Development and the Social Sciences: Essays on the History and Politics of Knowledge* (Berkeley: University of California Press, 1997).

24. James C. Scott, *Seeing like a State: How Certain Schemes to Improve the Human Condition Have Failed* (New Haven, CT: Yale University Press, 1998), 93–102.

25. Robert W. Cox, "Labor and Hegemony," *International Organization* 31, no. 3 (1977): 385–424; Lorenzo Mechi, *L'organizzazione internazionale del lavoro e la ricostruzione europea: Le basi sociali dell'integrazione economica (1931–1957)* (Rome: Ediesse, 2012).

26. Scott, *Seeing like a State*, 99.

27. Charles S. Maier, "Between Taylorism and Technocracy: European Ideologies and the Vision of Industrial Productivity in the 1920s," *Journal of Contemporary History* 5, no. 2 (1970): 27–61.

28. Christian Teichmann, "Cultivating the Periphery: Bolshevik Civilizing Missions and 'Colonialism' in Soviet Central Asia," *Comparativ* 19, no. 1 (2009): 34–52; Stephen Kotkin, *Magnetic Mountain: Stalinism as Civilization* (Berkeley: University of California Press, 1995); Niccolò Pianciola, *Stalinismo di frontiera: Colonizzazione agricola, sterminio dei nomadi e costruzione statale in Asia centrale (1905–1936)* (Rome: Viella, 2009).

29. Silvio Pons, *The Global Revolution: A History of International Communism, 1917–1991* (Oxford: Oxford University Press, 2014), 89; Paul Hollander, *Political Pilgrims: Travels of Western*

*Intellectuals to the Soviet Union, China, and Cuba, 1928–1978* (New York: Oxford University Press, 1981), 102–176.

30. Sidney Webb and Beatrice Webb, *Soviet Communism: A New Civilization?* (London: Longman, 1935).

31. Michael David-Fox, *Showcasing the Great Experiment: Cultural Diplomacy and Western Visitors to the Soviet Union, 1921–1941* (New York: Oxford University Press, 2012), 98–141.

32. David C. Engerman, "The Romance of Economic Development and New Histories of the Cold War," *Diplomatic History*, 28, no. 1 (2004): 28.

33. Jukka Gronow, *Caviar with Champagne: Common Luxury and the Ideals of the Good Life in Stalin's Russia* (Oxford, UK: Berg, 2003).

34. Jawaharlal Nehru, "The Importance of the National Idea," in *Decolonization: Perspectives from Now and Then*, ed. Prasenjit Duara (London: Routledge, 2004), 32–41.

35. "Presidential Address 1936," quoted in Arndt, *Economic Development*, 20.

36. Wolfgang Schivelbusch, *Three New Deals: Reflections on Roosevelt's America, Mussolini's Italy, and Hitler's Germany, 1933–1939* (New York: Metropolitan Books, 2006), 124–163.

37. Vittorio Santoianni, "Il razionalismo nelle colonie italiane 1928–1943: La nuova architettura delle Terre d'Oltremare" (PhD diss., University of Naples Federico II, 2008), accessed 6 May 2014, *http://www.fedoa.unina.it/1881/1/Santoianni_Progettazione_Architettonica.pdf*; Michela Wrong, *I Didn't Do It for You: How the World Betrayed a Small African Nation* (New York: Harper Collins, 2005), 52–77. On Libya, see Federico Cresti, "The Early Years of the Agency of Colonization of Cyrenaica (1932–1935)," in *Italian Colonialism*, ed. Ruth Ben-Ghiat and Mia Fuller (New York: Palgrave Macmillan, 2005), 73–82.

38. Nathan Reingold and Marc Rothenberg, eds., *Scientific Colonialism: A Cross-Cultural Comparison* (Washington, DC: Smithsonian Institution Press, 1987); Sebastian Conrad, "Die Zivilisierung des 'Selbst': Japans koloniale Moderne" in Barth and Osterhammel, *Zivilisierungsmissionen*, 254–255.

39. Ekbladh, *Great American Mission*, 43–48; Kiran Klaus Patel, *The New Deal: A Global History* (Princeton, NJ: Princeton University Press, 2016).

40. On Lilienthal, see David Ekbladh, "'Mr. TVA': Grass-Roots Development, David Lilienthal, and the Rise and Fall of the Tennessee Valley Authority as a Symbol for U.S. Overseas Development, 1933–1973," *Diplomatic History* 26, no. 3 (2002): 335–374.

41. Daniel Immerwahr, *Thinking Small: The United States and the Lure of Community Development* (Cambridge, MA: Harvard University Press, 2015), 42–44.

42. Nick Cullather, "Damming Afghanistan: Modernization in a Buffer State," in "History and September 11," special issue, *The Journal of American History* 89, no. 2 (September 2002): 524.

43. Patel, *New Deal*, 294–300.

44. On Eugene Staley, see Ekbladh, *Great American Mission*, 67–69; Greg Grandin, *Fordlandia* (New York: Metropolitan Books, 2009).

45. Frederick Cooper, *Decolonization and African Society: The Labor Question in French and British Africa* (Cambridge: Cambridge University Press, 1996), 23–170; Cooper, *Africa since 1940*, 30–35.

46. Joseph Morgan Hodge, *Triumph of the Expert: Agrarian Doctrines of Development and the Legacies of British Colonialism* (Athens: Ohio University Press, 2007), 144–178.

47. John G. Darwin, *Britain and Decolonisation: The Retreat from Empire in the Post-War World* (Basingstoke, UK: Macmillan), 131–140; Ronald Hyam, *Britain's Declining Empire: The Road to Decolonisation, 1918–1968* (Cambridge: Cambridge University Press, 2006), 87.

48. Martin Petter, "Sir Sydney Caine and the Colonial Office in the Second World War: A Career in the Making," *Canadian Journal of History* 16, no. 1 (1981): 67–86.

49. W. Arthur Lewis, *Sir William Arthur Lewis: Collected Papers, 1941–1988*, ed. Patrick A. M. Emmanuel, vol. 1 (Cave Hill, Barbados: Institute of Social and Economic Research [Eastern Caribbean], University of the West Indies, 1994), 604–622; John Michael Lee and Martin Petter, *The Colonial Office, War, and Development Policy: Organisation and the Planning of a Metropolitan Initiative, 1939–1945* (London: Maurice Temple Smith, Institute for Commonwealth Studies, 1982), 210–212.

50. David A. Low and John M. Lonsdale, "Towards the New Order, 1945–1963," introduction to *History of East Africa*, vol. 3, ed. David A. Low and Alison Smith (Oxford, UK: Clarendon Press, 1976), 13.

51. William Keith Hancock, *Argument of Empire* (Harmondsworth, UK: Penguin Books [1943]), 111, 120, 136.

52. Monica M. van Beusekom and Dorothy L. Hodgson, "Lessons Learned? Development Experiences in the Late Colonial Period," *Journal of African History*, 41, no. 1 (2000): 29–33.

53. Howard Johnson, "The British Caribbean from Demobilization to Constitutional Decolonization," in *Oxford History of the British Empire*, vol. 4, ed. Judith M. Brown and William Roger Louis (Oxford: Oxford University Press, 1999), 613.

54. Hodge, *Triumph of the Expert*, 209–230; Matteo Rizzo, "What Was Left of the Groundnut Scheme? Development Disaster and Labour Market in Southern Tanganyika, 1946–1952," *Journal of Agrarian Change* 6, no. 2 (April 2006): 205–238.

55. Myrdal, *Economic Theory*.

56. James Myall, "Britain and the Third World," in *The West and the World: Essays in Honour of JBD Miller*, ed. Robert O'Neill and Raymond John Vincent (Basingstoke, UK: Macmillan, 1990), 66–90.

57. Martin Thomas, "French Imperial Reconstruction and the Development of the Indochina War, 1945–1950," in *The First Vietnam War*, ed. Mark Atwood Lawrence and Fredrik Logevall (Cambridge, MA: Harvard University Press, 2007), 140.

58. Charles-Robert Ageron, *Histoire de la France coloniale*, vol. 3, *Le decline* (Paris: Armand Colin, 1991), 337–358.

59. Laurent Cesari, "The Declining Value of Indochina: France and the Economics of Empire, 1950–1955," in Lawrence and Logevall, *First Vietnam War*, 176.

60. Jacques Marseille, *Empire coloniale et capitalisme français* (Paris: Albin Michel, 1984).

61. Partha Chatterjee, *Nationalist Thought in the Colonial World: A Derivative Discourse* (Minneapolis: University of Minnesota Press, 1993), 30, 50–51; Bertrand Badie, *The Imported State: The Westernization of the Political Order* (Stanford, CA: Stanford University Press, 2000).

62. Crawford Young, "The End of the Post-Colonial State in Africa?," *African Affairs* 193, no. 410 (2004): 23–49.

## Chapter Two

1. Harry S. Truman, *Memoirs*, vol. 2 (Garden City, NY: Doubleday, 1955–56), 230–239.

2. "President Roosevelt to Ambassador Grew, Letter of 21 January 1941," in US Department of State, *Foreign Relations of the United States* (hereafter *FRUS*), vol. 4 (1941), 8.

3. Christopher D. O'Sullivan, *Sumner Welles, Postwar Planning, and the Quest for a New World Order, 1937–1943* (New York: Columbia University Press, 2003), chapter 5, accessed 17 May 2014, *http://www.gutenberg-e.org/osc01/*.

4. Economist Horace Belshaw, longtime collaborator of the FAO, quoted in Ekbladh, *Great American Mission*, 94.

5. Ronald Steel, "1919–1945–1989," prologue to *The Treaty of Versailles: A Reassessment after 75 Years*, ed. Manfred F. Boemeke, Gerald D. Feldman, and Elisabeth Glaser (Cambridge: Cambridge University Press, 1998), 22; David Reynolds, "FDR's Foreign Policy and the Construction of American History, 1945–1955," in *FDR's World: War, Peace, and Legacies*, ed. David B. Woolner, Warren F. Kimball, and David Reynolds (New York: Palgrave Macmillan, 2008), 16.

6. Jessica Reinisch, "Internationalism in Relief: The Birth (and Death) of UNRRA," *Past and Present* 210, suppl. 6 (2011): 258–289.

7. "Clayton Memorandum," 27 May 1947, in Ellen Garwood, *Will Clayton: A Short Biography* (Austin: University of Texas Press, [1958]), 118–121.

8. Marshall Plan speech, 5 June 1947, accessed 2 May 2017, *http://marshallfoundation.org /library/wp-content/uploads/sites/16/2014/06/Marshall_Plan_Speech_Complete.pdf*.

9. Literature on the Marshall Plan is abundant. For an iconic reading, see Greg Behrman, *The Most Noble Adventure: The Marshall Plan and the Time When America Helped Save Europe* (New York: Free Press, 2007); for a critical attitude, see Alan S. Milward, "Was the Marshall Plan Necessary?" *Diplomatic History* 13, no. 2 (1989): 231–252.

10. Ekbladh, *Great American Mission*, 4.

11. O'Sullivan, *Sumner Welles*, chapter 5; Mark Mazower, *Governing the World: The History of an Idea* (New York: Penguin Press, 2012), 200.

12. "Oral History Interview with John W. Snyder," Harry S. Truman Presidential Library and Museum, accessed December 2016, *https://www.trumanlibrary.org/oralhist/snyder31.htm*.

13. William Malcolm Hailey, *The Future of Colonial Peoples* (Princeton, NJ: Princeton University Press, 1944), 52.

14. The text is widely available, including at the Harry S. Truman Presidential Library and Museum, *https://www.trumanlibrary.org/whistlestop/50yr_archive/inagural20jan1949.htm*.

15. Truman, *Memoirs*, 231.

16. Louis J. Halle, "On Teaching International Relations," *Virginia Quarterly Review* 40, no. 1 (1964): 11–25.

17. Hardy's *Use of U.S. Technological Resources as a Weapon in the Struggle with International Communism* is quoted in Ekbladh, *Great American Mission*, 97–98.

18. Michael A. Heilperin, "Private Means of Implementing Point Four," in "Aiding Underdeveloped Areas Abroad," special issue, *Annals of the American Academy of Political and Social Science* 268 (March 1950): 54–65.

19. Truman, *Memoirs*, 233.

20. Sergei Y. Shenin, *The United States and the Third World: The Origins of Postwar Relations and the Point Four Program* (New York: Nova Science, 2000), 59.

21. "Oral History Interview with Douglas Ensminger," Harry S. Truman Presidential Library and Museum, accessed 20 May 2014, *http://www.trumanlibrary.org/oralhist/esmingr.htm*.

22. Lauchlin Currie, "Some Prerequisites for Success of the Point Four Program," in "Formulating a Point Four Program," special issue, *The Annals of the American Academy of Political and Social Science* 270 (July 1950): 102–108.

23. "Zusammenarbeit mit Entwicklungsfähigen Ländern," Politisches Archiv des Auswärtigen Amts (hereafter PA AA), B58 Ref. 407, 10; the plan was sketched by Robert Murphy (State Department), Struve Hensel (former assistant secretary of defense), and Berthold Beitz of A. Krupp.

24. Sergius Yakobson, "Soviet Concepts of Point Four," in "Aiding Underdeveloped Areas Abroad," special issue, *Annals of the American Academy of Political and Social Science* 268 (March 1950): 130.

25. "Oral History Interview with Joseph D. Coppock," Harry S. Truman Presidential Library and Museum, accessed December 2016, *https://www.trumanlibrary.org/oralhist/coppockj.htm.*

26. Sumner called it "the problem before us in South Asia." Sumner was chief economic officer, China Mission, Economic Cooperation Administration, 1948–1949. Quoted in Marc Frey, "Indoktrination, Entwicklungspolitik, und "State building": Die Vereinigten Staaten in Südostasien 1945–1961," in Barth and Osterhammel, *Zivilisierungsmissionen*: 342.

27. Truman, *Memoirs*, 239.

28. Willard L. Thorp, "The Objectives of Point Four," in "Aiding Underdeveloped Areas Abroad," special issue, *Annals of the American Academy of Political and Social Science* 268 (March 1950): 22–26.

29. "Formulating a Point Four Program," special issue, *Annals of the American Academy of Political and Social Science* 270 (July 1950).

30. Marc Frey, "Neo-Malthusianism and Development: Shifting Interpretations of a Contested Paradigm," *Journal of Global History* 6, 1 (2011): 77.

31. "Oral History Interview with Samuel P. Hayes," Harry S. Truman Presidential Library and Museum, 22, accessed December 2016, *https://www.trumanlibrary.org/oralhist/hayessp.htm.*

32. For this view, see Escobar, *Encountering Development*; Wolfgang Sachs, ed., *The Development Dictionary: A Guide to Knowledge as Power* (London: Zed Books, 1992).

33. Willard L. Thorp, "Practical Problems of Point Four," in "Formulating a Point Four Program," special issue, *Annals of the American Academy of Political and Social Science* 270 (July 1950): 95–101.

34. Frey, "Indoktrination, Entwicklungspolitik," 342.

35. Ekbladh, *Great American Mission*, 102.

36. Timothy Mitchell, *Rule of Experts: Egypt, Techno-politics, Modernity* (Berkeley: University of California Press, 2002).

37. Aurelio Peccei, "Un gran problema de nuestro tiempo: Los países subdesarrollados," Buenos Aires, 1959; Aurelio Peccei, "Como enfrentar los problemas de los paises subdesarrollados: Conferencia pronunciada en la Escuela Nacional de Guerra el 14 de julio de 1961," Buenos Aires, 1961.

38. Nick Cullather, "The Foreign Policy of the Calorie," *The American Historical Review* 112, no. 2 (2007).

39. Małgorzata Mazurek, " 'Crossroads of Capitalism': Eastern Europe, Ludwik Landau and His Interwar Vision of Global Inequalities," *Stan Rzeczy, Anti-disciplinary Journal*, no. 1 (2017): 127–143.

40. Daniel Speich, "The Use of Global Abstractions: National Income Accounting in the Period of Imperial Decline," *Journal of Global History* 6 (2011): 7–28.

41. Daniel Speich-Chassé, "Towards a Global History of the Marshall Plan: European Post-War Reconstruction and the Rise of Development Economic Expertise," in *Industrial Policy in Europe after 1945: Wealth, Power and Economic Development in the Cold War*, ed. Christian Grabas and Alexander Nützenadel (London: Palgrave Macmillan, 2014), 187–212.

42. Paul G. Hoffman, *Peace Can Be Won* (Garden City, NY: Doubleday, 1951), 65; see Alan R. Raucher, *Paul G. Hoffman: Architect of Foreign Aid* (Lexington: University Press of Kentucky, 1985).

43. Sara Lorenzini, "Ace in the Hole or Hole in the Pocket? The Italian Mezzogiorno and the Story of a Troubled Transition from Development Model to Development Donor," *Contemporary European History* 26, no. 3 (August 2017): 441–446.

44. Elisa Grandi, "'Una TVA per il Mezzogiorno': David Lilienthal e reti transnazionali nei piani di sviluppo della Cassa per il Mezzogiorno," *Annali della Fondazione Ugo La Malfa* 27 (2012): 215–232.

45. Jagdish N. Bhagwati and Richard S. Eckaus, eds., *Development and Planning: Essays in Honour of Paul Rosenstein Rodan* (London: Allen and Unwin, 1972), 7.

46. Luigi Paganetto and Pasquale Lucio Scandizzo, *La Banca Mondiale e l'Italia: Dalla ricostruzione allo sviluppo* (Bologna: Il Mulino, 2000), 118.

47. Leandra D'Antone, "L'interesse straordinario per il Mezzogiorno (1943–1960)," in *Meridiana*, no. 24 (1995): 17–64. See Michele Alacevich, *The World Bank's Early Reflections on Development: A Development Institution or a Bank?* Development Studies Working Papers, no. 221 (Centro Studi Luca d'Agliano, January 2007).

48. Gerald M. Meier and Dudley Seers, *Pioneers in Development* (New York: Oxford University Press, 1984).

49. W. Arthur Lewis, "Economic Development with Unlimited Supplies of Labour," *Manchester School of Economic and Social Studies* 22, 2 (May 1954): 139–191.

50. Albert O. Hirschmann to Manlio Rossi-Doria, 13 July 1952, in Manlio Rossi-Doria, *Una Vita per il Sud: Dialoghi epistolari 1944–1987*, ed. Emanuele Bernardi (Rome: Donzelli Editore, 2011), 63–65. On this also see Jeremy Adelman, Michele Alacevich, Victoria de Grazia, Ira Katznelson, and Nadia Urbinati, "Albert Hirschman and the Social Sciences: A Memorial Roundtable," *Humanity: An International Journal of Human Rights, Humanitarianism, and Development* 6, no. 2 (2015): 265–286.

51. Hollis B. Chenery, "From Engineering to Economics," *Banca Nazionale del Lavoro Quarterly Review*, no. 183 (December 1992); minutes and working materials are in collections of the Harvard University Archives, Faculty Archives, Papers of Hollis Burnley Chenery, unprocessed accession, Accession 12810, Box 2.

52. Pasquale Saraceno, Veniero Ajmone Marsan, Franco Pilloton, and Beppe Sacchi, eds., *Economic Effects of an Investment Program in Southern Italy* (Rome: Tip. F. Failli, 1951); also *Ricerche sullo sviluppo economico dell'Europa meridionale: Tre studi della Commissione Economica per l'Europa, Nazioni Unite—Divisione economica e sociale*, ed. Svimez (Rome: [publisher unknown], 1956).

53. Valeria Vitale, "L'attività della SVIMEZ dal 1946 al 1991," *Rivista economica del Mezzogiorno* 14, no. 2 (2000): 569, 604.

54. *Atti del congresso internazionale di studio sul problema delle aree arretrate, Milano, 10–15 ottobre 1954* (Milan: Giuffrè, 1954–56). An analysis is also in Claudia Villani, *La trappola degli aiuti: Sottosviluppo, Mezzogiorno e guerra fredda negli anni '50* (Bari, Italy: Progedit, 2008), 106–119.

55. *Atti del congresso internazionale*, vol. 1, 9.

56. Elena Calandri, "L'Italia e la questione dello sviluppo: Una sfida tra anni sessanta e settanta," in *L'Italia nella costruzione europea: Un bilancio storico 1957–2007*, ed. Piero Craveri and Antonio Varsori (Milan: FrancoAngeli, 2009), 267–290.

## Chapter Three

1. Ama Biney, *The Political and Social Thought of Kwame Nkrumah* (New York: Palgrave Macmillan, 2011), 81.

2. "Oral History Interview with Douglas Ensminger," Harry S. Truman Presidential Library and Museum, 65, accessed May 2014, *http://www.trumanlibrary.org/oralhist/esmingr.htm*.

3. Charles S. Maier, *Among Empires: American Ascendancy and Its Predecessors* (Cambridge, MA: Harvard University Press, 2006), 134.

4. Christian Koller, "Eine Zivilisierungsmission der Arbeiterklasse? Die Diskussion über eine 'Sozialistiche Kolonialpolitik' vor dem Ersten Weltkrieg," in Barth and Osterhammel, *Zivilisierungsmissionen*, 229–243.

5. Max Schippel in 1908 on the Herero and Nama uprisings, in Max Schippel, "Marxismus und Koloniale Eingeborenenfrage," *Sozialistische Monatshefte* 14 (1908): 273–285.

6. Karl Kautsky, *Sozialismus und Kolonialpolitik* (Berlin: Buchhandlung Vorwärts, 1907).

7. Eduard Bernstein, "Der Socialismus und die Colonialfrage," *Sozialistische Monatshefte* 4 (1900): 549–562.

8. In 1913 Lenin wrote an article in *Pravda*, "Backward Europe and Advanced Asia"—quoted in Vijay Prashad, *The Darker Nations: A People's History of the Third World* (New York: New Press, 2007), 20.

9. Kris Manjapra, *Age of Entanglement: German and Indian Intellectuals across Empire* (Cambridge, MA: Harvard University Press, 2014), 171–190; Kris Manjapra, "Communist Internationalism and Transcolonial Recognition," in *Cosmopolitan Thought Zones: South Asia and the Global Circulation of Ideas* (Basingstoke, UK: Palgrave Macmillan, 2010), 159–177. Manjapra has written a biography on Roy, *M. N. Roy: Marxism and Colonial Cosmopolitanism* (London: Routledge, 2010).

10. Westad, *Global Cold War*, 39–73, especially 52–53.

11. Quoted in Pankaj Mishra, *From the Ruins of Empire: The Revolt against the West and the Remaking of Asia* (London: Penguin, 2013), 202.

12. Sukarno in 1929, quoted in Westad, *Global Cold War*, 83.

13. Edward H. Carr, *A History of Soviet Russia: The Bolshevik Revolution, 1917–1923*, vol. 3 (London: Macmillan, 1953), 520–522.

14. Jerry F. Hough, *The Struggle for the Third World: Soviet Debates and American Options* (Washington, DC: Brookings Institution Press, 1986), 36.

15. Hough, 38–48.

16. George Padmore, ed., *History of the Pan-African Congress: Colonial and Coloured Unity* (London: Hammersmith Books, 1963), 5.

17. Westad, *Global Cold War*, 64–65; Odd Arne Westad, ed., *Brothers in Arms: The Rise and Fall of the Sino-Soviet Alliance, 1945–1963* (Washington, DC: Woodrow Wilson Center Press, 1998); Jian Chen, *Mao's China and the Cold War* (Chapel Hill: University of North Carolina Press, 2001), 49–64.

18. Pons, *Global Revolution*, 232.

19. Ragna Boden, "Soviet-Indonesian Relations in the First Postwar Decade (1945–1954)," Parallel History Project on Cooperative Security (PHP), ETH Zürich, 2009, accessed 31 May 2014, *http://www.php.isn.ethz.ch/lory1.ethz.ch/collections/coll_indonesia/Introduction7149.html ?navinfo=100702*.

20. Westad, *Global Cold War*, 81.

21. Andreas Hilger, "The Soviet Union and India: The Years of Late Stalinism," Parallel History Project on Cooperative Security (PHP), ETH Zürich, September 2008, accessed 31 May 2014, *http://www.php.isn.ethz.ch/lory1.ethz.ch/collections/coll_india/documents/Introduction_000.pdf*.

22. Surjit Mansingh, "Indo-Soviet Relations in the Nehru Years: The View from New Delhi," Parallel History Project (PHP), ETH Zürich, 2009, accessed 31 May 2014, *http://www.php.isn .ethz.ch/lory1.ethz.ch/collections/coll_india/NehruYears-Introduction3593.html?navinfo=96318*.

23. On ideas for India's development, see Benjamin Zachariah, *Developing India: An Intellectual and Social History, c. 1930–50* (New Delhi: Oxford University Press, 2005); Sugata Bose and Ayesha Jalal, eds., *Nationalism, Democracy, and Development: State and Politics in India* (New Delhi: Oxford University Press, 1997).

24. The article, by M. Marinin, is quoted in Sergius Yakobson, "Soviet Concepts of Point Four," 129.

25. Alvin Z. Rubinstein, "Soviet Policy toward Under Developed Areas in the Economic and Social Council," *International Organization* 9 , no. 2 (May 1955): 232–243.

26. David C. Engerman, "The Second World's Third World," *Kritika* 12, no. 1 (2011): 183–211.

27. Elizabeth Kridl Valkenier, *The Soviet Union and the Third World: An Economic Bind* (New York: Praeger, 1983), 1–3.

28. David C. Engerman, "Learning from the East: Soviet Experts and India in the Era of Competitive Coexistence," *Comparative Studies of South Asia, Africa and the Middle East* 33, no. 2 (2013): 227–238.

29. Joseph S. Berliner, *Soviet Economic Aid: The New Aid and Trade Policy in Underdeveloped Countries* (New York: Council on Foreign Relations, Praeger, 1958), 17.

30. David C. Engerman, "Development Politics and the Cold War," *Diplomatic History* 41, no. 1 (2017): 1–19; David C. Engerman, *The Price of Aid: The Economic Cold War in India* (Cambridge, MA: Harvard University Press, 2018), 89–116.

31. Engerman, "Learning from the East," 230; David C. Engerman, "Solidarity, Development, and Non-alignment: Foreign Economic Advisors and Indian Planning in the 1950s and 1960s," in Berthold Unfried and Eva Himmelstoss, eds., *Die Eine Welt schaffen: Praktiken von "Internationaler Solidarität" und "Internationaler Entwicklung"* [Create One World: Practices of "international solidarity" and "international development"] (Leipzig, Germany: Akademische Verlagsanstalt, 2012).

32. Michał Kalecki, "Introduction to Annex to Financial Problems of the Third Plan (1963)," in *Collected Works of Michał Kalecki, vol. 5, Developing Economies*, ed. Jerzy Osiatyński (Oxford, UK: Clarendon Press, 1993), 217–218.

33. Alfred Sauvy, "Trois mondes, une planète," *L'Observateur* 118 (August 1952), now reprinted in *Vingtième siècle, revue d'histoire* 12 (October–December 1986): 81–83, *https://www.persee.fr /doc/xxs_0294-1759_1986_num_12_1_1516*. For a discussion on the birth of the concept, see Marcin Wojciech Solarz, " 'Third World': The 60th Anniversary of a Concept That Changed History," *Third World Quarterly* 33, no. 9 (2012): 1561–1573.

34. Sukarno's speech is in Prashad, *Darker Nations*, 30.

35. Prashad, *Darker Nations*, 16–30, 34.

36. Dipesh Chakrabarty, "The Legacies of Bandung: Decolonization and the Politics of Culture," in *Making a World after Empire: The Bandung Moment and Its Political Afterlives*, ed. Christopher J. Lee (Athens: Ohio University Press, 2010), 45–68.

37. Richard Wright, *The Color Curtain: A Report on the Bandung Conference* (New York: World Publishing, 1956).

38. Carlos P. Romulo, *The Meaning of Bandung* (Chapel Hill: University of North Carolina Press, 1956), 11–12. On Romulo and Malik in Bandung, see Samuel Moyn, *The Last Utopia: Human Rights in History* (Cambridge, MA: Belknap Press of Harvard University Press, 2010).

39. "From the Diary of S. V. Chervonenko, Memorandum of Conversation with the General Secretary of the CC CCP, Deng Xiaoping, 17 May 1960," June 1960, History and Public Policy Program Digital Archive, AVPRF (Foreign Policy Archives of the Russian Federation) f. 0100 op. 53, p. 8, d. 454, ll. 165–9. Translated by Ben Aldrich-Moodie. *http://digitalarchive .wilsoncenter.org/document/112661*.

40. "Final Communiqué of the Asian-African Conference of Bandung (24 April 1955)," in *Asia-Africa Speaks from Bandung* (Djakarta: Ministry of Foreign Affairs, Republic of Indonesia, 1955), 161–169, accessed 5 May 2017, *http://www.cvce.eu/obj/final_communique_of_the_asian _african_conference_of_bandung_24_april_1955-en-676237bd-72f7-471f-949a-88b6ae 513585.html*.

41. Robert S. Walters, *American and Soviet Aid: A Comparative Analysis* (Pittsburgh: University of Pittsburgh Press, 1970), 30.

42. Henry Kissinger, "Reflections on American Diplomacy," *Foreign Affairs* 35, no. 1 (October 1956): 37–56.

43. Zbigniew Brzezinski, "The Politics of Underdevelopment," *World Politics* 9, no. 1 (October 1956): 55–75.

44. US State Department, *The Sino-Soviet Economic Offensive in the Less Developed Countries* (Washington, DC: US State Department, 1958).

45. Berliner, *Soviet Economic Aid*, 7; David C. Engerman, *Know Your Enemy: The Rise and Fall of America's Soviet Experts* (Oxford: Oxford University Press, 2009).

46. A list is in the meeting with L. Lara (MPLA), 8 September 1961, in Politisches Archiv des früheren Ministeriums für Auswärtige Angelegenheiten, Berlin (hereafter MfAA), A15964.

47. "Konsultationen über Beziehungen mit afrikanischen Ländern und Befreiungsbewegungen," MfAA, A14159.

48. In 1966–67 the CPSU asked the SED to take care of socialist education in "mixed or pro-Chinese" parties. MfAA, C521 /72.

49. Berliner, *Soviet Economic Aid*.

50. Evgenij Varga, "On Trends of Development of Contemporary Capitalism and Socialism," *World Economy and International Relations* 4 (1957): 36–48.

51. Alessandro Iandolo, "The Rise and Fall of the 'Soviet Model of Development' in West Africa, 1957–64," *Cold War History* 12, no. 4 (2012): 691.

52. Ragna Boden, "Globalisierung Sowjetisch: Der Kulturtransfer in die Dritte Welt," in *Globalisierung imperial und sozialistisch*, ed. Martin Aust (Frankfurt, Germany: Campus Verlag, 2013), 425–442.

53. Davidson, *Black Man's Burden*, 194–195.

54. Text of (Mikhail Andreevich) Suslov report to CPSU Plenum, 14 February 1964, [Washington] US Dept. of State, External Research Staff, foreign press and broadcast supplement, Sino-Soviet dispute. On Sino-Soviet relations, see Sergey Radchenko, *Two Suns in the Heavens: The Sino-Soviet Struggle for Supremacy, 1962–1967* (Stanford, CA: Stanford University Press, 2009).

55. Hans Siegfried Lamm and Siegfried Kupper, *DDR und Dritte Welt* (Munich: Oldenbourg, 1976), 95–96.

56. On the structure of Soviet trade agreements, see Walters, *American and Soviet Aid*, 96, 135–137, 144–145.

57. Walters, *American and Soviet Aid*, 39.

58. Robin Luckham, "Soviet Arms and African Militarization," in *Soviet Interests in the Third World*, ed. Robert Cassen (London: SAGE, 1985), 89.

59. Tobias Rupprecht, "La guerra fredda e l'avanzata modernità socialista," in *Contemporanea* 1 (2012): 141–142.

60. Khrushchev at the Twenty-First Party Congress in 1959, quoted in Walters, *American and Soviet Aid*, 42.

61. Tobias Rupprecht, "Socialist High Modernity and Global Stagnation: A Shared History of Brazil and the Soviet Union during the Cold War," *Journal of Global History* 6, no. 3 (2011): 505–528.

62. Artemy M. Kalinovsky, "Not Some British Colony in Africa: The Politics of Decolonization and Modernization in Soviet Central Asia, 1955–1964," *Ab Imperio*, no. 2 (2013): 191–222; Artemy M. Kalinovsky, *Laboratory of Socialist Development: Cold War Politics and Decolonization in Soviet Tajikistan* (Ithaca, NY: Cornell University Press, 2018).

63. Christopher J. Lee, "Tricontinentalism in Question: The Cold War Politics of Alex La Guma and the African National Congress," in Lee, *Making a World after Empire*, 266–286; Alex La Guma, *Soviet Journey* (Moscow: Progress Publishers, 1978).

64. Timothy Nunan, "Northern Crossings: Soviet Development in Afghan Turkestan" (paper presented at the conference "Rethinking Development," Trento, Italy, 30–31 May 2013); also in Timothy Nunan, *Humanitarian Invasion: Global Development in Cold War Afghanistan* (New York: Cambridge University Press, 2016), 46–118. On Soviet aid to Afghanistan, see Antonio Giustozzi and Artemy Kalinovsky, *Missionaries of Modernity: Advisory Missions and the Struggle for Hegemony in Afghanistan and Beyond* (London: Hurst, 2016), 165–191.

65. Ragna Boden, "Cold War Economics: Soviet Aid to Indonesia," *Journal of Cold War Studies* 10, no. 3 (2008): 125.

66. Bradley Simpson, *Economists with Guns: Authoritarian Development and U.S.-Indonesian Relations, 1960–1968* (Stanford, CA: Stanford University Press, 2008), 18–23; Clifford Geertz, *Agricultural Involution* (Berkeley: Association for Asian Studies by University of California Press, 1966).

67. On Soviet-Indonesia relations, see Ragna Boden, *Die Grenzen der Weltmacht: Sowjetische Indonesienpolitik von Stalin bis Brežnev* (Stuttgart, Germany: Franz Steiner Verlag, 2006); Boden, "Cold War Economics," 121.

68. The agreement was signed on 17 November 1958; MfAA, A11245. On trade relations between socialist countries and Guinea, see Bundesarchiv Berlin (hereafter BArchB), DL2 3313 and DL2 5349.

69. "Expertenbericht," Hans Georg Keiser, Gerd Friedrich, 4 August 1959, BArchB, DE1 VA 41784.

70. Details on negotiations are in BArchB, DL2 4308.

71. Bericht Schädlich, Gespräch Enkelmann-Melnikov, 1 December 1959, Gespräch Enkelmann-Quietzch, 10 December 1959, BArchB, DL2 5338.

72. Bericht Jansen-Bourgoin, PA AA, B34 Ref. 307, 85; Bericht Schroeder (FRG ambassador in Conakry), 8 December 1961, PA AA, B58 IIIB1 175.

73. Sergei Mazov, *A Distant Front in the Cold War: The USSR in West Africa and the Congo, 1956–1964* (Stanford, CA: Stanford University Press, 2010); on Soviet relations with African countries, see Christopher Stevens, *The Soviet Union and Black Africa* (London: Macmillan, 1976).

74. Alessandro Iandolo, "De-Stalinizing Growth: Decolonization and the Development of Development Economics in the Soviet Union," in *The Development Century*, ed. Stephen J. Macekura and Erez Manela (Cambridge, MA: Harvard University Press, 2018), 213–216; Chris Miller, "Georgii Mirskii and Soviet Theories of Authoritarian Modernization," *The International History Review* (2017), doi:10.1080/07075332.2017.1402803.

## Chapter Four

1. A. G. Hopkins, "Globalisation and Decolonisation," *Journal of Imperial and Commonwealth History* 45, no. 5 (2017): 737.

2. Martin Thomas, Bob Moore, and L. J. Butler, *Crises of Empire: Decolonization and Europe's Imperial States* (London: Bloomsbury, 2015).

3. Elizabeth Buettner, *Europe after Empire: Decolonization, Society, and Culture* (Cambridge: Cambridge University Press, 2016), 95–99.

4. Eugène L. Guernier, *L'Afrique: Champ d'expansion de l'Europe* (Paris: Armand Colin, 1933); Eugène L. Guernier, *Le destin des continents: Trois continents, trois civilisations, trois destins* (Paris: Librairie Felix Alcan, 1936). Eurafrica was listed as the French world utopia. In Italy, the debate was led by Paolo D'Agostino Orsini di Camerota. Peo Hansen and Stefan Jonsson, *Eurafrica: The Untold History of European Integration and Colonialism* (London: Bloomsbury, 2014), 44–68.

5. Anne Deighton, "Entente Neo-Coloniale? Ernest Bevin and the Proposals for an Anglo-French Third World Power, 1945–1949," *Diplomacy & Statecraft* 17, no. 4 (December 2006): 835–852; Anne Deighton, "Ernest Bevin and the Idea of Euro-Africa from the Interwar to the Postwar Period," in *L'Europe unie et l'Afrique: De l'idée d'Eurafrique à la convention de Lomé 1*, ed. Marie-Thérèse Bitsch and Gérard Bossuat (Brussels: Bruylant, 2005), 97–118; John Kent, "Bevin's Imperialism and the Idea of Euro-Africa," in *British Foreign Policy 1945–56*, ed. Michael Dockrill and John W. Young (Basingstoke, UK: Macmillan, 1989), 47–76; John Kent, *The Internationalization of Colonialism: Britain, France, and Black Africa, 1939–1956* (Oxford, UK: Clarendon Press, 1992).

6. "Ambiguity in France," *New York Times*, 15 June 1957, quoted in Hansen and Jonsson, *Eurafrica*, 267.

7. "Eisenhower Special Message on Foreign Economic Policy, March 30, 1954," in *Public Papers of the Presidents of the United States* (Washington, DC: Government Printing Office, 1954), 352.

8. Michael Adamson, "'The Most Important Single Aspect of Our Foreign Policy?' The Eisenhower Administration, Foreign Aid, and the Third World," in *The Eisenhower Administration, the Third World, and the Globalization of the Cold War*, ed. Kathryn C. Statler and Andrew L. Johns (Lanham, MD: Rowman & Littlefield, 2006), 49, 52; Michael E. Latham, *The Right Kind of Revolution: Modernization, Development, and U.S. Foreign Policy from the Cold War to the Present* (Ithaca, NY: Cornell University Press, 2011), 43.

9. Walters, *American and Soviet Aid*, 75–77.

10. David Bruce diary, Historical Archives of the European Union (hereafter HAEU), Jean Monnet American Sources (JMAS), Virginia Historical Archive, 149.

11. Gerhard Thomas Mollin, *Die USA und der Kolonialismus: Amerika als Partner und Nachfolger der belgischen Macht in Afrika 1939–1965* (Berlin: Akademie Verlag, 1996), 152.

12. Burton I. Kaufman, *Trade and Aid: Eisenhower's Foreign Economic Policy, 1953–1961* (Baltimore: Johns Hopkins University Press, 1982), 49–51.

13. Dulles to Cabot Lodge, Washington, 9 February 1955, FRUS 1955–1957, vol. 18, *Africa*, Doc. 2.

14. Aaron Dean Rietkerk, "In Pursuit of Development: The United Nations, Decolonization and Development Aid, 1949–1961" (PhD diss., London School of Economics, June 2015), 53–55.

15. Walt W. Rostow, *The Diffusion of Power: An Essay in Recent History* (New York: Macmillan, 1972), 92.

16. Current Economic Developments, 1 February 1955, US National Archives and Records Administration (hereafter NARA), RG 59, Lot 70D467, Box 6.

17. Yakobson, "Soviet Concepts of Point Four," 139.

18. Kenneth Alan Osgood, *Total Cold War: Eisenhower's Secret Propaganda Battle at Home and Abroad* (Lawrence: University Press of Kansas, 2006), 118–120.

19. Simpson, *Economists with Guns*, 17; Robert J. McMahon, "'The Point of No Return': The Eisenhower Administration and Indonesia, 1953–1960," in *The Eisenhower Administration, the Third World, and the Globalization of the Cold War*, ed. Kathryn C. Statler and Andrew L. Johns (Lanham, MD: Rowman & Littlefield, 2006), 88.

20. Nathan J. Citino, *Envisioning the Arab Future: Modernization in U.S.–Arab Relations, 1945–1967* (Cambridge: Cambridge University Press, 2017).

21. Adamson, "Most Important Single Aspect," 59–60.

22. Kaufman, *Trade and Aid*, 182.

23. Hansen and Jonsson, *Eurafrica*, 196–209.

24. NATO Restricted Working Paper AC/119-WP(58)58, 17 August 1958, PA AA, B34, Ref. 307, 114.

25. Robert L. Brown and Jeffrey M. Kaplow, "Talking Peace, Making Weapons: IAEA Technical Cooperation and Nuclear Proliferation," *Journal of Conflict Resolution* 58, no. 3 (2014): 403.

26. David Fisher, *History of the International Atomic Energy Agency: The First Forty Years* (Vienna: IAEA, 1997); Oral History Interview with Abdul Minty, IAEA History Research

Project, University of Vienna, accessed June 2018, *https://iaea-history.univie.ac.at/oral-history -videos/interviews-j-o/*.

27. Mishra, *From the Ruins of Empire*, 263.

28. Luns is quoted in Hansen and Jonsson, *Eurafrica*, 238.

29. Peo Hansen and Stefan Jonsson, "Another Colonialism: Africa in the History of European Integration," *Journal of Historical Sociology* 27 (2014): 451–453, doi:10.1111/johs.12055.

30. Uwe W. Kitzinger, "Europe: The Six and the Seven," *International Organization* 14, no. 1 (1960): 31; Carole A. Cosgrove, "The Common Market and Its Colonial Heritage," *Journal of Contemporary History* 4, no. 1 (1969): 76.

31. Yves Montarsolo, "Albert Sarraut et l'idée d'Eurafrique," in *L'Europe unie et l'Afrique: De l'idée d'Eurafrique à la convention de Lomé 1*, ed. Marie-Thérèse Bitsch and Gérard Bossuat (Brussels: Bruylant, 2005), 77–95.

32. Thomas Moser, *Europäische Integration, Dekolonisation, Eurafrika: Eine historische Analyse über Entstehungsbedingungen der Eurafrikanischen Gemeinschaft von der Weltwirtschaftskrise bis zum Jaunde-Vertrag, 1929–1963* (Baden-Baden, Germany: Nomos, 2000). Guy Mollet is quoted in Quinn Slobodian, *The Globalists: The End of Empire and the Birth of Neoliberalism* (Cambridge, MA: Harvard University Press, 2017), 195.

33. Alexandre Kojève, "Kolonialismus in europäischer Sicht: Vortrag gehalten vor dem Rhein-Ruhr-Klub e.V., am 16. Januar 1957," in *Schmittiana VII*, ed. Piet Tomissen (Berlin: Duncker & Humblot, 1999), 125–140; an English translation is in Erik de Vries, "Colonialism from a European Point of View," *Interpretation* 29, no. 1 (2001): 91–130; James H. Nichols, *Alexandre Kojève: Wisdom at the End of History* (Lanham, MD: Rowman & Littlefield, 2007).

34. Senghor in *Marchés coloniaux du monde*, 1953, quoted in Véronique Dimier, *The Invention of a European Aid Bureaucracy: Recycling Empire* (Basingstoke, UK: Palgrave Macmillan, 2014), 15; Slobodian, *Globalists*, 195.

35. Karis Muller, "Iconographie de l'Eurafrique," in *L'Europe Unie et l'Afrique: De l'idée d'Eurafrique à la convention de Lomé 1*, ed. Marie-Thérèse Bitsch and Gérard Bossuat (Brussels: Bruylant, 2005), 9–34.

36. On the origins of the EDF especially, see HAEU, BAC 25/1980, 1034.

37. Mareike Kleine, "Trading Control: International Fiefdoms in International Organizations," *International Theory* 5, no. 3 (November 2013): 321–346; Edward C. Page, *People Who Run Europe* (Oxford: Oxford University Press, 1997), 49.

38. Robert Lemaignen, *L'Europe au berceau: Souvenirs d'un technocrate* (Paris: Plon, 1964), 117.

39. Véronique Dimier, "Bringing the Neo-patrimonial State Back to Europe: Decolonization and the Construction of the EEC Development Policy," *Archiv für Sozialgeschichte*, no. 48 (2008): 433–460.

40. HAEU, BAC 25/1980, 1034.

41. Allardt quoted in "Läuft Afrika der EWG davon?," *Die Welt*, 2 June 1960, accessed May 2016, *http://www.cvce.eu/obj/"lauft_afrika_der_ewg_davon_"_in_die_welt_2_juni_1960-de-8c d03eec-c84b-4de4- 9694-0c7a36e4a4bc.htm*.

42. Helmut Allardt, *Politik vor und hinter den Kulissen* (Düsseldorf, Germany: Econ Verlag, 1979), 187–188.

43. Jean-Pierre Bat, *La fabrique des barbouzes: Histoire des réseaux Foccart en Afrique* (Paris: Nouveau Monde, 2015), 10–11, 26.

44. Jean-Pierre Bat, *Le syndrome Foccart: La politique française en Afrique, de 1959 à nos jours* (Paris: Gallimard, 2012), 253.

45. Bat, *Le syndrome Foccart*, 256.

46. Thomas, Moore, and Butler, *Crises of Empire*, 108–109.

47. "Läuft Afrika der EWG davon?," *Die Welt*, 2 June 1960, accessed May 2016, https://www .cvce.eu/de/obj/lauft_afrika_der_ewg_davon_in_die_welt_2_juni_1960-de-8cd03eec-c84b -4de4-9694-0c7a36e4a4bc.html.

48. Enzo R. Grilli, *The European Community and the Developing Countries* (Cambridge: Cambridge University Press, 1993), 18–21.

49. The quotes are from Hans J. Morgenthau, "A Political Theory of Foreign Aid," *American Political Science Review* 56, no. 2 (June 1962): 309; John Kenneth Galbraith, *The Nature of Mass Poverty* (Cambridge, MA: Harvard University Press, 1979), 29; Irene L. Gendzier, *Managing Political Change: Social Scientists and the Third World* (Boulder, CO: Westview Press, 1985), 22–48.

50. Federico Romero, *Storia della guerra fredda: L'ultimo conflitto per l'Europa* (Turin: Einaudi, 2009), 134–138.

51. Latham, *Modernization as Ideology*, 30–46.

52. David Milne, *America's Rasputin: Walt Rostow and the Vietnam War* (New York: Hill and Wang, 2008), 26–72.

53. Walt Whitman Rostow, "Marx Was a City Boy, or, Why Communism May Fail," *Harper's Magazine*, no. 2 (February 1955): 25–30.

54. Max F. Millikan and Walt W. Rostow, *A Proposal: Key to an Effective Foreign Policy* (New York: Harper and Brothers, 1957). A first draft was written in 1954, but the links to the Cold War are developed only in 1957; see James M. Hagen and Vernon W. Ruttan, "Development Policy under Eisenhower and Kennedy," *Bulletin of the Economic Development Center* 87, no. 10 (November 1987): 34–35. On this see also Gilman, *Mandarins of the Future*, 174–179.

55. Joseph S. Nye Jr., "Soft Power," *Foreign Policy*, no. 80 (Autumn 1990): 153–171.

56. William J. Lederer and Eugene Burdick, *The Ugly American* (New York: Norton, 1958).

57. "A note from the authors," Lederer and Burdick, *Ugly American*, 7. The later novel was William J. Lederer and Eugene Burdick, *Sarkhan* (New York: McGraw Hill, 1965).

58. Hubert H. Humphrey, *The Man and His Dream* (New York: Methuen, 1978), 234–237.

59. Immerwahr, *Thinking Small*, 40–65.

60. Henry S. Reuss, *When Government Was Good: Memories of a Life in Politics* (Madison: University of Wisconsin Press, 1999), 58–62.

61. Speech of Senator John F. Kennedy, Cow Palace, San Francisco, CA, 2 November 1960, The American Presidency Project, Gerhard Peters and John T. Woolley, https://www.presidency .ucsb.edu/documents/speech-senator-john-f-kennedy-cow-palace-san-francisco-ca.

62. Report quoted in Jeremy Friedman, *Shadow Cold War: The Sino-Soviet Competition for the Third World* (Chapel Hill: University of North Carolina Press, 2015), 31.

63. Memorandum, Kennedy to Rusk, quoted in Latham, *Modernization as Ideology*, 142.

64. Latham, *Modernization as Ideology*, 127–128. See Elizabeth Cobbs Hoffman, *All You Need Is Love: The Peace Corps and the Spirit of the 1960s* (Cambridge, MA: Harvard University Press, 1998).

65. Julius A. Amin, *The Peace Corps in Cameroon* (Kent, OH: Kent State University Press, 1992), 77, 164.

66. Ulrich van den Heyden, "FDJ-Brigaden der Freundschaft aus der DDR-Die Peace Corps des Ostens?," in Unfried and Himmelstoss, *Die eine Welt schaffen*, 99–122.

67. Latham, *Modernization as Ideology*, 164.

68. John F. Kennedy, *The Strategy of Peace* (New York, Harper [1960]), 6.

69. Rostow, *Diffusion of Power*, 189–207.

70. John F. Kennedy, "Address before the General Assembly of the United Nations, September 25, 1961," John F. Kennedy Presidential Library and Museum, *https://www.jfklibrary.org /Research/Research-Aids/JFK-Speeches/United-Nations_19610925.aspx*.

71. Examples are in Cullather, *Hungry World*, 77, 97, 140.

72. Mark Karp, *The Economics of Trusteeship in Somalia* (Boston: Boston University Press, 1960), 124–145.

73. Arthur Schlesinger in 1949, quoted in Cullather, "Damming Afghanistan," 524.

74. Walters, *American and Soviet Aid*, 156.

75. Latham, *Modernization as Ideology*, 69–108, especially 81.

76. Walt W. Rostow, "Economic Development," speech to the American Chamber of Commerce, Mexico City, 19 August 1963, quoted in Latham, *Modernization as Ideology*, 91–92.

77. Latham, *Modernization as Ideology*, 83.

78. Jeffrey F. Taffet, *Foreign Aid as Foreign Policy: The Alliance for Progress in Latin America* (Abingdon, UK: Routledge, 2007), 7, 29–65.

79. Kathryn C. Statler, "Building a Colony: South Vietnam and the Eisenhower Administration, 1953–1961," in *The Eisenhower Administration, the Third World, and the Globalization of the Cold War*, ed. Kathryn C. Statler and Andrew L. Johns (Lanham, MD: Rowman & Littlefield, 2006), 107–113.

80. Immerwahr, *Thinking Small*, 54.

81. Latham, *Modernization as Ideology*, 174.

82. Joseph J. Zasloff, "Rural Resettlement in South Viet Nam: The Agroville Program," *Pacific Affairs* 35, no. 4 (Winter 1962–1963): 327–340. On the colonial precedents of concentration villages, see also Stephan Malinowski and Moritz Feichtinger, " 'Eine Million Algerier lernen im 20. Jahrhundert zu leben' Umsiedlungslager und Zwangsmodernisierung im Algerienkrieg 1954–1962," in Malinowski and Unger, "Modernizing Missions," 107–133.

## Chapter Five

1. Cullather, "Damming Afghanistan," 528.

2. David C. Engerman, "Ideology and the Origins of the Cold War, 1917–1962," in *The Cambridge History of the Cold War*, ed. Melvyn P. Leffler and Odd Arne Westad (Cambridge: Cambridge University Press, 2010), 20–43.

3. Odd Arne Westad, "The New International History of the Cold War: Three (Possible) Paradigms," *Diplomatic History* 24, no. 4 (Fall 2000): 551–565, especially 563; David C. Engerman, *The Price of Aid: The Economic Cold War in India* (Cambridge, MA: Harvard University Press, 2018), 1–17; Frederick Cooper, *Africa since 1940*, 89.

4. Sara Lorenzini, *Due Germanie in Africa: La cooperazione allo sviluppo e la competizione per i mercati di materie prime e tecnologia* (Florence: Polistampa, 2003); William Glenn Gray, *Germany's Cold War: The Global Campaign to Isolate East Germany, 1949–1969* (Chapel Hill:

University of North Carolina Press, 2000); Massimiliano Trentin, *La guerra fredda tedesca in Siria: Diplomazia, economia e politica, 1963–1970* (Padua, Italy: CLEUP, 2015).

5. Bent Boel, *The European Productivity Agency and Transatlantic Relations, 1953–1961* (Copenhagen: Museum Tusculanum Press, 2003).

6. "Aufzeichnung," Bonn, 19 September 1959, PA AA, B58 IIIB1 324.

7. Willard L. Thorp, *The Reality of Foreign Aid* (New York: Council of Foreign Relations, Praeger, 1971), xiii.

8. Matthias Schmelzer, "A Club of the Rich to Help the Poor? The OECD, 'Development,' and the Hegemony of Donor Countries," in *International Organizations and Development, 1945–1990*, ed. Marc Frey, Sönke Kunkel, and Corinna R. Unger (Basingstoke, UK: Palgrave Macmillan, 2014), 180.

9. NATO Restricted Working Paper AC/119-WP(58)58, 17 August 1958, PA AA, B34 Ref. 307, 114.

10. Robert Cassen et al., *Does Aid Work? Report to an Intergovernmental Task Force* (Oxford, UK: Clarendon Press, 1986), 2.

11. "Bericht über die Dritte Sitzung der DAC-Arbeitsgruppe zur Vorbereitung der Welthandelskonferenz, BMWi," Bonn, 31 March 1964, PA AA, IIIB1 234.

12. Telegram 4485, Luciolli, 9 February 1963, Archivio Storico Diplomatico del Ministero degli Affari Esteri e della Cooperazione Internazionale (hereafter ASD MAECI), Telegrammi.

13. Mete Durdag, *Some Problems of Development Financing: The Turkish First Five-Year Plan, 1963–1967* (Dordrecht, Netherlands: Reidel, 1973), 64.

14. Telegram 21973, Ortona, 26 September 1964 and Telegram 1431, 22 January 1965, Diga Keban, Ortona, ASD MAECI, Telegrammi. Thomas C. Kuchenberg, "The OECD Consortium to Aid Turkey," *Studies in Law and Economic Development* 2, no. 1 (1967): 91–106.

15. Thorp, *Reality of Foreign Aid*, 8.

16. *Report to the President of the United States from the Committee to Strengthen the Security of the Free World: The Scope and Distribution of United States Military and Economic Assistance Programs*, 20 March 1963. Kennedy Library, personal papers of George Ball, box 1, Clay Report, p. 2.

17. "Your trip to Bonn, Paris and London," Myer Rashish to Mr. Ball, 27 February 1961, NARA, General Records of the Department of State (RG59), box 25.

18. "Sharing the Costs of Military Alliance and International Economic Aid," 16 April 1962, NARA, RG59, box 25.

19. McGhee, 28 January 1964, PA AA, B58 IIIB1 311.

20. In 1962 (Keller-Achilles) and in 1963 (Müller Roschach-Rostow), see PA AA, B58 IIIB1 924. The comparison of economic potential of the two blocs is in PA AA, B58 IIIB1 324, 325.

21. NARA, RG59, Bureau of European Affairs, records relating to the OECD and DAC, lot file 68D150, box 31; "Aufzeichnung 'Deutsch-amerikanische Zusammenarbeit bei der Hilfe für EL,' Legationsrat Dr. G. Pfeiffer," 7 April 1960, PA AA, Büro StS, B2 81.

22. Memorandum of conversation, 3 April 1961, "Under-Secretary Ball's trip to Europe, March 20 and March 21, 1961," NARA, RG59, Bureau of European Affairs, records relating to the OECD and DAC, lot file 68D83, box 25.

23. Memorandum of conversation, 3 April 1961.

24. IBRD, office memorandum, 27 January 1963, NARA, RG59, box 25.

25. "Tentative Programme of Work for the Development Assistance Committee," DAC (63)18 (Add.), Paris, 31 December 1963, PA AA, IIIB1 235.

26. "Record Atlantic Affairs Conference," 17 May 1965, NARA, RG59, box 26.

27. "FRG Aid Program and Budget Problem, AID Administrator's Trip," 21–27 February 1965, NARA, RG59, box 25.

28. "The US and Other Aid-Giving Countries," NARA, lot file 68D150, box 27.

29. Schmidt-Schlegel-Rostow talk, 27 December 1960; proposal originated by Rosenstein-Rodan, PA AA, B58 IIIB1 324.

30. "Strengthening DAC and Multilateral Aid Coordination," NARA, RG59, box 25.

31. "Fernschreiben Paris an AA," 20 February 1965, PA AA, B58 IIIB1 225.

32. "President Johnson's Equivalent of the Marshall Plan," 11 June 1965, and "Record Atlantic Affairs Conference," 17 May 1965, NARA, RG59, box 26.

33. Memorandum, Deane R. Hinton to Mr. Leddy, 15 June 1965, NARA, RG59, box 26.

34. Memorandum, W. W. Rostow to Mr. Bell, 29 January 1965, NARA, RG59, box 25.

35. "Proposal to Create a New Bilateral US-FRG Aid Relationship," NARA, RG59, box 25.

36. "OECD Ministerial Meeting, Paris, 25–26 November 1965, Scope Paper," NARA, RG59, entry A1–5605, b.3. On the Kennedy Round, see Lucia Coppolaro, *The Making of a World Trading Power: The European Economic Community (EEC) in the GATT Kennedy Round Negotiations (1963–67)* (Farnham, UK: Ashgate, 2013).

37. "Strengthening DAC and Multilateral Aid Coordination," NARA, RG59, box 25.

38. "The Growth of External Debt Service Liabilities of Less Developed Countries," DAC (65) 17, National Archives, OD9/150.

39. "Official Committee on Overseas Development, Summary of the DAC Annual Aid Review 1965," 19 July 1965, National Archives, OD9/150. Speech notes for the minister's statement to the DAC on 22 July, F. C. Mason, 19 July 1965, National Archives, OD9/150.

40. High-level DAC meetings, 1965; prospect of debt servicing, DAC (65)17; "Proposal for Development Finance," 15 July 1965; and statement of Mr. Woods at DAC ministerial meeting, 16 July 1965; National Archives, OD9/150.

41. Confidential telegram, UK Del to DAC, 27 July 1965, National Archives, OD9/151.

42. Goran Ohlin, "The Organization for Economic Cooperation and Development," in "The Global Partnership: International Agencies and Economic Development," special issue, *International Organization* 22, no. 1 (Winter 1968): 236.

43. Record Atlantic Affairs Conference, 17 May 1965; NARA, RG59, lot file 68D83, box 26.

44. Sara Lorenzini, "Globalising Ostpolitik," *Cold War History* 9, no. 2 (May 2009): 227–230.

45. Robert Delavignette, *Service Africaine* (Paris: Gallimard, 1946). On the influence of Delavignette, see Dimier, *Invention of a Development Aid Bureaucracy*, 33–34, 116–120.

46. HAEU, BAC 25/1980, 1034.

47. Rochereau address, 8–11 December 1964, quoted in Dimier, *Invention of a European Aid Bureaucracy*, 34.

48. Jacques Ferrandi, "La Communauté européenne et l'assistance technique," *International Development Review*, no. 8 (1964): 8–9.

49. Carlo Felice Casula, *Credere nello sviluppo sociale: La lezione intellettuale di Giorgio Ceriani Sebregondi* (Rome: Lavoro, 2010).

50. Development Assistance Policy of the European Economic Community, summary minutes, meeting held in Paris, 6 May 1964 (report dated 12 August 1964), DAC/AR M (64)8, PA AA, B58 IIIB1 381.

51. Durieux to Ferrandi, 28 February 1973, HAEU, BAC 25/1980 2947.

52. "External Aid to the Somali Republic, 10 May 1969, S. J. Whitwall," in *Somali Republic: Economic Affairs (External): Multilateral Aid*, National Archives, FCO (Foreign and Commonwealth Office) 31/429.

53. Aide à la production à Madagascar—Programme supplementaire de développement de la production rizicole, HAEU, BAC 25/1980_773 (1966–1972).

54. Project Alaotra, HAEU, BAC 25/1980_773 (1966–1972); Reports 1970: Aide à la production; Amenagement hydro-agricole des perimetres de Morafeno, Beholamena; Andranobe, Ranofotsy—Lovoka et Andragorona, BAC 25/1980 783 (1969–1971).

55. Note à l'attention de Monsieur Ferrandi, Bruxelles, 29 November 1966, signed J. Hecq, BAC 25/1980 773 (1966–1972).

56. Dimier, *Invention of a European Development Aid*, 36.

57. Auclert, Development Assistance Policy of the European Economic Community, summary minutes, DAC/M(64)8, PA AA, B58 IIIB1 381.

58. Dimier, *Invention of a European Development Aid*, 35–36.

59. L'hôpital de Mogadiscio (Somalie): Rapport de mission effectuée par la Direction générale du Développement de l'Outre-mer, HAEU, BAC 025/1980_1420; L'hôpital de Mogadiscio (Somalie): Rapports de missions effectuées par les fonctionnaires de la Direction générale du Développement de l'Outre-mer, HAEU, BAC 025/1980_1419; L'hôpital de Mogadiscio (Somalie): Mission de M. CARLIN chargé d'étudier les problèmes d'organisation administrative et d'exploitation afin de mettre en place un système administratif pour assurer un meilleur fonctionnement, HAEU, BAC 025/1980_1417.

60. Working Party on the Annual Aid Review of the Development Assistance Committee on the Development Assistance Efforts and Policies of the European Economic Community, DAC/AR/M(63)9, PA AA, B58 IIIB1 381.

61. Véronique Dimier and Mike McGeever, "Diplomats without a Flag: The Institutionalization of the Delegations of the Commission in African, Caribbean and Pacific Countries," *Journal of Common Market Studies* 44, no. 3 (2006): 483–505.

62. High-level DAC meeting, 1966, summary record of the 77th session, 20–21 July 1966, National Archives, OD9/153.

63. Martin Rempe, *Decolonization by Europeanization? The Early EEC and the Transformation of French-African Relations*, KFG Working Paper No. 27 (2011). On the reform of the peanut sector and the diversification projects (with the introduction of cotton as a new cash crop), see Martin Rempe, *Entwicklung im Konflikt: Die EWG und der Senegal 1957–1975* (Cologne: Böhlau Verlag, 2012), 139–178.

64. Ulf Engel and Hans-Georg Schleicher, *Die beiden deutschen Staaten in Afrika: Zwischen Konkurrenz und Koexistenz 1949–1990* (Hamburg, Germany: Institut für Afrika-Kunde im Verbund der Stiftung Deutsches Übersee-Institut, 1998), 243–246; Ralf Ahrens, *Gegenseitige Wirtschaftshilfe? Die DDR im RGW—Strukturen und handelspolitische Strategien 1963–1976* (Cologne: Böhlau, 2000).

65. Heinz Joswig, "Zur Perspektive der ökonomischen Zusammenarbeit zwischen den Ländern des RGW und den Entwicklungsländern," *Deutsche Aussenpolitik* 3 (March 1975): 331–339; Konstantin Ivanovich Mikulsky, *CMEA: International Significance of Socialist Integration* (Moscow: Progress Publishers, 1979 [English edition, 1982]), 316.

66. BArchB, DL2 3590; Bundesarchiv Koblenz Stiftung Archiv der Parteien und Massenorganisationen der DDR (hereafter SAPMO-BArchiv), DY 30 3462, Büro Ulbricht.

67. BArchB, DL2 VAN 224 and DL2 4307.

68. Direktive, *XIV Ratstagung* (March 1961), SAPMO-BArchiv, DY 30/J IV2/2A/800; also BArchB, DE1 VA 41795.

69. BArchB, DL2 1894.

70. "Direktive für das Auftreten der Delegation der DDR auf der 1. Sitzung der Ständigen Kommission des Rates für Gegenseitige Wirtschaftshilfe für die Koordinierung der technischen Unterstützung," BArchB, DL2 VAN 76.

71. Gerhard Wettig, *Community and Conflict in the Socialist Camp: The Soviet Union, East Germany and the German Problem, 1965–1972* (London: C. Hurst, 1975), 150.

72. 4. Tagung der SKTU, Moscow, 16–20 April 1963, BArchB, DL2 VAN 76.

73. John Michael Montias, "Background and Origins of the Rumanian Dispute with Comecon," *Soviet Studies* 16, no. 2 (October 1964): 132; Simon Godard, "Framing the Discourse on 'Backwardness': Tension about the Development Issue Considered within the Socialist Bloc or on a Global Scale" (paper presented at the conference "Development and Underdevelopment in Post-War Europe," Columbia University, 10 October 2014).

74. "Bericht, Konsultation der Stellvertretenden Minister für Außenhandel, Moskau, September 1965," BArchB, DL2 VAN 57.

75. Heinrich Machowski and Siegfried Schultz, *RGW-Staaten und Dritte Welt: Wirtschaftsbeziehungen und Entwicklungshilfe* (Bonn, Germany: Forschungsinstitut der Deutschen Gesellschaft für Auswärtige Politik e.V. Europa Union Verlag, 1981), 43.

76. Koordinationsplan, SKTU, 1963, BArchB, DE1 VA 42175.

77. "Aktennotiz-Auswertung der Reise Winzer in afrikanische Länder," 10 June 1963, BArchB, DL2 VAN 24.

78. "Analyse, MAI," 21 August 1963, BArchB, DL2 VAN 920 and "Information des MAI zur Entwicklung des Handels mit den ökonomisch schwach entwickelten Ländern," BArchB, DE1 VA 42174. Ulbricht's quote comes from "Aktennotiz-Auswertung der Reise Winzer in afrikanische Länder," 10 June 1963, BArchB, DL2 VAN 242.

79. "Bericht, 9. Sitzung der SKTU," Moscow, 11–14 January 1966, BArchB, DL2 VAN 37–38.

80. Elizabeth Bishop, "Talking Shop: Egyptian Engineers and Soviet Specialists at the Aswan High Dam" (PhD diss., University of Chicago, 1997), 281.

81. Bishop, 244.

82. "Kollegiumsitzung vom 19. Februar 1962," MfAA, LS-A447 160–184.

83. "Einige Bemerkungen und Schlußfolgerungen," SAPMO-BArchiv, DY 30 /IVA2/20/795.

84. Hans-Joachim Spanger and Lothar Brock, *Die beiden deutschen Staaten in der Dritten Welt: Die Entwicklungspolitik der DDR—eine Herausforderung für die Bundesrepublik Deutschland?* (Opladen, Germany: Westdeutscher Verlag, 1987), 230.

85. "Bericht, Handelsrat Hartmann," 25 September 1967, MfAA, C 1467/72.

86. "Gespräch Lessing-Lacik," MfAA, C 1467/72.

87. The Higher School of Economics Bruno Leuschner, see BArchB, DL2 4307; Spanger and Brock, *Die beiden deutschen Staaten*, 235.

88. 4. Tagung der SKTU, 16–20 April 1963, and 9. Tagung der SKTU, Moscow, January 1966, BArchB, DL2 VAN 37–38.

89. Kollegiumsitzung, 19 August 1963, MfAA, LS-A 488. The decision was taken with the *MR-Beschluß*, 10 October 1963, BArchB, DL2 VAN 57.

90. Hubertus Büschel, *Hilfe zur Selbsthilfe: Deutsche Entwicklungsarbeit in Afrika 1960–1975* (Frankfurt, Germany: Campus Verlag, 2014), 452–481.

91. Young-Sun Hong, *Cold War Germany, the Third World, and the Global Humanitarian Regime* (New York: Cambridge University Press, 2015).

92. "Bericht, 5. Sitzung SKTU," 1963, BArchB, DL2 VAN 76; "Bericht, 7. Sitzung SKTU," Moscow, 19–21 November 1964, BArchB, DL2 VAN 37–38.

93. In October 1966, Warsaw, BArchB, DL2 VAN 57; Machowski and Schultz, *RGW-Staaten und Dritte Welt*, 23.

94. "SKTU-Frage einer möglichen Beteiligung an der Organisierung und Erweiterung der Produktion von Kupfer, Nickel, Kautschuk, und Baumwolle in den EL (1964)," BArchB, DE1 VSII 12720.

95. Carol R. Saivetz and Sylvia Woodby, *Soviet-Third World Relations* (Boulder, CO: Westview Press, 1985), 135; "Zusammenarbeit der Handelsvertretungen der RGW-Länder in Entwicklungsländern," BArchB, DL2 VAN 50.

96. "Analyse 1970," BArchB, DL2 VA 1225; "Bericht, 3. Sitzung SKTU," Moscow, 21–22 September 1962, BArchB, DL2 VAN 37–38.

97. Colin W. Lawson, "The Soviet Union in North-South Negotiations: Revealing Preferences," in *Soviet Interests in the Third World*, ed. Robert Cassen (London, SAGE, 1985), 177–191.

98. "Bericht, Konsultation der Stellvertretenden Minister für Außenhandel," Warsaw, 25 October 1966, BArchB, DL2 VAN 57.

99. Raymond Aron, *Dix-huit leçons sur la société industrielle* (Paris: Gallimard, 1962); Zbigniew Brzezinski and Samuel P. Huntington, *Political Power: USA/USSR* (New York: Viking Press, 1964), 409–436; Ian Weinberg, "The Problem of the Convergence of Industrial Societies: A Critical Look at the State of a Theory," *Comparative Studies in Society and History* 11, no. 1 (January 1969): 1–15; Alfred G. Meyer, "Theories of Convergence," in *Change in Communist Systems*, ed. Chalmers Johnson (Stanford, CA: Stanford University Press, 1970), 313–341.

100. John Kenneth Galbraith, *The New Industrial State* (New York: New American Library, [1967]).

101. Herbert Meißner, *Konvergenztheorie und Realität* (Frankfurt, Germany: Verlag Marxistische Blätter, 1971); Günter Rose, *Konvergenz der Systeme: Legende und Wirklichkeit* (Cologne: Pahl-Rugenstein Verlag, 1970); Günter Rose, *"Industriegesellschaft" und Konvergenztheorie: Genesis Strukturen Funktionen* (Berlin: VEB Deutscher Verlag der Wissenschaften, 1973). A review of the reception of these ideas in Central and Eastern Europe is in Jörg Requate, "Visions of the Future during the 1960s: GDR, CSSR and the Federal Republic of Germany in Comparative Perspective," in *Comparative and Transnational History: Central European Approaches and New Perspectives*, ed. Heinz-Gerhard Haupt and Jürgen Kocka (New York: Berghahn Books, 2009), 178–203.

102. Léopold Sédar Senghor, *On African Socialism* (New York: Praeger, 1964), 133.

## Chapter Six

1. Interview with Richard Gardner, Columbia Center for Oral History Archive (hereafter CCOH), 12.

2. John F. Kennedy, "Address before the General Assembly of the United Nations, September 25, 1961," John F. Kennedy Presidential Library and Museum, *https://www.jfklibrary.org/Research/Research-Aids/JFK-Speeches/United-Nations_19610925.aspx*.

3. John Toye and Richard Toye, *The UN and Global Political Economy: Trade, Finance, and Development* (Bloomington: Indiana University Press, 2004), 178.

4. Daniel Maul, *Menschenrechte, Sozialpolitik und Dekolonisation: Die Internationale Arbeitsorganisation (IAO) 1940–1970* (Essen, Germany: Klartext, 2007), 55.

5. Stéphane Hessel, *Danse avec le siècle* (Paris, Seuil, 1997), 139.

6. Kunibert Raffer and Hans Wolfgang Singer, *The Foreign Aid Business: Economic Assistance and Development Co-operation* (Cheltenham, UK: Edward Elgar, 1996).

7. Maurice Bourquin, *Vers une nouvelle société des nations* (Neuchâtel, Switzerland: Éditions la Baconnière, 1945), 66–68.

8. Martin D. Dubin, "Toward the Bruce Report: The Economic and Social Programs of the League of Nations in the Avenol Era," in *The League of Nations in Retrospect: Proceedings of the Symposium* (Berlin: De Gruyter, 1983), 52–72.

9. Jamie Martin, "International Development before the Cold War: Corporatism and Planning between Europe and Asia in the 1930s" (paper presented at the conference "Cold War Economics," London, December 2015).

10. "Foreign Trade: No Cure for Hard Times," *Atlantic Monthly* 44 (1879): 477, quoted in Ninkovich, "Die Zivilisierungsmission der USA," 303.

11. William Easterly, *The Tyranny of Experts: Economists, Dictators, and the Forgotten Rights of the Poor* (New York, Basic Books, 2014), 53–54.

12. Margherita Zanasi, "Exporting Development: The League of Nations and Republican China," *Comparative Studies in Society and History* 49, no. 1 (2007): 143–169.

13. Paul B. Trescott, "H. D. Fong and the Study of Chinese Economic Development," *History of Political Economy* 34, no. 4 (Winter 2002): 789–809.

14. Cooper, *Africa since 1940*, 88.

15. Easterly, *Tyranny of Experts*, 68.

16. James Ferguson, *The Anti-Politics Machine: "Development," Depoliticization, and Bureaucratic Power in Lesotho* (Minneapolis: University of Minnesota Press, 1994).

17. Galbraith, *Nature of Mass Poverty*.

18. Paul W. Drake, ed., *Money Doctors, Foreign Debts and Economic Reforms in Latin America from the 1890s to the Present* (Wilmington, DE: SR Books, 1994).

19. Amy L. S. Staples, *The Birth of Development: How the World Bank, Food and Agriculture Organization, and World Health Organization Changed the World, 1945–1965* (Kent, OH: Kent State University Press, 2006); John Boyd Orr, *As I Recall* (London: MacGibbon and Kee, 1966), 123–131.

20. Joseph Hodge, "British Colonial Expertise, Post-Colonial Careering and the Early History of International Development," in Malinowski and Unger, "Modernizing Missions," 24–46.

21. Glenda Sluga, "The Human Story of Development: Alva Myrdal at the UN, 1949–1955," in *International Organizations and Development, 1945–1990*, ed. Marc Frey, Sönke Kunkel, and Corinna Unger (London: Palgrave Macmillan, 2014), 57.

22. *Our Responsibility for Poor Nations* (1961), quoted by Yvonne Hirdman, *Alva Myrdal: The Passionate Mind* (Bloomington: Indiana University Press, 2008), 319.

23. Sluga, "Human Story of Development," 53–54.

24. Alva Myrdal, *Nation and Family: The Swedish Experiment in Democratic Family and Population Policy* (New York: Harper, 1941).

25. Matthew Connelly, *Fatal Misconception: The Struggle to Control World Population* (Cambridge, MA: Belknap Press of Harvard University Press, 2008); Daniel Maul, *Human Rights, Development and Decolonization: The International Labour Organization, 1940–70* (London: Palgrave Macmillan, 2011); Richard Jolly, Louis Emmerij, and Frederic Lapeyre, *UN Contributions to Development Thinking and Practice* (Bloomington: University of Indiana Press, 2004), 188–192.

26. Escobar, *Encountering Development*, 4.

27. United Nations, Department of Social and Economic Affairs, *Measures for the Economic Development of Underdeveloped Countries*, 1951.

28. Staples, *Birth of Development*, 26.

29. Michele Alacevich, *The Political Economy of the World Bank: The Early Years* (Stanford, CA: Stanford University Press, 2009), 13.

30. Lorenzini, "Ace in the Hole?," 441–446.

31. "Gespräch Adenauer-Black," 3 July 1959, PA AA, B58 IIIB1 215.

32. Alacevich, *Political Economy*, 11–63.

33. Escobar, *Encountering Development*, 25.

34. Staples, *Birth of Development*, 37–42.

35. Jackson to Anstee, 31 January 1971, quoted in James Gibson, *Jacko, Where Are You Now? A Life of Robert Jackson* (Richmond, UK: Parsons Publishing, 2006), 239.

36. Sergei Y. Shenin, *America's Helping Hand: Paving the Way to Globalization* (New York: Nova Science, 2005), 147.

37. Ekbladh, *Great American Mission*, 88.

38. Sluga, "Human Story of Development," 50.

39. Mazower, *Governing the World*, 287.

40. Thomas G. Weiss, Tatiana Carayannis, Louis Emmerij, and Richard Jolly, eds., *UN Voices: The Struggle for Development and Social Justice* (Bloomington: Indiana University Press, 2005), 147.

41. W. Arthur Lewis, *The Principles of Economic Planning: A Study Prepared for the Fabian Society* (London: Dennis Dobson, George Allen & Unwin, 1949), accessed December 2014, *https://ia802607.us.archive.org/13/items/principlesofecon030862mbp/principlesofecon030862mbp.pdf*.

42. William Arthur Lewis, *Sir William Arthur Lewis: Collected Papers, 1941–1988*, vols. 1–3 (Cave Hill, Barbados: Institute of Social and Economic Research, University of the West Indies, 1994).

43. Craig N. Murphy, *The United Nations Development Programme: A Better Way?* (Cambridge: Cambridge University Press, 2006).

44. Jolly, Emmerij, and Lapeyre, *UN Contributions to Development Thinking*, 65.

45. Hans Singer, "The Distribution of Gains between Investing and Borrowing Countries," *American Economic Review* 40, no. 2 (1950): 473–485.

46. Louis Emmerij, Richard Jolly, and Thomas G. Weiss, *Ahead of the Curve? UN Ideas and Global Challenges* (Bloomington: Indiana University Press, 2001), 21.

47. United Nations, Economic Commission for Latin America, *The Economic Development of Latin America and Its Principal Problems* (Lake Success, NY: United Nations Department of Economic Affairs, 1950; reprinted in *Economic Bulletin for Latin America* 7, no. 1, 1962).

48. Edgar J. Dosman, *The Life and Times of Raúl Prebisch, 1901–1986* (Montreal: McGill-Queen's University Press, 2008).

49. Oral history interview with Hans Singer, 2 January 2000, CCOH.

50. Dosman, *Life and Times of Raúl Prebisch*, 251.

51. Murphy, *United Nations Development Programme*, 112; Raucher, *Paul G. Hoffman*, 120–154.

52. D. John Shaw, *Sir Hans Singer: The Life and Work of a Development Economist* (London: Palgrave Macmillan, 2002), 72–90.

53. Robert E. Elder and Forrest D. Murden, *Economic Cooperation: Special United Nations Fund for Economic Development (SUNFED)* (New York: Woodrow Wilson Foundation, 1954), 21.

54. Oral history interview with Hans Singer.

55. Letter to Eisenhower, quoted in Raucher, *Paul G. Hoffman*, 125. See Paul G. Hoffman, "Reply," *Christian Century* 74 (3 April 1957): 427.

56. Toye and Toye, *UN and Global Political Economy*, 173.

57. Shaw, *Sir Hans Singer*, 89.

58. Quoted in Toye and Toye, *UN and Global Political Economy*, 174.

59. Paul G. Hoffman, *One Hundred Countries, One and One Quarter Billion People: How to Speed Their Economic Growth, and Ours, in the 1960's* (New York: Albert D. and Mary Lasker Foundation, 1960), 23.

60. Robert L. Tignor, *W. Arthur Lewis and the Birth of Development Economics* (Princeton, NJ: Princeton University Press, 2006), 147–149.

61. Jeffrey W. Jacobs, "Mekong Committee History and Lessons for River Basin Development," *The Geographical Journal* 161, no. 2 (July 1995): 135–148; Jeffrey W. Jacobs, "The Mekong River Commission: Trans-boundary Water Resources Planning and Regional Security," *Geographical Journal* 168, no. 4 (December 2002): 354–364; Jeffrey W. Jacobs, "The United States and the Mekong Project," *Water Policy* 1, no. 6 (2000): 587–603.

62. Ekbladh, *Great American Mission*, 91; Simon Toner, "The Counter-Revolutionary Path: South Vietnam, the United States, and the Global Allure of Development, 1968–1973" (PhD diss., London School of Economics, 2015).

63. John Toye, "Assessing the G77: 50 Years after UNCTAD and 40 Years after the NIEO," *Third World Quarterly* 35, no. 10 (2014): 1762.

64. *Proceedings of the United Nations Conference for Trade and Development*, vol. 1, 101, accessed February 2015, *http://unctad.org/en/Docs/econf46d141vol1_en.pdf*.

65. *Towards a New Trade Policy for Development: Report by the Secretary-General of the United Nations Conference on Trade and Development*, United Nations Document E/Conf.46/3 (New York: United Nations, 1964). One chapter is devoted entirely to East-South trade (90–98).

66. Oral history interview with Hans Singer.

67. Sidney Dell, "The Origins of UNCTAD," in *UNCTAD and the North-South Dialogue: The First Twenty Years*, ed. Michael Zammit Cutajar (Oxford, UK: Pergamon Press, 1985), 19–21.

68. On UNCTAD, see Giuliano Garavini, *After Empires: European Integration, Decolonization, and the Challenge from the Global South, 1957–1986* (New York: Oxford University Press, 2012).

69. Pover Shahen Abrahamian, Edmar L. Bacha, Gerry Helleiner, Roger Lawrence, and Pedro Malan, eds., *Poverty, Prosperity and the World Economy: Essays in Memory of Sidney Dell* (Basingstoke, UK: Macmillan, 1995), 10–11.

70. Oral history interview with Hans Singer, 14.

71. Toye and Toye, *UN and Global Political Economy*, 203.

72. "The UN Role: Tinbergen and Jackson Reports," *Development Policy Review* A4, no. 1 (November 1970): 22–26.

73. Kevin Brushett, "Partners in Development? Robert McNamara, Lester Pearson, and the Commission on International Development, 1967–1973," *Diplomacy & Statecraft* 26, no. 1 (2015): 84–102.

74. Dosman, *Life and Times of Raúl Prebisch*, 438; Emmerij, Jolly, and Weiss, *Ahead of the Curve?*, 175.

75. Commission on International Development, *Partners in Development: Report of the Commission on International Development* (New York: Praeger, 1969).

76. Lester B. Pearson, "Partners in Development: A New Strategy for Global Development," *Unesco Courier*, February 1970, 10.

77. *The Widening Gap: Development in the 1970s.* Columbia Conference on International Economic Development, Williamsburg, Virginia, and New York, 15–21 February 1970 (New York: Columbia University Press, 1971).

78. "Richard Nixon, Special Message to the Congress on Foreign Aid, May 28, 1969," in *Public Papers of the President of the United States, Richard Nixon, 1969* (Washington, DC: Government Printing Office, 1970), 411.

79. Pearson, "Partners in Development," 14.

80. Lewis to Nkrumah, 1 August 1957, quoted in Murphy, *United Nations Development Programme*, 126–127; Volta River Project Preparatory Commission, *The Volta River Project* (London: H. M. Stationery Office, 1956); "The Volta River Project," *African Affairs* 55, no. 221 (October 1956): 287–293; James Moxon, *Volta: Man's Greatest Lake; The Story of Ghana's Akosombo Dam* (New York: Praeger, 1969). On the social consequences, see Jordan E. Shapiro, "Settling Refugees, Unsettling the Nation: Ghana's Volta River Project Resettlement Scheme and the Ambiguities of Development Planning, 1952–1970" (PhD diss., University of Michigan, 2003); *The Volta Resettlement Experience: Proceedings of a Symposium Held at the University of Science and Technology, Kumasi, March 21 to 27, 1965* (London: Pall Mall, 1970), 147–156.

81. Cooper and Packard, *International Development*, 83.

82. Robert Gillman Allen Jackson, *The Case for an International Development Authority* (Syracuse, NY: Syracuse University Press, 1959).

83. "Oral History Memoir," Robert G. A. Jackson, CCOH.

84. Margaret Joan Anstee, *Never Learn to Type: A Woman at the United Nations* (Chichester, UK: Wiley and Sons, 2003), 255–265.

85. Robert Jackson, *A Study of the Capacity of the United Nations Development System*, vols. 1 and 2 combined (Geneva: United Nations Geneva, 1969), 13.

## Chapter Seven

1. William Attwood, "What to Do about Africa?," *Princeton Alumni Weekly* 68 (September 1967): 39; also in William Attwood, *The Reds and the Blacks: A Personal Adventure* (New York: Harper & Row, 1967).

2. For example, Roger Parson, ed., *Sino-Soviet Intervention in Africa* (Washington, DC: Council on American Affairs, 1977).

3. Shmuel N. Eisenstadt, "Multiple Modernities," *Daedalus* 129, no. 1 (Winter 2000): 1–29.

4. Lawson, "Soviet Union in North-South Negotiations," 177–191.

5. Roger Kanet, *The Soviet Union and the Developing Nations* (Baltimore: Johns Hopkins University Press, 1974).

6. The model of the *mnogoukladnost* is described in Saivetz and Woodby, *Soviet-Third World Relations*, 12.

7. Sara Lorenzini, "Comecon and the South in the Years of Détente: A Study on East–South Economic Relations," *European Review of History: Revue européenne d'histoire* 21, no. 2 (2004): 183–199; Sara Lorenzini, "Modernisierung durch Handel: Der Ostblock und die Koordinierung der Entwicklungshilfe in der Ständigen Kommission für Technische Unterstützung," in *Osteuropäische Geschichte und Globalgeschichte*, ed. Martin Aust and Julia Obertreis (Stuttgart, Germany: Steiner-Verlag, 2014), 225–240.

8. "Information zur Konsultation der Vertreter der Minister für Aussenhandel im RGW," Moscow, 21–24 April 1971, BArchB, SKAH, DL2 VAN 57.

9. Yurii Konstantinov in 1977, quoted by David R. Stone, "CMEA's International Investment Bank and the Crisis of Developed Socialism," *Journal of Cold War Studies* 10, no. 3 (2008): 66.

10. "Direktive Konsultation der DDR mit der UdSSR—Import von Rohstoffen aus den EL in den RGW," 6 October 1970, BArchB, SKAH, DL2 VAN 489 and 489a.

11. "Information zur Konsultation der Vertreter der Minister für Aussenhandel im RGW," Moscow, 21–23 April 1971, BArchB, DL2 VAN 57; "Bericht, 23. SKTU," March 1972, BArchB, DE1 VA 52248.

12. "Bericht, 29. SKTU," Moscow, 13–15 November 1974, BArchB, DE1 VA 52056.

13. Stone, "CMEA's International Investment Bank," 48–77.

14. Simon Godard, "Framing the Discourse."

15. Rostislav A. Ulyanovsky, *Socialism in the Newly Independent Nations* (Moscow: Progress Publishers, 1974). For the East German concept of *überholen ohne einzuholen*, see André Steiner, *Von Plan zu Plan: Eine Wirtschaftsgeschichte der DDR* (Munich: Deutsche Verlags-Anstalt, 2004), 142.

16. *Information über die 60. Tagung des Executivkomittees des RGW*, SAPMO-BArchiv, DY 3023–1311, *Zusammenarbeit mit dem Rat für Gegenseitige Wirtschaftshilfe*, 1972–73; Giovanni Graziani, "The Non-European Members of the CMEA: A Model for Developing Countries?," in *The Soviet Union, Eastern Europe and the Third World*, ed. Roger E. Kanet (Cambridge: Cambridge University Press, 1988), 163–179.

17. Thomas P. M. Barnett, *Romanian and East German Policies in the Third World: Comparing the Strategies of Ceaușescu and Honecker* (Westport, CT: Praeger, 1992).

18. N. Shinkov, *Experience of the CMEA Activities over 25 Years* (Moscow: Council for Mutual Economic Assistance, 1975), 18.

19. Klaus Fritsche, *Sozialistische Entwicklungsländer in der 'internationalen sozialistischen Arbeitsteilung' des RGW: Zum Forschungsstand* (Cologne: Bundesinstitut für Ostwissenschaftliche und Internationale Studien, 1991), 27.

20. Aroon K. Basak's comments in Christopher T. Saunders, ed., *East-West-South: Economic Interaction between Three Worlds* (Basingstoke, UK: Macmillan, 1983), 369.

21. Philip Muehlenbeck, *Czechoslovakia in Africa, 1945–1968* (Basingstoke, UK: Palgrave Macmillan, 2016), 187.

22. "Politbüro-Beschluss, 20. Dezember 1977," BArchB, DL2 Bereich Kommerzielle Koordinierung (KOKO), Abteilung Handelspolitik (HP), 1; see Sara Lorenzini, "East-South Relations in the 1970s and the Added Value of GDR Involvement in Africa: Between Bloc Loyalty and Self Interest," in *The Globalization of the Cold War: Diplomacy and Local Confrontation, 1975–85*, ed. Massimiliano Guderzo and Bruna Bagnato (London: Routledge, 2010), 104–115.

23. Patrick Gutmann, "Tripartite Industrial Cooperation and Third World Countries," in Saunders, *East-West-South*, 337–364; Patrick Gutmann, "West-östliche Wirtschaftskooperationen in der Dritten Welt," in *Ökonomie im Kalten Krieg*, ed. Christian Th. Müller, Claudia Weber, and Bernd Greiner (Hamburg, Germany: Hamburger Edition, 2010), 395–412.

24. Kridl Valkenier, *Soviet Union and the Third World*, 59, 65.

25. Michał Kalecki, *Essays on Developing Economies* (Hassocks, UK: Harvester Press, 1976), 36.

26. M. Maximova, quoted in Kridl Valkenier, *Soviet Union and the Third World*, 55.

27. Quotation of Viktor Goncharev, a deputy director of the Soviet Institute for African Studies, in "Soviet Policy in Southern Africa: An Interview with Viktor Goncharev by Howard Barrell," *Work in Progress* 7, no. 4 (1987): 140–141.

28. N. N. Inozemtsev, quoted in Kridl Valkenier, *Soviet Union and the Third World*, 68.

29. Anatoli Olshany and Leon Z. Zevin, *CMEA Countries and Developing States: Economic Cooperation* (Moscow: Progress Publishers, 1984), 91.

30. An analysis including the attitude of Western European parties is in Christoph Kalter, *Die Entdeckung der Dritten Welt: Dekolonisierung und neue radikale Linke in Frankreich* (Frankfurt, Germany: Campus Verlag, 2011).

31. Karen Nersesovich Brutents, *The Newly Free Countries in the Seventies* (Moscow: Progress Publishers, 1983), 7.

32. Roy Allison, *The Soviet Union and the Strategy of Non-alignment in the Third World* (Cambridge: Cambridge University Press, 1988), 34.

33. Peter Willetts, *The Non-aligned Movement: The Origins of a Third World Alliance* (London: F. Pinter: 1978).

34. Piero Gleijeses, *Conflicting Missions: Havana, Washington, & Africa, 1959–1976* (Chapel Hill: University of North Carolina Press, 2002); Piero Gleijeses, "Moscow's Proxy? Cuba and Africa, 1975–1988," *Journal of Cold War Studies* 8, no. 2 (2006): 3–51.

35. John M. Kirk and H. Michael Erisman, "Cuba's Cold War Medical Aid Programs," in *Cuban Medical Internationalism: Origins, Evolution, and Goals* (Basingstoke, UK: Palgrave Macmillan, 2009), 59–96.

36. Piero Gleijeses, *The Cuban Drumbeat: Castro's Worldview; Cuban Foreign Policy in a Hostile World* (London: Seagull, 2009).

37. Conversation of third secretary of the Soviet Embassy in Cuba, D. Atabekov, with head of the MFA Cuba Department of International Organizations, A. Moreno, 10 February 1972, quoted in Jeremy Friedman, *Shadow Cold War*, 205.

38. SAPMO-BArchiv, Büro Lamberz, DY 30 IV 2/2.033, 122, 123; Sara Lorenzini, "East-South Relations in the 1970s," 104–115; Edward George, *The Cuban Intervention in Angola, 1965–1991: From Che Guevara to Cuito Cuanavale* (London: Frank Cass, 2005), 43, 260.

39. Allison, *Soviet Union and the Strategy of Non-alignment*, 35–36.

40. I. I. Kovalenko and R. A. Tuzmukhamedov, eds., *The Non-aligned Movement* (Moscow: Progress Publishers, 1985).

41. Mikulsky, *CMEA*, 316.

42. See Elizabeth Kridl Valkenier, "Revolutionary Change in the Third World: Recent Soviet Assessments," *World Politics* 38, no. 3 (1986): 415–434; also Kridl Valkenier, *Soviet Union and the Third World*, 136.

43. Oleg Bogolomov, "The CMEA Countries and the NIEO," in Saunders, *East-West-South*, 251.

44. Godard, "Framing the Discourse."

45. Easterly, *Tyranny of Experts*, 53–79.

46. Bruce D. Larkin, *China and Africa, 1949–1970: The Foreign Policy of the People's Republic of China* (Berkeley: University of California Press, 1971), 93.

47. Between December 1963 and February 1964 he visited the United Arab Republic (Egypt), Algeria, Morocco, Tunisia, Ghana, Mali, Guinea, Sudan, Ethiopia, and Somalia. He was in Asia 14–29 February 1964, in Burma (now Myanmar), Pakistan, and Ceylon (now Sri Lanka).

48. Quoted in Friedman, *Shadow Cold War*, 118–119.

49. Leslie James, *George Padmore and Decolonization from Below: Pan-Africanism, the Cold War, and the End of Empire* (Basingstoke, UK: Palgrave Macmillan, 2015).

50. On the talks with the Soviet Union before the Tricontinental Conference of AAPSO in Havana (1966), see SAPMO-BArchiv, DY30/ IV A2/20/113.

51. Jeremy Friedman, "Soviet Policy in the Developing World and the Chinese Challenge in the 1960s," *Cold War History* 10, no. 2 (2010): 247–272.

52. Fulbert Youlou, *J'accuse la Chine* (Paris: La Table Ronde, 1966).

53. Odd Arne Westad, "The Great Transformation: China in the Long 1970s," in *The Shock of the Global: The 1970s in Perspective*, ed. Charles Maier, Niall Ferguson, Erez Manela, and Daniel Sargent (Cambridge, MA: Belknap Press of Harvard University Press, 2010), 65–79.

54. Philip Snow, "China and Africa: Consensus and Camouflage," in *Chinese Foreign Policy*, ed. Thomas W. Robinson and David Sambaugh (Oxford, UK: Clarendon Press, 1994), 283–321.

55. Chen Jian, "China and the Bandung Conference," in *Bandung Revisited: The Legacy of the 1955 Asian-African Conference for International Order*, ed. See Seng Tan and Amitav Acharya (Singapore: NUS Press, 2008), 132–159.

56. "Cina: Ritorno in Africa," *Nigrizia* 89, no. 1 (January 1971): 40–41.

57. See Warren Weinstein and Thomas H. Henriksen, *Soviet and Chinese Aid to African Nations* (New York: Praeger, 1980).

58. In the introduction to Philip Snow, *China Returns to Africa: A Rising Power and a Continent Embrace* (London: Hurst, 2008), xviii.

59. Deborah Bräutigam, *The Dragon's Gift: The Real Story of China in Africa* (Oxford: Oxford University Press, 2009), 41; "Nous aidons les Chinois à nous aider," *Madagascar Matin*, 5 May 1982, quoted by Snow, "China and Africa," 306.

60. Chen Jian, "China's Changing Policies toward the Third World and the End of the Global Cold War," in *The End of the Cold War and the Third World: New Perspectives on Regional Conflict*, ed. Artemy M. Kalinovsky and Sergey Radchenko (Abingdon, UK: Routledge, 2011), 101–121.

61. Snow, "China and Africa," 305.

62. *Deng Xiaoping sixiang nianpu*, ed. CCP Central Institute of Historical Documents (Beijing: Zhongyang Wenxian, 1998), quoted in Chen, "China and the Bandung Conference," 149.

63. Andreas Eckert, "Julius Nyerere, Tanzanian Elites and the Project of African Socialism," in *Elites and Decolonization in the Twentieth Century*, ed. Jost Düffler and Marc Frey (London: Palgrave Macmillan, 2011), 226.

64. Rist, *History of Development*, 123–139.

65. Bräutigam, *Dragon's Gift*, 39.

66. On this, see Goran Hyden, *Beyond Ujamaa in Tanzania* (London: Heinemann, 1980).

67. Julius Nyerere, "Socialism and Rural Development, 1967," in *Freedom and Socialism: A Selection from Writings and Speeches, 1965–1967* (Oxford: Oxford University Press, 1968), 337–366.

68. A. Grande, "Un maestro in paradiso," *Nigrizia* 94, no. 23 (December 1976): 14–15.

69. The report is quoted in Andrew Coulson, *Tanzania: A Political Economy* (New York: Oxford University Press, 2013), 162.

70. Andreas Eckert, *Herrschen und Verwalten: Afrikanische Bürokraten, staatliche Ordnung und Politik in Tanzania, 1920–1970* (Munich: Oldenbourg, 2007), 253–258.

71. Mike Faber and Dudley Seers, eds., *The Crisis of Planning* (London: Chatto and Windus for Sussex University Press, 1972).

72. Padre R. Ballan, "Tanzania: La battaglia più dura," *Nigrizia* 86, no. 12 (December 1968): 16; also see "Speranze per il socialismo africano," *Nigrizia* 97, no. 20 (December 1979): 13.

73. A. De Carolis, "Dove va la Tanzania?," *Nigrizia* 90, no. 13–15 (July–August 1972): 11–12.

74. On Catholic bishops in Tanzania, see "Tanzania: Pace e comprensione reciproca," *Nigrizia* 90, no. 21 (November 1972): 40–43.

75. On the downsides of *Ujamaa*, see Michael Jennings, *Surrogates of the State: NGOs, Development, and Ujamaa in Tanzania* (Bloomfield, CT: Kumarian Press, 2008), 37–74, 139–157.

76. Padre Walbert Bühlmann, "Chiesa e socialismo in Africa: Speranze messianiche?," *Nigrizia* 97, no. 20 (1 December 1979): 32.

77. Jamie Monson, *Africa's Freedom Railway* (Bloomington: Indiana University Press, 2009), 15–20.

78. Jamie Monson, "Working ahead of Time: Labor and Modernization during the Construction of the Tazara Railway, 1968–86," in Lee, *Making a World after Empire*, 239.

79. Elisabeth Hsu, "Medicine as Business: Chinese Medicine in Tanzania," in *China Returns to Africa: A Rising Power and a Continental Embrace*, ed. Chris Alden, Daniel Large, and Ricardo Soares de Oliveira (London: C. Hurst, 2008), 226.

80. The project developed by Paul Fuchs (1904–5) is described in Scott, *Seeing Like a State*, 227–229.

81. G77 Doc. MM.77/I/SR.14, 25 October 1967, quoted in Daniel J. Whelan, "'Under the Aegis of Man': The Right to Development and the Origins of the New International Economic Order," *Humanity: An International Journal of Human Rights, Humanitarianism, and Development* 6, no. 1 (Spring 2015): 99.

82. Giuliano Garavini, "The Colonies Strike Back: The Impact of the Third World on Western Europe, 1968–1975," *Contemporary European History* 16, no. 3 (August 2007): 299–319.

83. Pierre Jalee, *The Pillage of the Third World* (Paris: François Maspero, 1965).

84. Christopher Dietrich, *Oil Revolution: Anticolonial Elites, Sovereign Rights, and the Economic Culture of Decolonization* (Cambridge: Cambridge University Press, 2017), 106–109, 116, 202.

85. Samuel Moyn, *Not Enough: Human Rights in an Unequal World* (Cambridge, MA: Belknap Press of Harvard University Press, 2018), 105.

86. Walden Bello, "Building an Iron Cage: The Bretton Woods Institutions, the WTO, and the South," in *Views from the South: The Effects of Globalization and the WTO on Third World Countries*, ed. Sarah Anderson (Chicago: Food First Books, 2000), 54–87.

87. Johan Galtung, "On the Relation between Military and Economic Non-alignment," December 1982, accessed 7 May 2014, *http://www.transcend.org/galtung/papers/On%20the%20 Relation%20Between%20Military%20and%20Economic%20Non-Alignment.pdf*. See also Changavalli Siva Rama Murthy, "Non-aligned Movement Countries as Drivers of Change in International Organizations," *Comparativ* 23, no. 4/5 (2013): 118–136.

88. Garavini, *After Empires*, 175–183.

89. Mohammed Bedjaoui, *Towards a New International Economic Order* (New York: Holmes & Meier, 1979). UN resolution 3281 is available at *http://www.un-documents.net/a29r3281 .htm*; the 1974 Declaration on the Establishment of a New International Economic Order is available at *http://www.un-documents.net/s6r3201.htm*. Antony Anghie, *Imperialism, Sovereignty and the Making of International Law* (Cambridge: Cambridge University Press, 2005), 212–216.

90. Nils Gilman, "The New International Economic Order: A Reintroduction," *Humanity: An International Journal of Human Rights, Humanitarianism, and Development* 6, no. 1 (Spring 2015): 7; Michael Crozier, Samuel P. Huntington, and Joji Watanuki, eds., *The Crisis of Democracy: Report on Governability of Democracies to the Trilateral Commission* (New York: New York University Press, 1975).

91. Consultations with the socialist countries were held in German—the representative for the group was Peter Florin, from the GDR. Summaries by Diego Cordovez are "Note for the Record: Progress of Informal Negotiations as of Tuesday 9 September" and "Note for the Record: Progress of Informal Negotiations as of Thursday 11 September [1975]," United Nations Archives (hereafter UNA), S 0908 b2 f10.

92. "Media Coverage," April 1974, UNA, S-0908-b2f7.

93. Gromyko's words were reported by *Pravda* in "Media Coverage," April 1974, UNA, S-0908-b2f7.

94. *Die Sozialistische Internationale zum antiimperialistischen Kampf in Afrika, Asien und Lateinamerika: Materialien des gemeinsamen wissenschaftlichen Kolloquiums des Problemrates "Ideologie und Politik der internationalen Sozialdemokratie" und der Kommission der Historiker der DDR und der UVR am 24. September 1987 in Berlin* (Berlin: Akademie für Gesellschaftswissenschaften beim ZK der SED, 1988), 241–248.

95. Kovalenko and Tuzmukhamedov, *Non-aligned Movement*, 134–135.

96. Allison, *Soviet Union and the Strategy of Non-alignment*, 116–119.

97. Mahbub ul Haq, *The Poverty Curtain: Choices for the Third World* (New York: Columbia University Press, 1976); Robert Cox, "Ideologies and the New International Economic Order: Reflections on Some Recent Literature," *International Organization* 33, no. 2 (March 1979): 263; Gilbert Rist, "The Not-So-New International Order," *Development (SID)* 20, no. 3–4 (1978): 48–51.

98. Cody Stephens, "The Accidental Marxist: Andre Gunder Frank and the 'Neo-Marxist' Theory of Underdevelopment, 1958–1967," *Modern Intellectual History*, Vol. 15, 2 (August 2018): 411–442.

99. Andre Gunder Frank, "Long Live Transideological Enterprise! The Socialist Economies in the Capitalist International Division of Labor," *Review (Fernand Braudel Center)* 1, no. 1 (1977): 91–140; Immanuel Wallerstein, "The Rise and Future Demise of the World Capitalist System: Concepts for Comparative Analysis," *Comparative Studies in Society and History* 16, no. 4 (September 1974): 387–415; Johanna Bockman, "Socialist Globalization against Capitalist Neocolonialism," *Humanity: An International Journal of Human Rights, Humanitarianism, and Development* 6, no. 1 (Spring 2015): 118.

## Chapter Eight

1. David Lilienthal, *The Armament of a Democracy* (Knoxville: Tennessee Valley Authority, 1940); James C. Scott, "High Modernist Social Engineering: The Case of the TVA," in *Experiencing the State*, ed. Lloyd I. Rudolph and John Kurt Jacobsen (New Delhi: Oxford University Press, 2007), 25.

2. Immerwahr, *Thinking Small*, 68, 82.

3. For a discussion on planning and its prospects, see Faber and Seers, *Crisis in Planning*.

4. Louis Armand and Michel Drancourt, *Plaidoyer pour l'avenir* (Paris: Calmann-Lévy, 1961).

5. Jacob Darwin Hamblin, *Arming Mother Nature: The Birth of Catastrophic Environmentalism* (New York: Oxford University Press, 2013), 152.

6. Laura K. Landolt, "Constructing Population Control: Social and Material Factors in Norm Emergence and Diffusion," *Global Society* 21, no. 3 (2007): 401.

7. Latham, *Right Kind of Revolution*, 95–109.

8. Connelly, *Fatal Misconception*.

9. Charles S. Elton, *The Ecology of Invasions by Animals and Plants* (London: Methuen, 1958).

10. Rachel Carson, *Silent Spring* (New York: Fawcett Crest, 1962).

11. Hamblin, *Arming Mother Nature*, 151–178. Barry Commoner, one of the leading figures of later environmentalism, was part of the 1958 working group on the social consequences of science.

12. In 1957, industrialist Gaston Berger founded the journal *Prospective* and a study center of the same name, while philosopher Bertrand de Jouvenel, with funding from the Ford Foundation, opened the Association Internationale Futuribles and the journal of the same name.

13. Sharon E. Kingsland, *Modeling Nature: Episodes in the History of Population Ecology* (Chicago: University of Chicago Press, 1985), 1–24.

14. Wolfgang Sachs, *Planet Dialectics* (London: Zed Books, 1999), 63.

15. Kingsley Davis, "Population Policy: Will Current Programs Succeed?," *Science, New Series* 158, no. 3802 (November 10, 1967): 739.

16. Garrett Hardin, "The Tragedy of the Commons," *Science, New Series* 162, no. 3859 (13 December 1968): 1243–1248; Paul R. Ehrlich, *The Population Bomb* (New York: Ballantine Books, [1968]). See Élodie Vieille Blanchard, "Les limites à la croissance dans un monde global: Modélisations, prospectives, réfutations" (PhD diss., École des Hautes Études en Sciences Sociales, 2011), 156–174.

17. "The Population Challenge of the '70s," *Population Bulletin* 26, no. 1 (February 1970).

18. "A Brief Guide to the 1970 AAAS Annual Meeting," *Science* 170, no. 3960 (20 November 1970): 873–899.

19. John Maddox, *The Doomsday Syndrome* (New York: McGraw-Hill, 1972).

20. René Dubos, *Reason Awake* (New York: Columbia University Press, 1970), 257–260.

21. On Peccei and the Club of Rome, see Gunter A. Pauli, *Crusader for the Future: A Portrait of Aurelio Peccei, Founder of the Club of Rome* (Oxford, UK: Pergamon Press, 1987); Adriana Castagnoli, ed., *Fra etica, economia e ambiente: Aurelio Peccei, un protagonista del Novecento* (Turin: SEB, 2009).

22. Aurelio Peccei, *The Chasm Ahead* (New York: Macmillan, 1969), 113.

23. Aurelio Peccei, "Considerazioni sulla necessità di una programmazione globale: Conferenza," *Mondo economico: Settimanale di economia, finanza, politica, cultura* 22, no. 40 (1967): 21–30.

24. Hasan Ozbekhan, "Toward a General Theory of Planning," in *Perspectives of Planning: Proceedings of the OECD Working Symposium on Long-Range Forecasting and Planning; Bellagio, Italy, 27th October–2nd November 1968*, ed. Erich Jantsch (Paris: Organisation for Economic Cooperation and Development, 1969), 45–155.

25. Carl Kaysen, "The Computer that Printed Out W*O*L*F*," *Foreign Affairs* 50, no. 4 (1972): 660–668.

26. Peter Passell, Marc Roberts, and Leonard Ross, "The Limits to Growth: A Review," in *Pollution, Resources, and the Environment*, ed. Alain C. Enthoven (New York: Norton, [1973]), 230.

27. *Newsweek*, 13 March 1972, 103.

28. "So geht die Welt zugrunde: Eine Bombe im Taschenbuchformat; Siebzehn Wissenschaftler sagen den Wachstumstod der Zivilisation voraus," *Die Zeit*, 17 March 1972. On German reception of the report, see Nils Freytag, "'Eine Bombe im Taschenbuchformat?' Die 'Grenzen des Wachstums' und die öffentliche Resonanz," *Zeithistorische Forschungen* [Studies in contemporary history] 3 (2006) no. 3, 465–469; and Jonas van der Straeten, *Der erste Bericht an den Club of Rome von 1972 und seine Rezeption in der Bundesrepublik Deutschland* (Altstadt, Germany: Grin Verlag, 2009).

29. "Ernest Stern to Robert McNamara, Report on the 'Limits to Growth,'" 6 September 1972, in Ernest Stern, Chronological Files (Development Policy), Correspondence 1972, 1850301, World Bank Group Archives.

30. Oral history interview with Dr. James A. Lee, 4 April 1985, World Bank–IFC Oral History Program, 6, accessed January 2017, *http://documents.worldbank.org/curated/en/3371 31468340887059/pdf/790710TRN0Lee00erview0April04001985.pdf.*

31. "Ernest Stern to Mr. Haq, Limits to Growth," 15 May 1972, in Ernest Stern, Chronological Files (Development Policy), Economic Advisory Correspondence, 1850312, World Bank Group Archives.

32. "President's Council Meeting," 26 January 1970, in Records of the Office of the President, 1770818, World Bank Group Archives.

33. Matthias Schmelzer, "The Crisis before the Crisis: The 'Problems of Modern Society' and the OECD, 1968–74," *European Review of History: Revue européenne d'histoire* 19, no. 6 (1 December 2012): 999–1020. On cultural complexity of the crisis, see Fredric Jameson, *Postmodernism, or, The Cultural Logic of Late Capitalism* (Durham, NC: Duke University Press, 1991).

34. Gilman, *Mandarins of the Future*, 241–276.

35. Dudley Seers, "The Meaning of Development," *International Development Review* 11, no. 4 (December 1969): 2–3.

36. NSC Undersecretaries Committee, 25 March 1970, Memorandum for the President (Elliot Richardson), NARA, Nixon Presidential Materials Staff, National Security Council Institutional (H) Files, National Security Study Memorandums, H 146.

37. Schmelzer, "Crisis before the Crisis," 1008. The document quoted here is *The Problems of Modern Society*, attributed to Alexander King. On discussion in the OECD, see Matthias Schmelzer, *The Hegemony of Growth: The OECD and the Making of the Economic Growth Paradigm* (Cambridge: Cambridge University Press, 2016), 289–312.

38. Henry A. Kissinger, Talking Points National Security Council, Aid, 27 April 1970, NARA, Nixon Presidential Materials Staff, National Security Council Institutional (H) Files, National Security Council Meetings, H 028.

39. *U.S. Foreign Assistance in the 1970s: A New Approach; Report to the President from the Task Force on International Development*, 4 March 1970, 2; NARA, Nixon Presidential Materials Staff, National Security Council Institutional (H) Files, National Security Council Meetings, H 028.

40. NARA, Nixon Presidential Materials Staff, National Security Council Institutional (H) Files, National Security Study Memorandums, H 146.

41. Latham, *Right Kind of Revolution*, 112. On agricultural development see Corinna R. Unger, *International Development: A Postwar History* (London: Bloomsbury, 2018), 109–115.

42. Cullather, *Hungry World*, 232–262; Vandana Shiva, *The Violence of the Green Revolution: Third World Agriculture, Ecology and Poverty* (London: Zed Books, 1991).

43. NARA, Nixon Presidential Materials Staff, National Security Council Institutional (H) Files, National Security Study Memorandums, H 146.

44. Stephen Macekura, "The Limits of the Global Community: The Nixon Administration and Global Environmental Politics," *Cold War History* 11, no. 4 (2011): 489–518; Mazower, *Governing the World*, 334.

45. Jan-Henrik Meyer, "Appropriating the Environment: How the European Institutions Received the Novel Idea of the Environment and Made It Their Own," KFG Working Paper No. 31 (September 2011), 11, accessed May 2016, *http://userpage.fu-berlin.de/kfgeu/kfgwp/wpseries/WorkingPaperKFG_31.pdf*.

46. Schmelzer, "Crisis before the Crisis," 1004–1006.

47. Macekura, "Limits of the Global Community," 493–496.

48. Thorsten Schulz-Walden, *Anfänge globaler Umweltpolitik: Umweltsicherheit in der internationalen Politik (1969–1975)* (Munich: Oldenbourg Verlag, 2013), 91.

49. Linda Risso, "NATO, and the Environment: The Committee on the Challenges of Modern Society," *Contemporary European History* 25, no. 3 (2016): 517.

50. Willy Brandt, "Brief vom 17. September 1972," in Willy Brandt, Bruno Kreisky, and Olof Palme, *Briefe und Gespräche, 1972–1975* (Frankfurt, Germany: Europäische Verlagsanstalt, 1975), 40.

51. George Kennan, "To Prevent World Wasteland," *Foreign Affairs* 48, no. 3 (April 1970): 401–413.

52. Schulz-Walden, *Anfänge globaler Umweltpolitik*, 64.

53. Antonio Cederna, *La distruzione della natura in Italia* (Turin: Einaudi, [1975]).

54. Key L. Ulrich, "Der Himmel über der Ruhr geriet etwas zu blau," *Frankfurter Allgemeine Zeitung*, 5 June 1972.

55. Schulz-Walden, *Anfänge Globaler Umweltpolitik*, 80–152.

56. Giorgio Nebbia, introduction to *I pionieri dell'ambiente: L'avventura del movimento ecologista italiano; Cento anni di storia*, ed. Edgar H. Meyer (Milan: Carabà Edizioni, 1995), 8.

57. Sicco Mansholt, "Lettre à FM Malfatti," in Laurence Reboul, *La lettre Mansholt: Réactions et commentaires* (Paris: J. J. Pauvert, 1972). See also Sicco Mansholt, *Die Krise: Europa und die Grenzen des Wachstums; Aufzeichnung von Gesprächen mit Janine Delaunay und Freimut Duve* (Reinbek, Germany: Rowohlt-Taschenbuch-Verlag, 1974).

58. Giovanni Berlinguer, "Ecologia e politica," *Rinascita* 25 (23 June 1972): 20–21.

59. *Economic Costs and Benefits of an Antipollution Project in Italy: Summary Report of a Preliminary Evaluation; Special Issue for the United Nations Conference on the Human Environment, Stockholm, June 5–16, 1972* (Rome: Istituto per gli Studi Sviluppo Economico e il Progresso Tecnico-Ente Nazionale Idrocarburi, 1972); Sara Lorenzini, "Ecologia a parole? L'Italia, l'ambientalismo globale e il rapporto ambiente-sviluppo intorno alla conferenza di Stoccolma," *Contemporanea* 3 (2016): 395–418; Sara Lorenzini, "The Emergence of Global Environmentalism: A Challenge for Italian Foreign Policy?," in *Italy in the International System from Détente to the End of the Cold War: The Underrated Ally*, ed. Antonio Varsori and Benedetto Zaccaria (Basingstoke, UK: Palgrave Macmillan, 2017), 207–225.

60. Gianni Scaiola, *L'intervento pubblico contro l'inquinamento: Valutazione dei costi e dei benefici economici connessi a un progetto di eliminazione delle principali forme di inquinamento atmosferico e idrico in Italia* (Milan: FrancoAngeli, 1971); Gianni Scaiola, Paolo Gardin, and Martino Lo Cascio, eds., *Lineamenti di una politica di intervento pubblico contro l'inquinamento* (Milan: FrancoAngeli, 1975).

61. Simone Neri Serneri, "L'impatto ambientale dell'industria 1950–2000: Risorse e politiche," in *Industria ambiente e territorio: Per una storia ambientale delle aree industriali in Italia*, ed. Salvatore Adorno and Simone Neri Serneri (Bologna: Il Mulino, 2009), 46.

62. GA Res. 2581 (XXIV), United Nations Conference on the Human Environment, *http://www.un.org/documents/ga/res/24/ares24.htm*. For a discussion, see Louis B. Sohn, "The Stockholm Declaration on the Human Environment," *Harvard International Law Journal* 14, no. 3 (Summer 1973): 423.

63. Maurice Strong, *Where on Earth Are We Going?* (Toronto: Alfred A. Knopf, 2000).

64. Centre de l'information économique et sociale à l'Office Européen des Nations Unies Genève, *Environment—Stockholm: Une seule terre, Conference des Nations Unies sur l'Environnement, Stockholm 5–6 juin 1972*; Archivio Centrale dello Stato, Italia Nostra, b.279.

65. "Historique de la conférence," in *Environment—Stockholm*, 16.

66. *Development and Environment: Report and Working Papers of a Panel of Experts Convened by the Secretary-General of the United Nations Conference on the Human Environment, Founex, Switzerland, 4–12 June 1971* (Paris; Mouton, 1972).

67. "Working Paper 4: Environmental Costs and Priorities," Environmental Science and Public Policy Archives, Harvard College Library (hereafter ESPPA), Strong Papers, Box 40.

68. UN Doc. A/CONF.48/10 Annex I at 20, 33, 1971.

69. Soraya Boudia, "Environnement et construction du global," in *La mondialisation des risques: Une histoire politique et transnationale des risques sanitaires et environnementaux*, ed. Soraya Boudia and Emmanuel Henry (Rennes, France: Presses Universitaires de Rennes, 2015), 61–76.

70. Barbara Ward and René Dubos, *Only One Earth: The Care and Maintenance of a Small Planet* (New York: Norton, 1972).

71. Ward and Dubos, xvi.

72. Barry Commoner, "Motherhood in Stockholm," *Harper's Magazine*, no. 6 (June 1972): 49–54.

73. Richard Jolly, Louis Emmerij, and Thomas G. Weiss, *UN Ideas That Changed the World* (Bloomington: Indiana University Press, 2009), 153.

74. Vieille Blanchard, "Les limites à la croissance," 447.

75. Maurice F. Strong, ed., *Who Speaks for Earth?* (New York: Norton, 1973).

76. "Man and Environment," Plenary Session of United Nations Conference on Human Environment, Stockholm, 14 June 1972, accessed February 2014, *http://lasulawsenvironmental .blogspot.it/2012/07/indira-gandhis-speech-at-stockholm.html*.

77. "Message of His Holiness Paul VI to Mr. Maurice F. Strong, Secretary-General of the Conference on the Environment," accessed August 2017, *https://w2.vatican.va/content/paul-vi /en/messages/pont-messages/documents/hf_p-vi_mess_19720605_conferenza-ambiente.html*.

78. Vieille Blanchard, "Les limites à la croissance," 446.

79. Annex 3, p. 3, A/CONF.48/10 Development and Environment (Area V), ESPPA, Strong Papers, Box 42.

80. Stephen Macekura, *Of Limits and Growth: The Rise of Global Sustainable Development in the Twentieth Century* (New York: Cambridge University Press, 2015), 115; Lars-Göran Engfeldt, *From Stockholm to Johannesburg and Beyond* (Stockholm: Government Offices of Sweden, Ministry of Foreign Affairs, 2009).

81. Jolly, Emmerij, and Weiss, *UN Ideas*, 169–185.

82. Wassily W. Leontief and Marvin Hoffenberg, "The Economic Effects of Disarmament," *Scientific American* 204, no. 4 (1961): 47–55.

83. "Office Memorandum, Nicholas G. Carter to Hollis B. Chenery, Back-to-Office Report, Meeting of the Ad Hoc Expert Group on the Future of the World Economy," 26 October 1976, Hollis B. Chenery Papers—McNamara discussions, 30235183, World Bank Archives.

84. United Nations, Centre for Disarmament, *The Relationship between Disarmament and Development: Report of the Secretary-General* (New York: United Nations, 1982).

85. Antonio Donini, "Conversion, Is It a Problem?," in *The Future Role of the United Nations in an Interdependent World*, ed. John P. Renninger (Dordrecht, Netherlands: Martinus Nijhoff, 1989), 151–171.

86. Nicholas Georgescu-Roegen, *The Entropy Law and the Economic Process* (Cambridge, MA: Harvard University Press, 1971), 19; Nicholas Georgescu-Roegen, "Energy and Economic Myths," *Southern Economic Journal* 41, no. 3 (1974): 347–381.

87. R. E. Levien, "Welcoming Address," in *Carbon Dioxide, Climate and Society: Proceedings of a IIASA Workshop Cosponsored by WMO, UNEP, and SCOPE*, ed. Jill Williams (Oxford, UK: Pergamon Press, 1978), 5.

88. "Jermen Mikhailovich Gvishiani, Zhermen Mikhailovich," in *The Great Soviet Encyclopedia*, 3rd ed. (Farmington Hills, MI: St. James Press/GALE, 1970–1979).

89. Wolfgang Geierhos, "Die Sowjetunion und der Club of Rome," *Deutsche Studien Vierteljahreshefte*, no. 67 (1979): 213–230.

90. Howard Raiffa, "Creating an International Research Institution," in *IIASA Conference, International Institute for Applied Systems Analysis* 1, no. 1 (1976): 25; Howard Raiffa, "IIASA: An Experiment in International Cooperation," *Vortrag, Österreichische Zeitschrift für Außenpolitik* 14, no. 4 (1974): 253–259.

91. Dzermen Gvishiani, "The Concept of IIASA," in *IIASA Conference, International Institute for Applied Systems Analysis* 1, no. 1 (1976): 11–18.

92. Hans Knop, "Large Scale Planning Projects: The Tennessee Valley Authority and the Bratsk-Ilimsk Complex," in *IIASA Conference, International Institute for Applied Systems Analysis* 1, no. 1 (1976): 187–202.

93. Titles in *Der Spiegel*: "Die Erdöl Erpressung," 5 November 1973; "Öl Scheichs gegen Europa," 12 November 1973; "Folge der Ölkrise: Ende der Überfluss-Gesellschaft," 19 November 1973; "Energiekrise: Rettung durch die Kohle?," 3 December 1973.

94. Brandt, Kreisky, and Palme, *Briefe und Gespräche*.

95. Charles Maier, "Malaise: The Crisis of Capitalism in the 1970s," in *The Shock of the Global: The 1970s in Perspective*, ed. Charles S. Maier, Niall Ferguson, Erez Manela, and Daniel Sargent (Cambridge, MA: Belknap Press of Harvard University Press, 2010), 25–48.

96. Thomas Robertson, *The Malthusian Moment: Global Population Growth and the Birth of American Environmentalism* (New Brunswick, NJ: Rutgers University Press, 2012).

97. Alan Grainger, "Assessing the Environmental Impacts of National Development," in *Sustainable Development in a Developing World*, ed. Colin Kirkpatrick and Norman Lee (Cheltenham, UK: Edward Elgar, 1997), 61–87.

98. Peccei to Strong, 3 November 1976, ESPPA, Strong Papers, Box 58; the report was published as Jan Tinbergen, *Reshaping the International Order: A Report to the Club of Rome* (New York: Dutton, 1976).

99. Douglas Weiner, *A Little Corner of Freedom: Russian Nature Protection from Stalin to Gorbachëv* (Berkeley: University of California Press, 1999).

100. "Tass Communiqué: Soviet Scientists Meet with the Club of Rome," Moscow, 30 August–1 September 1977, ESPPA, Strong Papers, Box 58, f567.

101. Report on "The Stockholm Colloquium on World Situations and Prospects," 27–28 September 1977, ESPPA, Strong Papers, Box 58.

102. Eduard Pestel, *Beyond the Limits to Growth: A Report to the Club of Rome* (New York: Universe, 1989).

103. Independent Commission on International Development Issues (Willy Brandt Commission), *North-South: A Programme for Survival; Report of the Independent Commission on International Development Issues* (Cambridge, MA: MIT Press, 1980); Independent Commission on International Development Issues (Willy Brandt Commission), *Common Crisis North-South: Cooperation for World Recovery* (Cambridge, MA: MIT Press, 1983); Independent Commission on Disarmament and Security Issues (Palme Commission), *Common Security: A Blueprint for Survival* (New York: Simon and Schuster, 1982); World Commission on Environment and Development (Brundtland Commission), *Our Common Future* (Oxford: Oxford University Press, 1987).

## Chapter Nine

1. Odd Arne Westad, *The Cold War: A World History* (London: Allen Lane, 2017), 475.

2. Mahbub ul Haq, "Employment and Income Distribution in the 1970's: A New Perspective," *Pakistan Economic and Social Review* 9, no. 1/2 (June–December 1971): 1–9.

3. "The Cocoyoc Declaration," *International Organization* 29, no. 3 (1975): 896.

4. Mahbub ul Haq in the introduction to Paul Streeten, *First Things First: Meeting Basic Human Needs in Developing Countries*, with Shahid Javed Burki, Mahbub ul Haq, Norman Hicks, and Frances Stewart (New York: World Bank and Oxford University Press, 1981), ix, accessed December 2016, *http://documents.worldbank.org/curated/en/882331468179936655 /pdf/997710english.pdf*.

5. *Towards Accelerated Development: Proposals for the Second United Nations Development Decade*, Report of the Sixth Session of the Committee for Development Planning (New York: United Nations, 1970).

6. David A. Morse is quoted in Heinz W. Arndt, "Economic Development," 92. His ideas on the relations between growth and employment are in David A. Morse, "The Employment Problem in Developing Countries," *Political Science Quarterly* 85, no. 1 (March 1970): 1–16; Matthias Schmelzer, "The Growth Paradigm: History, Hegemony, and the Contested Making of Economic Growthmanship," *Ecological Economics* 118 (2015): 262–271.

7. Maul, *Human Rights*.

8. *U.S. Foreign Assistance in the 1970s: A New Approach—Report to the President from the Task Force on International Development*. Department of State Bulletin, 6 April 1970, 447–467; also see *FRUS, 1969–1976*, vol. 4, *Foreign Assistance, International Development, Trade Policies, 1969–1972*, doc. 128, *https://history.state.gov/historicaldocuments/frus1969-76v04/d128*.

9. Robert A. Pastor, *Congress and the Politics of U.S. Foreign Economic Policy, 1929–1976* (Berkeley: University of California Press, 1982), 278.

10. Jolly, Emmerij, and Lapeyre, *UN Contributions*, 112.

11. Patrick Allen Sharma, *Robert McNamara's Other War: The World Bank and International Development* (Philadelphia: University of Pennsylvania Press, 2017), 54, 57.

12. ["Global Review"], Robert S. McNamara Personal Chronological Files, World Bank Group Archives, *http://pubdocs.worldbank.org/en/326111383057012137/wbg-archives-1772420.pdf*.

13. François Duchêne, "The European Community and the Uncertainties of Interdependence," in *A Nation Writ Large? Foreign Policy Problems before the European Community*, ed. Max Kohnstamm and Wolfgang Hager (London: Macmillan, 1973), 20.

14. "Statement from the Paris Summit," *Bulletin of the European Communities*, no. 10 (10 October 1972): 14–26, accessed 24 March 2016, *http://www.cvce.eu/content/publication/1999/1/1 /b1dd3d57-5f31-4796-85c3-cfd2210d6901/publishable_en.pdf*.

15. Jacques Giri, *Du tiers monde aux mondes émergents: Un demi-siècle d'aide au développement* (Paris: Karthala, 2012), 91–92; Kent, *Internationalization of Colonialism*.

16. Georges Sunier, "Claude Cheysson: Histoire d'une pensée politique (1940–1981)" (PhD diss., Université de Paris VII, 1995).

17. "Declaration at Yaoundé, 29 December 1973," in Sunier, "Claude Cheysson," 91.

18. Max Liniger-Goumaz, *L'Eurafrique: Utopie ou réalité? Les métamorphoses d'une idée* (Yaoundé, Cameroon: Éditions CLE, 1972).

19. "Lomé Dossier," *The Courier*, no. 31, special issue (March 1975); Éric Bussière, Vincent Dujardin, Michel Dumoulin, Piers N. Ludlow, Jan W. Brouwer, and Élizabeth Palmero, eds., *La Commission européenne 1973–1986: Histoire et mémoires d'une institution* (Luxembourg: Publications Office of the EU, 2014), 401–421.

20. Lorenzo Ferrari, "Speaking with a Single Voice: The Assertion of the EC as a Distinctive International Actor, 1969–79" (PhD diss., IMT Lucca, 2014), 131.

21. *The Courier* 38 (July–August 1976): 55.

22. Quoted in Rempe, *Entwicklung im Konflikt*, 318.

23. *The Courier* 30 (January 1975): 4.

24. "Communication de Claude Cheysson à la reunion tenue à Rotterdam, le 9 avril 1974, dés Comittes Directeurs d'organisations privées tournées vers l'Afrique," HAEU, BAC 25/1980-1876, 188.

25. HAEU, SGCI 8765, Note, Brussels, 18 July 1974 I/96/74 (ACP 30) (FIN 24). Oral history interview with Klaus Roeh, Historical Archives of the European Union, *http://archives .eui.eu/en/oral_history/INT254.*

26. On the history of *The Courier*, see HAEU, BAC 25/1980 n.1614 and 1615. Especially numbers 8/1971, 12/1972, and 32/1975.

27. Edgar Pisani, *La main et l'outil: Le développement du Tiers Monde et l'Europe* (Paris: Éditions R. Laffont, 1984), 137.

28. "Communication de M. Claude Cheysson à la réunion tenue à Rotterdam des Comités Directeurs d'Organisations Privées tournés vers l'Afrique, 9 Avril 1974," in Sunier, "Claude Cheysson," 101.

29. "Meeting with Trade Unions, Geneva 22 June 1974," HAEU, BAC 25/1980 n.1878.

30. "Ou en est la politique globale de coopération au développement à l'échelle mondiale," HAEU, BAC 25/1980 n.1897.

31. *The Courier* 38 (July–August 1976): 54.

32. Claude Cheysson, "An Agreement Unique in History," *The Courier* 31, special issue (March 1975): 13.

33. "Intervention de M. Claude Cheysson, débat organisé par la revue Croissance des jeunes nations," 18 March 1979, HAEU, BAC 25/1980 n.1878.

34. "Préparation du Conseil européen de Dublin: Document de Travail de la Commission sur les problèmes des relations avec les PVD, 21 février 1975," quoted in Sunier, "Claude Cheysson," 98; Claude Cheysson, "La contribution du Tiers Monde à la relance de l'économie mondiale," *Studia diplomatica* 31, no. 1 (1978): 98.

35. "Interview with La Croix [Jacques Docquiert]," *La Croix*, 14 January 1978, 4, accessed September 2017, *http://aei.pitt.edu/12710/.*

36. *Rapport, Jean Durieux*, HAEU, BAC 25/1980, 304, 305.

37. Vladimir Kollontaj and Iakov I. Etinger, *The European Common Market and the Developing Countries* (Moscow: Oriental Literature, 1963); Peter Føge Jensen, *Soviet Research on Africa with Special Reference to International Relations* (Uppsala: Scandinavian Institute of African Studies, 1973), accessed January 2017, *http://nai.diva-portal.org/smash/get/diva2:276760/FULLTEXT01.pdf.*

38. C. M. Tibazarwa, *From Berlin to Brussels: 100 Years of Afro-European Cooperation* (Durham: Pentland Press, 1994); Evgeny Anatolevich Tarabrin, *The New Scramble for Africa* (Moscow: Progress Publishers, 1974); V. [Vladimir Mikhaĭlovich] Kazakevicius, "The Common Market and the Developing Countries," *International Affairs*, June 1979, 57–66.

39. Frans A. M. Alting von Geusau, *The Lomé Convention and a New International Economic Order* (Leiden, Netherlands: Sijthoff, 1977), 153.

40. Garavini, *After Empires*, 185.

41. The concept of European exceptionalism is in David S. Landes, *The Wealth and Poverty of Nations: Why Some Are So Rich and Some So Poor* (New York: W. W. Norton, 1998), where it

is used to define European success in the eighteenth and nineteenth centuries. Some authors expand it to today's Europe. A definition is in Kalypso Nicolaïdis, "Southern Barbarians? A Post-Colonial Critique of EUniversalism," in *Echoes of Empire: Memory, Identity and Colonial Legacies*, ed. Kalypso Nicolaïdis, Berny Sèbe, and Gabrielle Maas (London: I. B. Tauris, 2015), 292. For its use in connection with the European Court of Human Rights; see Georg Nolte and Helmut Philipp Aust, "European Exceptionalism?," *Global Constitutionalism* 2, no. 3 (2013): 407–436.

42. Massimiliano Trentin, "Divergence in the Mediterranean: The Economic Relations between the EC and the Arab Countries in the Long 1980s," *Journal of European Integration History* 21, no. 1 (2015): 91.

43. On the Euro-Arab Dialogue, see Silvio Labbate, *Illusioni mediterranee: Il dialogo Euro-Arabo* (Florence: Mondadori-Le Monnier, 2016); and Maria Eleonora Guasconi, "Europe and the Mediterranean in the 1970s: The Setting Up of the Euro-Arab Dialogue," *Les cahiers Irice* 1, no. 10 (2013): 163–175.

44. "Lomé Dossier," 169.

45. Document de travail des services de la Commission "Dialogue Euro-Arabe," 28 January 1975, HAEU, SEC (75) 415, Klaus Mayer (KM) 40.

46. David Allen, "The Euro-Arab Dialogue," *Journal of Common Market Studies* 16, no. 4 (December 1977): 323–342.

47. *Le Courier* 38 (July–August 1976): 54.

48. Ali A. Mazrui, "Eurafrica, Eurabia, and African-Arab Relations: The Tensions of Tripolarity," in *Interdependence in a World of Unequals: African-Arab-OECD Economic Cooperation for Development*, ed. Dunstan M. Wai (Boulder, CO: Westview Press, 1982), 17–46.

49. Editorial in *The Courier* 44 (July–August 1977).

50. ESPPA, Strong Papers, box 103, f. 975.

51. Claude Cheysson, "Partial Summary of Remarks November 29, 1975," in "Economic Cooperation and Resource Management," *Trialogue*, no. 9 (1976): 10–11.

52. L. S. Senghor, "Pour une Afrique qui integre le Moyen-Orient, Club de Rome, Colloque de Stockholm, 27–28 Septembre 1977," ESPPA, Strong Papers, box 58, f. 567.

53. Memorandum of conversation, Rambouillet, 15–17 November 1975, in *FRUS, 1969–1976*, vol. 31, *Foreign Economic Policy, 1973–1976*, https://history.state.gov/historicaldocuments/frus1969-76v31/d125.

54. Memorandum from Robert Hormats of the National Security Council Staff to Secretary of State Kissinger, 24 October 1975, *FRUS, 1969–1976*, vol. 31, *Foreign Economic Policy, 1973–1976*, 354, https://history.state.gov/historicaldocuments/frus1969-76v31/d112.

55. Memorandum from Edward Fried and Henry Owen to President-Elect Carter, 26 November 1976, "Redirecting Foreign Aid," https://history.state.gov/historicaldocuments/frus1977-80v03/d253.

56. Federico Romero, "Refashioning the West to Dispel Its Fears," in *International Summitry and Global Governance: The Rise of the G7 and the European Council, 1974–1991*, ed. Emmanuel Mourlon-Druol and Federico Romero (London: Routledge, 2014), 128.

57. Christopher M. Andrew and Vasili Mitrokhin, *The World Was Going Our Way: The KGB and the Battle for the Third World* (New York: Basic Books, 2005). The memoranda of conversation used for this section are available at https://history.state.gov/historicaldocuments/frus1969

*-76v31/d148;  https://history.state.gov/historicaldocuments/frus1969-76v31/d149;  https://history.state.gov/historicaldocuments/frus1969-76v31/d150;* all in *FRUS, 1969–1976,* vol. 31, *Foreign Economic Policy, 1973–1976.*

58. "A Note on the General Discussion Held during the First Week of the Seventh Special General Assembly on Development and International Economic Co-operation," UNA, 0908S2f9.

59. Memorandum of conversation, Rambouillet, 16 November 1975, *FRUS, 1969–1976,* vol. 31, *Foreign Economic Policy, 1973–1976, https://history.state.gov/historicaldocuments/frus1969-76v31/d124.*

60. "Development aid: Fresco of community action tomorrow; Communication of the Commission transmitted to the Council on 5 November 1974," COM(74) 1728, 30 October 1974, in *Bulletin of the European Communities,* Supplement 8/74. The new policy is described by Director-General Hans-Broder Krohn in his editorial in *The Courier* 44 (July–August 1977).

61. Memorandum from the President's Assistant for National Security Affairs (Brzezinski) to President Carter, 14 April 1977, *https://history.state.gov/historicaldocuments/frus1977-80v03/d263.*

62. Jahangir Amuzegar, "A Requiem for the North-South Conference." *Foreign Affairs,* 56, no. 1 (October 1977), 136–159.

63. Memorandum from the Under Secretary of State for Economic Affairs (Cooper) to Secretary of State Vance, 11 June 1977, "Post-mortem on CIEC," *https://history.state.gov/historicaldocuments/frus1977-80v03/d266.*

64. Memorandum of conversation, Rambouillet, France, 17 November 1975, *FRUS, 1969–1976,* vol. 31, *Foreign Economic Policy, 1973–1976, https://history.state.gov/historicaldocuments/frus1969-76v31/d125;* Memorandum of conversation, Dorado Beach, Puerto Rico, 28 June 1976, Second Session of Summit Meeting, *FRUS, 1969–1976,* vol. 31, *Foreign Economic Policy, 1973–1976, https://history.state.gov/historicaldocuments/frus1969-76v31/d149.*

65. Letter from President Carter to Soviet General Secretary Brezhnev (1977–1980, vol. 6, Soviet Union) *https://history.state.gov/historicaldocuments/frus1977-80v06/d1.*

66. ESPPA, Strong Papers, box 103; Trilateral Commission, f. 972–1977.

67. "Draft Joint Statement Trilateral Commission, 1976," ESPPA, Strong Papers, box 102, f. 971, Trilateral Commission; "Z. Brzezinski, Trilateral Commission," 25 October 1977, ESPPA, Strong Papers, box 103, Trilateral Commission.

68. "Report of the Task Force on Constructive Communist Global Involvement," ESPPA, Strong Papers, box 103, Trilateral Commission.

69. Briefing Memorandum from the Director of the Policy Planning Staff (Lake) to Secretary of State Vance, 17 June 1977, "Prospects for Expanded Soviet Bloc Role in North-South Problems," *https://history.state.gov/historicaldocuments/frus1977-80v02/d215.*

70. Antony Anghie, "Legal Aspects of the New International Economic Order," *Humanity: An International Journal of Human Rights, Humanitarianism, and Development* 6, no. 1 (Spring 2015): 145–149.

71. Liliana Obregon, "Noted for Dissent: The International Life of Alejandro Alvarez," *Leiden Journal of International Law* 19 (2006): 983–1016.

72. Gilman, "New International Economic Order," 5; Mohammed Bedjaoui, *Pour un nouvel ordre économique international* (Paris: UNESCO, 1979); Umut Özsu, " 'In the Interests of Mankind

as a Whole': Mohammed Bedjaoui's New International Economic Order," *Humanity: An International Journal of Human Rights, Humanitarianism, and Development* 6, no. 1 (2015): 129–143.

73. Paul Berthoud, "UNCTAD and the Emergence of International Development Law," in *UNCTAD and the South-North Dialogue: The First Twenty Years*, ed. M. Zammit Cutajar (Oxford, UK: Pergamon Press, 1985), 75.

74. Moyn, *Last Utopia*; Klaas Dykmann, "Only with the Best Intentions: International Organizations as Global Civilizers," *Comparativ* 23, no. 4/5 (2013): 21–46. On human rights in the 1970s (but with hardly any mention of economic and social rights), see Akira Iriye, Petra Goedde, and William I. Hitchcock, eds., *The Human Rights Revolution: An International History* (Oxford: Oxford University Press, 2012).

75. Whelan, " 'Under the Aegis of Man,' " 93–106.

76. Amuzegar, "Requiem for the North-South Conference."

77. Zbigniew Brzezinski, *Power and Principle: Memoirs of the National Security Adviser, 1977–1981* (New York: Farrar, McGraw-Hill Ryerson, 1983), 7.

78. "Foreign Policy Priorities November 3, 1976–May 1, 1977: A Memorandum to the President Elect," Jimmy Carter Presidential Library (JCPL), Plains Files, b.41, f.7.

79. Memorandum from Edward Fried and Henry Owen to President-Elect Carter, 26 November 1976, Redirecting Foreign Aid, *https://history.state.gov/historicaldocuments/frus1977-80 v03/d253*.

80. Michael Franczak, "Human Rights and Basic Needs: Jimmy Carter's North-South Dialogue, 1977–81," *Cold War History* 18, no. 4 (2018): 450–451.

81. Memorandum from Roger Hansen of the National Security Council Staff to the President's Assistant for National Security Affairs (Brzezinski) and the President's Deputy Assistant for National Security Affairs (Aaron), 26 July 1977, *https://history.state.gov/historicaldocuments /frus1977-80v03/d271*.

82. David F. Schmitz and Vanessa Walker, "Jimmy Carter and the Foreign Policy of Human Rights: The Development of a Post-Cold War Foreign Policy," *Diplomatic History* 28, no. 1 (January 2004): 130.

83. Cyrus Vance's address in March 1979, "America's Commitment to Third World Development," *FRUS*, 1977–1980, vol. 1, *Foundations of Foreign Policy*.

84. Memorandum from Guy Erb of the National Security Council Staff to the President's Assistant for National Security Affairs (Brzezinski), 11 February 1978, "North-South Policies: Assessment and Recommendations," *https://history.state.gov/historicaldocuments/frus1977-80v03/d295*.

85. Memorandum from the Under Secretary of State for Economic Affairs (Cooper) to Secretary of State Vance, 18 August 1978, "A Possible Orientation to North/South Issues in 1979," *https://history.state.gov/historicaldocuments/frus1977-80v03/d315*.

86. Franczak, "Human Rights and Basic Needs," 5.

87. Johan Galtung, "The New International Economic Order and the Basic Needs Approach," *Alternatives* 4, no. 4 (1978–79): 462.

88. Moyn, *Not Enough*, 138–139.

89. Paul Streeten, "Basic Needs and Human Rights," *World Development* 8, no. 2 (1980): 107.

90. Upendra Baxi, "The New International Economic Order, Basic Needs, and Rights: Notes toward Development of the Right to Development," *Indian Journal of International Law* 23, no. 2 (1983): 25–45.

91. Umberto Tulli, *Tra diritti umani e distensione: L'amministrazione Carter e il dissenso in Urss* (Milan: FrancoAngeli, 2013), 105.

92. Sarah B. Snyder, "'A Call for U.S. Leadership': Congressional Activism on Human Rights," *Diplomatic History* 37, no. 2 (2013): 372–397.

93. Aurélie Élisa Gfeller, "Champion of Human Rights: The European Parliament and the Helsinki Process," *Journal of Contemporary History* 49, no. 2 (2014): 407.

94. Claude Cheysson, "Europe, the Third World and Human Rights," in "The Politics of Human Rights," *Trialogue*, no. 19 (1978), accessed January 2018, *http://trilateral.org/file/101*.

95. Interview with Claude Cheysson, in *La Croix*, 14 January 1978, accessed January 2017, *http://aei.pitt.edu/12710/*; Bradley Simpson, "Self-Determination, Human Rights, and the End of Empire in the 1970s," *Humanity: An International Journal of Human Rights, Humanitarianism, and Development* 4, no. 2 (2013): 239–260.

96. Cheysson, "Europe, the Third World and Human Rights," 23.

97. Lorenzo Ferrari, *Sometimes Speaking with a Single Voice: The European Community as an International Actor, 1969–1979* (Brussels: Peter Lang, 2016), 191–197.

98. Discussions in the European Parliament on this topic are in HAEU, PE0 2955.

99. Moyn, *Not Enough*, 121; Helen E. S. Nesadurai, "Bandung and the Political Economy of North-South Relations: Sowing the Seeds for Re-visioning International Society," in *Bandung Revisited: The Legacy of the 1955 Asian-African Conference for International Order*, ed. See Seng Tan and Amitav Acharya (Singapore: NUS Press, 2008), 68–101; "Paper Prepared by Thomas Thornton of the National Security Council Staff [undated, 1980], North-South Affairs: Evaluative Comments—Retrospective and Prospective," *https://history.state.gov/historicaldocuments/frus1977-80v03/d354*.

100. Nyerere's words are quoted in Moyn, *Not Enough*, 117.

101. Peter Worsley, "How Many Worlds?," *Third World Quarterly* 1, no. 2 (April 1979): 100–108.

102. Uwe Andersen, "Neue Weltwirtschaftsordnung—von alten Konzepten zu neuen Realitäten?," *Politische Bildung* 24, no. 1 (1991): 31–42.

103. Tor Krever, "The Legal Turn in Late Development Theory: The Rule of Law and the World Bank's Development Model," *Harvard International Law Journal* 52, no. 1 (2011): 287–319, accessed January 2017, *http://www.harvardilj.org/wp-content/uploads/2011/02/HILJ_52-1_Krever.pdf*. On the right to development, see also Amartya Sen, *Development as Freedom* (New York: Anchor Books, 1999), 146–159.

## Chapter Ten

1. "Address to the 42d Session of the United Nations General Assembly in New York, New York, September 21, 1987," Ronald Reagan Presidential Library, National Archives and Records Administration, accessed February 2019, *https://www.reaganlibrary.gov/research/speeches/092187b*.

2. Gilbert Rist, "Development as a Buzzword," *Development in Practice* 17, no. 4–5 (2007): 485–491.

3. Barbara Ward and Peter T. Bauer, *Two Views on Aid to Developing Countries* (Bombay: Vora, 1968).

4. Peter Bauer and Basil S. Yamey, "The Harm That Foreign Aid Can Do in the Name of Fuelling Development," *The Guardian*, 1 August 1983.

5. Peter T. Bauer, "The Case Against Foreign Aid," *Intereconomics* 8, no. 5 (1973): 154–157.

6. Peter T. Bauer, "Creating the Third World: Foreign Aid and Its Offspring," *Journal of Economic Growth* 2, no. 4 (1987): 3–9.

7. Peter T. Bauer, "Reflections on Western Technology and 'Third World' Development," *Minerva* 15, no. 2 (1977): 144.

8. Peter T. Bauer, "Foreign Aid, Forever? Critical Reflections on a Myth of Our Time," *Encounter*, May 1974, 25.

9. Robert D. Putnam, *Making Democracy Work: Civic Traditions in Modern Italy* (Princeton, NJ: Princeton University Press, 1993).

10. Bauer, "Case against Foreign Aid," 155.

11. Dambisa Moyo, *Dead Aid: Why Aid Is Not Working and How There Is a Better Way for Africa* (London: Allen Lane, 2009); William Easterly, *The White Man's Burden: Why the West's Efforts to Aid the Rest Have Done So Much Ill and So Little Good* (New York: Penguin Press, 2006).

12. Eric Helleiner, "From Bretton Woods to Global Finance: A World Turned Upside Down," in *Political Economy and the Changing Global Order*, ed. Richard Stubbs and Geoffrey Underhill (London: Macmillan, 1994), 163–174.

13. Ivan Illich, *Medical Nemesis: The Expropriation of Health* (London: Calder & Boyars, 1975), 20.

14. "Workshop on National Preparedness for Acute and Large Scale Food Shortages in Central and West African Countries, Dakar, Senegal, 28 October–1 November 1985," ESPPA, Strong Papers, box 308, f. 2915.

15. For an analysis of the report, see *Third World Quarterly* 2, no. 4 (October 1980), especially "Editorial: Third World Options: Brandt Report," xxiv–xxvii; Andre Gunder Frank, "North-South and East-West Keynesian Paradoxes in the Brandt Report," 669–680; Dudley Seers, "Muddling Morality and Mutuality," 681–693; H. W. Singer, "A 'Northwestern' Point of View," 694–700.

16. "Notes on a Meeting Held in the Secretary General's Conference Room on Tuesday, 12 February 1980," UNA, S-0913 b23 f2 91/5, NIEO.

17. "Vienna, UNIDO, to United Nations New York Secretary General Executive Office, 10/11," UNA, S-0913 b23 f2, 91/5 NIEO—Summit Cancun.

18. According to resolution 34/138 adopted unanimously by the thirty-fourth General Assembly in 1979; see "Global Negotiations," UNA, S-0972 b5 f1.

19. UNA, S-0972 b5 f3.

20. "Summary of Remarks made by President Reagan in Philadelphia on 15 October 1981," UNA, S-0972 b5 f3.

21. "Notes on a Meeting Held in the Secretary General's Conference Room on Tuesday, 12 February 1980," UNA, S-0913 b23 f2 91/5, NIEO.

22. "Notes on the Breakfast Meeting Held at the Secretary-General's Residence on Wednesday, 19 November 1980," UNA, S-0913 b23 f2 91/5, NIEO—Summit Cancun.

23. The document "The Mexico Summit" is quoted in Toye and Toye, *UN and Global Political Economy*, 257.

24. Joseph Morgan Hodge, "Writing the History of Development (Part 1: The First Wave)," *Humanity: An International Journal of Human Rights, Humanitarianism and Development* 6, no. 3 (2015): 434–437.

25. Wallerstein, *Politics of the World Economy*, 9.

26. Brigitte Erler, *Tödliche Hilfe: Bericht von meiner letzten Dienstreise in Sachen Entwicklungshilfe* (Freiburg, Germany: Dreisam Verlag, 1985).

27. Patrick Sharma, "The United States, the World Bank, and the Challenges of International Development in the 1970s," *Diplomatic History* 37, no. 3 (2013): 572–604; Garavini, *After Empires*, 215.

28. Sharma, *Robert McNamara's Other War*, 101.

29. On accelerated development in Sub-Saharan Africa, see *Accelerated Development in Sub-Saharan Africa: An Agenda for Action* (Washington, DC: World Bank, 1981), 4–8; Antony G. Hopkins, "The World Bank in Africa: Historical Reflections on the African Present," *World Development* 14 (December 1986): 1477.

30. Research news, quoted by John Toye, *Dilemmas of Development: Reflections on the Counter-Revolution in Development Theory and Policy* (Oxford, UK: Basil Blackwell, 1987), 47–49.

31. David Reed, ed., *Structural Adjustment, the Environment, and Sustainable Development* (London: Earthscan, 1996), 8.

32. Devesh Kapur, John P. Lewis, and Richard Webb, *The World Bank: Its First Half Century*, vol. 1, *History* (Washington, DC: Brookings Institution Press, 1997).

33. Paul Mosley, Jane Harrigan, and John Toye, *Aid and Power: The World Bank and Policy-Based Lending* (London: Routledge, 1991).

34. William Easterly, "IMF and World Bank Structural Adjustment Programs and Poverty," in *Managing Currency Crises in Emerging Markets*, ed. Michael P. Dooley and Jeffrey A. Frankel (Chicago: University of Chicago Press, 2003), doi:10.7208/chicago/9780226155425.001.0001.

35. Oral history interview with Gamani Corea, 1 February 2000, CCOH archives.

36. Robert Wade, *Governing the Market: Economic Theory and the Role of Government in East Asian Industrialization* (Princeton, NJ: Princeton University Press, 1990).

37. *Proceedings of the United Nations Conference on Trade and Development*, Fifth Session, Manila, 7 May–3 June 1979, vol. 1, *Report and Annexes, https://www.unog.ch/80256EDD006 B8954/(httpAssets)/DFF6C32F5D46E1E1C1257CF5005B65CE/$file/TD-269.Vol.1.pdf.*

38. Kriedl Valkenier, *Soviet Union and the Third World*, 33.

39. Karl Wohlmuth, *Structural Adjustment and East-West-South Economic Cooperation: Key Issues* (Bremen, Germany: Weltwirtschaftlichen Colloquium der Universität Bremen, Fachbereich Wirtschaftswissenschaft, [1989]).

40. Boris S. Vaganov and Abram B. Froumkin, "East-West Relations and Their Impact on Development: Is the International Development Strategy Feasible?," in Renninger, *Future Role of the United Nations*, 201.

41. Nodari Simonia, *Destiny of Capitalism in the Orient* (Moscow: Progress Publishing, 1985), 215–217.

42. *Die Sozialistische Internationale.*

43. Kridl Valkenier, *Soviet Union and the Third World*, 127.

44. Kridl Valkenier, "Revolutionary Change in the Third World," 417.

45. Simonia, *Destiny of Capitalism in the Orient*, 205–214.

46. Nodari Simonia, "Newly-Free Countries: Problems of Development," *International Affairs*, May 1982, 83–91; Simonia, *Destiny of Capitalism in the Orient*, 250–252.

47. Vernon V. Aspaturian, "Gorbachev's 'New Political Thinking' and Foreign Policy," in *Gorbachev's New Thinking and Third World Conflicts*, ed. Jiri Valenta and Frank Cibulka (New Brunswick, NJ: Transaction Publishers, 1990), 15, 33.

48. W. Donald Bowles, "Perestroika and Its Implications for Soviet Foreign Aid," in *The Soviet Union and Eastern Europe in the Global Economy*, ed. Marie Lavigne (Cambridge: Cambridge University Press, 1992), 66–85. Data are all net debt reimbursement (68–69).

49. A conversion rate of 1.58 USD/ruble, 1987 data, is in Philip Taubman, "In Soviet: Rubles, Coupons and "Real Money,'" *New York Times*, 22 July 1987, accessed December 2016, *http://www.nytimes.com/1987/07/22/world/in-soviet-rubles-coupons-and-real-money.html*.

50. Nodari Simonia, "On the Character of Change in the USSR, Eastern Europe and the Third World," *European Journal of Development Research* 2, no. 2 (1990): 176.

51. Ivan Illich, "The Delinking of Peace and Development," *Alternatives* 7, no. 4 (1 January 1981).

52. Vaganov and Froumkin, "East-West Relations," 202.

53. A famous discussion of this took place at the 1983 conference on the long-term consequences of a nuclear war held in Washington, DC, included in Paul Ehrlich, Carl Sagan, Donald Kennedy, and Walter Orr Roberts, *The Cold and the Dark: The World after Nuclear War* (New York: Norton, 1984); Carl Sagan, *A Path Where No Man Thought: Nuclear Winter and the End of the Arms Race* (New York: Random House, 1990).

54. Sveneld A. Evteev, Renat A. Perelet, and Vadim P. Voronin, "Ecological Security of Sustainable Development," in Renninger, *Future Role of the United Nations*, 162–171.

## Conclusions

1. George H. W. Bush, *Speaking of Freedom: The Collected Speeches* (New York: Scribner, 2009), 47.

2. This reference is to Francis Fukuyama, *The End of History and the Last Man* (New York: Free Press, 1992).

3. "Angela Merkel and the History Book That Helped Inform Her Worldview," *The Guardian*, 29 December 2016, accessed December 2016, *https://www.theguardian.com/world/2016/dec/29/angela-merkel-jurgen-osterhammel-the-transformation-of-the-world-book-germany*; Jürgen Osterhammel, *The Transformation of the World: A Global History of the Nineteenth Century* (Princeton, NJ: Princeton University Press, 2016).

4. Such as Arturo Escobar, Gilbert Rist, or Immanuel Wallerstein, who see development as a global ideology of Western dominance imposed by the United States—see Escobar, *Encountering Development*; Rist, *History of Development*; and Wallerstein, *Politics of the World Economy*.

5. "Foreign Aid: Debating the Uses and Abuses," *New York Times*, 1 March 1981.

6. Bauer, "Creating the Third World," 3–9.

7. Jürgen Osterhammel and Niels P. Petersson, *Geschichte der Globalisierung: Dimensionen, Prozesse, Epochen* (Munich: Verlag C. H. Beck, 2003), 7–15. See also Dipesh Chakrabarty, "The Politics of Climate Change Is More Than the Politics of Capitalism," *Theory, Culture & Society* 34, no. 2–3 (2017): 25–37.

8. Odd Arne Westad, "The Cold War and the Third World," epilogue to *The Cold War in the Third World*, ed. Robert J. McMahon (Oxford: Oxford University Press, 2013), 217.

9. Cassen, *Does Aid Work?*

10. "Poverty and Equity Data Portal," The World Bank, *http://povertydata.worldbank.org /poverty/home/.*

11. Ravi Kanbur and Andy Sumner, "Poor Countries or Poor People? Development Assistance and the New Geography of Global Poverty," *Journal of International Development* 24 (2012): 686–695.

12. Wade, *Governing the Market,* 345–381.

13. "Aid Brought Liberia Back from the Brink," *The Economist,* 29 June 2017.

14. "Review of the International Aid System in Mali: Synthesis and Analysis," Bamako, 1998, *http://unpan1.un.org/intradoc/groups/public/documents/cafrad/unpan011311.pdf.*

15. Judy L. Baker, *Evaluating the Impact of Development Projects on Poverty: A Handbook for Practitioners* (Washington, DC: World Bank, 2000).

16. Deborah A. Bräutigam and Stephen Knack, "Foreign Aid, Institutions, and Governance in Sub-Saharan Africa," *Economic Development and Cultural Change* 52, no. 2 (January 2004): 255–285.

17. "Aid Brought Liberia Back from the Brink," *The Economist,* 29 June 2017.

18. "The Very Poor Are Now Concentrated in Violent Countries: Aid Policy Must Evolve," *The Economist,* 16 March 2017.

19. "The Hard Man on the Hills, Briefing: Rwanda," *The Economist,* 15 July 2017.

20. Brook Larmer, "Is China the World's New Colonial Power?" *New York Times,* 2 May 2017.

21. Deborah Bräutigam and Haisen Zhang, "Green Dreams: Myth and Reality in China's Agricultural Investment in Africa," *Third World Quarterly* 34, no. 9 (2013): 1676–1696.

22. "Diplomacy and Aid in Africa," *The Economist,* 14 April 2016.

23. Deborah Bräutigam and Sigrid-Marianella Stensrud Ekman, "Briefing: Rumours and Realities of Chinese Agricultural Engagement in Mozambique," *African Affairs* 111, no. 444 (2012): 483–492.

24. Bräutigam, *Dragon's Gift,* 46–67.

25. "AD122: China's Growing Presence in Africa Wins Largely Positive Popular Reviews," Afrobarometer, *http://afrobarometer.org/publications/ad122-chinas-growing-presence-africa-wins -largely-positive-popular-reviews.*

26. Kartik Jayaram, Omid Kassiri, and Irene Yuan Sun. "Dance of the Lions and Dragons: How Are Africa and China Engaging, and How Will the Partnership Evolve?," McKinsey Report (June 2017), 9; accessed August 2017, *http://www.mckinsey.com/Global-Themes /Middle-East-and-Africa/The-closest-look-yet-at-Chinese-economic-engagement-in-Africa.*

27. David Dollar, "China's Engagement with Africa: From Natural Resources to Human Resources," John L. Thornton China Center at Brookings, accessed August 2017, *https://www .brookings.edu/wp-content/uploads/2016/07/Chinas-Engagement-with-Africa-David-Dollar -July-2016.pdf.*

28. "Development Aid Rises Again in 2016 but Flows to Poorest Countries Dip," OECD, accessed August 2017, *http://www.oecd.org/dac/development-aid-rises-again-in-2016-but-flows -to-poorest-countries-dip.htm.*

29. "Misplaced Charity," *The Economist,* 11 June 2016.

30. For this kind of evidence, see Jean-Claude Berthélemy, Monica Beuran, and Mathilde Maurel, "Aid and Migration: Substitutes or Complements?" *World Development* 37, no. 10

(2009): 1589–1599; also Michael A. Clemens, "Does Development Reduce Migration?," IZA Discussion Paper No. 8592 (October 2014), accessed August 2017, *http://ftp.iza.org/dp8592 .pdf.*

31. "Special Eurobarometer 375: Making a Difference in the World; Europeans and the Future of Development Aid," EU Open Data Portal, accessed August 2017, *https://data.europa .eu/euodp/en/data/dataset/S987_76_1_EBS375.*

32. Marie de Vergès, "L'Afrique attend un 'plan Merkel' pour le continent," *Le Monde*, 13 June 2017, *http://www.lemonde.fr/economie/article/2017/06/13/l-afrique-attend-un-plan-merkel-pour-le -continent_5143625_3234.html#iOdbo3LZDRJs49SD.99.*

33. *Africa and Europe—A New Partnership for Development, Peace and a Better Future* (Berlin: Federal Ministry for Economic Cooperation and Development, 2017), *https://www.bmz .de/en/publications/type_of_publication/information_flyer/information_brochures/Materialie 270_africa_marshallplan.pdf.*

34. Doug Porter, Bryant Allen, and Gaye Thompson, *Development in Practice: Paved with Good Intentions* (London: Routledge, 1991), xv.

35. Jo Guldi and David Armitage, *The History Manifesto* (Cambridge: Cambridge University Press, 2014).

# BIBLIOGRAPHY

## Archive Collections

### ARCHIVIO CENTRALE DELLO STATO (ACS) (ROME)

Agenzia per lo Sviluppo Economico della Somalia (ASES) (1957–1960)
Amministrazione Fiduciaria della Somalia (1959–1960)
Consiglio Nazionale delle Ricerche (CNR) (1911–1990)
Italia Nostra
Ministero del Bilancio e della Programmazione Economica (1950–1972)
Ministero per il Commercio con l'Estero
Presidenza del Consiglio dei Ministri

### ARCHIVIO STORICO DEL CNR (ROME)

### ARCHIVIO STORICO DIPLOMATICO DEL MINISTERO DEGLI AFFARI ESTERI E DELLA COOPERAZIONE INTERNAZIONALE (ASD MAECI) (ROME)

Archivio di Gabinetto 1944–1958
Direzione Generale Affari Economici
Direzione Generale Affari Politici
Telegrammi

### ARQUIVO HISTÓRICO-DIPLOMÁTICO, MINISTERIO DOS NEGOCIOS ESTRANGEIROS (LISBON)

Repartiçao das Questoes Economicas, Asia e Africa (EAA)

### ARQUIVO HISTÓRICO ULTRAMARINO (LISBON)

### BUNDESARCHIV KOBLENZ—ABTEILUNGEN DDR (BERLIN)

Ministerium für Außenwirtschaft (DL2)
Ministerium für Land-, Forst-, und Nahrungsgüterwirtschaft (DK1)
Politisches Archiv des früheren Ministeriums für Auswärtige Angelegenheiten (Berlin)
Staatliche Plankommission (DE1)

## COLUMBIA CENTER FOR ORAL HISTORY (CCOH) (NEW YORK) ORAL HISTORY COLLECTION, UNITED NATIONS INTELLECTUAL HISTORY PROJECT (UNIHP)

## HARVARD ENVIRONMENTAL SCIENCE AND PUBLIC POLICY ARCHIVES (ESPPA) (CAMBRIDGE, MA)

Maurice F. Strong Papers
Peter S. Thacher Environment Collection

## HARVARD UNIVERSITY ARCHIVES (CAMBRIDGE, MA)

Faculty Archives, Papers of Hollis Burnley Chenery

## HISTORICAL ARCHIVES OF THE EUROPEAN UNION (HAEU) (FLORENCE)

Edoardo Martino (EM)
Emanuele Gazzo (EG)
Emile Nöel (EN)
The European Commission—Fonds BAC
Franco Maria Malfatti (FMM)
François-Xavier Ortoli (FXO)
Klaus Meyer (KM)
Oral History Holdings (Voices on Europe; European Commission 1958–1973 and European Commission 1973–1986)
Organes parlementaires pour la coopération au développement (ACP)
Uwe Kitzinger and Noël Salter Fonds (UWK/NS)

## JOHN F. KENNEDY PRESIDENTIAL LIBRARY (BOSTON)

John F. Kennedy Presidential Papers—President's office files, National Security Files
Oral history collection
Personal Papers of George W. Ball
Papers of David E. Bell

## LONDON SCHOOL OF ECONOMICS ARCHIVES (LONDON)

Fabian Society
Duncan Lyall Burn
Peter David Shore
Royal Economic Society

## NATIONAL ARCHIVES AND RECORDS ADMINISTRATION (NARA) (COLLEGE PARK, MD)

Nixon Presidential Materials Project—Country Files, NSC files, Henry A. Kissinger Office files (HAK files)

Records of the Department of State, RG 59
Records of the Agency for International Development (AID), RG 286

## THE NATIONAL ARCHIVES (KEW GARDENS, UK)

Foreign and Commonwealth Office (FCO)
Foreign Office (FO)
Ministry of Overseas Development (OD)

## POLITISCHES ARCHIV DES AUSWÄRTIGEN AMTS (PA AA) (BERLIN)

Abteilung für Handels- und Entwicklungspolitik (B58 e B68)
Ausrüstungshilfe (B57)
Politische Abteilung (B34)

## STIFTUNG ARCHIV DER PARTEIEN UND MASSENORGANISATIONEN IN DER DDR (SAPMO-BARCHIV) (BERLIN)

Nachlass Ulbricht
Nachlass Verner
Zentral Politisches Archiv der SED (DY30)

## UNITED NATIONS ARCHIVES (UNA) (NEW YORK)

Fonds Department of Economic and Social Affairs (DESA) (1955–present)
Fonds UN Secretary-General Kurt Waldheim (1972–1981)

## WORLD BANK GROUP ARCHIVES (WASHINGTON, DC)

Ernest Stern Files (Development Policy)
Personal Papers of Hollis B. Chenery
Records of the Office of the President, Records of President Eugene R. Black
Records of the Office of the President, Records of President George D. Woods
Records of the Office of the President, Records of President Robert S. MacNamara

## Published Primary and Secondary Sources

Abrahamian, Pover Shahen, Edmar L. Bacha, Gerry Helleiner, Roger Lawrence, and Pedro Malan, eds. *Poverty, Prosperity and the World Economy: Essays in Memory of Sidney Dell.* Basingstoke, UK: Macmillan, 1995.

*Accelerated Development in Sub-Saharan Africa: An Agenda for Action.* Washington, DC: World Bank, 1981.

Adamson, Michael. "'The Most Important Single Aspect of Our Foreign Policy?' The Eisenhower Administration, Foreign Aid, and the Third World." In *The Eisenhower Administration, the Third World, and the Globalization of the Cold War,* edited by Kathryn C. Statler and Andrew L. Johns, 47–73. Lanham, MD: Rowman & Littlefield, 2006.

Adelman, Jeremy, Michele Alacevich, Victoria de Grazia, Ira Katznelson, and Nadia Urbinati. "Albert Hirschman and the Social Sciences: A Memorial Roundtable." *Humanity: An International Journal of Human Rights, Humanitarianism, and Development* 6, no. 2 (Summer 2015): 265–286.

*Africa and Europe—A New Partnership for Development, Peace and a Better Future.* Berlin: Federal Ministry for Economic Cooperation and Development (BMZ), 2017. *https://www.bmz.de /en/publications/type_of_publication/information_flyer/information_brochures/Materialie270 _africa_marshallplan.pdf.*

Agarwala, Amar N., and Sampat P. Singh, eds. *The Economics of Underdevelopment: A Series of Articles and Papers.* New York: Oxford University Press, 1958.

Ageron, Charles-Robert. *Histoire de la France coloniale.* Vol. 3, *Le decline.* Paris: Armand Colin, 1991.

Ahrens, Ralf. *Gegenseitige Wirtschaftshilfe? Die DDR im RGW—Strukturen und handelspolitische Strategien 1963–1976.* Cologne: Böhlau, 2000.

Alacevich, Michele. *The Political Economy of the World Bank: The Early Years.* Stanford, CA: Stanford University Press, 2009.

———. *The World Bank's Early Reflections on Development: A Development Institution or a Bank?* Development Studies Working Papers, no. 221. Centro Studi Luca d'Agliano, January 2007.

Allardt, Helmut. *Politik vor und hinter den Kulissen.* Düsseldorf, Germany: Econ Verlag, 1979.

Allen, David. "The Euro-Arab Dialogue," *Journal of Common Market Studies* 16, no. 4 (December 1977): 323–342.

Allison, Roy. *The Soviet Union and the Strategy of Non-alignment in the Third World.* Cambridge: Cambridge University Press, 1988.

Alting von Geusau, Frans A. M. *The Lomé Convention and a New International Economic Order.* Leiden, Netherlands: Sijthoff, 1977.

Amin, Julius A. *The Peace Corps in Cameroon.* Kent, OH: Kent State University Press, 1992.

Amrith, Sunil. *Crossing the Bay of Bengal: The Furies of Nature and the Fortunes of Migrants.* Cambridge, MA: Harvard University Press, 2013.

Amuzegar, Jahangir. "A Requiem for the North-South Conference." *Foreign Affairs,* 56, no. 1 (October 1977): 136–159.

Andersen, Uwe. "Neue Weltwirtschaftsordnung—von alten Konzepten zu neuen Realitäten?" *Politische Bildung* 24, no. 1 (1991): 31–42.

Andrew, Christopher M., and Vasili Mitrokhin. *The World Was Going Our Way: The KGB and the Battle for the Third World.* New York: Basic Books, 2005.

Anghie, Antony. *Imperialism, Sovereignty and the Making of International Law.* Cambridge: Cambridge University Press, 2005.

———. "Legal Aspects of the New International Economic Order." *Humanity: An International Journal of Human Rights, Humanitarianism, and Development* 6, no. 1 (Spring 2015): 145–158.

Anstee, Margaret Joan. *Never Learn to Type: A Woman at the United Nations.* Chichester, UK: Wiley and Sons, 2003.

Armand, Louis, and Michel Drancourt. *Plaidoyer pour l'avenir*. Paris: Calmann-Lévy, 1961.

Arndt, Heinz W. "Economic Development: A Semantic History." *Economic Development and Cultural Change* 29, no. 3 (1981): 457–466.

———. *Economic Development: The History of an Idea*. Chicago: University of Chicago Press, 1987.

Aron, Raymond. *Dix-huit leçons sur la société industrielle*. Paris: Gallimard, 1962.

Aspaturian, Vernon V. "Gorbachev's 'New Political Thinking' and Foreign Policy." In *Gorbachev's New Thinking and Third World Conflicts*, edited by Jiri Valenta and Frank Cibulka, 3–44. New Brunswick, NJ: Transaction Publishers, 1990.

*Atti del congresso internazionale di studio sul problema delle aree arretrate, Milano, 10–15 ottobre 1954*. Milan: Giuffrè, 1954–56.

Attwood, William. *The Reds and the Blacks: A Personal Adventure*. New York: Harper & Row, 1967.

———. "What to Do about Africa?" *Princeton Alumni Weekly* 68 (September 1967): 39.

Badie, Bertrand. *The Imported State: The Westernization of the Political Order*. Stanford, CA: Stanford University Press, 2000.

Baker, Judy L. *Evaluating the Impact of Development Projects on Poverty: A Handbook for Practitioners*. Washington, DC: World Bank, 2000.

Ballantyne, Tony, and Antoinette Burton. "Empires and the Reach of the Global." In *A World Connecting, 1870–1945*, edited by Emily S. Rosenberg, 285–431. Cambridge, MA: Belknap Press of Harvard University Press, 2012.

Barnett, Thomas P. M. *Romanian and East German Policies in the Third World: Comparing the Strategies of Ceaușescu and Honecker*. Westport, CT: Praeger, 1992.

Barth, Boris, and Jürgen Osterhammel, eds. *Zivilisierungsmissionen: Imperiale Weltverbesserung seit dem 18. Jahrhundert*. Konstanz, Germany: UVK Verlagsgesellschaft, 2005.

Bat, Jean-Pierre. *La fabrique des barbouzes: Histoire des réseaux Foccart en Afrique*. Paris: Nouveau Monde, 2015.

———. *Le syndrome Foccart: La politique française en Afrique, de 1959 à nos jours*. Paris: Gallimard, 2012.

Bauer, Peter T. "The Case against Foreign Aid." *Intereconomics* 8, no. 5 (1973): 154–157.

———. "Creating the Third World: Foreign Aid and Its Offspring." *Journal of Economic Growth* 2, no. 4 (1987): 3–9.

———. "Foreign Aid, Forever? Critical Reflections on a Myth of Our Time." *Encounter*, May 1974, 15–28.

———. "Reflections on Western Technology and 'Third World' Development." *Minerva* 15, no. 2 (1977): 144–154.

Bauer, Peter T., and Basil S. Yamey. "The Harm That Foreign Aid Can Do in the Name of Fuelling Development." *The Guardian*, 1 August 1983.

Baxi, Upendra. "The New International Economic Order, Basic Needs, and Rights: Notes toward Development of the Right to Development." *Indian Journal of International Law* 23, no. 2 (1983): 25–45.

Bedjaoui, Mohammed. *Pour un nouvel ordre économique international*. Paris: UNESCO, 1979.

———. *Towards a New International Economic Order*. New York: Holmes & Meier, 1979.

Behrman, Greg. *The Most Noble Adventure: The Marshall Plan and the Time When America Helped Save Europe*. New York: Free Press, 2007.

Bello, Walden. "Building an Iron Cage: The Bretton Woods Institutions, the WTO, and the South." In *Views from the South: The Effects of Globalization and the WTO on Third World Countries*, edited by Sarah Anderson, 54–87. Chicago: Food First Books, 2000.

Berliner, Joseph S. *Soviet Economic Aid: The New Aid and Trade Policy in Underdeveloped Countries.* New York: Council on Foreign Relations, Praeger, 1958.

Berlinguer, Giovanni. "Ecologia e politica." *Rinascita* 25 (23 June 1972).

Bernstein, Eduard. "Der Socialismus und die Colonialfrage." *Sozialistische Monatshefte* 4 (1900): 549–562.

Berthélemy, Jean-Claude, Monica Beuran, and Mathilde Maurel. "Aid and Migration: Substitutes or Complements?" *World Development* 37, no. 10 (2009): 1589–1599.

Berthoud, Paul. "UNCTAD and the Emergence of International Development Law." In *UNCTAD and the South-North Dialogue: The First Twenty Years*, edited by Michael Zammit Cutajar: 71–98. Oxford, UK: Pergamon Press, 1985.

Betts, Raymond F. *The False Dawn: European Imperialism in the Nineteenth Century.* Minneapolis: University of Minnesota Press, 1975.

Bhagwati, Jagdish N., and Richard S. Eckaus, eds. *Development and Planning: Essays in Honour of Paul Rosenstein Rodan.* London: Allen and Unwin, 1972.

Biney, Ama. *The Political and Social Thought of Kwame Nkrumah.* New York: Palgrave Macmillan, 2011.

Bishop, Elizabeth. "Talking Shop: Egyptian Engineers and Soviet Specialists at the Aswan High Dam." PhD diss., University of Chicago, 1997.

Bockman, Johanna. "Socialist Globalization against Capitalist Neocolonialism." *Humanity: An International Journal of Human Rights, Humanitarianism, and Development* 6, no. 1 (2015): 109–128.

Boden, Ragna. "Cold War Economics: Soviet Aid to Indonesia." *Journal of Cold War Studies* 10, no. 3 (2008): 110–128.

———. *Die Grenzen der Weltmacht: Sowjetische Indonesienpolitik von Stalin bis Brežnev.* Stuttgart, Germany: Franz Steiner Verlag, 2006.

———. "Globalisierung Sowjetisch: Der Kulturtransfer in die Dritte Welt." In *Globalisierung imperial und sozialistisch*, edited by Martin Aust, 425–442. Frankfurt, Germany: Campus Verlag, 2013.

———. "Soviet-Indonesian Relations in the First Postwar Decade (1945–1954)." Parallel History Project on Cooperative Security (PHP). ETH Zürich, 2009. *http://www.php.isn.ethz .ch/lory1.ethz.ch/collections/coll_indonesia/Introduction7149.html?navinfo=100702.*

Boel, Bent. *The European Productivity Agency and Transatlantic Relations, 1953–1961.* Copenhagen: Museum Tusculanum Press, 2003.

Bogolomov, Oleg. "The CMEA Countries and the NIEO." In *East-West-South: Economic Interaction between Three Worlds*, edited by Christopher T. Saunders, 246–256. Basingstoke, UK: Macmillan, 1983.

Bose, Sugata, and Ayesha Jalal, eds. *Nationalism, Democracy, and Development: State and Politics in India.* New Delhi: Oxford University Press, 1997.

Boudia, Soraya. "Environnement et construction du global." In *La mondialisation des risques: Une histoire politique et transnationale des risques sanitaires et environnementaux*, edited by Soraya Boudia and Emmanuel Henry, 61–76. Rennes, France: Presses Universitaires de Rennes, 2015.

Bourquin, Maurice. *Vers une nouvelle société des nations.* Neuchâtel, Switzerland: Éditions la Baconnière, 1945.

Bowles, W. Donald. "Perestroika and Its Implications for Soviet Foreign Aid." In *The Soviet Union and Eastern Europe in the Global Economy*, edited by Marie Lavigne, 66–85. Cambridge: Cambridge University Press, 1992.

Brandt, Willy, Bruno Kreisky, and Olof Palme. *Briefe und Gespräche, 1972–1975*. Frankfurt, Germany: Europäische Verlagsanstalt 1975.

Bräutigam, Deborah. *The Dragon's Gift: The Real Story of China in Africa*. Oxford: Oxford University Press, 2009.

Bräutigam, Deborah A., and Stephen Knack. "Foreign Aid, Institutions, and Governance in Sub-Saharan Africa." *Economic Development and Cultural Change* 52, no. 2 (January 2004): 255–285.

Bräutigam, Deborah, and Sigrid-Marianella Stensrud Ekman. "Briefing: Rumours and Realities of Chinese Agricultural Engagement in Mozambique." *African Affairs* 111, no. 444 (2012): 483–492.

Bräutigam, Deborah, and Haisen Zhang. "Green Dreams: Myth and Reality in China's Agricultural Investment in Africa." *Third World Quarterly* 34, no. 9 (2013): 1676–1696.

"A Brief Guide to the 1970 AAAS Annual Meeting." *Science* 170, no. 3960 (20 November 1970): 873–899.

Brown, Robert L., and Jeffrey M. Kaplow. "Talking Peace, Making Weapons: IAEA Technical Cooperation and Nuclear Proliferation." *Journal of Conflict Resolution* 58, no. 3 (2014): 402–428.

Brushett, Kevin. "Partners in Development? Robert McNamara, Lester Pearson, and the Commission on International Development, 1967–1973." *Diplomacy & Statecraft* 26, no. 1 (2015): 84–102.

Brutents, Karen Nersesovich. *The Newly Free Countries in the Seventies*. Moscow: Progress Publishers, 1983.

Brzezinski, Zbigniew, and Samuel P. Huntington. *Political Power: USA/USSR*. New York: Viking Press, 1964.

———. "The Politics of Underdevelopment." *World Politics* 9, no. 1 (October 1956): 55–75.

———. *Power and Principle: Memoirs of the National Security Adviser, 1977–1981*. New York: Farrar, McGraw-Hill Ryerson, 1983.

Buettner, Elizabeth. *Europe after Empire: Decolonization, Society, and Culture*. Cambridge: Cambridge University Press, 2016.

Büschel, Hubertus. *Hilfe zur Selbsthilfe: Deutsche Entwicklungsarbeit in Afrika 1960–1975*. Frankfurt, Germany: Campus Verlag, 2014.

Bush, George H. W. *Speaking of Freedom: The Collected Speeches*. New York: Scribner, 2009.

Bussière, Éric, Vincent Dujardin, Michel Dumoulin, Piers N. Ludlow, Jan W. Brouwer, and Élizabeth Palmero, eds. *La Commission européenne 1973–1986: Histoire et mémoires d'une institution*. Luxembourg: Publications Office of the EU, 2014.

Calandri, Elena. "L'Italia e la questione dello sviluppo: Una sfida tra anni sessanta e settanta." In *L'Italia nella costruzione europea: Un bilancio storico 1957–2007*, edited by Piero Craveri and Antonio Varsori, 267–290. Milan: FrancoAngeli, 2009.

———. *Prima della globalizzazione: L'Italia, la cooperazione allo sviluppo e la Guerra Fredda 1955–1995*. Padua, Italy: CEDAM, 2013.

Carr, Edward H. *A History of Soviet Russia: The Bolshevik Revolution, 1917–1923*. Vol. 3. London: Macmillan, 1953.

Carson, Rachel. *Silent Spring*. New York: Fawcett Crest, 1962.

Cassen, Robert, et al. *Does Aid Work? Report to an Intergovernmental Task Force.* Oxford, UK: Clarendon Press, 1986.

Castagnoli, Adriana, ed. *Fra etica, economia e ambiente: Aurelio Peccei, un protagonista del Novecento.* Turin: SEB, 2009.

Casula, Carlo Felice. *Credere nello sviluppo sociale: La lezione intellettuale di Giorgio Ceriani Sebregondi.* Rome: Lavoro, 2010.

Cederna, Antonio. *La distruzione della natura in Italia.* Turin: Einaudi, 1975.

Cesari, Laurent. "The Declining Value of Indochina: France and the Economics of Empire, 1950–1955." In *The First Vietnam War,* edited by Mark A. Lawrence and Fredrik Logevall, 175–195. Cambridge, MA: Harvard University Press, 2007.

Chakrabarty, Dipesh. "The Legacies of Bandung: Decolonization and the Politics of Culture." In *Making a World after Empire: The Bandung Moment and Its Political Afterlives,* edited by Christopher J. Lee, 45–68. Athens: Ohio University Press, 2010.

———. "The Politics of Climate Change Is More Than the Politics of Capitalism." *Theory, Culture & Society* 34, no. 2–3 (2017): 25–37.

Chatterjee, Partha. *Nationalist Thought in the Colonial World: A Derivative Discourse.* Minneapolis: University of Minnesota Press, 1993.

Chen, Jian. "China and the Bandung Conference." In *Bandung Revisited: The Legacy of the 1955 Asian-African Conference for International Order,* edited by See Seng Tan and Amitav Acharya, 132–159. Singapore: NUS Press, 2008.

———. "China's Changing Policies toward the Third World and the End of the Global Cold War." In *The End of the Cold War and the Third World: New Perspectives on Regional Conflict,* edited by Artemy M. Kalinovsky and Sergey Radchenko, 101–121. Abingdon, UK: Routledge, 2011.

———. *Mao's China and the Cold War.* Chapel Hill: University of North Carolina Press, 2001.

Chenery, Hollis B. "From Engineering to Economics." *Banca Nazionale del Lavoro Quarterly Review,* no. 183 (December 1992): 369–406.

Cheysson, Claude. "An Agreement Unique in History." *The Courier* 31 (1975): 12–13.

———. "Europe, the Third World and Human Rights." In "The Politics of Human Rights," *Trialogue,* no. 19 (1978).

———. "La contribution du Tiers Monde à la relance de l'économie mondiale." *Studia diplomatica* 31, no. 1 (1978): 3–19.

———. "Partial Summary of Remarks November 29, 1975." In "Economic Cooperation and Resource Management," *Trialogue* no. 9 (1976): 10–11.

Chomsky, Noam. *American Power and the New Mandarins.* New York: Pantheon Books, 1969.

Citino, Nathan J. *Envisioning the Arab Future: Modernization in U.S.–Arab Relations, 1945–1967.* Cambridge: Cambridge University Press, 2017.

Clemens, Michael A. "Does Development Reduce Migration?" IZA Discussion Paper No. 8592, October 2014. Accessed August 2017. *http://ftp.iza.org/dp8592.pdf.*

Cobbs Hoffman, Elizabeth. *All You Need Is Love: The Peace Corps and the Spirit of the 1960s.* Cambridge, MA: Harvard University Press, 1998.

*Collected Works of Michał Kalecki.* Vol. 5, *Developing Economies,* edited by Jerzy Osiatyński. Oxford, UK: Clarendon Press, 1993.

Commission on International Development. *Partners in Development: Report of the Commission on International Development.* New York: Praeger, 1969.

Commoner, Barry. "Motherhood in Stockholm." *Harper's Magazine*, no. 6 (June 1972): 49–54.

Connelly, Matthew James. *A Diplomatic Revolution: Algeria's Fight for Independence and the Origins of the Post-Cold War Era*. Oxford: Oxford University Press, 2002.

———. *Fatal Misconception: The Struggle to Control World Population*. Cambridge, MA: Belknap Press of Harvard University Press, 2008.

Conrad, Sebastian. "Die Zivilisierung des 'Selbst': Japans koloniale Moderne." In *Zivilisierungsmissionen: Imperiale Weltverbesserung seit dem 18. Jahrhundert*, edited by Boris Barth and Jürgen Osterhammel, 245–268. Konstanz, Germany: UVK Verlagsgesellschaft, 2005.

Cooper, Frederick. *Africa since 1940: The Past of the Present*. Cambridge: Cambridge University Press, 2002.

———. *Decolonization and African Society: The Labor Question in French and British Africa*. Cambridge: Cambridge University Press, 1996.

———. "Writing the History of Development." In "Modernizing Missions: Approaches to 'Developing' the Non-western World after 1945," edited by Stephan Malinowski and Corinna R. Unger, 5–23. Special issue, *Journal of Modern European History* 8, 1 (2010).

Cooper, Frederick, and Randall Packard, eds. *International Development and the Social Sciences: Essays on the History and Politics of Knowledge*. Berkeley: University of California Press, 1997.

Coppolaro, Lucia. *The Making of a World Trading Power: The European Economic Community (EEC) in the GATT Kennedy Round Negotiations (1963–67)*. Farnham, UK: Ashgate, 2013.

Cosgrove, Carol Ann. "The Common Market and Its Colonial Heritage." *Journal of Contemporary History* 4, no. 1 (1969): 73–87.

Cot, Jean-Pierre. *À l'épreuve du pouvoir: Le tiers-mondisme, pour quoi faire?* Paris: Seuil, 1984.

Coulson, Andrew. *Tanzania: A Political Economy*. New York: Oxford University Press, 2013.

Cox, Robert W. "Ideologies and the New International Economic Order: Reflections on Some Recent Literature." *International Organization* 33, no. 2 (March 1979): 257–302.

———. "Labor and Hegemony." *International Organization* 31, no. 3 (1977): 385–424.

Cresti, Federico. "The Early Years of the Agency of Colonization of Cyrenaica (1932–1935)." In *Italian Colonialism*, edited by Ruth Ben-Ghiat and Mia Fuller, 73–82. New York: Palgrave Macmillan, 2005.

Crozier, Michael, Samuel P. Huntington, and Joji Watanuki. *The Crisis of Democracy: Report on Governability of Democracies to the Trilateral Commission*. New York: New York University Press, 1975.

Cullather, Nick. "Damming Afghanistan: Modernization in a Buffer State." In "History and September 11." Special issue, *The Journal of American History* 89, no. 2 (September 2002): 512–537.

———. "The Foreign Policy of the Calorie." *The American Historical Review* 112, no. 2 (2007): 337–364.

———. *The Hungry World: America's Cold War Battle against Poverty in Asia*. Cambridge, MA: Harvard University Press, 2010.

Currie, Lauchlin. "Some Prerequisites for Success of the Point Four Program." In "Formulating a Point Four Program." Special issue, *The Annals of the American Academy of Political and Social Science* 270 (July 1950): 102–108.

D'Antone, Leandra. "L'interesse straordinario per il Mezzogiorno (1943–1960)." In *Meridiana*, no. 24 (1995): 17–64.

Darwin, John G. *Britain and Decolonisation: The Retreat from Empire in the Post-War World*. Basingstoke, UK: Macmillan, 1988.

David-Fox, Michael. *Showcasing the Great Experiment: Cultural Diplomacy and Western Visitors to the Soviet Union, 1921–1941*. New York: Oxford University Press, 2012.

Davidson, Basil. *The Black Man's Burden: Africa and the Curse of the Nation-State*. Oxford, UK: James Currey, 1992.

———. *Black Star: A View of the Life and Times of Kwame Nkrumah*. London: Allen Lane, 1973.

Davis, Kingsley. "Population Policy: Will Current Programs Succeed?" *Science, New Series* 158, no. 3802 (10 November 1967): 730–739.

de Vries, Erik. "Colonialism from a European Point of View." *Interpretation* 29, no. 1 (2001): 91–130.

"The Cocoyoc Declaration." *International Organization* 29, no. 3 (1975): 893–901.

Deighton, Anne. "Entente Neo-Coloniale? Ernest Bevin and the Proposals for an Anglo–French Third World Power, 1945–1949." *Diplomacy & Statecraft* 17, no. 4 (2006): 835–852.

———. "Ernest Bevin and the Idea of Euro-Africa from the Interwar to the Postwar Period." In *L'Europe unie et l'Afrique: De l'idée d'Eurafrique à la convention de Lomé 1*, edited by Marie-Thérèse Bitsch and Gérard Bossuat, 97–118. Brussels: Bruylant, 2005.

Delavignette, Robert. *Service Africaine*. Paris: Gallimard, 1946.

Dell, Sidney. "The Origins of UNCTAD." In *UNCTAD and the North-South Dialogue: The First Twenty Years*, edited by Michael Zammit Cutajar. Oxford, UK: Pergamon Press, 1985.

Department of Information—FRELIMO, Lourenço Marques. *Mozambique Revolution*, Independence Issue, no. 61, [1975].

*Development and Environment: Report and Working Papers of a Panel of Experts Convened by the Secretary-General of the United Nations Conference on the Human Environment, Founex, Switzerland, 4–12 June 1971*. Paris: Mouton, 1972.

*Die Sozialistische Internationale zum antiimperialistischen Kampf in Afrika, Asien und Lateinamerika: Materialien des gemeinsamen wissenschaftlichen Kolloquiums des Problemrates "Ideologie und Politik der internationalen Sozialdemokratie" und der Kommission der Historiker der DDR und der UVR am 24. September 1987 in Berlin*. Berlin: Akademie für Gesellschaftswissenschaften beim ZK der SED, 1988.

Dietrich, Christopher. *Oil Revolution: Anticolonial Elites, Sovereign Rights, and the Economic Culture of Decolonization*. Cambridge: Cambridge University Press, 2017.

Dimier, Véronique. "Adieu les artistes, here are the managers: Les réformes managériales au sein de la DG Développement." *Sociologie du travail* 52 (2010): 234–254.

———. "Bringing the Neo-patrimonial State Back to Europe: Decolonization and the Construction of the EEC Development Policy." *Archiv für Sozialgeschichte*, no. 48 (2008): 433–460.

———. *The Invention of a European Development Aid Bureaucracy: Recycling Empire*. Basingstoke, UK: Palgrave Macmillan, 2014.

———. *Le gouvernement des colonies, regards croisés franco-britanniques*. Brussels: Éditions de l'Université de Bruxelles, 2004.

———. "Négocier avec les 'Rois nègres': L'influence des administrateurs coloniaux français sur la politique européenne de développement." In *L'Europe unie et l'Afrique: De l'idée d'Eurafrique à la convention de Lomé 1*, edited by Marie-Thérèse Bitsch and Gérard Bossuat, 392–409. Brussels: Bruylant, 2005.

Dimier, Véronique, and Mike McGeever. "Diplomats without a Flag: The Institutionalization of the Delegations of the Commission in African, Caribbean and Pacific Countries." *Journal of Common Market Studies* 44, no. 3 (2006): 483–505.

Dollar, David. *China's Engagement with Africa: From Natural Resources to Human Resources.* Washington, DC: Brookings Institution Press, 2016.

Donini, Antonio. "Conversion, Is It a Problem?" In *The Future Role of the United Nations in an Interdependent World*, edited by John P. Renninger, 151–171. Dordrecht, Netherlands: Martinus Nijhoff, 1989.

Dosman, Edgar J. *The Life and Times of Raúl Prebisch, 1901–1986.* Montreal: McGill-Queen's University Press, 2008.

Drake, Paul W., ed. *Money Doctors, Foreign Debts and Economic Reforms in Latin America from the 1890s to the Present.* Wilmington, DE: SR Books, 1994.

Duara, Prasenjit, ed. *Decolonization: Perspectives from Now and Then.* London: Routledge, 2004.

Dubin, Martin D. "Toward the Bruce Report: The Economic and Social Programs of the League of Nations in the Avenol Era." In *The League of Nations in Retrospect: Proceedings of the Symposium.* Berlin: De Gruyter, 1983.

Dubos, René. *Reason Awake.* New York: Columbia University Press, 1970.

Duchêne, François. "The European Community and the Uncertainties of Interdependence." In *A Nation Writ Large? Foreign Policy Problems before the European Community*, edited by Max Kohnstamm and Wolfgang Hager, 1–21. London: Macmillan, 1973.

Durdag, Mete. *Some Problems of Development Financing: The Turkish First Five-Year Plan, 1963–1967.* Dordrecht, Netherlands: Reidel, 1973.

Dykmann, Klaas. "Only with the Best Intentions: International Organizations as Global Civilizers." *Comparativ* 23, no. 4/5 (2013): 21–46.

Easterly, William. "IMF and World Bank Structural Adjustment Programs and Poverty." In *Managing Currency Crises in Emerging Markets*, edited by Michael P. Dooley and Jeffrey A. Frankel, 361–391. Chicago: University of Chicago Press, 2003.

———. *The Tyranny of Experts: Economists, Dictators, and the Forgotten Rights of the Poor.* New York: Basic Books, 2014.

———. *The White Man's Burden: Why the West's Efforts to Aid the Rest Have Done So Much Ill and So Little Good.* New York: Penguin Press, 2006.

Eckert, Andreas. "Die Verheißung der Bürokratie: Verwaltung als Zivilisierungsagentur im kolonialen Westafrika." In *Zivilisierungsmissionen: Imperiale Weltverbesserung seit dem 18. Jahrhundert*, edited by Boris Barth and Jürgen Osterhammel, 269–284. Konstanz, Germany: UVK Verlagsgesellschaft, 2005.

———. *Herrschen und Verwalten: Afrikanische Bürokraten, staatliche Ordnung und Politik in Tanzania, 1920–1970.* Munich: Oldenbourg, 2007.

———. "Julius Nyerere, Tanzanian Elites and the Project of African Socialism." In *Elites and Decolonization in the Twentieth Century*, edited by Jost Düffler and Marc Frey, 216–240. London: Palgrave Macmillan, 2011.

*Economic Costs and Benefits of an Antipollution Project in Italy: Summary Report of a Preliminary Evaluation; Special Issue for the United Nations Conference on the Human Environment, Stockholm, June 5–16, 1972.* Rome: Istituto per gli Studi Sviluppo Economico e il Progresso Tecnico-Ente Nazionale Idrocarburi, 1972.

Ehrlich, Paul R. *The Population Bomb.* New York: Ballantine Books, [1968].

Ehrlich, Paul, Carl Sagan, Donald Kennedy, and Walter Orr Roberts. *The Cold and the Dark: The World after Nuclear War.* New York: Norton, 1984.

"Eisenhower Special Message on Foreign Economic Policy, March 30, 1954." In *Public Papers of the Presidents of the United States*. Washington, DC: Government Printing Office, 1954.

Eisenstadt, Shmuel N. "Multiple Modernities." *Daedalus* 129, no. 1 (Winter 2000): 1–29.

Ekbladh, David. *The Great American Mission: Modernization and the Construction of an American World Order*. Princeton, NJ: Princeton University Press, 2011.

———. " 'Mr. TVA': Grass-Roots Development, David Lilienthal, and the Rise and Fall of the Tennessee Valley Authority as a Symbol for U.S. Overseas Development, 1933–1973." *Diplomatic History* 26, no. 3 (2002): 335–374.

Elder, Robert E., and Forrest D. Murden. *Economic Cooperation: Special United Nations Fund for Economic Development (SUNFED)*. New York: Woodrow Wilson Foundation, 1954.

Elton, Charles S. *The Ecology of Invasions by Animals and Plants*. London: Methuen, 1958.

Emmerij, Louis, Richard Jolly, and Thomas G. Weiss. *Ahead of the Curve? UN Ideas and Global Challenges*. Bloomington: Indiana University Press, 2001.

Engel, Ulf, and Hans-Georg Schleicher. *Die beiden deutschen Staaten in Afrika: Zwischen Konkurrenz und Koexistenz 1949–1990*. Hamburg, Germany: Institut für Afrika-Kunde im Verbund der Stiftung Deutsches Übersee-Institut, 1998.

Engerman, David C. "Development Politics and the Cold War." *Diplomatic History* 41, no. 1 (2017): 1–19.

———. "Ideology and the Origins of the Cold War, 1917–1962." In *The Cambridge History of the Cold War*, edited by Melvyn P. Leffler and Odd Arne Westad, 20–42. Cambridge: Cambridge University Press, 2010.

———. *Know Your Enemy: The Rise and Fall of America's Soviet Experts*. Oxford: Oxford University Press, 2009.

———. "Learning from the East: Soviet Experts and India in the Era of Competitive Coexistence." *Comparative Studies of South Asia, Africa and the Middle East* 33, no. 2 (2013): 227–238.

———. *The Price of Aid: The Economic Cold War in India*. Cambridge, MA: Harvard University Press, 2018.

———. "The Romance of Economic Development and New Histories of the Cold War." *Diplomatic History* 28, no. 1 (2004): 23–54.

———. "The Second World's Third World." *Kritika* 12, no. 1 (2011): 183–211.

———. "Solidarity, Development, and Non-alignment: Foreign Economic Advisors and Indian Planning in the 1950s and 1960s." In *Praktiken von Internationaler Solidarität und Internationaler Entwicklung* [Practices of international solidarity and international development], edited by Berthold Unfried and Eva Himmelstoss. Leipzig, Germany: Akademische Verlagsanstalt, 2012.

Engfeldt, Lars-Göran. *From Stockholm to Johannesburg and Beyond*. Stockholm: Government Offices of Sweden, Ministry of Foreign Affairs, 2009.

Enthoven, Alain C. *Pollution, Resources, and the Environment*. New York: Norton, [1973].

Erler, Brigitte. *Tödliche Hilfe: Bericht von meiner letzten Dienstreise in Sachen Entwicklungshilfe*. Freiburg, Germany: Dreisam Verlag, 1985.

Escobar, Arturo. *Encountering Development: The Making and Unmaking of the Third World*. Princeton, NJ: Princeton University Press, 2012.

Evteev, Sveneld A., Renat A. Perelet, and Vadim P. Voronin. "Ecological Security of Sustainable Development." In *The Future Role of the United Nations in an Interdependent World*, edited by John P. Renninger, 162–171. Dordrecht, Netherlands: Martinus Nijhoff, 1989.

Faber, Mike, and Dudley Seers, eds. *The Crisis in Planning*. London: Chatto and Windus for Sussex University Press, 1972.

Ferguson, James. *The Anti-Politics Machine: "Development," Depoliticization, and Bureaucratic Power in Lesotho*. Minneapolis: University of Minnesota Press, 1994.

Ferrandi, Jacques. "La Communauté européenne et l'assistance technique." *International Development Review*, no. 8 (1964): 8–9.

Ferrari, Lorenzo. *Sometimes Speaking with a Single Voice: The European Community as an International Actor, 1969–1979*. Brussels: Peter Lang, 2016.

———. "Speaking with a Single Voice: The Assertion of the EC as a Distinctive International Actor, 1969–79." PhD diss., IMT Lucca, 2014.

Fisher, David. *History of the International Atomic Energy Agency: The First Forty Years*. Vienna: IAEA, 1997.

Franczak, Michael. "Human Rights and Basic Needs: Jimmy Carter's North-South Dialogue, 1977–81." *Cold War History* 18, no. 4 (2018): 447–464.

Frank, Andre Gunder. "Long Live Transideological Enterprise! The Socialist Economies in the Capitalist International Division of Labor." *Review (Fernand Braudel Center)* 1, no. 1 (1977): 91–140.

———. "North-South and East-West Keynesian Paradoxes in the Brandt Report." *Third World Quarterly* 2, no. 4 (1980): 669–680.

Frey, Marc. *Dekolonisierung in Südostasien: Die Vereinigten Staaten und die Auflösung der europäischen Kolonialreiche*. Munich: Oldenbourg Verlag, 2006.

———. "Indoktrination, Entwicklungspolitik, und 'State Building': Die Vereinigten Staaten in Südostasien 1945–1961." In *Zivilisierungsmissionen: Imperiale Weltverbesserung seit dem 18. Jahrhundert*, edited by Boris Barth and Jürgen Osterhammel, 335–362. Konstanz, Germany: UVK Verlagsgesellschaft, 2005.

———. "Neo-Malthusianism and Development: Shifting Interpretations of a Contested Paradigm." *Journal of Global History* 6 (2011): 75–97.

Freytag, Niels. " 'Eine Bombe im Taschenbuchformat?' Die 'Grenzen des Wachstums' und die öffentliche Resonanz." *Zeithistorische Forschungen* [Studies in contemporary history] 3, no. 3 (2006): 465–469.

Friedman, Jeremy. *Shadow Cold War: The Sino-Soviet Competition for the Third World*. Chapel Hill: University of North Carolina Press, 2015.

———. "Soviet Policy in the Developing World and the Chinese Challenge in the 1960s." *Cold War History* 10, no. 2 (2010): 247–272.

Frimpong-Ansah, Jonathan H. *The Vampire State in Africa: The Political Economy of Decline in Ghana*. London: J. Currey, 1991.

Fritsche, Klaus. *Sozialistische Entwicklungsländer in der 'internationalen sozialistischen Arbeitsteilung' des RGW: Zum Forschungsstand*. Cologne: Bundesinstitut für Ostwissenschaftliche und Internationale Studien, 1991.

Fukuyama, Francis. *The End of History and the Last Man*. New York, Free Press, 1992.

Furia, Annalisa. *The Foreign Aid Regime: Gift-Giving, States and Global Dis/order*. Basingstoke, UK: Palgrave Macmillan, 2015.

Galbraith, John Kenneth. *The Nature of Mass Poverty*. Cambridge, MA: Harvard University Press, 1979.

———. *The New Industrial State*. New York: New American Library, [1967].

Galtung, Johan. "The New International Economic Order and the Basic Needs Approach." *Alternatives* 4, no. 4 (1978–79): 455–476.

———. "On the Relation between Military and Economic Non-alignment." December 1982. http://www.transcend.org/galtung/papers/On%20the%20Relation%20Between%20Mili tary%20and%20Economic%20Non-Alignment.pdf.

Garavini, Giuliano. *After Empires: European Integration, Decolonization, and the Challenge from the Global South, 1957–1986*. New York: Oxford University Press, 2012.

———. "The Colonies Strike Back: The Impact of the Third World on Western Europe, 1968–1975." *Contemporary European History* 16, no. 3 (August 2007): 299–319.

Garwood, Ellen. *Will Clayton: A Short Biography*. Austin: University of Texas Press, [1958].

Geertz, Clifford. *Agricultural Involution*. Berkeley: Association for Asian Studies by University of California Press, 1966.

Geierhos, Wolfgang. "Die Sowjetunion und der Club of Rome." *Deutsche Studien Vierteljahreshefte*, no. 67 (1979): 213–230.

Gendzier, Irene L. *Managing Political Change: Social Scientists and the Third World*. Boulder, CO: Westview Press, 1985.

George, Edward. *The Cuban Intervention in Angola, 1965–1991: From Che Guevara to Cuito Cuanavale*. London: Frank Cass, 2005.

Georgescu-Roegen, Nicholas. "Energy and Economic Myths." *Southern Economic Journal* 41, no. 3 (1974): 347–381.

———. *The Entropy Law and the Economic Process*. Cambridge, MA: Harvard University Press, 1971.

Gerlach, Christian. "Der Versuch zur globalen entwicklungspolitischen Steuerung auf der World Food Conference von 1974." *Werkstattgeschichte* 11, no. 31 (2002): 50–91.

Gerschenkron, Alexander. *Economic Backwardness in Historical Perspective*. Cambridge, MA: Harvard University Press, 1966.

Gfeller, Aurélie Élisa. "Champion of Human Rights: The European Parliament and the Helsinki Process." *Journal of Contemporary History* 49, no. 2 (2014): 390–409.

Gibson, James. *Jacko, Where Are You Now? A Life of Robert Jackson*. Richmond, UK: Parsons Publishing, 2006.

Gilman, Nils. *Mandarins of the Future: Modernization Theory in Cold War America*. Baltimore: Johns Hopkins University Press, 2003.

———. "The New International Economic Order: A Reintroduction." *Humanity: An International Journal of Human Rights, Humanitarianism, and Development* 6, no. 1 (Spring 2015): 1–16.

Girault, René. "La France entre l'Europe et l'Afrique." In *Il rilancio dell'Europa e i trattati di Roma = La relance européenne et les traités de Rome: Actes du colloque de Rome, 25–28 Mars 1987*, edited by Enrico Serra, 351–378. Brussels: Bruylant, 1989.

Giri, Jacques. *Du tiers monde aux mondes émergents: Un demi-siècle d'aide au développement*. Paris: Karthala, 2012.

Giustozzi, Antonio, and Artemy Kalinovsky. *Missionaries of Modernity: Advisory Missions and the Struggle for Hegemony in Afghanistan and Beyond*. London: C. Hurst, 2016.

Gleijeses, Piero. *Conflicting Missions: Havana, Washington, & Africa, 1959–1976*. Chapel Hill: University of North Carolina Press, 2002.

———. *The Cuban Drumbeat: Castro's Worldview; Cuban Foreign Policy in a Hostile World*. London: Seagull, 2009.

———. "Moscow's Proxy? Cuba and Africa, 1975–1988." *Journal of Cold War Studies* 8, no. 2 (2006): 3–51.

Glenn Gray, William. *Germany's Cold War: The Global Campaign to Isolate East Germany, 1949–1969*. Chapel Hill: University of North Carolina Press, 2000.

Grainger, Alan. "Assessing the Environmental Impacts of National Development." In *Sustainable Development in a Developing World*, edited by Colin Kirkpatrick and Norman Lee, 61–87. Cheltenham, UK: Edward Elgar, 1997.

Grandi, Elisa. " 'Una TVA per il Mezzogiorno': David Lilienthal e reti transnazionali nei piani di sviluppo della Cassa per il Mezzogiorno." *Annali della Fondazione Ugo La Malfa* 27 (2012): 215–232.

Grandin, Greg. *Fordlandia*. New York: Metropolitan Books, 2009.

Graziani, Giovanni. "The Non-European Members of the CMEA: A Model for Developing Countries?" In *The Soviet Union, Eastern Europe and the Third World*, edited by Roger E. Kanet, 163–179. Cambridge: Cambridge University Press, 1988.

Grilli, Enzo R. *The European Community and the Developing Countries*. Cambridge: Cambridge University Press, 1993.

Gronow, Jukka. *Caviar with Champagne: Common Luxury and the Ideals of the Good Life in Stalin's Russia*. Oxford, UK: Berg, 2003.

Guasconi, Maria Eleonora. "Europe and the Mediterranean in the 1970s: The Setting Up of the Euro-Arab Dialogue." *Les cahiers Irice* 1, no. 10 (2013): 163–175.

Guernier, Eugène L. *L'Afrique: Champ d'expansion de l'Europe*. Paris: Armand Colin, 1933.

———. *Le destin des continents: Trois continents, trois civilisations, trois destins*. Paris: Librairie Felix Alcan, 1936.

Guldi, Jo, and David Armitage. *The History Manifesto*. Cambridge: Cambridge University Press, 2014.

Gunter, Pauli A. *Crusader for the Future: A Portrait of Aurelio Peccei, Founder of the Club of Rome*. Oxford, UK: Pergamon Press, 1987.

Gutmann, Patrick. "Tripartite Industrial Cooperation and Third World Countries." In *East-West-South: Economic Interaction between Three Worlds*, edited by Christopher T. Saunders, 337–364. Basingstoke, UK: Macmillan, 1983.

———. "West-östliche Wirtschaftskooperationen in der Dritten Welt." In *Ökonomie im Kalten Krieg*, edited by Christian Th. Müller, Claudia Weber, and Bernd Greiner, 395–412. Hamburg, Germany: Hamburger Edition, 2010.

Gvishiani, Dzermen. "The Concept of IIASA." *IIASA Conference, International Institute for Applied Systems Analysis* 1, no. 1 (1976): 11–18.

Hagen, James M., and Vernon W. Ruttan. "Development Policy under Eisenhower and Kennedy." *Bulletin of the Economic Development Center* 87, no. 10 (November 1987).

Hailey, William Malcolm. *The Future of Colonial Peoples*. Princeton, NJ: Princeton University Press, 1944.

Halle, Louis J. "On Teaching International Relations." *Virginia Quarterly Review* 40, no. 1 (1964): 11–25.

Hamblin, Jacob Darwin. *Arming Mother Nature: The Birth of Catastrophic Environmentalism.* New York: Oxford University Press, 2013.

Hancock, William Keith. *Argument of Empire.* Harmondsworth, UK: Penguin Books, [1943].

Hansen, Peo, and Stefan Jonsson. "Another Colonialism: Africa in the History of European Integration." *Journal of Historical Sociology* 27 (2014): 442–461.

———. *Eurafrica: The Untold History of European Integration and Colonialism.* London: Bloomsbury, 2014.

Hardin, Garrett. "The Tragedy of the Commons." *Science* 162, no. 3859 (13 December 1968): 1243–1248.

Hayes, Samuel P. "An Appraisal of Point Four." *Proceedings of the Academy of Political Science* 25, no. 3 (1953): 31–46.

———. "The United States Point Four Program." *Milbank Memorial Fund Quarterly* 28, no. 3 (1950): 263–272.

Heilperin, Michael A. "Private Means of Implementing Point Four." In "Aiding Underdeveloped Areas Abroad." Special issue, *Annals of the American Academy of Political and Social Science* 268 (March 1950): 54–65.

Helleiner, Eric. "From Bretton Woods to Global Finance: A World Turned Upside Down." In *Political Economy and the Changing Global Order*, edited by Richard Stubbs and Geoffrey Underhill, 163–174. London: Macmillan, 1994.

Herrera, Amílcar Oscar, ed. *Catastrophe or New Society? A Latin American World Model.* Ottawa: International Development Research Centre, 1976.

Hessel, Stéphane. *Danse avec le siècle.* Paris: Seuil, 1997.

Hevia, James. *English Lessons: The Pedagogy of Imperialism in Nineteenth-Century China.* Durham, NC: Duke University Press, 2003.

Hilger, Andreas. "The Soviet Union and India: The Years of Late Stalinism." Parallel History Project on Cooperative Security (PHP). Zürich: ETH, 2008. *http://www.php.isn.ethz.ch /lory1.ethz.ch/collections/coll_india/documents/Introduction_000.pdf.*

Hirdman, Yvonne. *Alva Myrdal: The Passionate Mind.* Bloomington: Indiana University Press, 2008.

Hodge, Joseph. "British Colonial Expertise, Post-Colonial Careering and the Early History of International Development." In "Modernizing Missions: Approaches to 'Developing' the Non-western World after 1945," edited by Stephan Malinowski and Corinna R. Unger. Special issue, *Journal of Modern European History* 8, no. 1 (2010): 24–46.

Hodge, Joseph Morgan. *Triumph of the Expert: Agrarian Doctrines of Development and the Legacies of British Colonialism.* Athens: Ohio University Press, 2007.

———. "Writing the History of Development (Part 1: The First Wave)." *Humanity: An International Journal of Human Rights, Humanitarianism and Development* 6, no. 3 (2015): 429–463.

———. "Writing the History of Development (Part 2: Longer, Deeper, Wider)." *Humanity: An International Journal of Human Rights, Humanitarianism, and Development* 7, no. 1 (2016): 125–174.

Hoffman, Paul G. *One Hundred Countries, One and One Quarter Billion People: How to Speed Their Economic Growth, and Ours, in the 1960's.* New York: Albert D. and Mary Lasker Foundation, 1960.

———. *Peace Can Be Won.* Garden City, NY: Doubleday, 1951.

————. "Reply." *Christian Century* 74 (3 April 1957).

Hollander, Paul. *Political Pilgrims: Travels of Western Intellectuals to the Soviet Union, China, and Cuba, 1928–1978*. New York: Oxford University Press, 1981.

Hong, Young-Sun. *Cold War Germany, the Third World, and the Global Humanitarian Regime*. New York: Cambridge University Press, 2015.

Hopkins, A. G. "Globalisation and Decolonisation." *Journal of Imperial and Commonwealth History* 45, no. 5 (2017): 729–745.

Hopkins, Antony G. "The World Bank in Africa: Historical Reflections on the African Present." *World Development* 14 (December 1986): 1473–1487.

Hough, Jerry F. *The Struggle for the Third World: Soviet Debates and American Options*. Washington, DC: Brookings Institution Press, 1986.

Hsu, Elisabeth. "Medicine as Business: Chinese Medicine in Tanzania." In *China Returns to Africa: A Rising Power and a Continental Embrace*, edited by Chris Alden, Daniel Large, and Ricardo Soares de Oliveira, 221–235. London: Hurst, 2008.

Humphrey, Hubert H. *The Man and His Dream*. New York: Methuen, 1978.

Hyam, Ronald. *Britain's Declining Empire: The Road to Decolonisation, 1918–1968*. Cambridge: Cambridge University Press, 2006.

Hyden, Goran. *Beyond Ujamaa in Tanzania*. London: Heinemann, 1980.

Iandolo, Alessandro. "De-Stalinizing Growth: Decolonization and the Development of Development Economics in the Soviet Union." In *The Development Century*, edited by Stephen J. Macekura and Erez Manela, 197–219. Cambridge, MA: Harvard University Press, 2018.

————. "The Rise and Fall of the 'Soviet Model of Development' in West Africa, 1957–64." *Cold War History* 12, no. 4 (2012): 683–704.

Illich, Ivan. "The Delinking of Peace and Development." *Alternatives* 7, no. 4 (1 January 1981): 409–416.

————. *Medical Nemesis: The Expropriation of Health*. London: Calder & Boyars, 1975.

Immerwahr, Daniel. *Thinking Small: The United States and the Lure of Community Development*. Cambridge, MA: Harvard University Press, 2015.

Independent Commission on Disarmament and Security Issues (Palme Commission). *Common Security: A Blueprint for Survival*. New York: Simon and Schuster, 1982.

Independent Commission on International Development Issues (Willy Brandt Commission). *Common Crisis North-South: Cooperation for World Recovery*. Cambridge, MA: MIT Press, 1983.

————. *North-South: A Programme for Survival; Report of the Independent Commission on International Development Issues*. Cambridge, MA: MIT Press, 1980.

Iriye, Akira, Petra Goedde, and William I. Hitchcock, eds. *The Human Rights Revolution: An International History*. Oxford: Oxford University Press, 2012.

Isaacman, Allen F., and Barbara S. Isaacman. *Dams, Displacement and the Delusion of Development: Cahora Bassa and Its Legacies in Mozambique, 1965–2007*. Athens: Ohio University Press, 2013.

Jackson, Robert Gillman Allen. *The Case for an International Development Authority*. Syracuse, NY: Syracuse University Press, 1959.

————. *A Study of the Capacity of the United Nations Development System*. Vols. 1 and 2. Geneva: United Nations Geneva, 1969.

Jacobs, Jeffrey W. "Mekong Committee History and Lessons for River Basin Development." *The Geographical Journal* 161, no. 2 (July 1995): 135–148.

————. "The Mekong River Commission: Trans-boundary Water Resources Planning and Regional Security." *Geographical Journal* 168, no. 4 (December 2002): 354–364.

————. "The United States and the Mekong Project." *Water Policy* 1, no. 6 (2000): 587–603.

Jalee, Pierre. *The Pillage of the Third World*. Paris: François Maspero, 1965.

James, Leslie. *George Padmore and Decolonization from Below: Pan-Africanism, the Cold War, and the End of Empire*. Basingstoke, UK: Palgrave Macmillan, 2015.

Jameson, Fredric. *Postmodernism, or, The Cultural Logic of Late Capitalism*. Durham, NC: Duke University Press, 1991.

Jennings, Michael. *Surrogates of the State: NGOs, Development, and Ujamaa in Tanzania*. Bloomfield, CT: Kumarian Press, 2008.

Jensen, Peter Føge. *Soviet Research on Africa with Special Reference to International Relations*. Uppsala: Scandinavian Institute of African Studies, 1973.

Johnson, Howard. "The British Caribbean from Demobilization to Constitutional Decolonization." In *Oxford History of the British Empire*, vol. 4, edited by Judith M. Brown and William Roger Louis, 597–622. Oxford: Oxford University Press, 1999.

Jolly, Richard, Louis Emmerij, and Frederic Lapeyre. *UN Contributions to Development Thinking and Practice*. Bloomington: University of Indiana Press, 2004.

Jolly, Richard, Louis Emmerij, and Thomas G. Weiss. *UN Ideas That Changed the World*. Bloomington: Indiana University Press, 2009.

Joswig, Heinz. "Zur Perspektive der ökonomischen Zusammenarbeit zwischen den Ländern des RGW und den Entwicklungsländern." *Deutsche Aussenpolitik* 3 (March 1975): 331–339.

Kalecki, Michał. *Essays on Developing Economies*. Hassocks, UK: Harvester, 1976.

————. "Introduction to Annex to Financial Problems of the Third Plan." In *Collected Works of Michał Kalecki*. Vol. 5, *Developing Economies*, edited by Jerzy Osiatyński. Oxford, UK: Clarendon Press, 1993.

Kalinovsky, Artemy M. *Laboratory of Socialist Development: Cold War Politics and Decolonization in Soviet Tajikistan*. Ithaca, NY: Cornell University Press, 2018.

————. "Not Some British Colony in Africa: The Politics of Decolonization and Modernization in Soviet Central Asia, 1955–1964." *Ab Imperio*, no. 2 (2013): 191–222.

Kalter, Christoph. *Die Entdeckung der Dritten Welt: Dekolonisierung und neue radikale Linke in Frankreich*. Frankfurt, Germany: Campus Verlag, 2011.

Kanbur, Ravi, and Andy Sumner. "Poor Countries or Poor People? Development Assistance and the New Geography of Global Poverty." *Journal of International Development* 24 (2012): 686–695.

Kanet, Roger. *The Soviet Union and the Developing Nations*. Baltimore: Johns Hopkins University Press, 1974.

Kapur, Devesh, John P. Lewis, and Richard Webb. *The World Bank: Its First Half Century*. Vol. 1, *History*. Washington, DC: Brookings Institution Press, 1997.

Karp, Mark. *The Economics of Trusteeship in Somalia*. Boston: Boston University Press, 1960.

Kaufman, Burton I. *Trade and Aid: Eisenhower's Foreign Economic Policy, 1953–1961*. Baltimore: Johns Hopkins University Press, 1982.

Kautsky, Karl. *Sozialismus und Kolonialpolitik*. Berlin: Buchhandlung Vorwärts, 1907.

Kaysen, Carl. "The Computer That Printed Out W*O*L*F*." *Foreign Affairs* 50, no. 4 (1972): 660–668.

Kazakevicius, V. [Vladimir Mikhaĭlovich]. "The Common Market and the Developing Countries." *International Affairs*, June 1979, 57–66.

Kennan, George F. "To Prevent World Wasteland." *Foreign Affairs* 48, no. 3 (1970): 401–413.

Kennedy, John F. *The Strategy of Peace*. New York: Harper, [1960].

Kent, John. "Bevin's Imperialism and the Idea of Euro-Africa." In *British Foreign Policy 1945–56*, edited by Michael Dockrill and John W. Young, 47–76. Basingstoke, UK: Macmillan, 1989.

———. *The Internationalization of Colonialism: Britain, France, and Black Africa, 1939–1956*. Oxford, UK: Clarendon Press, 1992.

Kingsland, Sharon E. *Modeling Nature: Episodes in the History of Population Ecology*. Chicago: University of Chicago Press, 1985.

Kirk, John M., and H. Michael Erisman. "Cuba's Cold War Medical Aid Programs." In *Cuban Medical Internationalism: Origins, Evolution, and Goals*, edited by John M. Kirk and H. Michael Erisman, 59–96. Basingstoke, UK: Palgrave Macmillan, 2009.

Kirk-Greene, Anthony. "The Thin White Line: The Size of the British Colonial Service in Africa." *African Affairs* 79 (1980): 25–44.

Kissinger, Henry A. "Reflections on American Diplomacy." *Foreign Affairs* 35, no. 1 (October 1956): 37–56.

Kitzinger, Uwe W. "Europe: The Six and the Seven." *International Organization* 14, no. 1 (1960).

Kleine, Mareike. "Trading Control: International Fiefdoms in International Organizations." *International Theory* 5, no. 3 (November 2013): 321–346.

Knop, Hans. "Large Scale Planning Projects: The Tennessee Valley Authority and the Bratsk-Ilimsk Complex." *IIASA Conference, International Institute for Applied Systems Analysis* 1, no. 1 (1976): 187–202.

Kojève, Alexandre. "Kolonialismus in europäischer Sicht: Vortrag gehalten vor dem Rhein-Ruhr-Klub e.V., am 16. Januar 1957." In *Schmittiana VII*, edited by Piet Tomissen, 125–140. Berlin: Duncker & Humblot, 1999.

Koller, Christian. "Eine Zivilisierungsmission der Arbeiterklasse? Die Diskussion über eine 'Sozialistiche Kolonialpolitik' vor dem Ersten Weltkrieg." In *Zivilisierungsmissionen: Imperiale Weltverbesserung seit dem 18. Jahrhundert*, edited by Boris Barth and Jürgen Osterhammel, 229–243. Konstanz, Germany: UVK Verlagsgesellschaft, 2005.

Kollontaj, Vladimir, and Iakov I. Etinger. *The European Common Market and the Developing Countries*. Moscow: Oriental Literature, 1963.

Koselleck, Reinhart. *Vergangene Zukunft: Zur Semantik geschichtlicher Zeiten*. Frankfurt, Germany: Suhrkamp, 1992.

Koskenniemi, Martti. *The Gentle Civilizer of Nations: The Rise and Fall of International Law, 1870–1960*. Cambridge: Cambridge University Press, 2001.

Kößler, Reinhart. *Entwicklung*. Munich: Westfälisches Dampfboot, 1998.

Kotkin, Stephen. *Magnetic Mountain: Stalinism as Civilization*. Berkeley: University of California Press, 1995.

Kovalenko, I. I., and R. A. Tuzmukhamedov, eds. *The Non-aligned Movement*. Moscow: Progress Publishers, 1985.

Krever, Tor. "The Legal Turn in Late Development Theory: The Rule of Law and the World Bank's Development Model." *Harvard International Law Journal* 52, no. 1 (2011): 287–319.

Kridl Valkenier, Elizabeth. "Revolutionary Change in the Third World: Recent Soviet Assessments." *World Politics* 38, no. 3 (1986): 415–434.

———. *The Soviet Union and the Third World: An Economic Bind.* New York: Praeger, 1983.

Kuchenberg, Thomas C. "The OECD Consortium to Aid Turkey." *Studies in Law and Economic Development* 2, no. 1 (1967): 91–106.

Labbate, Silvio. *Illusioni mediterranee: Il dialogo Euro-Arabo.* Florence: Mondadori-Le Monnier, 2016.

La Guma, Alex. *Soviet Journey.* Moscow: Progress Publishers, 1978.

Lake, Marilyn, and Henry Reynolds. *Drawing the Global Colour Line: White Men's Countries and the International Challenge of Racial Equality.* Cambridge: Cambridge University Press, 2008.

Lamm, Hans Siegfried, and Siegfried Kupper. *DDR und Dritte Welt.* Munich: Oldenbourg, 1976.

Lancaster, Carol. *Foreign Aid: Diplomacy, Development, Domestic Politics.* Chicago: University of Chicago Press, 2007.

Landes, David S. *The Wealth and Poverty of Nations: Why Some Are So Rich and Some So Poor.* New York: W. W. Norton, 1998.

Landolt, Laura K. "Constructing Population Control: Social and Material Factors in Norm Emergence and Diffusion." *Global Society* 21, no. 3 (2007): 393–414.

Larkin, Bruce D. *China and Africa, 1949–1970: The Foreign Policy of the People's Republic of China.* Berkeley: University of California Press, 1971.

Latham, Michael E. *Modernization as Ideology: American Social Science and "Nation Building" in the Kennedy Era.* Chapel Hill: University of North Carolina Press, 2000.

———. *The Right Kind of Revolution: Modernization, Development, and U.S. Foreign Policy from the Cold War to the Present.* Ithaca, NY: Cornell University Press, 2011.

Lawrence, Mark A., and Fredrik Logevall, eds. *The First Vietnam War.* Cambridge, MA: Harvard University Press, 2007.

Lawson, Colin W. "The Soviet Union in North-South Negotiations: Revealing Preferences." In *Soviet Interests in the Third World,* edited by Robert Cassen, 177–191. London: SAGE, 1985.

League of Nations, Secretariat. *The Aims, Methods, and Activity of the League of Nations.* Geneva: Secretariat of the League of Nations, 1935.

Lederer, William J., and Eugene Burdick. *Sarkhan.* New York: McGraw Hill, 1965.

———. *The Ugly American.* New York: Norton, 1958.

Lee, Christopher J., ed. *Making a World after Empire: The Bandung Moment and Its Political Afterlives.* Athens: Ohio University Press, 2010.

———. "Tricontinentalism in Question: The Cold War Politics of Alex La Guma and the African National Congress." In *Making a World after Empire: The Bandung Moment and Its Political Afterlives,* 266–286. Athens: Ohio University Press, 2010.

Lee, David. *Stanley Melbourne Bruce: Australian Internationalist.* London: Continuum, 2010.

Lee, John Michael, and Martin Petter. *The Colonial Office, War, and Development Policy: Organisation and the Planning of a Metropolitan Initiative, 1939–1945.* London: Maurice Temple Smith, Institute for Commonwealth Studies, 1982.

Lemaignen, Robert. *L'Europe au berceau: Souvenirs d'un technocrate.* Paris: Plon, 1964.

Leontief, Wassily W., and Marvin Hoffenberg. "The Economic Effects of Disarmament." *Scientific American* 204, no. 4 (1961): 47–55.

Levien, R. E. "Welcoming Address." In *Carbon Dioxide, Climate and Society: Proceedings of a IIASA Workshop Cosponsored by WMO, UNEP, and SCOPE*, edited by Jill Williams. Oxford, UK: Pergamon Press, 1978.

Lewis, W. Arthur. "Economic Development with Unlimited Supplies of Labour." *Manchester School of Economic and Social Studies* 22, 2 (May 1954): 139–191.

———. *The Principles of Economic Planning: A Study Prepared for the Fabian Society*. London: Dennis Dobson, George Allen & Unwin, 1949. Accessed December 2014. *https://ia802607 .us.archive.org/13/items/principlesofecon030862mbp/principlesofecon030862mbp.pdf.*

———. *Sir William Arthur Lewis: Collected Papers, 1941–1988*. Vols. 1–3, edited by Patrick A. M. Emmanuel. Cave Hill, Barbados: Institute of Social and Economic Research (Eastern Caribbean), University of the West Indies, 1994.

Lilienthal, David. *The Armament of a Democracy*. Knoxville: Tennessee Valley Authority, 1940.

Lindner, Ulrike. *Koloniale Begegnungen: Deutschland und Großbritannien als Imperialmächte in Afrika, 1880–1914*. Frankfurt, Germany: Campus Verlag, 2011.

Liniger-Goumaz, Max. *L'Eurafrique: Utopie ou réalité? Les métamorphoses d'une idée*. Yaoundé, Cameroon: Éditions CLE, 1972.

Lorenzini, Sara. "Ace in the Hole or Hole in the Pocket? The Italian Mezzogiorno and the Story of a Troubled Transition from Development Model to Development Donor." *Contemporary European History* 26, no. 3 (August 2017): 441–463.

———. "Comecon and the South in the Years of Détente: A Study on East–South Economic Relations." *European Review of History: Revue européenne d'histoire* 21, no. 2 (2004): 183–199.

———. *Due Germanie in Africa: La cooperazione allo sviluppo e la competizione per i mercati di materie prime e tecnologia*. Florence: Polistampa, 2003.

———. "East-South Relations in the 1970s and the Added Value of GDR Involvement in Africa: Between Bloc Loyalty and Self Interest." In *The Globalization of the Cold War: Diplomacy and Local Confrontation, 1975–85*, edited by Massimiliano Guderzo and Bruna Bagnato, 104–115. London: Routledge, 2010.

———. "Ecologia a parole? L'Italia, l'ambientalismo globale e il rapporto ambiente-sviluppo intorno alla conferenza di Stoccolma." *Contemporanea* 3 (2016): 395–418.

———. "The Emergence of Global Environmentalism: A Challenge for Italian Foreign Policy?" In *Italy in the International System from Détente to the End of the Cold War: The Underrated Ally*, edited by Antonio Varsori and Benedetto Zaccaria. 207–225. Basingstoke, UK: Palgrave Macmillan, 2017.

———. "Globalizing Ostpolitik." *Cold War History* 9, no. 2 (2009): 223–242.

———. "Modernisierung durch Handel: Der Ostblock und die Koordinierung der Entwicklungshilfe in der Ständigen Kommission für Technische Unterstützung." In *Osteuropäische Geschichte und Globalgeschichte*, edited by Martin Aust and Julia Obertreis, 225–240. Stuttgart, Germany: Steiner-Verlag, 2014.

Low, David A., and John M. Lonsdale. "Towards the New Order, 1945–1963." Introduction to *History of East Africa*. Vol. 3, edited by David A. Low and Alison Smith. Oxford, UK: Clarendon Press, 1976.

Luckham, Robin. "Soviet Arms and African Militarization." In *Soviet Interests in the Third World*, edited by Robert Cassen, 89–113. London: SAGE, 1985.

Ludlow, Piers. "History Aplenty but Still Too Isolated." In *Research Agendas in EU Studies: Stalking the Elephant*, edited by Michelle Egan, Neill Nugent, and William E. Paterson, 14–37. Basingstoke, UK: Palgrave Macmillan, 2009.

Lundestad, Geir. "Empire by Invitation? The United States and Western Europe, 1945–1952." *Journal of Peace Research* 23, no. 3 (1986): 263–277.

Macekura, Stephen. "The Limits of the Global Community: The Nixon Administration and Global Environmental Politics." *Cold War History* 11, no. 4 (2011): 489–518.

———. *Of Limits and Growth: The Rise of Global Sustainable Development in the Twentieth Century*. New York: Cambridge University Press, 2015.

Machowski, Heinrich, and Siegfried Schultz. *RGW-Staaten und Dritte Welt: Wirtschaftsbeziehungen und Entwicklungshilfe*. Bonn, Germany: Forschungsinstitut der Deutschen Gesellschaft für Auswärtige Politik e.V., Europa Union Verlag, 1981.

Maddox, John. *The Doomsday Syndrome*. New York: McGraw-Hill, 1972.

Maier, Charles S. *Among Empires: American Ascendancy and Its Predecessors*. Cambridge, MA: Harvard University Press, 2006.

———. "Between Taylorism and Technocracy: European Ideologies and the Vision of Industrial Productivity in the 1920s." *Journal of Contemporary History* 5, no. 2 (1970): 27–61.

———. "Malaise: The Crisis of Capitalism in the 1970s." In *The Shock of the Global: The 1970s in Perspective*, edited by Charles S. Maier, Niall Ferguson, Erez Manela, and Daniel Sargent, 25–48. Cambridge: Belknap Press of Harvard University Press, 2010.

Malinowski, Stephan, and Moritz Feichtinger. "'Eine Million Algerier lernen im 20. Jahrhundert zu leben': Umsiedlungslager und Zwangsmodernisierung im Algerienkrieg 1954–1962." In "Modernizing Missions: Approaches to 'Developing' the Non-western World after 1945," edited by Stephan Malinowski and Corinna R. Unger. Special issue, *Journal of Modern European History* 8, 1 (2010): 107–133.

Malinowski, Stephan, and Corinna R. Unger, eds. "Modernizing Missions: Approaches to 'Developing' the Non-western World after 1945." Special issue, *Journal of Modern European History* 8, 1 (2010).

Manela, Erez. *The Wilsonian Moment: Self-Determination and the International Origins of Anticolonial Nationalism*. New York: Oxford University Press, 2007.

Manjapra, Kris. *Age of Entanglement: German and Indian Intellectuals across Empire*. Cambridge, MA: Harvard University Press, 2014.

———. "Communist Internationalism and Transcolonial Recognition." In *Cosmopolitan Thought Zones: South Asia and the Global Circulation of Ideas*, 159–177. Basingstoke, UK: Palgrave Macmillan, 2010.

———. *M. N. Roy: Marxism and Colonial Cosmopolitanism*. London: Routledge, 2010.

Mansholt, Sicco. *Die Krise: Europa und die Grenzen des Wachstums; Aufzeichnung von Gesprächen mit Janine Delaunay und Freimut Duve*. Reinbek, Germany: Rowohlt-Taschenbuch-Verlag, 1974.

Mansingh, Surjit. "Indo-Soviet Relations in the Nehru Years: The View from New Delhi." Parallel History Project on Cooperative Security (PHP). Zürich: ETH, 2009. *http://www.php.isn.ethz .ch/lory1.ethz.ch/collections/coll_india/NehruYears-Introduction3593.html?navinfo=96318*.

Marseille, Jacques. *Empire coloniale et capitalisme français*. Paris: Albin Michel, 1984.

Maul, Daniel. *Human Rights, Development and Decolonization: The International Labour Organization, 1940–70*. London: Palgrave Macmillan, 2011.

————. *Menschenrechte, Sozialpolitik und Dekolonisation: Die Internationale Arbeitsorganisation (IAO) 1940–1970*. Essen, Germany: Klartext, 2007.

Mazov, Sergei. *A Distant Front in the Cold War: The USSR in West Africa and the Congo, 1956–1964*. Stanford, CA: Stanford University Press, 2010.

Mazower, Mark. *Governing the World: The History of an Idea*. New York: Penguin, 2012.

————. *No Enchanted Palace: The End of Empire and the Ideological Origins of the United Nations*. Princeton, NJ: Princeton University Press, 2009.

Mazrui, Ali A. "Eurafrica, Eurabia, and African-Arab Relations: The Tensions of Tripolarity." In *Interdependence in a World of Unequals: African-Arab-OECD Economic Cooperation for Development*, edited by Dunstan M. Wai, 17–46. Boulder, CO: Westview Press, 1982.

Mazurek, Małgorzata. "'Crossroads of Capitalism': Eastern Europe, Ludwik Landau and His Interwar Vision of Global Inequalities." *Stan Rzeczy, Anti-disciplinary Journal*, no. 1 (2017): 127–143.

McMahon, Robert J. "'The Point of No Return': The Eisenhower Administration and Indonesia, 1953–1960." In *The Eisenhower Administration, the Third World, and the Globalization of the Cold War*, edited by Kathryn C. Statler and Andrew L. Johns, 75–100. Lanham, MD: Rowman & Littlefield, 2006.

Mechi, Lorenzo. *L'organizzazione internazionale del lavoro e la ricostruzione europea: Le basi sociali dell'integrazione economica (1931–1957)*. Rome: Ediesse, 2012.

Meier, Gerald M., and Robert E. Baldwin. *Economic Development: Theory, History, Policy*. New York: Wiley, 1957.

Meier, Gerald M., and Dudley Seers. *Pioneers in Development*. New York: Oxford University Press, 1984.

Meißner, Herbert. *Konvergenztheorie und Realität*. Frankfurt, Germany: Verlag Marxistische Blätter, 1971.

Meyer, Alfred G. "Theories of Convergence." In *Change in Communist Systems*, edited by Chalmers Johnson, 313–341. Stanford, CA: Stanford University Press, 1970.

Meyer, Jan-Henrik. *Appropriating the Environment: How the European Institutions Received the Novel Idea of the Environment and Made It Their Own*. KFG Working Paper No. 31, September 2011. *http://userpage.fu-berlin.de/kfgeu/kfgwp/wpseries/WorkingPaperKFG_31.pdf*.

Migani, Guia. *La France et l'Afrique sub-saharienne, 1957–1963: Histoire d'une décolonisation entre idéaux eurafricains et politique de puissance*. Brussels: P.I.E. Peter Lang, 2008.

————. "Lomé and the North-South relations (1975–1984): From the New International Economic Order to a New Conditionality." In *Europe in a Globalising World: Global Challenges and European Responses in the 'Long' 1970s*, edited by Claudia Hiepel, 123–146. Baden-Baden, Germany: Nomos, 2014.

Mikulsky, Konstantin Ivanovich. *CMEA: International Significance of Socialist Integration*. Moscow: Progress Publishers, 1982.

Miller, Chris. "Georgii Mirskii and Soviet Theories of Authoritarian Modernization." *The International History Review* (2017). doi:10.1080/07075332.2017.1402803.

Millikan, Max F., and Walt W. Rostow. *A Proposal: Key to an Effective Foreign Policy*. New York: Harper and Brothers, 1957.

Milne, David. *America's Rasputin: Walt Rostow and the Vietnam War*. New York: Hill and Wang, 2008.

Milward, Alan S. "Was the Marshall Plan Necessary?" *Diplomatic History* 13, no. 2 (1989): 231–252.

Mishra, Pankaj. *From the Ruins of Empire: The Revolt against the West and the Remaking of Asia.* London: Penguin, 2013.

Mitchell, Timothy. *Rule of Experts: Egypt, Techno-politics, Modernity.* Berkeley: University of California Press, 2002.

Mollin, Gerhard Thomas. *Die USA und der Kolonialismus: Amerika als Partner und Nachfolger der belgischen Macht in Afrika 1939–1965.* Berlin: Akademie Verlag, 1996.

Monson, Jamie. *Africa's Freedom Railway.* Bloomington: Indiana University Press, 2009.

———. "Working ahead of Time: Labor and Modernization during the Construction of the Tazara Railway, 1968–86." In *Making a World after Empire: The Bandung Moment and Its Political Afterlives,* edited by Christopher J. Lee, 235–265. Athens: Ohio University Press, 2010.

Montarsolo, Yves. "Albert Sarraut et l'idée d'Eurafrique." In *L'Europe unie et l'Afrique: De l'idée d'Eurafrique à la convention de Lomé 1,* edited by Marie-Thérèse Bitsch and Gérard Bossuat, 77–95. Brussels: Bruylant, 2005.

Montias, John Michael. "Background and Origins of the Rumanian Dispute with Comecon." *Soviet Studies* 16, no. 2 (October 1964): 125–151.

Morgenthau, Hans J. "A Political Theory of Foreign Aid." *American Political Science Review* 56, no. 2 (June 1962): 301–309.

Morse, David A. "The Employment Problem in Developing Countries." *Political Science Quarterly* 85, no. 1 (March 1970): 1–16.

Moser, Thomas. *Europäische Integration, Dekolonisation, Eurafrika: Eine historische Analyse über Entstehungsbedingungen der Eurafrikanischen Gemeinschaft von der Weltwirtschaftskrise bis zum Jaunde-Vertrag, 1929–1963.* Baden-Baden, Germany: Nomos, 2000.

Moses, Dirk. "Partitions and the Sisyphean Making of Peoples." *Refugee Watch* 46 (December 2015): 36–60.

Mosley, Paul, Jane Harrigan, and John Toye. *Aid and Power: The World Bank and Policy-Based Lending.* London: Routledge, 1991.

Moxon, James. *Volta: Man's Greatest Lake; The Story of Ghana's Akosombo Dam.* New York: Praeger, 1969.

Moyn, Samuel. *The Last Utopia: Human Rights in History.* Cambridge, MA: Belknap Press of Harvard University Press, 2010.

———. *Not Enough: Human Rights in an Unequal World.* Cambridge, MA: Belknap Press of Harvard University Press, 2018.

Moyo, Dambisa. *Dead Aid: Why Aid Is Not Working and How There Is a Better Way for Africa.* London: Allen Lane, 2009.

Muehlenbeck, Philip. *Czechoslovakia in Africa, 1945–1968.* Basingstoke, UK: Palgrave Macmillan, 2016.

Muller, Karis. "Iconographie de l'Eurafrique." In *L'Europe unie et l'Afrique: De l'idée d'Eurafrique à la convention de Lomé 1,* edited by Marie-Thérèse Bitsch and Gérard Bossuat, 9–34. Brussels: Bruylant, 2005.

Murphy, Craig N. *The United Nations Development Programme: A Better Way?* Cambridge: Cambridge University Press, 2006.

Murthy, Changavalli Siva Rama. "Non-aligned Movement Countries as Drivers of Change in International Organizations." *Comparativ* 23, no. 4/5 (2013): 118–136.

Myall, James. "Britain and the Third World." In *The West and the World: Essays in Honour of JBD Miller*, edited by Robert O'Neill and Raymond John Vincent, 66–90. Basingstoke, UK: Macmillan, 1990.

Myrdal, Alva. *Nation and Family: The Swedish Experiment in Democratic Family and Population Policy*. New York: Harper, 1941.

Myrdal, Gunnar. *Economic Theory and Underdeveloped Regions*. London: Gerald Duckworth, 1957.

Nebbia, Giorgio. Introduction to *I pionieri dell'ambiente: L'avventura del movimento ecologista italiano; Cento anni di storia*, edited by Edgar H. Meyer. Milan: Carabà Edizioni, 1995.

Nehru, Jawaharlal. "The Importance of the National Idea." In *Decolonization: Perspectives from Now and Then*, edited by Prasenjit Duara, 32–41. London: Routledge, 2004.

Neri Serneri, Simone. "L'impatto ambientale dell'industria 1950–2000: Risorse e politiche." In *Industria, ambiente e territorio: Per una storia ambientale delle aree industriali in Italia*, edited by Salvatore Adorno and Simone Neri Serneri, 33–86. Bologna: Il Mulino, 2009.

Nesadurai, Helen E. S. "Bandung and the Political Economy of North-South Relations: Sowing the Seeds for Re-visioning International Society." In *Bandung Revisited: The Legacy of the 1955 Asian-African Conference for International Order*, edited by See Seng Tan and Amitav Acharya, 68–101. Singapore: NUS Press, 2008.

Nichols, James H. *Alexandre Kojève: Wisdom at the End of History*. Lanham, MD: Rowman & Littlefield, 2007.

Nicolaïdis, Kalypso. "Southern Barbarians? A Post-Colonial Critique of EUniversalism." In *Echoes of Empire: Memory, Identity and Colonial Legacies*, edited by Kalypso Nicolaïdis, Berny Sèbe, and Gabrielle Maas, 283–304. London: I. B. Tauris, 2015.

Ninkovich, Frank. "Die Zivilisierungsmission der USA im 19. Jahrhundert." In *Zivilisierungsmissionen: Imperiale Weltverbesserung seit dem 18. Jahrhundert*, edited by Boris Barth and Jürgen Osterhammel, 285–310. Konstanz, Germany: UVK Verlagsgesellschaft, 2005.

Nkrumah, Kwame. *Neo-colonialism: The Last Stage of Imperialism*. New York: International Publishers, 1965.

Nolte, Georg, and Helmut Philipp Aust. "European Exceptionalism?" *Global Constitutionalism* 2, no. 3 (2013): 407–436.

Nunan, Timothy. *Humanitarian Invasion: Global Development in Cold War Afghanistan*. New York: Cambridge University Press, 2016.

Nye, Joseph S., Jr. "Soft Power." *Foreign Policy* 80 (Autumn 1990): 153–171.

Nyerere, Julius. "Socialism and Rural Development, 1967." In *Freedom and Socialism: A Selection from Writings and Speeches, 1965–1967*, edited by Julius Nyerere, 337–366. Oxford: Oxford University Press, 1968.

Obregon, Liliana. "Noted for Dissent: The International Life of Alejandro Alvarez." *Leiden Journal of International Law* 19 (2006): 983–1016.

Ohlin, Goran. "The Organization for Economic Cooperation and Development." In "The Global Partnership: International Agencies and Economic Development." Special issue, *International Organization* 22, no. 1 (1968): 231–243.

Olshany, Anatoli, and Leon Z. Zevin. *CMEA Countries and Developing States: Economic Cooperation*. Moscow: Progress Publishers, 1984.

Oral History Interview with Abdul Minty. IAEA History Research Project, University of Vienna. Accessed June 2018. *https://iaea-history.univie.ac.at/oral-history-videos/interviews-j-o/*.

Orr, John Boyd. *As I Recall*. London: MacGibbon and Kee, 1966.

Osgood, Kenneth Alan. *Total Cold War: Eisenhower's Secret Propaganda Battle at Home and Abroad*. Lawrence: University Press of Kansas, 2006.

Osterhammel, Jürgen. " 'The Great Work of Uplifting Mankind': Zivilisierungsmission und Moderne." In *Zivilisierungsmissionen: Imperiale Weltverbesserung seit dem 18. Jahrhundert*, edited by Boris Barth and Jürgen Osterhammel, 363–426. Konstanz, Germany: UVK Verlagsgesellschaft, 2005.

———. *The Transformation of the World: A Global History of the Nineteenth Century*. Princeton, NJ: Princeton University Press, 2016.

Osterhammel, Jürgen, and Niels P. Petersson. *Geschichte der Globalisierung: Dimensionen, Prozesse, Epochen*. Munich: Verlag C. H. Beck, 2003.

O'Sullivan, Christopher D. *Sumner Welles, Postwar Planning, and the Quest for a New World Order, 1937–1943*. New York: Columbia University Press, 2003.

Ozbekhan, Hasan. "Toward a General Theory of Planning." In *Perspectives of Planning: Proceedings of the OECD Working Symposium on Long-Range Forecasting and Planning; Bellagio, Italy, 27th October–2nd November 1968*, edited by Erich Jantsch, 45–155. Paris: Organisation for Economic Cooperation and Development, 1969.

Özsu, Umut. " 'In the Interests of Mankind as a Whole': Mohammed Bedjaoui's New International Economic Order." *Humanity: An International Journal of Human Rights, Humanitarianism, and Development* 6, no. 1 (2015): 129–143.

Padmore, George, ed. *History of the Pan-African Congress: Colonial and Coloured Unity*. London: Hammersmith Books, 1963.

Paganetto, Luigi, and Pasquale Lucio Scandizzo. *La Banca Mondiale e l'Italia: Dalla ricostruzione allo sviluppo*. Bologna: Il Mulino, 2000.

Page, Edward C. *People Who Run Europe*. Oxford: Oxford University Press, 1997.

Palayret, Jean-Marie. "Da Lomé I a Cotonou: Morte e trasfigurazione della Convenzione Cee-Acp." In *Il primato sfuggente: L'Europa e l'intervento per lo sviluppo, 1957–2007*, edited by Elena Calandri, 35–52. Milan: FrancoAngeli, 2009.

"The Paris Conference on International Economic Co-operation (CIEC)." Overseas Development Institute Briefing Paper. https://www.odi.org/sites/odi.org.uk/files/odi-assets/publications-opinion-files/6602.pdf.

Parson, Roger, ed. *Sino-Soviet Intervention in Africa*. Washington, DC: Council on American Affairs, 1977.

Passell, Peter, Marc Roberts, and Leonard Ross. "The Limits to Growth: A Review." In *Pollution, Resources, and the Environment*, edited by Alain C. Enthoven, 230–234. New York: Norton, [1973].

Pastor, Robert A. *Congress and the Politics of U.S. Foreign Economic Policy, 1929–1976*. Berkeley: University of California Press, 1982.

Patel, Kiran Klaus. *The New Deal: A Global History*. Princeton, NJ: Princeton University Press, 2016.

Pearson, Lester B. "Partners in Development: A New Strategy for Global Development." *Unesco Courier*, February 1970, 4–15.

Peccei, Aurelio. *The Chasm Ahead*. New York: Macmillan, 1969.

———. "Como enfrentar los problemas de los paises subdesarrollados: Conferencia pronunciada en la Escuela Nacional de Guerra el 14 de julio de 1961." Buenos Aires, 1961.

———. "Considerazioni sulla necessità di una programmazione globale: Conferenza." *Mondo economico: Settimanale di economia, finanza, politica, cultura* 22, no. 40 (1967): 21–30.

———. "Un gran problema de nuestro tiempo: Los países subdesarrollados." Buenos Aires, 1959.

Pedersen, Susan. *The Guardians: The League of Nations and the Crisis of Empire*. New York: Oxford University Press, 2015.

Pestel, Eduard. *Beyond the Limits to Growth: A Report to the Club of Rome*. New York: Universe, 1989.

Petter, Martin. "Sir Sydney Caine and the Colonial Office in the Second World War: A Career in the Making." *Canadian Journal of History* 16, no. 1 (1981): 67–86.

Pianciola, Niccolò. *Stalinismo di frontiera: Colonizzazione agricola, sterminio dei nomadi e costruzione statale in Asia centrale (1905–1936)*. Rome: Viella, 2009.

Pisani, Edgar. *La main et l'outil: Le développement du Tiers Monde et l'Europe*. Paris: Éditions R. Laffont, 1984.

Pons, Silvio. *The Global Revolution: A History of International Communism, 1917–1991*. Oxford: Oxford University Press, 2014.

"The Population Challenge of the '70s," *Population Bulletin* 26, no. 1 (February 1970).

Porter, Doug, Bryant Allen, and Gaye Thompson. *Development in Practice: Paved with Good Intentions*. London: Routledge, 1991.

Prashad, Vijay. *The Darker Nations: A People's History of the Third World*. New York: New Press, 2007.

*Proceedings of the United Nations Conference for Trade and Development*. Vol. 1. New York: United Nations, 1964.

*Public Papers of the President of the United States, Richard Nixon, 1969*. Washington, DC: Government Printing Office, 1970.

Putnam, Robert D. *Making Democracy Work: Civic Traditions in Modern Italy*. Princeton, NJ: Princeton University Press, 1993.

Radchenko, Sergey. *Two Suns in the Heavens: The Sino-Soviet Struggle for Supremacy, 1962–1967*. Stanford, CA: Stanford University Press, 2009.

Raffer, Kunibert, and Hans Wolfgang Singer. *The Foreign Aid Business: Economic Assistance and Development Co-operation*. Cheltenham, UK: Edward Elgar, 1996.

Raiffa, Howard. "Creating an International Research Institution." *IIASA Conference, International Institute for Applied Systems Analysis* 1, no. 1 (1976): 19–27.

———. "IIASA: An Experiment in International Cooperation." *Vortrag, Österreichische Zeitschrift für Außenpolitik* 14, no. 4 (1974): 253–259.

Raucher, Alan R. *Paul G. Hoffman: Architect of Foreign Aid*. Lexington: University Press of Kentucky, 1985.

Ravenhill, John. *Collective Clientelism: The Lomé Conventions and North-South Relations*. New York: Columbia University Press, 1985.

Reagan, Ronald. "Address to the 42d Session of the United Nations General Assembly in New York, September 21, 1987." Ronald Reagan Presidential Library, National Archives and Records Administration. Accessed February 2019. *https://www.reaganlibrary.gov/research/speeches/092187b*.

Reboul, Laurence. *La lettre Mansholt: Réactions et commentaires*. Paris: J. J. Pauvert, 1972.

Reed, David, ed. *Structural Adjustment, the Environment, and Sustainable Development*. London: Earthscan, 1996.

Reingold, Nathan, and Marc Rothenberg, eds. *Scientific Colonialism: A Cross-Cultural Comparison*. Washington, DC: Smithsonian Institution Press, 1987.

Reinisch, Jessica. "Internationalism in Relief: The Birth (and Death) of UNRRA." *Past and Present* 210, suppl. 6 (2011): 258–289.

Rempe, Martin. *Decolonization by Europeanization? The Early EEC and the Transformation of French-African Relations*. KFG Working Paper No. 27, 2011.

———. *Entwicklung im Konflikt: Die EWG und der Senegal 1957–1975*. Cologne: Böhlau Verlag, 2012.

Renninger, John P., ed. *The Future Role of the United Nations in an Interdependent World*. Dordrecht: Martinus Nijhoff, 1989.

Requate, Jörg. "Visions of the Future during the 1960s: GDR, CSSR and the Federal Republic of Germany in Comparative Perspective." In *Comparative and Transnational History: Central European Approaches and New Perspectives*, edited by Heinz-Gerhard Haupt and Jürgen Kocka, 178–203. New York: Berghahn Books, 2009.

Reuss, Henry S. *When Government Was Good: Memories of a Life in Politics*. Madison: University of Wisconsin Press, 1999.

Reynolds, David. "FDR's Foreign Policy and the Construction of American History, 1945–1955." In *FDR's World: War, Peace, and Legacies*, edited by David B. Woolner, Warren F. Kimball, and David Reynolds, 5–34. New York: Palgrave Macmillan, 2008.

*Ricerche sullo sviluppo economico dell'Europa meridionale: Tre studi della Commissione Economica per l'Europa, Nazioni Unite—Divisione economica e sociale*. Rome: Svimez, 1956.

Rietkerk, Aaron Dean. "In Pursuit of Development: The United Nations, Decolonization and Development Aid, 1949–1961." PhD diss., London School of Economics, June 2015.

Risso, Linda. "NATO and the Environment: The Committee on the Challenges of Modern Society." *Contemporary European History* 25, no. 3 (2016): 505–535.

Rist, Gilbert. "Development as a Buzzword." *Development in Practice* 17, no. 4–5 (2007): 485–491.

———. *The History of Development: From Western Origins to Global Faith*. London: Zed Books, 1997.

———. "The Not-So-New International Order." *Development (SID)* 20, no. 3–4 (1978): 48–51.

Rizzo, Matteo. "What Was Left of the Groundnut Scheme? Development Disaster and Labour Market in Southern Tanganyika, 1946–1952." *Journal of Agrarian Change* 6, no. 2 (April 2006): 205–238.

Robertson, Thomas. *The Malthusian Moment: Global Population Growth and the Birth of American Environmentalism*. New Brunswick, NJ: Rutgers University Press, 2012.

Romero, Federico. "Refashioning the West to Dispel Its Fears." In *International Summitry and Global Governance: The Rise of the G7 and the European Council, 1974–1991*, edited by Emmanuel Mourlon-Druol and Federico Romero, 117–137. London: Routledge, 2014.

———. *Storia della guerra fredda: L'ultimo conflitto per l'Europa*. Turin: Einaudi, 2009.

Romulo, Carlos P. *The Meaning of Bandung*. Chapel Hill: University of North Carolina Press, 1956.

Rose, Günter. *"Industriegesellschaft" und Konvergenztheorie: Genesis Strukturen Funktionen*. Berlin: VEB Deutscher Verlag der Wissenschaften, 1973.

———. *Konvergenz der Systeme: Legende und Wirklichkeit.* Cologne: Pahl-Rugenstein Verlag, 1970.

Rosenstein Rodan, Paul N. "Natura Facit Saltum: Analysis of the Disequilibrium Growth Process." In *Pioneers in Development,* edited by Gerald M. Meier and Dudley Seers, 207–221. New York: Oxford University Press, 1984.

———. "Problems of Industrialisation of Eastern and South-Eastern Europe." *Economic Journal* 53, no. 210/211 (1943): 202–211.

Rossi-Doria, Manlio. *Una vita per il Sud: Dialoghi epistolari 1944–1987.* Edited by Emanuele Bernardi. Rome: Donzelli Editore, 2011.

Rostow, Walt W. *The Diffusion of Power: An Essay in Recent History.* New York: Macmillan, 1972.

———. "Marx Was a City Boy, or, Why Communism May Fail." *Harper's Magazine,* no. 2 (February 1955): 25–30.

———. *The Stages of Economic Growth: A Non-Communist Manifesto.* Cambridge: Cambridge University Press, 1960.

Rubinstein, Alvin Z. "Soviet Policy toward Under Developed Areas in the Economic and Social Council." *International Organization* 9, no. 2 (May 1955): 232–243.

Rupprecht, Tobias. "La guerra fredda e l'avanzata modernità socialista." *Contemporanea* 1 (2012): 137–145.

———. "Socialist High Modernity and Global Stagnation: A Shared History of Brazil and the Soviet Union during the Cold War." *Journal of Global History* 6, no. 3 (2011): 505–528.

Sachs, Wolfgang, ed. *The Development Dictionary: A Guide to Knowledge as Power.* London: Zed Books, 1992.

———. *Planet Dialectics.* London: Zed Books, 1999.

Sagan, Carl. *A Path Where No Man Thought: Nuclear Winter and the End of the Arms Race.* New York: Random House, 1990.

Saivetz, Carol R., and Sylvia Woodby. *Soviet-Third World Relations.* Boulder, CO: Westview Press, 1985.

Santoianni, Vittorio. "Il razionalismo nelle colonie italiane 1928–1943: La 'nuova architettura' delle Terre d'Oltremare." PhD diss., University of Naples Federico II, 2008.

Saraceno, Pasquale, Veniero Ajmone Marsan, Franco Pilloton, and Beppe Sacchi, eds. *Economic Effects of an Investment Program in Southern Italy.* Rome: Tip. F. Failli, 1951.

Sarraut, Albert. *La mise en valeur des colonies françaises.* Paris: Payot, 1923.

Saunders, Christopher T., ed. *East-West-South: Economic Interaction between Three Worlds.* Basingstoke, UK: Macmillan, 1983.

Sauvy, Alfred. "Trois mondes, une planète." *Observateur* 118 (August 1952): 14.

Scaiola, Gianni. *L'intervento pubblico contro l'inquinamento: Valutazione dei costi e dei benefici economici connessi a un progetto di eliminazione delle principali forme di inquinamento atmosferico e idrico in Italia.* Milan: FrancoAngeli, 1971.

Scaiola, Gianni, Paolo Gardin, and Martino Lo Cascio, eds. *Lineamenti di una politica di intervento pubblico contro l'inquinamento.* Milan: FrancoAngeli, 1975.

Schippel, Max. "Marxismus und Koloniale Eingeborenenfrage." *Sozialistische Monatshefte* 14 (1908): 273–285.

Schivelbusch, Wolfgang. *Three New Deals: Reflections on Roosevelt's America, Mussolini's Italy, and Hitler's Germany, 1933–1939.* New York: Metropolitan Books, 2006.

Schmelzer, Matthias. "A Club of the Rich to Help the Poor? The OECD, 'Development,' and the Hegemony of Donor Countries." In *International Organizations and Development, 1945–1990*, edited by Marc Frey, Sönke Kunkel, and Corinna Unger, 171–195. Basingstoke, UK: Palgrave Macmillan, 2014.

———. "The Crisis before the Crisis: The 'Problems of Modern Society' and the OECD, 1968–74." *European Review of History: Revue européenne d'histoire* 19, no. 6 (1 December 2012): 999–1020.

———. "The Growth Paradigm: History, Hegemony, and the Contested Making of Economic Growthmanship." *Ecological Economics* 118 (2015): 262–271.

———. *The Hegemony of Growth: The OECD and the Making of the Economic Growth Paradigm*. Cambridge: Cambridge University Press, 2016.

Schmitz, David F., and Vanessa Walker. "Jimmy Carter and the Foreign Policy of Human Rights: The Development of a Post-Cold War Foreign Policy," *Diplomatic History* 28, no. 1 (January 2004): 113–144.

Schulz-Walden, Thorsten. *Anfänge globaler Umweltpolitik: Umweltsicherheit in der internationalen Politik (1969–1975)*. Munich: Oldenbourg Verlag, 2013.

Scott, James C. "High Modernist Social Engineering: The Case of the TVA." In *Experiencing the State*, edited by Lloyd I. Rudolph and John Kurt Jacobsen. New Delhi: Oxford University Press, 2007.

———. *Seeing Like a State: How Certain Schemes to Improve the Human Condition Have Failed*. New Haven, CT: Yale University Press, 1998.

Seers, Dudley. "The Meaning of Development." *International Development Review* 11, no. 4 (December 1969): 2–3.

———. "Muddling Morality and Mutuality." *Third World Quarterly* 2, no. 4 (1980): 681–693.

Sen, Amartya. *Development as Freedom*. New York: Anchor Books, 1999.

Senghor, Léopold Sédar. *On African Socialism*. New York: Praeger, 1964.

Shapiro, Jordan E. "Settling Refugees, Unsettling the Nation: Ghana's Volta River Project Resettlement Scheme and the Ambiguities of Development Planning, 1952–1970." PhD diss., University of Michigan, 2003.

Sharma, Patrick. "The United States, the World Bank, and the Challenges of International Development in the 1970s." *Diplomatic History* 37, no. 3 (2013): 572–604.

Sharma, Patrick Allen. *Robert McNamara's Other War: The World Bank and International Development*. Philadelphia: University of Pennsylvania Press, 2017.

Shaw, D. John. *Sir Hans Singer: The Life and Work of a Development Economist*. London: Palgrave Macmillan, 2002.

Shenin, Sergei Y. *America's Helping Hand: Paving the Way to Globalization*. New York: Nova Science, 2005.

———. *The United States and the Third World: The Origins of Postwar Relations and the Point Four Program*. New York: Nova Science, 2000.

Shinkov, N. *Experience of the CMEA Activities over 25 Years*. Moscow: Council for Mutual Economic Assistance, 1975.

Shiva, Vandana. *The Violence of the Green Revolution: Third World Agriculture, Ecology and Poverty*. London: Zed Books, 1991.

Simonia, Nodari. *Destiny of Capitalism in the Orient*. Moscow: Progress Publishing, 1985.

———. "Newly-Free Countries: Problems of Development." *International Affairs*, May 1982, 83–91.

———. "On the Character of Change in the USSR, Eastern Europe and the Third World." *European Journal of Development Research* 2, no. 2 (1990): 176–185.

Simpson, Bradley R. *Economists with Guns: Authoritarian Development and U.S.-Indonesian Relations, 1960–1968*. Stanford, CA: Stanford University Press, 2008.

———. "Self-Determination, Human Rights, and the End of Empire in the 1970s." *Humanity: An International Journal of Human Rights, Humanitarianism, and Development* 4, no. 2 (2013): 239–260.

Singer, H. W. "A 'Northwestern' Point of View." *Third World Quarterly* 2, no. 4 (1980): 694–700.

Singer, Hans. "The Distribution of Gains between Investing and Borrowing Countries." *American Economic Review* 40, no. 2 (1950): 473–485.

Skeet, Ian. *Opec: Twenty-Five Years of Prices and Politics*. Cambridge: Cambridge University Press, 1988.

Slobodian, Quinn. *The Globalists: The End of Empire and the Birth of Neoliberalism*. Cambridge, MA: Harvard University Press, 2017.

Sluga, Glenda. "The Human Story of Development: Alva Myrdal at the UN, 1949–1955." In *International Organizations and Development, 1945–1990*, edited by Marc Frey, Sönke Kunkel, and Corinna Unger, 46–74. London: Palgrave Macmillan, 2014.

Smuts, Jan Christian. *The League of Nations: A Practical Suggestion*. London: Hodder and Stoughton, 1918.

Snow, Philip. "China and Africa: Consensus and Camouflage." In *Chinese Foreign Policy*, edited by Thomas W. Robinson and David Shambaugh, 283–321. Oxford, UK: Clarendon Press, 1994.

———. *China Returns to Africa: A Rising Power and a Continent Embrace*. London: Hurst, 2008.

Snyder, Sarah B. " 'A Call for U.S. Leadership': Congressional Activism on Human Rights." *Diplomatic History* 37, no. 2 (2013): 372–397.

Sohn, Louis B. "The Stockholm Declaration on the Human Environment." *Harvard International Law Journal* 14, no. 3 (Summer 1973): 423–515.

Solarz, Marcin Wojciech. " 'Third World': The 60th Anniversary of a Concept That Changed History." *Third World Quarterly* 33, no. 9 (2012): 1561–1573.

Sorensen, Theodore C. *Let the World Go Forth: The Speeches, Statements and Writings of John F. Kennedy, 1947–1963*. New York: Laurel, 1988.

"Soviet Policy in Southern Africa: An Interview with Viktor Goncharev by Howard Barrell." *Work in Progress* 7, no. 4 (1987): 140–141.

Spanger, Hans-Joachim, and Lothar Brock. *Die beiden deutschen Staaten in der Dritten Welt: Die Entwicklungspolitik der DDR—eine Herausforderung für die Bundesrepublik Deutschland?* Opladen, Germany: Westdeutscher Verlag, 1987.

Speich, Daniel. "The Use of Global Abstractions: National Income Accounting in the Period of Imperial Decline." *Journal of Global History* 6 (2011): 7–28.

Speich-Chassé, Daniel. "Towards a Global History of the Marshall Plan: European Post-War Reconstruction and the Rise of Development Economic Expertise." In *Industrial Policy in Europe after 1945: Wealth, Power and Economic Development in the Cold War*, edited by Christian Grabas and Alexander Nützenadel, 187–212. London: Palgrave Macmillan, 2014.

Staples, Amy L. S. *The Birth of Development: How the World Bank, Food and Agriculture Organization, and World Health Organization Changed the World, 1945–1965*. Kent, OH: Kent State University Press, 2006.

Statler, Kathryn C. "Building a Colony: South Vietnam and the Eisenhower Administration, 1953–1961." In *The Eisenhower Administration, the Third World, and the Globalization of the Cold War*, edited by Kathryn C. Statler and Andrew L. Johns, 101–123. Lanham, MD: Rowman & Littlefield, 2006.

Steel, Ronald. "1919–1945–1989." Prologue to *The Treaty of Versailles: A Reassessment after 75 Years*, edited by Manfred F. Boemeke, Gerald D. Feldman, and Elisabeth Glaser. Cambridge: Cambridge University Press, 1998.

Steiner, André. *Von Plan zu Plan: Eine Wirtschaftsgeschichte der DDR*. Munich: Deutsche Verlags-Anstalt, 2004.

Stephens, Cody. "The Accidental Marxist: Andre Gunder Frank and the 'Neo-Marxist' Theory of Underdevelopment, 1958–1967." *Modern Intellectual History*, Vol. 15, 2 (August 2018): 411–442.

Stevens, Christopher. *The Soviet Union and Black Africa*. London: Macmillan, 1976.

Stoddard, Lothrop. *The Rising Tide of Color against White World-Supremacy*. New York: Scribner, 1922.

Stone, David R. "CMEA's International Investment Bank and the Crisis of Developed Socialism." *Journal of Cold War Studies* 10, no. 3 (2008): 48–77.

Streeten, Paul. "Basic Needs and Human Rights." *World Development* 8, no. 2 (1980): 107–111.

———. *First Things First: Meeting Basic Human Needs in Developing Countries*. With Shahid Javed Burki, Mahbub ul Haq, Norman Hicks, and Frances Stewart. New York: World Bank and Oxford University Press, 1981. *http://documents.worldbank.org/curated/en/882331468179936655/pdf/997710english.pdf*.

Strong, Maurice. *Where on Earth Are We Going?* Toronto: Alfred A. Knopf, 2000.

Strong, Maurice F., ed. *Who Speaks for Earth?* New York: Norton, 1973.

Sunier, Georges. "Claude Cheysson: Histoire d'une pensée politique (1940–1981)." PhD diss., Université de Paris VII, 1995.

Taffet, Jeffrey F. *Foreign Aid as Foreign Policy: The Alliance for Progress in Latin America*. Abingdon, UK: Routledge, 2007.

Tarabrin, Evgeny Anatolevich. *The New Scramble for Africa*. Moscow: Progress Publishers, 1974.

Teichmann, Christian. "Cultivating the Periphery: Bolshevik Civilizing Missions and 'Colonialism' in Soviet Central Asia." *Comparativ* 19, no. 1 (2009): 34–52.

Thelen, Kathleen. "How Institutions Evolve: Insights from Comparative Historical Analysis." In *Comparative Historical Analysis in the Social Sciences*, edited by James Mahoney and Dietrich Reuschemeyer, 208–240. Cambridge: Cambridge University Press, 2003.

"Third World Options: Brandt Report." *Third World Quarterly* 2, no. 4 (1980): 681–693.

Thomas, Martin. "French Imperial Reconstruction and the Development of the Indochina War, 1945–1950." In *The First Vietnam War*, edited by Mark Atwood Lawrence and Fredrik Logevall, 130–151. Cambridge, MA: Harvard University Press, 2007.

Thomas, Martin, Bob Moore, and L. J. Butler. *Crises of Empire: Decolonization and Europe's Imperial States*. London: Bloomsbury, 2015.

Thorp, Willard L. "The Objectives of Point Four." In "Aiding Underdeveloped Areas Abroad." Special issue, *Annals of the American Academy of Political and Social Science* 268 (March 1950): 22–26.

————. "Practical Problems of Point Four." In "Formulating a Point Four Program." Special issue, *Annals of the American Academy of Political and Social Science* 270 (July 1950): 95–101.

————. *The Reality of Foreign Aid.* New York: Council of Foreign Relations, Praeger, 1971.

Tibazarwa, C. M. *From Berlin to Brussels: 100 Years of African-European Cooperation.* Durham, UK: Pentland Press, 1994.

Tignor, Robert L. *W. Arthur Lewis and the Birth of Development Economics.* Princeton, NJ: Princeton University Press, 2006.

Tinbergen, Jan. *Reshaping the International Order: A Report to the Club of Rome.* New York: Dutton, 1976.

Toner, Simon. "The Counter-Revolutionary Path: South Vietnam, the United States, and the Global Allure of Development, 1968–1973." PhD diss., London School of Economics, 2015.

Tornimbeni, Corrado. *Cento anni su una frontiera africana: Dal sogno dell'oro al parco naturale tra Mozambico e Zimbabwe.* Milan: FrancoAngeli, 2017.

*Towards Accelerated Development: Proposals for the Second United Nations Development Decade.* Report of the Sixth Session of the Committee for Development Planning. New York: United Nations, 1970.

*Towards a New Trade Policy for Development: Report by the Secretary-General of the United Nations Conference on Trade and Development.* United Nations Document E/Conf.46/3. New York: United Nations, 1964.

Toye, John. "Assessing the G77: 50 Years after UNCTAD and 40 Years after the NIEO." *Third World Quarterly* 35, no. 10 (2014): 1759–1774.

————. *Dilemmas of Development: Reflections on the Counter-Revolution in Development Theory and Policy.* Oxford, UK: Basil Blackwell, 1987.

Toye, John, and Richard Toye. *The UN and Global Political Economy: Trade, Finance, and Development.* Bloomington: Indiana University Press, 2004.

Trentin, Massimiliano. "Divergence in the Mediterranean: The Economic Relations between the EC and the Arab Countries in the Long 1980s." *Journal of European Integration History* 21, no. 1 (2015): 89–108.

————. *La guerra fredda tedesca in Siria: Diplomazia, economia e politica, 1963–1970.* Padua, Italy: CLEUP, 2015.

Trescott, Paul B. "H. D. Fong and the Study of Chinese Economic Development." *History of Political Economy* 34, no. 4 (Winter 2002): 789–809.

Truman, Harry S. *Memoirs.* Vol. 2. Garden City, NY: Doubleday, 1955–56.

Tulli, Umberto. *Tra diritti umani e distensione: L'amministrazione Carter e il dissenso in Urss.* Milan: FrancoAngeli, 2013.

ul Haq, Mahbub. "Employment and Income Distribution in the 1970's: A New Perspective." *Pakistan Economic and Social Review* 9, no. 1/2 (June–December 1971): 1–9.

————. *The Poverty Curtain: Choices for the Third World.* New York: Columbia University Press, 1976.

Ulyanovsky, Rostislav A. *Socialism in the Newly Independent Nations.* Moscow: Progress Publishers, 1974.

Unfried, Berthold, and Eva Himmelstoss, ed. *Die eine Welt schaffen: Praktiken von "Internationaler Solidarität" und "Internationaler Entwicklung"* [Create one world: Practices of "international solidarity" and "international development"]. Leipzig, Germany: Akademische Verlagsanstalt, 2012.

Unger, Corinna R. *International Development: A Postwar History*. London: Bloomsbury, 2018.

———. "Postwar European Development Aid: Defined by Decolonization, the Cold War, and European Integration?" In *The Development Century*, edited by Stephen J. Macekura and Erez Manela, 240–260. Cambridge: Cambridge University Press, 2018.

United Nations, Centre for Disarmament. *The Relationship between Disarmament and Development: Report of the Secretary-General*. New York: United Nations, 1982.

United Nations, Department of Social and Economic Affairs. *Measures for the Economic Development of Underdeveloped Countries*. 1951.

United Nations, Economic Commission for Latin America. *The Economic Development of Latin America and Its Principal Problems*. Lake Success, NY: United Nations Department of Economic Affairs, 1950. Reprinted in *Economic Bulletin for Latin America* 7, no. 1 (1962).

"The UN Role: Tinbergen and Jackson Reports." *Development Policy Review* A4, no. 1 (November 1970): 22–26.

*U.S. Foreign Assistance in the 1970s: A New Approach—Report to the President from the Task Force on International Development*. Department of State Bulletin, 6 April 1970, 447–467.

US State Department. *The Sino-Soviet Economic Offensive in the Less Developed Countries*. Washington, DC: US State Department, 1958.

Vaganov, Boris S., and Abram B. Froumkin. "East-West Relations and Their Impact on Development: Is the International Development Strategy Feasible?" In *The Future Role of the United Nations in an Interdependent World*, edited by John P. Renninger, 191–203. Dordrecht, Netherlands: Martinus Nijhoff, 1989.

van Beusekom, Monica M., and Dorothy L. Hodgson. "Lessons Learned? Development Experiences in the Late Colonial Period." *Journal of African History* 41, no. 1 (2000): 29–33.

van den Heyden, Ulrich. "FDJ-Brigaden der Freundschaft aus der DDR-Die Peace Corps des Ostens?" In *Die eine Welt schaffen: Praktiken von Internationaler Solidarität und Internationaler Entwicklung* [Create One World: Practices of international solidarity and international development], edited by Berthold Unfried and Eva Himmelstoss, 99–122. Leipzig, Germany: Akademische Verlagsanstalt, 2012.

van der Straeten, Jonas. *Der erste Bericht an den Club of Rome von 1972 und seine Rezeption in der Bundesrepublik Deutschland*. Altstadt, Germany: Grin Verlag, 2009.

Varga, Evgenij. "On Trends of Development of Contemporary Capitalism and Socialism." *World Economy and International Relations* 4 (1957): 36–48.

Vieille Blanchard, Élodie. "Les limites à la croissance dans un monde global: Modélisations, prospectives, réfutations." PhD diss., École des Hautes Études en Sciences Sociales, 2011.

Villani, Claudia. *La trappola degli aiuti: Sottosviluppo, Mezzogiorno e guerra fredda negli anni '50*. Bari, Italy: Progedit, 2008.

Vitale, Valeria. "L'attività della SVIMEZ dal 1946 al 1991." *Rivista economica del Mezzogiorno* 14, no. 2 (2000): 541–652.

*The Volta Resettlement Experience: Proceedings of a Symposium Held at the University of Science and Technology, Kumasi, March 21 to 27, 1965*. London: Pall Mall, 1970.

"The Volta River Project." *African Affairs* 55, no. 221 (October 1956): 287–293.

Volta River Project Preparatory Commission. *The Volta River Project*. London: H. M. Stationery Office, 1956.

Wade, Robert. *Governing the Market: Economic Theory and the Role of Government in East Asian Industrialization*. Princeton, NJ: Princeton University Press, 1990.

Wallerstein, Immanuel. *The Politics of the World Economy*. Cambridge: Cambridge University Press, 1984.

———. "The Rise and Future Demise of the World Capitalist System: Concepts for Comparative Analysis." *Comparative Studies in Society and History* 16, no. 4 (September 1974): 387–415.

Walters, Frances P. *A History of the League of Nations*. New York: Oxford University Press, 1952.

Walters, Robert S. *American and Soviet Aid: A Comparative Analysis*. Pittsburgh: University of Pittsburgh Press, 1970.

Ward, Barbara, and Peter T. Bauer. *Two Views on Aid to Developing Countries*. Bombay: Vora, 1968.

Ward, Barbara, and René Dubos. *Only One Earth: The Care and Maintenance of a Small Planet*. New York: Norton, 1972.

Watanabe, Shino. "Implementation System: Tools and Institutions." In *A Study of China's Foreign Aid: An Asian Perspective*, edited by Yasutami Shimomura and Hideo Ohashi, 58–81. London: Palgrave Macmillan, 2013.

Webb, Sidney, and Beatrice Webb. *Soviet Communism: A New Civilization?* London: Longman, 1935.

Weinberg, Ian. "The Problem of the Convergence of Industrial Societies: A Critical Look at the State of a Theory." *Comparative Studies in Society and History* 11, no. 1 (January 1969): 1–15.

Weiner, Douglas. *A Little Corner of Freedom: Russian Nature Protection from Stalin to Gorbachev*. Berkeley: University of California Press, 1999.

Weinstein, Warren, and Thomas H. Henriksen. *Soviet and Chinese Aid to African Nations*. New York: Praeger, 1980.

Weiss, Thomas G., Tatiana Carayannis, Louis Emmerij, and Richard Jolly, eds. *UN Voices: The Struggle for Development and Social Justice*. Bloomington: Indiana University Press, 2005.

Westad, Odd Arne, ed. *Brothers in Arms: The Rise and Fall of the Sino-Soviet Alliance, 1945–1963*. Washington, DC: Woodrow Wilson Center Press, 1998.

———. *The Cold War: A World History*. London: Allen Lane, 2017.

———. "The Cold War and the International History of the Twentieth Century." In *The Cambridge History of the Cold War*, edited by Melvyn P. Leffler and Odd Arne Westad, 1–19. Cambridge: Cambridge University Press, 2010.

———. "The Cold War and the Third World." Epilogue to *The Cold War in the Third World*, edited by Robert J. McMahon, 208–219. Oxford: Oxford University Press, 2013.

———. *The Global Cold War: Third World Interventions and the Making of Our Times*. Cambridge: Cambridge University Press, 2007.

———. "The Great Transformation: China in the Long 1970s." In *The Shock of the Global: The 1970s in Perspective*, edited by Charles S. Maier, Niall Ferguson, Erez Manela, and Daniel Sargent, 65–79. Cambridge, MA: Belknap Press of Harvard University Press, 2010.

———. "The New International History of the Cold War: Three (Possible) Paradigms." *Diplomatic History* 24, no. 4 (Fall 2000): 551–565.

Wettig, Gerhard. *Community and Conflict in the Socialist Camp: The Soviet Union, East Germany and the German Problem, 1965–1972*. London: C. Hurst, 1975.

Whelan, Daniel J. " 'Under the Aegis of Man': The Right to Development and the Origins of the New International Economic Order." *Humanity: An International Journal of Human Rights, Humanitarianism, and Development* 6, no. 1 (Spring 2015): 93–108.

Whitehead, Clive. *Colonial Educators*. London: I. B. Tauris, 2003.

*The Widening Gap: Development in the 1970s*. Columbia Conference on International Economic Development, Williamsburg, Virginia, and New York, February 15–21, 1970. New York: Columbia University Press, 1971.

Willetts, Peter. *The Non-aligned Movement: The Origins of a Third World Alliance*. London: F. Pinter, 1978.

Wirz, Albert. "Die humanitäre Schweiz im Spannungsfeld zwischen Philantropie und Kolonial-ismus: Moynier, Afrika und das IRKK." *Traverse* 5 (1998): 95–111.

Wohlmuth, Karl. *Structural Adjustment and East-West-South Economic Cooperation: Key Issues*. Bremen, Germany: Weltwirtschaftlichen Colloquium der Universität Bremen, Fachbereich Wirtschaftswissenschaft, [1989].

World Commission on Environment and Development (Brundtland Commission). *Our Common Future*. Oxford: Oxford University Press, 1987.

Worsley, Peter. "How Many Worlds?" *Third World Quarterly* 1, no. 2 (1979): 100–108.

Wright, Richard. *The Color Curtain: A Report on the Bandung Conference*. New York: World Publishing, 1956.

Wrong, Michela. *I Didn't Do It for You: How the World Betrayed a Small African Nation*. New York: Harper Collins, 2005.

Yakobson, Sergius. "Soviet Concepts of Point IV." In "Aiding Undeveloped Areas Abroad." Special issue, *Annals of the American Academy of Political and Social Science* 268 (March 1950): 129–139.

Yat-sen, Sun. *The International Development of China*. New York: Putnam, 1922.

Youlou, Fulbert. *J'accuse la Chine*. Paris: La Table Ronde, 1966.

Young, Crawford. "The End of the Post-Colonial State in Africa?" *African Affairs* 193, no. 410 (2004): 23–49.

Yuan Sun, Irene, Kartik Jayaram, and Omid Kassiri. *Dance of the Lions and Dragons: How Are Africa and China Engaging, and How Will the Partnership Evolve?* McKinsey Report, June 2017.

Zachariah, Benjamin. *Developing India: An Intellectual and Social History, c. 1930–50*. New Delhi: Oxford University Press, 2005.

Zanasi, Margherita. "Exporting Development: The League of Nations and Republican China." *Comparative Studies in Society and History* 49, no. 1 (2007): 143–169.

Zasloff, Joseph J. "Rural Resettlement in South Viet Nam: The Agroville Program," *Pacific Affairs* 35, no. 4 (Winter 1962–1963): 327–340.

# INDEX

A NOTE ON THE TYPE

This book has been composed in Arno, an Old-style serif typeface in the
classic Venetian tradition, designed by Robert Slimbach at Adobe.